OFF THE RECORD

OFF THE RECORD

Tim Skubick

The University of Michigan Press
Ann Arbor

and

The Petoskey Publishing Company
Traverse City

To those I deeply love.
Mom and Dad, Eleanor and Arnie.
Children: Shawn, Nicole, Mike and Carly
and to my wife, Gayle, for the inspiration to write

Contents

Foreword

Michigan citizens have a right to know, and need to know, about the workings of their state government. For more than three decades Tim Skubick has opened the door of state government with reporting that has taken us behind the scenes, onto the legislative floor and even into the Governor's office. His passionate brand of journalism has made an indelible mark on Lansing and on Michigan's political history.

—GOVERNOR JENNIFER M. GRANHOLM

From 1971 through 2002, I served as an elected official, first in the Michigan House, then in the Michigan Senate, and finally as a three term governor. I had one of the longer public careers in Lansing, and I know of only one reporter who covered state government that entire time: Tim Skubick. Tim, a fixture in Lansing for 34 years, has covered four gubernatorial administrations and 17 election cycles. This has given him a remarkable cache of stories and insights . . . not to mention his inimitable style.

Tim's career has coincided with one of the more troubling changes to occur in Lansing over the past three decades: decreasing media coverage of state government. When Tim and I began our careers in Lansing, there were numerous Lansing bureaus. Michigan citizens could receive information from a variety of perspectives. Now only a handful of bureaus are left, a situation that has not served the public well and, indeed, may have contributed to cynicism among citizens. Tim is the undisputed Dean of the Lansing journalists. The stories and insights he offers in his book will give readers a valuable perspective from a newsman who knows his business . . . and who deeply cares about our state and nation.

—GOVERNOR JOHN ENGLER
(1991–2002)

Since 1969, Tim Skubick has been an untiring and dedicated correspondent and analyst in our state capitol. No one in recent memory has witnessed so much in state government politics. While he and I may disagree from time to time on events and interpretations, we both share a deep love for the State of Michigan and its people.

—GOVERNOR JAMES J. BLANCHARD
(1983–1990)

Tim Skubick has had a special window on Capitol affairs for 34 years. He has earned great respect from elected officials, their staffs, and his media colleagues. His is a unique perspective from which to comment on both public and behind-the-scenes stories which should make compelling reading.

—GOVERNOR WILLIAM J. MILLIKEN
(1969–1982)

Acknowledgments

"So, you must be retiring."

Much to my surprise that was the most common reaction when folks in town discovered this book was in the works.

On and off the record, nothing could be more wrong. There is still plenty to learn, discover, and enjoy on this political beat and frankly I can see at least another twenty years before the "must be retiring" line has any validity.

I come away from this project with a renewed respect for the politicians I get to cover. The vast majority have made a personal commitment to make life better for everyone. It is a noble calling although few citizens see it that way anymore. But even against that backdrop, some are still willing to serve. Without them, I'd be selling pencils on the street corner.

So the first thank you is to all the politicians who have graced the stage in Lansing. Thank you for allowing me to grill you, laugh with you, and watch your every move. A special note of appreciation to all the former governors and the current chief executive. Even though they play the game at the highest level, I have found each one to be down to earth, accessible, and understanding of the role journalism has in helping to make government better.

Thank you to my wife, Gayle, for truly moving me to complete this assignment. "Do it before you forget it," she warned me the night that I drafted the first chapter. I can remember taking that chapter upstairs and reading it to her. The smile on her face was all the encouragement I needed. Thanks for the inspiration, love.

In 32 years of anchoring *Off the Record*, I also owe a huge debt of appreciation to all the capitol correspondents who make the show work. Without them, there is no program. Thanks guys, and an equal amount of gratitude to all the colleagues at WKAR-TV who help produce the program including Dick Best, Mike Lewis, Paul Pierantozzi, Ken Merley, Kurtis Kaechele, Diane Hutchins, Jeanie Croope, Cynthia Schneider, Bill Kinney, Scott Remington, Steve Meuche, and Tim Zeko.

And then there are a whole host of contacts, sources, and advisors who helped restore my memory and helped to reconstruct this 34 year compendium of Michigan political history. Patrick Anderson, Rick Albin, Keith Bassar, Lu Battaglieri, Lorraine Beebee, Dawson Bell, Loren Bennett, Connie Binsfield, Paula Blanchard, Bill Bobier, Bob Bowman, Liz Boyd, Joyce Braithwaite, Ken Brock, Bill Bryant, Mike Busch, Charlie Cain, Mike Cavanagh, Dennis Cawthrone, Chris Christoff, Tom Clay, Mora Corrigan, Jerry Crandall, Doug Cruce, Bob Danhof, Lew Dodak, Dan DeGrow, Betsy DeVos, Chris DeWitt, Joe Forbes, Mark Fox, Edgar Geerlings, Tommy Guastello, Rusty Hills, Frank Kelley, John Kelly, Robert Kolt, Pat "P.C." Laughlin, Larry Lee, Charles Levin, Bill Martin, Bill McMaster, Hugh McDiarmid, Gary Mitchell, Keith Molin, Dan Mulhern, Susan Grimes Munsell, Colleen McNamara, Ernie Nash, Mike Nye, Brain O'Connell, Ralph Ostling, Gary Owen, Larry Owen, Laurie Packard, Jeff Padden, Stu Patterson, Dan Pero, Lana Pollack, Gary Randall, Debbie Stabenow, Al Short, John Smietanka, Andy Such, Howard Anderson, Robert Vanderlaan, George Weeks, Gleaves Whitney, and to the University of Michigan Press and Petoskey Publishing for having the nerve to tackle this assignment with dedication, professionalism, and laughter.

And finally and not least, thank you to you for watching, listening, and reading these many years. With someone "out there" it is all worthwhile.

—TIM SKUBICK

1

A Granholm
Wake-Up Call

The candidate turned champion was engulfed by a sea of humanity as the spontaneous victory celebration reached a fever pitch in a downtown Detroit hotel. The center of attention had just captured the Democratic nomination for governor, and the joint was rockin'.

Jennifer Mulhern Granholm had just done what no other woman in state history had ever accomplished—she had won a major party's nomination for governor. The primary victory ended phase one of what she affectionately labeled, "The longest job interview of my life."

After shaking as many hands and exchanging as many hugs as she could, her campaign entourage whisked her away. Safely away from the maddening crowd, an exhausted Jennifer Granholm leaned against the back of the dingy freight elevator as the closing door shut her off from the pandemonium. She exclaimed, "That was crazy. I want a Strohs!"

Who said she didn't have Michigan values?

A long and arduous sojourn ended that warm August night some 18 months after it began on March 6, 2001 . . . with a phone call from me. I dialed the private number of the Granholm residence in Northville, just outside of Motown. It was 7:30 A.M. I was ready to break a huge political story. She and I needed to talk.

After three or four rings somebody picked up the receiver. "Hello," said the female voice on the other end of the line. It was State Attorney General Jennifer Granholm. I was in luck or so I hoped.

"Madam attorney general, this is Tim Skubick in Lansing. How are you?"

She blurted out, "I've got to get this number changed," and then she laughed. She probably did not remember giving me the number after taking office in 1998. There is an unwritten rule about using private phone numbers: Never abuse it, but use if it you have to. I had to. The story I was working on was very important to Ms. Granholm.

It was March 6, 2001 and speculation was approaching critical mass that Ms. Granholm wanted to exchange that title for something with a little more pop . . . governor. Everyone pretty much knew she would go for it, but nobody knew where or when.

I did.

"Ms. Granholm, I want to give you a heads up. In about half an hour, I'm going to air a story on WWJ Newsradio 950 that you are running for governor and you will make the formal announcement in about three weeks." There was a cold silence on the other end of the line that lasted for at least a minute.

Finally, and calmly, she spoke: "Where did you get that information?" She was thinking there was a leak in her organization and long afterward she told me, "Not that I thought you would tell me, mind you."

Coming from an attorney and a savvy politician it was not an unexpected dodge and exactly the right retort. "I can't tell you, but I'm very comfortable with the information," I returned the dodge. (I'm comfortable enough to risk my credibility by blasting it all over southeast Michigan during morning drive time. Then I would follow it up with an in-depth commentary in my weekly political column in the *Lansing State Journal* and make it the lead story on our *Off the Record* public TV program that Friday.)

She did not want me on the line. Like any potential candidate she wanted to control every aspect of her candidacy—including when to announce it. Delaying that proclamation allows the candidate to gobble up free media as the press speculates day after day about the impending statement. That in turn creates a crescendo of public anticipation, which produces a bigger audience for announcement day. However, once her hat is in the ring, the media is obliged to take everything she says and seek reaction from her opponents. That gives them free time, which she doesn't want. As long as she is a non-candidate, she could use her office to stage news conferences all over the state. She was getting a ton of free media doing that, and here I was with a story that would change all that.

The phone conversation was at a critical point. The way I figured, she had several options: Wish me well and hang up the phone. Not wish me well and still hang up. Play along to see if I was bluffing or help me out.

Had it been Governor John Engler, he would have given me a sardonic laugh and click. In covering Engler for three decades, he never once confirmed an exclusive story and never came close to even whispering one in my ear. Former Governor William Milliken would have been reluctant to confirm the story but would not have hung up, and ex-Governor Jim Blanchard and I would have worked out a deal whereby I'd protect him and he'd give me the inside skinny.

Granholm did what I hoped she'd do. She easily took me into her confidence. But it wouldn't have happened if there wasn't some trust there. The only way to move inside this political game and be somewhat successful is to establish that bond and instill a sense of fair play with the persons you cover. It is not done overnight. Like any human relationship it takes time.

Lansing is a very small town where word gets around real fast. If some reporter is perceived as "out to get" some politician, the journalist will have a tough time getting anyone to talk, let alone giving guidance on a critical story. That doesn't mean you have to be a wimp to survive, but it does mean you have to be fair.

I think I sort of apologized for having to bother her at that early morning hour and then I asked some questions to make sure I had the story right. She told me the date I had written was wrong and then promptly gave me the right one. I read smidgens of my column to her. She made some minor suggestions. Fact is she was under no obligation to do it.

Here's what she was thinking during the give and take. First, she wanted to make sure I was not bluffing, but when I read accounts of what I was going to broadcast, she knew I wasn't bluffing. Second, and in typical Granholm fashion she turned a lemon into lemonade. "I figured that a Skubick story on WWJ was not all bad as long as the facts were generally correct and I could control the formal announcement later."

After we talked I was more comfortable than ever. Even though I had a good source, there is always that lingering doubt just before you break a story. There were times in the last thirty-four years that I goofed big time. What if the story turns out to be wrong? It's possible that the source had it right, but by the time it was funneled along to me, the story could have changed six ways from Sunday. Those nagging doubts were gone on this one. I had it right from the candidate's mouth. I did not quote her as the source. That gave her the option to fend off the rest of the press corps by saying, she couldn't confirm or deny the report. Or she could trot out her "stay tuned" quote that she often used when she didn't want to say anything. She also had the option to confirm it or do whatever she wanted. I didn't ask and she didn't tell. But what she decided after the conversation caught me by surprise.

I sincerely thanked her for helping me and wished her well. I told her I looked forward to covering her along with the other three guys in the race, former Governor Jim Blanchard, Michigan congressman David Bonior, and state senator Gary Peters and the other woman, Senator Alma Wheeler Smith.

I also promised not to use her private number on a regular basis. I was hoping she wouldn't change it because I was pretty sure she would not hand it over again. She hung up and I just sat in the chair for a second. Even though I've been at this game for some 34 years, there is still a rush knowing that you've got something that nobody else has. Yeah, it sounds silly but in the political news game, it's one of the only games we have. It's as phony as hell to judge a reporter's worth based on getting a story first, but everybody does it nonetheless.

I reflected for a moment on the tenor of our conversation. You are always listening to see if the other person is getting angry. You worry about the response because it could impact your future relationship. In this case, I was going to be covering the Granholm for Governor campaign and if she got elected, I'd be on her story for four years. You don't want to start out with any bad blood. There was no hint of that with her.

It was about ninety minutes after I put the story on the air that I got word that the attorney general had filed papers that morning to form an exploratory committee for governor. That was not an announcement of candidacy but it was only an eyelash away. She did not wake up planning to do that, but her inner circle huddled and came up with that strategy after I spilled the beans.

When she finally announced later that month, Ms. Granholm got a ton of free media. She was taking the first step onto a history making road. Sure there had been other female candidates for governor. Democrat Debbie Stabenow of Lansing tried and failed. Republican Colleen Engler, then wife of John, tried and failed, but as this Granholm juggernaut got rolling, you sensed the outcome might be different. There was a long way to go before that chapter was finalized.

My phone call was actually the second time in her infant candidacy that her time table got rocked. Jim Blanchard was the culprit the first time.

All during 2000 on the rubber chicken circuit I was telling audiences that James J. Blanchard would never run again for governor. Been there, done that. The way I figured it, here was a guy who was dragging down a pretty good salary with his legal/lobbying gig in Washington D.C. He could pretty much come and go as he pleased and did no visible heavy lifting in the process. Why put that at risk by coming back to a job he had lost in 1990? That was my story and for months I incorrectly stuck to it until one night outside a public library, I discovered I was dead wrong.

The former governor and I ended up on the same program one night in Oakland County. He was on a panel debating the pros and cons of the voucher ballot proposal. That was the hot button, school funding proposal to fund private and or religious schools with state tax dollars. I was the referee between both sides.

Blanchard was the co-chair of the anti-voucher coalition, and was consuming lots of media space as he went on his crusade to help "save public education" from the right wing GOP led by former party chair Betsy DeVos and pals.

He was also hoping to stash away some chits from the state's largest teachers union, the Michigan Education Association, which was helping to bankroll the anti-voucher effort. No doubt he was thinking about a possible endorsement down the line. Blanchard's high visibility should have been a clue that my analysis about his not running was wrong. I missed it.

Anyhow, after the program, Blanchard and I found ourselves standing in the parking lot after everyone had gone home. It was a great Michigan eve and Blanchard was in one of his talkative moods and I was more than eager to listen. I told him I was telling citizens he'd never run again.

"You better change your story." He shocked me.

"Say what?"

"I'm thinking about running," he disclosed and for the next twenty minutes or so, he rearranged my thinking on the subject. He said he had learned a lot being away from Lansing and had constructed a portfolio of new experiences that made him the best qualified candidate in the bunch.

We discussed what would be the obvious media take on his candidacy, i.e., he was doing it to redeem himself from that razor thin upset loss to John Engler. He confided that was not his major motivation. He had convinced himself that he could do a better job and was in this thing to stay. The early polling data seemed to buttress his convictions. He was in the lead.

So Blanchard was really the first guy into the hunt and he did it in part to smoke out Ms. Granholm. But before he got in, they held a private meeting at his request in December of 2000. He wanted some sense of where she was. Was she in or out? His version of the session has her in effect telling him to go for it. Her version suggests she gave him no reason to conclude she would stay out. The two agreed to disagree but it's clear Blanchard came out encouraged that she might not run. As the old year ended and the new one began,

Granholm made a private decision to run and intended to reveal it around Labor Day 2001. She did not email Blanchard with the news. But the more Blanchard ping-ponged around the state trying to secure votes, the Granholm folks got more nervous, especially her husband Dan Mulhern. Eventually when it appeared the former governor might be making significant headway, she decided to move the date up to March 28.

Covering the historic race was going to be a total hoot and the first item on my agenda was to get the five Democrats to debate on public TV. I had my sights set on August of 2001. Traditionally we always did a debate in August a year before the primary the next year. The hook was we'd be the first to have at the candidates. We had no competition since the rest of the commercial TV stations didn't even know there was an election, which is a snarly way of saying, they didn't care.

The four other Democrats were more than eager to have at Ms. Granholm who shamelessly promoted herself as the only one who could win. I was more than eager to provide the forum. Usually there is some nif-nawing on the format, but each candidate bought into my standard pitch for no rules. I found the best debates are the ones that just happen unencumbered by time restraints, rebuttals and re-rebuttals, and a host of other nightmarish constraints. Remember, most good candidates are control freaks and sitting there, naked to the world with no format rules to hide behind, can be a disconcerting experience. I loved the format for that very reason, but the August debate was not to be.

The phone rang at home and candidate Jim Blanchard was on the other end. He and I had many a conversation over the years so the call was not a surprise. What he had to say was.

"Tim, I can't do your debate in August," he started out. "I want to do it, that date just won't work. Janet [his wife] and I are taking her mom on a vacation. We won't be near East Lansing. Can we change the date?"

I knew that Blanchard rarely took a vacation and on a personal level, I was sympathetic to his plight. But on a professional level, which is where we were, I had real concerns. What I didn't know, was that Janet's dad had just passed on, and this vacation with Janet's mom was especially important. Had I known that, I would have been a bit more cooperative. However, I didn't, so I didn't sign off on the Blanchard request immediately.

The first thought through my head was very selfish. It is a total pain to rework a date with five candidates when you have one in place. It's endless back and forth phone calls. Three can make it on such and such a date but the other two can't. Then two can but the others can't and so it goes. Plus there is always the risk the whole shebang will just implode and nobody can make it at all. Secondly, I didn't want it to appear I was playing favorites. If Blanchard asked for this and then one of the others asked for something else, all of a sudden I'm in the middle of an ethical mess, and I was not happy about those prospects either.

I told the former governor that I'd have to get back to him. He made it very clear that he still wanted to do the thing, just not on that date. I believed him.

I checked with my TV folks at WKAR. We certainly didn't have a program if one of the five was not there and we could not do it without him, so I called him back and agreed to a date shift. He was relieved and gave me a gracious thank you. I could tell he wanted that vacation. I thought that meant he had grown. Twenty years ago confronted with the same choice, I figured he would have chucked the mother-in-law. I concluded that maybe this was a different Jim Blanchard running for governor as he had been telling me. To underscore his gratefulness, he sent along a warm post card from wherever he was to thank me again for making the change. It was a very nice touch. It was only afterward he explained about the death in the family.

The date that everyone eventually agreed to was the Fifth of November . . . which was almost one year away from the actual general election date in 2002.

Prior to that first TV debate, the Democratic candidates for governor met in their first joint appearance in Grand Rapids. Everyone was there except David Bonior who was confined to his duties in the Congress. I was there to moderate the exchange. It was an unusual forum in that the topic was limited to retirement issues per the sponsoring group's wishes. My job was to fill an hour with questions from the audience. The sponsors were adamant about sticking to the subject but I did secure the ability to do follow up questions when I felt the original audience question had been skirted or unanswered. Everyone was on the same page and on September 24th the quasi debate was staged in DeVos Hall. I still joke that I wonder if Betsy DeVos, the state GOP chair, had the joint bugged.

I had the story pretty much to myself. I think one of the local TV stations sent a crew, but that was about it. The format was working just fine. I got questions from the audience, relayed them to the candidates, and each had a turn to answer and I would jump in occasionally with a clarifying question. The bad news was nobody was making any news. The good news was nobody in the audience appeared to be nodding off.

Then there was a question about not having enough state revenue to fund retirement programs, which in my mind, opened the door to one of my favorite debate questions: The no tax pledge. Even if you've only followed national and state politics from afar, you're still familiar with the promise: The office seeker looks you right in the eye and promises never, ever, no matter what, to raise your taxes. I never had any qualms about asking the darn thing, but it always bothered me when somebody said yes. To be honest, I feel that pledge is the worst form of political pandering. It sounds so good to a tax weary citizenry, but it's also the height of irresponsibility and any solid and forthright candidate knows it.

Needless to say I was shocked and dove for my note pad when Jim Blanchard took the oath! He had never done that before to my knowledge. In fact during his first campaign for governor he addressed the tax increase issue when his 1982 challenger Dick Headlee forced him. Headlee, of course, took the pledge without batting an eyelash. Blanchard said he would only hike taxes as a last resort. His response was not as popular as Headlee's , but it was the right thing to do and to his credit he did it.

Now almost twenty years later, I was hearing something I had not expected. The other candidates refused to join Blanchard. I recall Granholm suggesting that he was wrong to make such a promise in that there was no way a governor could predict the future. What if there was a war or state disaster that drained the treasury? She made it clear she didn't want to raise taxes either but declined to do the politically expedient thing, and Peters and Smith concurred.

Since the rest of the debate had zippo appeal to my statewide TV and radio audiences, I decided to go with the tax promise story.

After the debate, I had my cameraman there and I asked Blanchard to repeat the pledge on tape and got responses from the others as well. It had been a good day. The debate went well. I got a pretty good story and rolled back into Lansing ready to get it on the air. However, just before I left, I got a hint that not everyone was as pleased as I was.

And sure enough, a few days later, I received another phone call. This time from the retirement organization that sponsored the event. They were livid because I had deviated from the format rules.

"Come again?" I questioned.

And so commenced a lengthy conversation where I allowed them to vent and get it out of their system. As the discussion went on, it became clear that somebody had blown the whistle and I was pretty sure it wasn't Granholm, Peters, or Smith. Sure enough it was Blanchard's guy Bob Kolt blowing the whistle. He had belly ached to the sponsors that I had broken the rules by asking the tax question. Hey, it's a free country and I respected his right to beef. I just didn't agree. I felt the tax issue fit neatly into the format, which is why I never gave it a second thought before putting it into play. Unfortunately, the sponsors sided with Blanchard, which they had a right to do.

I apologized saying it had never been my intent to violate the rules and I was sorry they had reached that conclusion. I firmly believed I was just doing my job. We ended the conversation agreeing to disagree. They eventually got over the thing and invited me back to conduct a similar forum with the two GOP candidates for governor later that same year.

The silly thing about the flap was, if I had not asked Blanchard about the tax promise there, I would have eventually done it somewhere else. Either way I would get the story, but rules were rules, and he felt I had broken some.

I have covered eight governor's sweepstakes and this was number nine. However this one had lots of new twists. There was the first female candidate for governor who really had a shot at winning; a former governor trying to win back a job he should never have lost; two worthy state senators, one of whom had already chastised Granholm for not having enough experience and a pit bull from D.C. known for taking no hostages. David Bonior almost single-handedly brought former GOP House Speaker Newt Gingrich to his knees. Since he had missed the Grand Rapids event, I was left to wonder what his conduct would be toward the emerging front runner. Would he have the nerve to take on Granholm?

Even though the election was just about a year away, the capital press corps' interest was well above normal for the very reasons outlined above. When the public TV debate rolled around, the general public may have been out to lunch, but reporters in Lansing were ecstatic.

The drill was pretty much the way we had done debates since the early 1970s. The candidates would be with me in one studio and next door in Studio A we would set up a feed for the press corps, the campaign staffers from the various camps, and we added seats for the local sponsor of *Off the Record*. Kelly Rossman and Roger Martin, who run a local political consulting and public relations company, were told by station management they could invite clients to view the taping. It was a perk for helping to underwrite the series.

In all there must have been over a hundred folks waiting patiently to see what would unfold in this first televised meeting between the five Democrats.

Before the taping even began, I heard rumblings about Granholm having more folks in the peanut gallery than anyone else. The station had not imposed any restrictions but someone from the Blanchard team complained. "We would have had more people here too, had we known it was OK" was the observation. It was an image thing. Blanchard's crowd looked scrawny compared to hers and his camp didn't like it. She probably did.

Granholm also attempted to upstage the other candidates by holding a news conference just before the taping. She told the press corps that former speakers of the Michigan State House of Representatives Bobby Don Crim, Curtis Hertel, and Lewis Dodak were endorsing her that very day. Never mind that there weren't three voters in the state who knew who these guys were and even if they did, they could have cared less. But it was still a great ploy because every reporter knew who they were. Some whispered it was a smooth move by the governor wannabe to gain a little momentum and psychological advantage going into this televised event.

Now get inside my head for a moment on how I prep for a debate. The prime objective is to frame questions so that viewers can compare and contrast the candidates. After all we are doing the program to assist voters making a decision on whom to support. The second goal is to make some news.

Some stations do debates live. We found over the years that on a statewide level, if you tape the debate one day and show it the next, you build a bigger audience. What's the sense of doing it if nobody watches? The reasoning is pretty simple. We do the show. The media reports on it the next day. Readers see the story and find out that the debate will be on that night and voila . . . more people watch . . . or so goes the theory.

I also try to develop questions that are completely new to the candidates. It's typical that during a campaign each candidate will get the same question over and over again to the point they can regurgitate the answer without even thinking. I like to see how candidates perform on their feet dealing with questions that have not been rehearsed.

I also avoid any open ended questions such as, "What is your position on education?" Yikes. Any candidate can do an hour and a half with that softball. It usually reveals very little and eats up valuable time for the rest of the program.

The key to a good debate is having the ability to cross examine. The candidate's first response to a question often needs to be refined so that viewers can understand it. That's also because a lot of questions don't get answered the first time around. Take the follow-up away from a debate and you basically have a free commercial for the candidate's which is why many candidates try to negotiate rules that limit, if not eliminate, that tool.

Every candidate goes through a debate prep. Many of the questions can be anticipated, but that was not the case with my first one for Mr. Blanchard.

Prior to the taping we drew numbers for seating positions. Blanchard got number one, Peters two, Smith three, Granholm four, and Bonior got seat five. We rotated each round of questions so that Blanchard would not get stuck with the first inquiry every time.

As it turned out, being first did not work to his advantage, as everyone else benefited from the mess the former governor quickly found himself in.

The first toss up seemed pretty straight forward.

"Mr. Blanchard," I began after explaining to the audience that there were no rules for this debate, "do you promise never to tell a lie if you are elected?"

First he let out a gasp and launched into it, "First of all promises are things that are only broken by politicians. But I don't believe as governor that I ever told any kind of a serious falsehood . . . ."

I couldn't let that one slipped by so I interrupted to ask, "A serious falsehood?"

What he wanted to say but what didn't come out was that sometimes people tell little white lies in order to avoid hurting someone. His answer was, "There's always white things [now his thumb and index finger are in the air to show a small lie] people talk about not to hurt people's feelings." Then he explains that in Congress and in Lansing he had an honest record. Then he actually took the pledge not to lie, although it was sort of lost in the rest of his answer.

"Sure. Absolutely," he responded.

To which I tried to clarify, "So you won't lie to us?"

"I have no intention of sitting here and lying or serving as governor and lying," he said.

"You might not have any intention of doing that, but maybe you might have to lie sometimes?" I continued.

"In extreme cases . . . national security or personal security," he continued. He's making sense here.

"So it's a promise with an asterisk?" I asked.

"Jimmy Carter . . . .Everybody says that. Politicians are prone . . . I'm wary of politicians that [sic] make promises. I promise to do my best . . . ."

At the time I had no idea how this answer was playing over in studio A where the assembled political insiders were watching. I was told afterward that everyone had a grand laugh as he struggled to find just the right touch on the touchy issue of lying.

More on his reaction to the question in a moment but here's how Jennifer Granholm tackled the question with the benefit of seeing her colleague struggle with it.

"You bet," as she took the pledge right off the bat. She noted that "if for some reason I can't say the answer, I'll say I can't tell you now."

"So you'll offer a no comment?" I stupidly asked. What I did was wrong. I in effect tossed her a life line and she took it. I'm not sure why that happened but it did. There would be no more softballs for her as you will read in a moment.

"Sure if it's something sensitive, but absolutely be honest," she concluded in a clearer and less confusing answer than Blanchard's.

By the time the loaded bomb got around to Bonior, he had this sucker diffused, "I won't lie to the American people or the people of the State of Michigan." End of statement.

I reminded him that Blanchard had just said that all politicians say that, "and none of them keep it."

Bonior responded with, "I've kept my promise," Blanchard jumped in for another bite of the apple being unable to just let this thing die.

"Tim, what I meant by that is there are little things here and there that may not have been intended as a falsehood" and he goes into boilerplate about how all five of them are honorable folks, etc., etc., etc.

To be sure it was not a fatal error for Blanchard. The debate was one year before the election and would be quickly forgotten by media, audience, and others. The Blanchard camp was not in a forgetting or forgiving mood however. Word got back to me within days that they were not only upset with me but felt I was supporting another candidate.

Ouch. That's something you never want to hear. My job now was to go to the horse's mouth and try to resolve this smoldering mess.

After playing phone tag, he and I finally connected.

"I hear you are not happy with me regarding the lying question during the debate," I started out getting right to the point.

He said that was the case as he labeled the question "stupid."

I defended the inquiry and suggested that his answer probably could have been clearer. Bottom line: we agreed to disagree. I also made it very clear that I was not in anyone else's corner and had made a career out of being neutral. I reminded him that when he was in office we might have had disagreements on this or that, but I felt I had always been fair to him and he concurred. We decided to move forward.

Subsequently, I obtained a deeper insight into why he answered the question as he did. He felt I was setting him up. Going on in his head at the time was the concern that once I got him to take the promise, I would confront him with a "lie" that I had uncovered from his earlier days in office. So to cover all the bases, he tried to answer the question from every possible whichway to minimize the damage when I lowered the boom.

Fact was I had no boom. There was no hidden agenda. I didn't have the goods on him, but now at least I had all the candidates on the record promising never to lie, with certain exceptions. I saved the tape waiting for the day when they did. It never happened.

Then we were back to the rest of the hour long debate. While Blanchard was stumbling over his first question, it was candidate Granholm's turn in the barrel on question three, where she looked evasive and uncomfortable. She should have done much better because she knew the question was coming. In fact, she rehearsed her answer during debate prep. Granholm had been corporation counsel, or the chief lawyer, for Wayne County Executive Ed McNamara, who at the time was embroiled in a GOP investigation into contract irregularities at Detroit Metropolitan Airport. Cronyism was the allegation. No one on the Republican committee ever conceded the point, but most in the media correctly concluded if they could ever uncover a smoking gun with Granholm's meat hooks on it, they could end her bid for governor before she could say "vote for me." The debate question was, "If you were governor, would you investigate the airport allegations?"

She said as attorney general she could not launch such an investigation because "nothing has been referred to me criminally."

"Can't you investigate on your own?" I interrupted.

"Well, I'm not an investigating agency. I am a prosecutor," she said.

I tried again, "Can't you file a complaint to investigate?"

She said the senator who chairs the investigation has the "right or obligation to do that."

Then she tried to shift the discussion to the new terminal that was under construction. "They have followed the bidding procedures in the new mid-field terminal . . . the stuff that is being dragged out now is stuff from years ago."

"On your watch?" I inquired

"Much of it before my watch."

Once more, "Any of it on your watch?"

"You know I haven't even seen the report (from the legislature) to be honest with you, Tim. I've not even looked at the report."

Pause for just a second. This exchange is exhibit A on why you want an unstructured format in a debate. Imagine if you will, that the rules allowed only one follow up question, which many formats demand. The viewer would have gotten an incomplete picture and the candidate would have been taken off the hot seat. Because of those follow ups you saw Granholm on the spot.

The airport questioning continued.

Having said that she had not seen the report and knew nothing about it, I asked if she expected some Republican to raise the issue if she got the nomination. She said, "I have doubts there will an effort to do that."

And when they do, "You'll say, you don't know?"

"No, [she responded with her voice rising on the 'o'] I am going to . . . this is what I know, Tim." Now she goes into an explanation of her role as corporation counsel saying she did not set policy for the county but merely reviewed contracts for "form, etc."

"You found no irregularities on your watch?"

"No. This is what I found. Absolutely." She discloses that when she learned there were some old contracts that had not been bid for awhile, "We pulled a swat team of people. We implemented an entirely new process in the mid-field terminal. So the fact that all of these contracts are now bid is a result of what I did as corporation counsel."

As for the GOP probe she offered, "I do think it is part of a witch hunt. You bet."

Now it was Bonior's turn and he was more blunt.

"The airport has been a mess in terms of contracts, cronyism. All those types of irregularities have come to light in the press and something has to be done about it."

I turned back to Granholm, "Is there cronyism going on there or was there?"

She still does not give a direct response. "You know what, Tim, this to me is such a bit of a red herring because the new terminal has abided by all the procedures." When on the ropes, this was one of her techniques that all good politicians use: talk about what you want to talk about. Her only life line was the new terminal, which she returned to time and time again when she was in trouble regarding problems at the old terminal.

"So there's no cronyism?"

"Well" . . . and at that critical point Bonior jumps in, "We're not talking about the new terminal. We're talking about the old terminal."

"Exactly."

But with that interruption she was off the hook and never answered the follow up cronyism question because Blanchard got into the act saying he agreed with Granholm that Republicans were "on a witch hunt." He called for an independent investigation into the matter noting that "public confidence in that airport was very low."

Debating the airport mess and McNamara's alleged involvement must have been uncomfortable for everyone to a certain extent. Granholm had worked for the guy and he was responsible for her running for governor. Bonior and Blanchard knew McNamara from way back, though by this point Blanchard and McNamara had already exchanged nasty public charges about each other.

Blanchard was asked if the current attorney general should investigate. He said he was talking about the airport and not whether the attorney general should investigate.

Granholm was asked the same question and gave the same answer as before. "Tim, the attorney general does not investigate . . . I don't have investigators in my office to do that." Everyone else seemed to think otherwise.

Seeing an opening, Bonior tried to pin her down, "What did you do when you investigated gas price gouging?" Didn't she have investigators for that? was his implied inquiry.

She demurred claiming "the citizens did that."

Granholm managed to get through the ten minute grilling about the airport without a major mistake, but a major impression remained that she could have done better. A notion confirmed by her own camp afterward. In their debriefing, Granholm told her team she was "glad it was over." This was really her maiden voyage in a debate with four other contenders. Heretofore she had only done a one-on-one format with her opponent for attorney general.

"It was not the best answer," one of her aides confessed as they reviewed the airport discussion. "You know what happens when you get in front of the camera . . . you don't always say what you want to say." The Granholm team also went to school and studied the other candidates and how they did.

"Blanchard did a meltdown," was one of the assessments from her side. They also discovered that the former governor was "thin-skinned" regarding his eight year record in office. Finding that weakness, "gave us a road map on how to deal with him in the future," was their conclusion. The Granholm team felt Bonior was one "cool, cold, assassin . . . with a dark side." He appeared to be the least "warm and fuzzy" of the five, which was a fair conclusion. In a word, Bonior was tough to get next to.

There was one other noteworthy line of questioning during this first encounter and it related to the issue of charisma vs. experience. Granholm's opponents had broadly hinted that she had more of the former than the latter, suggesting she was not ready for prime time. Months before this debate, state senator Alma Wheeler Smith, who had years of experience in the legislative trenches, had said so on *Off the Record.*

So I asked Granholm which was more important, charisma or experience? She said both. I asked her to evaluate her charisma quotient. She said she never considered it. There wasn't a soul in the building who bought that from someone who had not taken a bad photograph in her life. Then I asked her about Smith's earlier criticism. Granholm said she had not heard that from the senator. I said "hold on" as I turned to Smith. At first, Smith retreated, but when I reminded her I had her on tape, she confirmed her comments. Don't kid yourself, Granholm was very much aware of Smith's criticism, just as much as she was very much aware of her charisma. Granholm explained that she had plenty of solid experience even though she had been in state government for only three years. The "experience" thing would dog her on the campaign trail, but frankly, much of the public didn't give a hoot. It's the same public that supported term limits, so they treat experience like it's a capital crime.

There was a chemistry of sorts going on between the candidates as I peppered them with questions and they bounced off each other's responses. Perhaps one of the most humorous and spontaneous moments came as Bonior was waxing on about his experience in Congress.

"How does that qualify you to run the state?" I tried to get to the heart of the point.

"It doesn't qualify me," he honestly answered again without beating around the bushy. But he added the experience he got in a variety of situations in the nation's capital would "help him do the business of the state."

As he responded, I noticed that Granholm raised her eyebrows. So I said to Bonior, "Look at her eyebrows right now." Then turning back to Granholm, I asked, "Why are your eyebrows raised?" I am thinking those eyebrows were up because Granholm is not buying Bonior's experience monologue. Wrong.

"I'm listening," she innocently replied.

But Bonier topped her with his comeback. "It's part of her charisma!"

Everyone laughs and she lets out her patented "aaahhh" that starts in a high octave and descends from there.

As the debate drew to a close, the most cantankerous exchange erupted between Blanchard and Bonior over slant drilling in the Great Lakes. They fought to a draw, and then it was over.

One of the fun things to watch is what happens right after the taping. Everyone sat there as we waited for the all-clear from the director. The University of Michigan and Michigan State football game was on tap for that weekend so the chit chat quickly turned to who would win. Blanchard being an MSU graduate did what you expected. The others jumped in, but Granholm refused to be drawn into a prediction. Everyone tried, but she would not budge. Turns out she is not a sports nut, and during one campaign stop she didn't remember who had won the big showdown the year before, and she wasn't, even in a relaxed setting, about to go there again. This lady learns fast.

The debate answered one question—how aggressive would Bonior and Blanchard be on Granholm? On a scale of one to ten, Blanchard was a zero. He took no swipes. Bonior was about a two or three. That would change as the campaign wore on. Granholm had a lead and the two boys had no other political choice but to raise the needle higher.

If there was a fallout from her airport answers, Granholm moved quickly to erase any residue. Within two weeks, she ordered an investigation by the state police into the airport situation. She said she finally acted because she had received a letter from a legislator requesting action. Within that same time frame, Senator Gary Peters dropped out. Most considered him a very qualified contender, but Granholm had gobbled up so much labor money, there were only crumbs leftover for Peters. He knew he would drop out before he did the debate, but delayed the announcement until after his appearance. Sometime later, Smith said adios, too. But in an interesting twist that made news for a couple of news cycles, Bonior asked her to be his running mate and she agreed. It was a smart move, but it did not cut into the "inevitability" factor that Granholm was unbeatable.

There were still some more interesting moments on the way down the campaign trail. The next time I met all the candidates, it was a very unusual forum in Detroit, sponsored by the Michigan Association of School Administrators (MASA). About five hundred school superintendents attended a winter conference and I was there in an unusual role . . . instant analysis of the candidates performances. The affable executive director of MASA, Mike Flannigan, had invited the four Democrats and the two Republicans in the contest, Dick Posthumus and John Schwarz. The former was lt. governor with John Engler, and Schwarz was the widely respected state senator from Battle Creek, who was a candidate, but in name only. Nobody expected him to win the nomination.

The drill was unique. Each candidate would be given twenty minutes to say whatever he or she wanted. I would listen to each one, and then deliver my comments to the audience. I had never done that before and thought it was an interesting challenge. Posthumus got points for just showing up. The organized school lobby was not a big fan of the lt. governor's boss—Engler. Posthumus knew that, so in effect, he was entering the lion's den. He began by telling them that "things had changed" since 9–11, some six months earlier. He then launched into a personal story about his teenage son to underscore the point.

Just after America went into Afghanistan to root out terrorism, Posthumus said his son came to him with a surprising announcement . . . he thought he might join the Marines. Posthumus said he was proud to hear that, but as any parent might be, he had concerns about having his son in harm's way. My wife, Gayle, was with me at the table, and we both remarked that it was a touching and effective story. After that, he recounted his accomplishments; "twenty-four tax cuts that put people to work" and his three proudest; 1) Proposal A, 2) rewriting the school code, and 3) helping to resolve a multi-year legal suit over funding for special education students.

There was his usual stuff about growing up on the farm and having a blue collar background and then he ventured into the touchiest part of his presentation—his support for public education. He noted that all of his children attended public schools and as a parent he had been very active—even allowing himself to be dunked in the school carnival dunk tank.

The superintendents seemed unmoved. They knew that Posthumus, over the previous year, had been the mouth piece for a school voucher proposal that was roundly deep-sixed at the polls. To his credit, he hit it head on.

"You probably heard I voted for vouchers," he tried feebly to bring some humor into the exchange. No one laughed. He forged ahead by saying, "Vouchers are dead. Vouchers aren't for Michigan."

When he finished, there was one question from the audience. "Will you promise never to support vouchers or any variation thereof?"

He said yes, but not one of the five hundred in attendance believed him! During my analysis, I asked the audience about the promise, asking them to applaud if they bought the pledge. Dead silence. They felt because of his very close ties to fellow west Michigan Republican, Betsy Devos, who bankrolled a huge chunk of the pro voucher campaign, that if he got elected, he would renege under pressure from her. I suppose the mistrust was not that surprising, but the next audience response was. I asked them to react to his story about his son. A majority felt he had used it to score political points. More bluntly, he was pandering for votes using 9–11 and his son's comments. Wow ! I could not have disagreed more. I had a different perspective than the audience. I had known Posthumus since he entered the Senate in 1982. I knew he was a true family man and would not "use" his children to win votes. The problem for Posthumus, none of the voters in that room had the same insight, so when he trotted out the touching story, it got him nowhere. In fact, it actually hurt him. Welcome to the rough and tumble world of politics. Even if you are sincere, if you don't have the "charisma" to make them believe you, the public won't buy it. It would haunt Posthumus throughout the entire campaign against Granholm.

Granholm did not give a stunning performance herself. She tried to stuff thirty minutes of you know what into a twenty minute bag and it resulted in a rushed presentation that had very little focus and audience impact. She talked about her five values for running. She spoke so fast, I could only copy down four of them. I didn't see anyone else in the audience even trying to write them down. She explained that her tone toward education would be different than John Engler's. She reflected that Engler had created an atmosphere in which more people believed that Elvis was alive than believed in government. She spoke about reopening health care clinics in schools, teaching parents how to teach, and "tweaking" Proposal A. She, however, had no specifics on what that meant.

In my post speech analysis, I had very little to say because she had very little to say. It was not a great presentation.

Blanchard had some baggage he wanted to unload. He had been questioned repeatedly about why he was in the race, so he told the audience that he "had a passion for the state" . . . and he hyped his experience for his third term. He got in his Engler bashing too, noting that he led the anti-voucher campaign and wanted to form bi-partisan partnerships to get things done. That was Granholm's theme too, to which he said "Everyone tells you they want you at the table. I have had you at the table before and will again."

It wasn't a lousy presentation like Granholm's. He did appear to have a good deal of zest and you could see signs that it was a new Jim Blanchard up there. For one thing, he was one time. When he was in office, this was never the case. The press corps was convinced he'd be late to his own funeral. He seemed to be more at ease with himself and overall got a good reception.

Ditto for Senator Smith who boasted that she was the "most qualified, but least known" . . . a perfect prescription for losing. She did have a good and solid grasp of the issues and nobody could fault her depth of knowledge, but I informed the audience she had no money and therefore would be the next one to drop out.

The "nice" David Bonior appeared at this event. He told the

superintendents that he had a solid record of voting in school elections, but he did not mention Granholm's lackluster record, which he had done on other occasions. He made points for supporting a freeze on a scheduled income tax and single business tax rollbacks. He and Blanchard also wanted to revisit Proposal A, but they didn't use the "T" word for tax increase. I said he did a good job of establishing his credibility with the education community and noted that he had a shot at the nomination vis-a-vis his labor support, which in any Democratic primary was a key factor.

The last guy on the podium was Schwarz. By this time, the audience was on empty, having plodded through almost an hour of boilerplate bromides and rhetoric from the other five, but the underdog Republican brought them back to life.

"I am never going to win the Ms. Congeniality title," he warned the educators. "I may be the last moderate Republican going down in the quick sand, but I will do it with my middle finger in the air" as he brought down the house. It was vintage Schwarz. He said he didn't give a shit what he said. Then he proceeded to take about five minutes to list off his positions on issues, such as vouchers—against them; charter schools—no objection to them, but wanted more accountability before creating more; Department of Education—make it bigger and put MEAP back there.

Then he told the audience he was ready for their questions and he egged them on with, "give me a little chin music . . . a little high hard one never hurt anybody!" He finished with his performance the way the others wished they had. The audience, in a show of hands, gave the day to him. It wasn't even close.

During the analysis, I hinted that there had been some chatter about some Democrat actually selecting Schwarz as a running mate, at which point Blanchard popped up. I didn't even know he was still there! He asked if I would help him recruit Schwarz. It was his best line of the day, and the audience laughed. I said I would not. More laughter.

Herein, lies one of the ironies of politics that has been repeated several times in this state. I laid it out for the audience. In the GOP field there was no question that Schwarz would have been the stronger candidate to challenge whoever got the Democratic nomination. All of the Democrats conceded that point publicity and privately. But he had no chance of getting the nomination. He was pro choice and Right to Life controlled a large piece of real estate in the state GOP. Schwarz was a moderate and clearly out of step with his more conservative compatriots. He had no name recognition outside of Lansing and his home town and he had no money to buy it. He spoke his mind in an unedited fashion and often in a coarse manner, which would offend some Casper Milktoast types in the body politic. Yet he was widely respected among his peers and had a ton of experience, moxy, and all the other elements you look for in a governor. The only problem was he could not win.

Schwarz was relegated to having three debates with Posthumus. In the negotiations, he tried to land one of those on our program. "Skubick, I tried. They would have no part of it," he told me afterward. Instead, they debated in Kalamazoo, Petoskey, and some other out of the way place I can't even remember. They were non-events designed to give him as little exposure as possible. One was on a Friday night at 6 P.M . . . .not exactly prime time. Posthumus knew Schwarz was good, so why risk letting others find that out too.

The Schwarz candidacy was a Don Quixote affair and even he knew it. "From the get-go I knew I would not win, but every once in a while, I would lapse into an illusionary world, but never in the real world. I knew it would not happen," he had said. He still wanted to push his party from what he termed the "Republican moral absolutists" who applied a litmus test to every candidate. If you flunked their exam, you were out. Schwarz knew that attitude would not play well with women in Oakland and western Wayne County. "They would never go for Dick," he figured and even the Posthumus team all but conceded that female vote. Posthumus campaign manager Katie Packer who ran the Posthumus campaign said, "There was no way we could out-woman a woman," referring to Granholm's powerful hold on the gender front.

During the three joint appearances that masqueraded as debates, Schwarz contends, "I could have dismantled him, but I didn't because I knew the outcome had already been decided." Instead, the two formed a rather collegial approach as they bantered about the issues in front of audiences that wouldn't fill a phone booth. Aside from his 'win' at the school forum, Schwarz's other victories, however hollow they might prove, were getting the *Detroit Free Press'* endorsement for the GOP primary and getting John McCain to visit the state on three occasions on his behalf.

Playing everything out, maybe in case of a miracle, Schwarz asked astronaut Jack Lousma to be on the list of possible running mates. There was also a female candidate that Schwarz never disclosed until I pried it out of him for this book. It was Cynthia Wilbanks, the vice president for government relations for the University of Michigan. She had worked for former Michigan Congressmen Carl Pursell and Marv Esch. Lousma said yes to the suggestion. Schwarz says Wilbanks knew about his idea but it was never offered. Had he somehow gotten the nomination, he adds, "I probably would have gone with her."

Since everyone knew he would not win, there was widespread speculation that Schwarz might land a job in Granholm's administration. He reports that he was never approached by anybody for any position. In retrospect, he concluded, "I did the right thing by running for governor." My guess is had the election been decided by the capital press corps, Schwarz might have defeated Posthumus. Even Packer conceded he was immensely popular with the scribes in town, but that doesn't win you any elections. So much for the power of the press.

Schwarz finished in the low double digits with the voters and Posthumus clobbered his Senatemate.

Over on the Democratic side, the three Democrats were hustling for primary votes and political endorsements as well. Frankly, those are not what they used to be. In the 40s and 50s when a union boss embraced a candidate, there was a pretty good chance rank and file would follow his or her lead . . . or else.

Nowadays, there is no "or else." Sure the bosses still endorse, but workers are more independent and stubborn. The Michigan political landscape is riddled with candidates who won the endorsement of the union upper echelon, only to have the minions send them to the showers. George Wallace was an anathema to the United Auto Workers (UAW) and the AFL-CIO, but when the union heads went after him, he showed them. He won the presidential primary with lots of blue collar support. Ditto for Geoffrey Fieger, who despised union leaders. The feeling was mutual. But the angry white males thought he was Mr. Wonderful. He got the Democratic nomination for governor in 1998 with them.

Granholm, Blanchard and Bonior knew the Michigan Education Association (MEA) under its new and savvy president Lu Battaglieri offered a plum of an endorsement. It carries bucks and the promise of grassroots teacher backing. Each candidate wanted it despite the teacher union's track record of some nagging miscues. In 1994, the giant union got out front early and loudly for Democrat Larry Owen. Despite a ton of money, and in-kind contributions stacked high, Owen lost to Howard Wolpe who had UAW and other union backing.

After that, the MEA went into a deep funk. It unloaded its then executive director, who had engineered the Owen endorsement, and the new president sent his union into hiding. It refused to endorse in 1998 even though Owen was back in the hunt. The union discovered that it had many members who didn't want to play the political game. So with the MEA on the sidelines, the aggressive Battaglieri quickly moved to get the union back in the game in 2002. He correctly understood that the MEA could help influence the outcome of the primary and if the right horse was picked, it would mean benefits for the union down the road. Consequently, he announced a screening process for May 2002 in which all the contenders, Democratic and Republican, were invited. To no one's surprise, each agreed to attend.

There was a story sitting out there that I wanted before the interviews took place. I wanted to know who would get the nod and proceeded to work the story until I got it. There were several teachers on the screening committee and if you made enough calls, I figured, the story would emerge. About two weeks before the screening process took place, I ran a story revealing Granholm would get the MEA approval. Just after the paper hit the stands, my phone rang at home. It was Blanchard. He wanted to know if the story was accurate, or just smoke. The essence of his call boiled down to a simple fact. If the outcome was rigged from the start, Blanchard wouldn't waste his time with the "interviews." I obviously could not disclose how I reached that conclusion, but I indicated that obviously I felt the story was true or I would not have run it.

On the very day for the interviews, I staked out a position in front of the MEA building in East Lansing to get a sound bite with each of the participants. It had been revealed to me that Granholm had done something unusual just before the interviews. She had sent freebie fund raiser tickets to all nine members of the screening committee. But this was no ordinary run of the mill fund raiser. It was not a one hundred dollar VFW hall event, but one thousand dollars in the candidate's *own home*. And to top it off, it was held the night *before* the candidate's interviews.

Going into the MEA session Blanchard was direct in his criticism of the Granholm invite. "I think it was wrong. It's another episode in the whole Wayne County airport ethics engulfing the attorney general's office." And then he delivered his best line, "It was like jury tampering."

Bonior didn't go there but he too concluded, "It doesn't feel right . . . . I wouldn't have done it."

Even Republican Dick Posthumus had a take but seemed to cut her some slack. "I think it's a little inappropriate . . . . but what she does is her business."

Granholm reported that no one on the committee attended, which ethically was beside the point. She called it a "gesture to underscore the importance of the education support in her campaign . . . . people invite people to their events all the time. This was a way for them to see how I would want them to come to my home."

Pleazzzze! The whole thing smelled like Limburger cheese. And insiders at the union agreed. "It was wrong," confided one source who sat in all the meetings and reports the Granholm invite was discussed at length. To the MEA's credit, it had warned screening members weeks earlier not to attend anything like the Granholm fundraiser for obvious reasons. If she needed to make a "gesture" the only proper thing to do was to do it after the screening or do it months before the interviews.

The story never got legs and was forgotten. That was a common consequence for her.

Blanchard came out of the meeting with a perplexed look. "It didn't take very long," he recounted "and there were not a lot of follow-up questions" to his presentation. There was a reason for that. Nobody on the screening committee supported the ex-governor, and his interview was described as "pro forma," i.e., just going through the motions.

We next waited in front of the MEA entrance for Bonior to appear after his screening. After a while I got suspicious that he might be trying to duck our interview. Sure enough. Keith Bassar my cameraman and I drove to the parking lot behind the headquarters. There he was trying to get into his car. I ran over and requested a comment which he gave, but it was just a standard "the interview went well." I was certainly hoping for something more, but maybe he knew the writing was one the wall.

The Granholm MEA endorsement was not a slam dunk. There were three Bonior supporters on the panel. They had long and strong ties to their guy and weren't in a mood to cave in. There was an intense discussion about who could win the race and the MEA had a raft of internal polling to show there was only one choice. When the final count was taken, one Bonior backer flipped to the majority and the other two hung tough. The 7–2 vote was not the solidarity the president wanted. But he took it and instructed everyone to keep it secret until the formal announcement. The outcome appeared in the media the next day, the day before the news conference.

Prior to the announcement, Granholm stayed with her message that she shared with every group, "They have a real opportunity here to really make a data-based decision about who is most likely to win." That was precisely the basis for the union's decision even though Blanchard and Bonior had carried the water for the MEA over the years, loyalty was not the overriding consideration. Winning was.

Battaglieri also wanted to bless the candidacy of GOP underdog Schwarz and the panel went along. He had two reasons for that: One it was for the GOP members of his union who had complained for eons about the MEA being a Democratic shop. Secondly, the union head had visions of promoting Schwarz for lt. governor on the Democratic ticket after he lost the GOP primary to Posthumus.

That was another story I stumbled into. Somebody called and told me to ask Schwarz about being approached on the lt. governor possibility. I thought what a great political story and what a great move to entice a Republican onto the Democratic ticket to broaden the ticket's appeal. Independent and moderate GOP voters would surely have taken notice of that.

Hot on the story, I caught up with Schwarz outside a committee room on the third floor of the capitol.

"We need to talk." I suggested walking up to him.

"About what?" he asked.

Now in a softer voice, "About running for lt. governor with the Democrats."

He motioned me into a room nearby and closed the door. He confirmed that he had had two phone calls from unnamed sources who were "feeling him out" on what he might do if asked. "This is great stuff," I said in my head as he proceeded to fill in some of the details. I couldn't get the names out of him, but I had enough to run the story, which I told him I would do. He was concerned about what impact that might have on his relationship with other Republicans. He had to work with them as they were in the middle of the budget writing process. I gave him cover on the story by agreeing not to mention his name which gave him the option to say, "There goes that crazy Skubick again with a wild eyed piece of speculation," or something along the same lines.

Before I ran the article I ran into Granholm and ran it by her. She had not heard it and sarcastically thanked me for "helping me put my ticket together." Of course that was not my intention, but she confided that while it might be a novel idea, "I could never get it through a Democratic convention."

So provocative the notion, the story lasted longer than most. Ultimately it died on the vine.

I was also chasing another endorsement story. In a Democratic election the vote in Detroit is important and winning the support of the mayor can help. Ask Blanchard. He lost the 1990 election, in part, because then Mayor Coleman Young was hacked at Blanchard and didn't lift a finger for him . . . well maybe one finger. Kwame Kilpatrick was now in the mayor's seat and was being courted by the three Democrats. Of the trio, Granholm had the least entree in the city. While she and her husband boasted about once living in the Motor City, they quietly moved out to the suburbs when husband Dan took a job with Congressman Sandy Levin. They could have stayed in Detroit but didn't.

Kilpatrick showed up in the capitol one day and I ambushed him in the hallway outside the Speaker's office. After I did an interview on another issue, we quietly went on regarding his endorsement. He whispered in my ear that Granholm would get the nod that weekend. I asked if I could run with that on the radio. He nodded yes, but again the deal was, leave his name out of it. This is when you trot out the time-worn stuff about "sources close to the mayor."

The story ran on Thursday and I sat back and waited to have it confirmed over the weekend. Saturday came and went. No word. Then Sunday went by. No confirmation. I'm a little hard of hearing, so I'm wondering if I misunderstood Mr. Mayor. Somebody in the Granholm camp called at home reminding me that while I was correct on the MEA thing, they had not gotten any word from the mayor that I was right this time. I couldn't reveal my source, but felt comfortable that the mayor wouldn't misled me.

Turns out he didn't. The big guy just chickened out. I firmly believe that at the time he talked with me, he had every intention of siding with her, but something happened on the way to the endorsement. One unconfirmed theory in the Granholm campaign suggests that Kilpatrick was worried about his own political standing if he picked a horse that didn't win in his town. If Kilpatrick embraces Granholm and he spends a ton of his political capital to deliver the vote and she loses, then he loses a ton of prestige too. So rather than take the risk, he takes the easy way out. Much to my chagrin, Kilpatrick stages a news conference and invites all three candidates and with them standing joyfully at his side, he announces he'll remain neutral and wishes each of them well—so much for my exclusive report. Thanks Mr. Mayor. You owe me one, big guy.

As a result of the non-endorsement, Granholm took a hit. My story created the expectation that she would be blessed and when she wasn't, it looked bad. Not fatal, just clumsy. It was not her only run in with the mayor. He once publicly criticized her debate performance. Meanwhile, Blanchard and Bonior were pleased as punch because they were now on equal footing with her in Motown.

Bottom line, the Detroit vote was up for grabs. When they counted those votes on primary election night, Granholm finished dead last. In fact her showing was such that Blanchard refused to concede defeat on election night. He was hoping that a strong showing in other urban areas, coupled with his strong outing in Detroit, might prove the polls wrong and he would be declared the primary winner.

It was not to be.

Former governor candidate Geoffrey Fieger had an accurate post-election analysis: Granholm was the first Democrat to win a primary without the Detroit vote. That means she did so well in out-state Michigan that it was enough to overcome her dead last showing in the state's largest city.

Blanchard was also quizzed on the feeling that he had gone too far in his attacks on the winner and his take was equally as interesting. He called it a "too far" notion and "hocus pocus." Then he suggested this: The race would have been a lot easier had Alma Wheeler Smith stayed in and there were two women and two men. We could have had a serious dialogue. Instead, every time there was any criticism, you had Granholm supporters and the apologists in the media saying, "Oh you shouldn't criticize her." His theory, which holds some water, was that with two women, that would have been muted.

For years Democrats have staged a "Unity Breakfast" the day after the primary, where all the combatants are encouraged to attend to display a united front as they rally behind the victor. That was the script for the 2002 get together at the Pontchartrain Hotel in downtown Detroit. It is always an awkward event. Here you have three candidates who have been whacking away at one another for months. Feelings have been bruised. Bad blood has flown and now the day after, they magically are supposed to forget all that and put on a happy face.

In the back of my mind was the question, would Bonior and Blanchard show up? When I caught sight of Blanchard and wife Janet, I had my answer and of course shoved a microphone in his face to get his comments. He was very gracious and said all the right things about working for the ticket and doing whatever he could to help deliver the state for Granholm. I felt he was very sincere and was not putting on an act, although I knew it must be tough on him. At one point in the Oakland County parking lot, he was the front runner. Now he had finished last.

Bonior was not nearly as bouncy but just as sincere in his congratulations to Granholm. The B-Boys moved into the room to shake hands with the winner. Blanchard gave her a hug and shook hands with members of the Granholm team . . . some of whom had been with him when he first won twenty years earlier. Bonior joined in and the program began.

About halfway through I noticed that the Blanchards were not in the room. I figured they had been taking an understandable break outside. The script for this event had a climatic photo opt where the three candidates stand together, arms up high, as they acknowledge the thundering applause. But one of the three musketeers was nowhere to be found. Turns out the Blanchards were catching a plane to D.C. Bonior and Granholm embraced, thanked the crowd and held their arms up high, but it was obvious one set of arms was missing. The press corps circulated the room asking, "Where's Blanchard?" Even worse for Granholm, she had to vamp an answer on his mysterious vanishing act. She was as surprised as everyone else.

The Blanchard unexpected exit was the top story on *Off the Record* that week. The consensus of the panel was: Bad form . . . understandable but still bad form. Bad Boy Jamie had managed to steal some of her thunder on the very day "Unity" was on the menu. He did reappear and did earnestly work for the ticket, and the flap blew over. But it's the sort of stuff folks stick in the back of their memory banks. The conclusion was Blanchard was no longer interested in running for any other office because he had burned his bridges with the party faithful that fateful day in August 2002.

If the press corps saw it as a snub, Democratic party chair Mark Brewer did not, and Granholm tried to switch the subject to her Republican opponent. Word was already out that Posthumus was trying to make an issue of her Canadian birthplace. She was not shy about saying, "I think it's a completely phony issue . . . and 85 percent of the people agree with me." She correctly noted that if it were a problem for voters, "I would not be standing here today" as the victor in the Democratic primary.

2

The Mauling
in Marquette

The 2002 election cycle did not have many debates. There were only two Democratic primary debates and three forgettable GOP debates, and then only two in the general election for governor. The first Democratic debate between Blanchard, Bonior and Granholm was staged hundred of miles away from East Lansing—the original spot it was to be held at. In retrospect, the Granholm team called it "the turning point in the campaign."

It was a one-hour special edition of *Off the Record* and we were in Marquette because that's where Blanchard wanted it to be. He told the Granholm folks that there should be at least one meeting in the Upper Peninsula. Her handlers had a different take—that he wanted to "run them around the state." Regardless, when I was asked if we could do the thing up there, I checked with the public TV folks at WNMU-TV and got the green light. This was not my first choice, but frankly I didn't care if we did it in Minnesota as long as we got a chance to do it.

The debate itself is only one element of the story. Some of the stuff leading up to it is also newsworthy. Bonior's team made no demands on format, location, lighting, etc. Blanchard wanted the U.P. site and got it. Granholm's debate squad was really interested in having a podium. I preferred chairs. It is much less formal. Podiums are like being in a court room, which is why her side, with Granholm being an attorney, wanted her standing behind one. She was at home. Granholm's group also felt she would look more like a leader if she stood up. They also worried about the height of the trio. Had she been shorter than Blanchard and Bonior, they may have chucked the podium. Someone recalled that when former Democratic candidate for president, Michael Dukakis debated George Bush, Sr., the Massachusetts governor stood on a box behind his podium. When he stepped over to shake hands, you could see Bush was at least a foot taller than Dukakis. "She works better standing up," one source explained. Her side was also very image sensitive. Blanchard was not far behind. It appeared Bonior didn't give a hoot. He just wanted a debate.

Sitting in Granholm's office, her team plotting the strategy before the debate, they assumed that the two guys would "go after her." By this time she was ahead in the polls and on her way to victory if her opponents didn't do some damage to her. She was advised to be cool, and if she just held her own, she would do well. Granholm had briefing books on issues and on her opponent's records and practiced in several mock debates. Mitch Irwin, who became her management and budget director, played Blanchard. An attorney out of Wayne County, played Bonior and Rick Wiener and Mark Fox traded off playing me. Come to find out, Wiener, the former state Democratic party chair, had made a cottage industry out of being Skubick for a variety of candidates over the years. Fox, the affable Lansing attorney, had been on the inside negotiations on debates for three decades and was the guy dealing with me on format and set. He got his podiums and I got what I wanted—a format with no rules!

Going into this debate, the take on Granholm in the press corps, was that she was untested. She clearly did not have the experience the other two had. She was young and nobody knew if she was tough enough to take some hits and dish it back. They questioned how she would do on the issues. I recalled that during her candidacy announcement tour, she was asked about term limits, a ten year old issue, and she responded, "I'll have to get back to you on that."

The taping was set for 10A.M. on July 18. We got into town the night before and went over to the TV station to check out the set. Some minor adjustments were made and we told the three camps if they wanted to view the studio they could, too. Everyone seemed content. It doesn't always go that way. Come the next morning, I tried to get a copy of the two Detroit newspapers. Turns out the *Free Press* was the only one in the newsstand. I found out afterward that the *Detroit News* arrived a day later. Anyway, it was a good thing I read the *Free Press*, because there was a great question sitting in an article by Chris Christoff. He had written a piece on one of the criticisms Granholm had faced, she was not saying a whole lot about issues . . . not taking any controversial stands on a lot of stuff. There was a clear impression that the less she said, the less chance there was for a slip up. And much to my surprise she in essence confirmed it in the article.

"I would like to give people bushels of specific proposals except that's not what the political experts have said I should be doing." I can't believe she said that. I quickly got on the phone and called Christoff to confirm it. He did, and I wrote down notes knowing I would pop it on her somewhere in the debate.

The broadcast also made news even before the program aired. The local newspaper, the *Marquette Mining Journal*, had done an editorial complaining that the impending event was staged. The editor reamed us for "controlling" all aspects of the program from when reporters could talk to the candidates and a host of other stuff they had a right to print even though none of it was accurate. Had anyone bothered to contact me, some of the misconceptions could have been eradicated. The hidden agenda in the piece was that they didn't have one of their reporters asking the questions. Our regular *Off the Record* director, Dick Best, the WKAR-TV executive producer, Tim Zeko, my wife Gayle, and I arrived at the studio about an hour before the taping. Gayle went to the room where the press corps and the three campaigns would be watching the program. I asked her to take copious notes on where in the program there was an audience reaction to either a question or an answer. I remembered what had happened in the November debate when the audience reacted in so many different ways to what it saw.

I then went around to each room to say good morning to each candidate. I caught Bonior in the middle of rehearsing his closing remarks. I apologized and wished him good luck. Ditto for Blanchard and Granholm. I asked them if they had gotten my list of questions that I had sent to them earlier. They looked startled for a moment before realizing I had never sent them any. I knew they had anticipated some of the questions, but I was sure I had some they weren't ready for.

I returned to the studio to do a mike check. On cue, my first question was . . . if you were a tree, what kind would you be? It was the ole Barbara Walters question from her touchy feely interviews with movie stars that always made me gag. I found out later that Chris DeWitt, Granholm's media guy, was lurking in the control room when he heard the question and then dashed back to their room and announced, "I don't know if this is the first question or not, but Skubick asked what kind of tree would you be" during his mike check. They quickly went to work to construct an answer. I think they came up with an oak . . . strong, solid, etc. Of course, the question never came.

It came time for them to come in and the technicians proceeded to mike them. The week before we drew lots to see where they would stand. Granholm's team had wanted to know well in advance where everyone would be. Their attention to detail was above the curve. Bonior got podium one, Blanchard two, and Granholm three. She won the lottery and picked the last spot because she wanted to go last on closing statements. That would give her the final word and a chance to refute any knock out punches her opponents might have landed.

None of these preparations were seen in the viewing room. It wasn't exactly tense in the studio but it was not a picnic either. Each wrote down some notes on the pad they were allowed to have. There was some good natured back and forth about all the loaded questions I would ask and then it was time to do it.

No it wasn't.

The hidden ear piece that I was to wear to take time cues from the director wasn't working. The engineers assured me it wouldn't take long to fix it. The candidates got more nervous by the minute, and I was getting uncomfortable as well, trying to encourage them to be patient and hang in there. Blanchard didn't. He got up and went to the bathroom. I quickly offered the same to the other two, but they declined. By the time Blanchard got back, it still wasn't working, so I said to pitch it, which is what I should have said earlier.

In the viewing room, Gayle said a lot of speculation was going on. Put twenty reporters and political handlers all in one room and give them time with a blank television screen and you'll get rumors sprouting up like mushrooms.

"Granholm had a meltdown," was one of the rumors, coming from the opposing team.

"Skubick was in make-up and they wouldn't let him out," could have been another guess.

Anyway, I heard the program opening tape roll and I knew we were finally underway. I wished everyone luck again and I said a little prayer under my breath asking for the wisdom to be fair. I had crafted a first question that I thought would get us off to a good start. Lots of charges had flown between the three up to that point, and I wanted to know if there was one question the candidates wanted answered before we finished the debate.

In my thirty-four years of doing this stuff, it was probably the worst question I had ever developed. There was only one person in the place who understood it, and that was me. I wanted them to say something like, "My opponent has called me a 'so and so' and I just want the audience to know the truth." What I got wasn't even close. Poor Bonior had to figure out what the question meant and finally went into a blurb about why he was best for the job. Blanchard didn't give me much better. Granholm did what amounted to an opening statement and all I could do was sit there and wish I had developed a better opening shot.

The second question started with Blanchard. One of the knocks on him was that he spent many of his years in the governor's office doing what his polling told him to do, not what he believed he should do. Rightly or wrongly, it was an issue that led me to ask: "If you had a strong personal conviction on an issue, yet the polls told you that the people were dead set against it, which factor would be more important in making your decision?"

"You care about what people think, but what's right for the state is the key question," he suggested. Stop the tape for some background. Remember that in this race the female vote was emerging as a dominant factor. Blanchard was smart enough to know that abortion resonated with segments of that voting block, so he effectively segued from my question into what he wanted to talk about, which was Granholm's stance on abortion. Roll tape. "I'm the only candidate standing here who has been unwaveringly and clearly pro-choice," he tells the camera.

Granholm jumps in asking for permission to "allow some free exchange." She didn't need it; the rules were designed to provide just that. "I have been 100 percent pro-choice, too, Jim. And you darn well know that your secret committee has taken out ads against me that say I'm not pro-choice, and that is a lie." She proceeds to tick off four women's groups that have endorsed her, but Blanchard overrides her.

"Name three things you've done as attorney general to protect a woman's right to choose . . . name one thing," as he looks her square in the eye.

Granholm, as she did several times during the broadcast, ignored the direct question and did the ol' switch-eroo.

"Jim, my question to you is, will you call upon your committee to take down ads that are lies?"

Blanchard then accuses her of airing an ad that is "misleading and false." We are now eight minutes into the debate and the fat is already in the fire. Granholm admonishes him for trying to take female votes away from her and remembering her opposition research on him, she hits him for voting for the Hyde Amendment in Congress to deny the right of poor women to have an abortion.

Watching all this, while his handlers in the back room are screaming for him to get into the battle, is Bonior, who finally says he wants to answer my earlier question on convictions vs. polls.

He does a nice job of pointing out a courageous stand he had taken on calling for a freeze in two tax rollbacks slated to take effect. He argues you can't give back money you don't have and chastises his opponents for being afraid to take that stance. On polls vs. convictions, Bonior was scoring some points. "Their handlers basically told them you can't take that posture," driving the point home.

Granholm is asked about her convictions. She points to her

strong beliefs about family, faith, and core issues "that are fundamental to who I am." But she also says there are other issues in the
"public domain" where you need input from stakeholders to make a
good decision. To illustrate her point she brings up the concealed
weapons permit issue that had gone though the legislature. She says
she took an unpopular stand to oppose the measure thus acting on
her convictions—she felt that more concealed guns on the streets
might produce more suffering.

Bonior and Blanchard do a tag team attack on her. Bonior says
she "waffled" on the issue and Blanchard concurs claiming she
wants to be on both sides of guns, choice, vouchers, and campaign
finance reform.

"What waffle?" she retorts.

Stop tape. One of the fascinating elements in this race was how
the two gentlemen treated the lone female in the debate. The rules
of engagement are different than they are if the candidates are all
men. I had the sense that nobody was quite sure what the new
engagement rules were. Thus, neither of the men knew where the
line was on attacking her. They didn't want to offend voters, but
they also didn't want to let her off the hook.

Where the line was became clearer after the broadcast. I would
find out that my role as inquisitor was also under the microscope
vis-a-vis my questions to Granholm, which drew some interesting
viewer comments. You should know that the Granholm debate prep
team told her the two men would come after her and they did. She
was prepared. Not only did she take the hits, but she did not flinch
at striking back. Roll tape.

The next question was for Granholm and it was out of left field.
There is no way she could have anticipated this one. Her answer
turned out to be the best of the debate, because it came from her
heart and not her debate prep book. The question was, "Had you
been governor at the time, would you have opposed cross district
busing?"

I took some heat after the debate for asking this one. Brian Dick-
erson in a *Detroit Free Press* column thought it was silly to raise an
issue that was over thirty years old and others readily nodded their
heads in agreement. On the surface they were right. However, there
was a reason for the question that went beyond the mere issue. In
my research before the debate, I came across an article on

Granholm where she had been a negotiator at her California high school where busing was being used to integrate the school. Her assignment was to make it work and bring both races together. After reading that, I thought it was fair to ask about her views on the issue as it related to Michigan.

During the 1970s busing was "the" emotional issue of the decade. Suburbs were lined up against the concept, but a federal judge was for it, and Detroit school children were caught in the cross fire. A constitutional amendment on the issue was put up for a vote in Congress and I knew both Blanchard and Bonior had been involved. Granholm was not a Michigan resident during all this so my question had several objectives. One, would her answer be consistent today with her beliefs when she was in high school? Second, her answer could not have been rehearsed and I wanted viewers and myself to see what she did on her feet being forced to formulate a response on the spot.

I knew immediately after asking the question that she had not anticipated it because, as any good debater does when time is needed to think, she repeated the question to herself. "Hum. Had I been governor at the time, would I have opposed cross district busing? Hum . . . No, I would not have. I think that busing was at the time a very important part of having children interact . . . an attempt to get people to come together." But what about somebody from the suburbs who might have said, I fear for my children? Granholm noted that this was not an issue today and I suggested I wanted to get at the "essence of her civil rights beliefs."

She took it and ran for a touchdown. There was no waffling here. Speaking from the heart, which is where the best answers come from, she noted that while at Harvard Law School she was on the *Law Review Journal.* What she didn't say was she got into trouble with the administration when she endorsed the divestiture of university funds in South Africa. She said she had been a law clerk for Judge Damon Keith who had a distinguished civil rights record and she added, "I wanted to be a civil rights attorney."

She then masterfully moved into comments about needing a governor who was "not afraid to have a dialogue about race." She hit the Engler administration for having "disenfranchised" cities and criticized Lansing, "which had turned its back on our urban cities."

Then reworking the line that former Governor William Milliken liked to use, she said "We can't have a vibrant state without vibrant cities."

Bonior agreed on the need for such an agenda and then he tackled the busing issue. He conceded afterward that his answer was "twisted" and I wasn't really sure what he had said. He did reveal that his own child was bused but Bonior preferred "different options" and could not support busing in all cases.

Blanchard's son was also voluntarily bused, but the former congressman opposed the concept when it was debated in Washington.

Bonior then moved the debate into its most contentious segment. All three candidates were arguing at once over her role as attorney general on an obscure state body called the Administrative Board. There were not three viewers in TV land that had heard of it, but both Bonior and Blanchard tried to paint her as a rubber stamp for John Engler's policies that passed through the board rather than standing up to him.

She explained the board does not make policy and her role was to merely sign off on the "form" of various contracts. Blanchard took the first shot, "I don't know why you are running for governor if you don't know the duties of attorney general." Granholm, now frustrated said, "Oh my goodness." Blanchard says he has more experience in the A.G.'s office than she does and next she delivered a line that her advisors told her not to deliver.

"And you were Frank Kelley's driver."

"I wish I had been," Blanchard cut in, "because I would have had more power frankly."

"Bonior accused her of fronting for Engler and she retorts, "Its part of the problem with being a congressman from Washington, coming in to see how state government works." It's getting really good now.

He interrupted her, "I served in the legislature for four years. You don't have to lecture me on how state government works!"

She dismissed the whole discussion as a "red herring" but Bonior refused to let it go. His debate handlers and he had decided their agenda was to show her as someone who "goes along to get along." Bonior used a quote from the *Free Press* to slam home his point . . . the quote I was going to use. She was not giving a "bushel of specifics" . . . "that's not what the political experts have said I should be doing," then Bonior added this, "She isn't her own person. She wasn't in Wayne County with McNamara. She isn't now."

It was the hardest hitting comment of the debate, but rather than respond to the quote, Granholm delivers a rehearsed line she had been waiting to use.

Remember she had been told that the guys would go on the attack, but her retort had to be delivered after that fact was firmly established in the viewers' minds. She saw the opening and looked right into the camera lens to talk to the voters at home: "This is what's going on here, so that everybody understands. The polling reflects that I am doing very well and so the object here is to try to take apart the person who is in first place." The line was delivered without malice, but with just the right touch to drive home her point.

But she is not done as she then attempts to smudge her challengers. "These are all good people and unfortunately politics sometimes does terrible things to otherwise good people." Bonior has had enough. "That's a very patronizing remark and I resent it as well." He tries to continue his line of attack, but once more she steps in to redirect the discussion, and she accuses him of violating the spirit of the public funding campaign law. "A classic case of hypocrisy" she tells him and he tells her she did the same thing when she ran for attorney general.

Just as I am ready to move onto something else, Blanchard decides he's not done with the "being a rubber stamp for Engler" subject, and we're right back into her role on the Administrative Board.

Eventually we moved onto other issues and near the end I popped them a question that was designed to test their knowledge of current events. The Michigan Chamber of Commerce two weeks earlier had staged a news conference opposing legislation to change the definition of "sinking funds." Those are monies used by school districts for non-operating expenditures. It was in all the papers so the intent of the question was to see if they knew it and, if not, would they try to fake an answer or just admit they didn't know.

To their credit each one said they didn't know. The Granholm handlers, sensitive to the criticism that she was not up to speed on the issues were thrilled to hear Blanchard confess his ignorance because if he didn't know after eight years in the executive office, how could she know?

In their closing remarks, Bonior went first. "It's been a joy to be with you . . . well maybe not a joy, but interesting . . . I will fight for the people of Michigan. I will be your leader." Blanchard said, "I've done it before, I can do it again." Granholm noted that "I'm not a legislator. I am just somebody who is a regular person . . . we need a new generation of leadership and I'm ready to take it on."

I thanked the trio for participating and then made one last miscue, I reminded people to be sure and "vote on April 6." Of course, the primary was on August 6, which all three candidates reminded me, as the credits rolled. We all laughed.

The formal debate was in the can, but the entire shooting match wasn't over by a long shot. A debate is really divided into three parts. Part one is the preparation. Granholm, as noted earlier, went through extensive preparation that began by having meetings with key advisors, going over strategy and books on issues and her opponents' stances on the same. Then she progressed to mock debate rehearsals we mentioned earlier. Bonior took a different tack. He conferred on issues with his handlers but then retired to review the material by himself, much like you might cram for a final exam.

I also did lots of debate prep. Every news item involving the candidates was clipped out. I would keep a list of potential questions on my desk and would add to it whenever one popped into my head. Sometimes that would be in the middle of the night. I would literally wake up with a question floating around in my head and I'd either jot it down on a pad or get up and write it out before I could go back to sleep. I always ended up with more questions than could be used, so I had to cull out the ones I thought would give the audience the most insight. I sometimes ran questions past my wife, who acted as a one person focus group. Sometimes I ran them by people I trusted who followed the Lansing scene closely. In addition, many times other reporters would call with suggestions.

The second phase is the debate itself and then comes the final portion, the post debate spin session. That was next as the candidates headed for the big viewing room at NMU where the reporters waited to grill them some more. My role was to be quiet and listen. I would go from huddle to huddle where each candidate was adding their observations to the story. I remember Granholm commented that there wasn't much time for issues the voters wanted to know about. A good criticism, but I also knew in the next debate slated for

Southfield in three days, there would be plenty of that and very little of the intense cross examination she and the two men had just gone through.

I retreated to Gayle. She remains my most honest critic. I could tell from the smile on her face that she thought it had gone well.

The spin session is like the floor of a political convention. Reporters are trying to get more angles to their stories and the candidates and their handlers are trying to present their performance in the best light possible—which is why all three candidates declared victory.

The Bonior declaration was the most interesting in that his campaign team said publicly.

They concluded privately. "We thought we lost," confessed a Bonior insider. "We kept waiting for him to get into the act. At one point it seemed like fifteen minutes before he said anything."

In a word the Bonior team was deflated. What they saw on the screen was not what they wanted to see. They labored through the spin session with reporters, trying to conceal the notion that they figured he had finished dead last.

Then something unexpected happened. Bonior got outside the debate bubble and people approached him on the campaign trail congratulating him on his stellar performance.

My stellar, what? he must have mumbled to himself.

The comments kept coming. "You stayed above the fray." "You did a great job."

Suddenly his squad reversed its thinking. It was not as bad as they thought. "Sometimes you get too close to these things," one aide confessed.

How true. The same thing can happen to reporters covering a race. You get so up close and personal that you lose that vital connection to the guy at home who is not.

Prior to this surprising audience reaction, Bonior's folks suggested he had "dominated the debate." What, by keeping his mouth shut for fifteen solid minutes? Go figure.

Meanwhile the other two candidates were hurriedly grinding out their press releases, too. Granholm's claimed, "She scored a victory as she highlighted her record of accomplishment as attorney general that gets real results for real people . . . ." She also took a swipe at the challengers saying, "It's unfortunate that my opponents would rather have a confrontational discussion about politics, than talk about the issues that count!" Take that.

Ironically it was the very confrontational nature of the program that helped Granholm the most. It established in the press' mind that she was no light-weight. Blanchard and Bonior tried to make mince meat out of her and she emerged smelling like a rose. It was just the results her handlers had hoped for.

Blanchard's media hound, Eric Mueller, got into the act. "Today we saw the beginning of the Granholm meltdown. Now I see why they wanted to negotiate for less [sic] debates. She was really rattled," claimed Mueller. He couldn't stop putting in a plug for the guy who signed his checks, "It was obvious who the governor was on that stage. Governor Blanchard was the clear winner."

You would expect each candidate to declare victory and head for the Lower Peninsula. They can say all they want, but the reality is that the final arbiters of who won are the media, the audience, and word of mouth in the general public.

The media play on the story was critical of the candidates. Most of the state would not see the program but many more would read about it. Kathy Barks Hoffman, the veteran correspondent for the Associated Press, told newspapers and radio listeners around the state, "It was a heated debate." She recounted the attacks on Granholm as the two guys suggested "she was not being her own person . . . and was too closely tied to John Engler." Then she quoted Granholm's finely rehearsed line, "The object here is to take apart the person who's in first place."

Veteran and insightful *Detroit News* columnist George Weeks had a different take. He called it "One of the most contentious gubernatorial debates in recent years." And quoting Granholm about the match, she called it "a tag team verbal attack." Then she boasted, "I stood toe to toe. Bring it on. Who let the dogs out?"

I talked with each candidate as the post debate session wore down and thanked them. I sincerely meant my thank yous. Doing these events is what I enjoy most but it would never happen if the candidates did not agree to appear. I wished them well and said I would see them at the WXYZ-TV forum in three days for the second and final debate.

The candidates moved onto other events. I thought if anybody bothers to watch they will see the candidates as they have never seen them before . . . and given the limited number of debates, probably never again.

Best, Zeko, Gayle and I hopped in the car. They were headed for East Lansing as the tape had to be driven back to make the satellite uplink time. The two of us headed for Mackinac Island to belatedly celebrate our anniversary which was the day of the debate. Some anniversary gift, hey babe?

On US-2 between Marquette and Mackinac the consensus of the foursome was, "We had all done good." In the TV audience's mind, nothing could have been further from the truth. But I would not discover that, until after we got home later that weekend.

Over the years viewer reaction to any one program is fairly predictable. Very few bother to say anything, preferring to get on with their lives. Those who really hate a production are usually the ones to complain but their numbers are relatively small.

When we got home the email box was humming. There was a ton of extremely unhappy and upset folks out there and these were not the run of the mill, "we didn't like your program" genre either. Many were nasty. Some hinted they would stop contributing to public TV. Others took after me personally. The one I liked the most was, "There weren't two men debating Granholm, there were three." Meaning me.

Nobody had ever written that about me covering men running for governor.

As the weekend moved on, the emails kept rolling in. I lost count after about 50. I was shocked, disappointed and knew I had another assignment . . . answering all these people who took their time to express themselves—even if it wasn't to fan my ego.

Zeko was gracious enough to take the ones that had a general beef. It was only appropriate that I tackle the ones who personally had it in for me.

To maintain my sense of humor, at a decidedly unfunny moment, I reminded myself of the way L. Brooks Patterson used to answer unfriendly mail. He'd write, "I regret to inform you that some jerk is writing nasty letters and is signing your name at the bottom."

Obviously I could not say that, but it helped to keep this matter in perspective. I had learned over the year that it's fruitless to attempt changing a person's mind once it's made up. So my tack was to share with them why I had done what I did. I began by thanking them for taking the time to share their thoughts. I explained that one of the missions of our program was to stimulate public discussion, to jolt viewers out of their lethargy and get involved in the process. Clearly these folks were doing that and I applauded the effort. And I really meant it.

I tried to explain the genesis of some of the questions and my role as a moderator to pursue the candidates whenever I felt they had not answered the question. I said I did not treat Ms. Granholm any differently from all the other governors I had covered (just ask them).

Clearly there was a reservoir of sympathy for Granholm which I had not confronted before. It was a wake up call that having a woman in the race touched a nerve with voters that I had never seen before. The point was really driven home a few days later when I made a call to Fraser, Michigan.

We were on the way to Ann Arbor to baby sit the grandkids when I decided to call my Mom.

"Hey, mom. How ya' doing?"

"Why were you so rough on Granholm in that debate?"

There was no "Hi Timmy, how are you?" And certainly no, "You were fabulous, son." I double checked the cell phone to make sure I had the right number.

Having lost my mom, I knew this thing was serious. She went on to join in with the other folks who didn't like my performance either. Being an understanding son, I let her go on. And the more she talked, the more I concluded that I had to write a column on this whole experience.

The column that week began, "Dear Mom." I wrote as if I was talking to her and tried to explain the role of a journalist. What she and my other "friends" were indirectly telling me was to cut Granholm some slack. Give her a little break. I explained I could not do that. Doing so would violate my journalistic duty to treat everyone the same regardless of gender. I concluded the letter by making sure Mom still loved me.

Before the piece went in the paper I ran into Jerome Marks from the Granholm campaign and gave him a heads up on the "Dear Mom" letter. A few days after the piece ran, I ran into Ms.

Granholm. She walked right up to me and said, "I really like your mom. Where did she go wrong with you?" she pulled my chain.

I told her I was adopted. We both laughed.

The good news is Granholm was not upset with my role in the debate. She was used to it. She did not want to be treated any differently. She knew I was just doing my job and told me so. I appreciated that and secretly thought to myself, well then call off all your zealots who don't. I was not in this business to win a popularity contest. I was a big boy and could take some hits but I must say the intensity of the hits this time was a new experience.

Your first human reaction when pelted with bricks is to throw them back, but after a while, I re-evaluated it. Had I gone too far? Was I unfair to her? Should I have blown the whistle more often to interrupt the verbal battles between the three? As I reviewed the tape again before writing this chapter, I felt there were a couple of times I became too engaged in cross examining her, but, in the heat of the moment when I think a candidate is not answering a question, it is my style to jump in and try to get one. Remember, these are folks who don't always *want* to answer. Frankly, some viewers like it, and some don't. Political journalism is not a popularity contest. You do what you think is right at the time and let the chips fall where they may.

I remain convinced that I was not unfair to anyone in the debate. I dished it out to the two men as much as I did to her. After the shock of all the negative comments was allowed to settle, I took much of the criticism to heart, but on balance I was able to sleep at night. It was still exciting to anchor such an event. My next assignment would be back in my regular role as observer, not participant.

The three Democrats had agreed to only two televised debates and the last one was in Southfield, four days after the "Mauling in Marquette." The three would again stand behind podiums but the format this time featured Chuck Stokes, the editorial director at WXYZ, Channel 7, and their two main anchors Guy Gordon and Diana Lewis. The latter two would provide the questions and Stokes would jump in for clarification when needed. The candidates' answers were limited to ninety seconds and there was not much, if any, opportunity for them to verbally interact with each other. This would not be a free for all.

The program was done live and I joined my colleagues in an

adjoining studio to watch the festivities. There was a whispered groan in the group when Ms. Lewis asked the first question. . . . "Should God remain in the Pledge of Allegiance?" Not exactly a cutting edge question that would determine the outcome of the election, but it's a free country and reporters can ask whatever they want. To no one's surprise, none of the three candidates came out against God.

Question two was better. It dealt with the sorry state of Michigan's financially strapped budget and the need for a possible tax hike. Reporters in the bull pen knew the answers before the candidates opened their mouths. We had heard it countless times on the campaign trail, but it was still a good question in that many of the viewers where getting their first glimpse at the candidates and were hearing the answers for the first time.

And there-in lies a constant dilemma in political journalism. Reporters who cover the candidates day to day have heard the same clap trap on the same issues over and over again. We are always looking for a new top, a new lead, something different for today's story. Sometimes we forget that the typical voter is not following the race as closely as we are and we lose sight of the fact that they probably haven't heard the answer on taxes. But by the same token we can't and don't want to run the same story over and over again, although candidates would love that. Finding the middle ground between something new and something the voters need to hear is a challenge and I don't think we get it right all the time.

The exchange went on fairly routinely with the trio discussing Canadian trash, the Detroit reform school board, and roads. Finally at 8:43 . . . some forty-three minutes into the debate, Jim Blanchard fired a shot. Taking a question on public health, he turned it into an accusation aimed at Granholm's husband, Dan Mulhern. Blanchard suggested that because Mulhern had been a paid consultant to Michigan Blue Cross and Blue Shield, Granholm, if elected, could not regulate the insurance giant.

She retorted that her husband's work was "separate from my role," as she actively rejected her opponents thinly veiled conflict of interest charge. She was much more animated in the post debate spin. The attack was "over the edge" an angered Granholm told the press corps eager to find a new angle on an old story. "To attack one's husband," she warmed to the counterattack, "is totally garbage and crosses the line." She noted that Blanchard was behind in the polls and hinted that he was desperate . . . the same thing she said in Marquette . . . and she was right.

In their closing remarks, Bonior said the state needed "more than a lawyer." Blanchard remained on the attack suggesting that Granholm was not new, but part of the "old Democratic machine out of Wayne County." Granholm said, "I want you to hire me." She then accused the two men of talking the talk, but not walking the walk when it comes to getting things done. "If you want the same old, same old," she concluded, "I am not your man!"

They covered twelve different questions on the program and it was much more orderly than the one in Marquette. Granholm's folks liked this format much better because there was more control and she was not put on the defensive. As one aide said during an interview for this book, "We had proven in your debate that she could go toe to toe with these guys. There was no need to prove it again."

The WXYZ debate had a wonderfully large audience. It won its time slot that night, which was a very encouraging sign. Given a chance, voters will watch a debate, but they need to have more. Two debates in a race for an open seat is not enough. The debates came just two weeks before the election. Much of the research suggests that many voters don't begin to focus on a race until ten days or so before. Granholm's people would not agree to holding a debate closer to the election. It was too risky. Why take the chance? Good political judgment, but bad for the uninformed public. That's the way it's always been, and short of getting a court order to control the broadcast date, which is impossible, that's the way it will be. Too bad.

The rest of the Democratic primary was waged on the airwaves with commercials the candidates controlled, which is just the way they like it. That's the stuff that uninformed voters saw days before they voted. Basing a decision on those ads is a disservice to our democracy. It boils the race down to image and not much more, which is a lousy way to pick our leaders. None of those final day commercials dealt with the most pressing issues of the election: What would the candidates do about the whopping state deficit?

There were only two candidates who hit it head on with direct and easy to understand answers. Bonior and Schwarz got it right.

Bonior talked about freezing the scheduled tax rollbacks and Schwarz told his opponent Posthumus in one debate, "We have tax cut ourselves to death . . . we need to pause the tax cuts." The others did not agree, but they also didn't offer even a hint of how they would address the mushrooming red ink and its impact on state services.

Once the primary was over, and it was Posthumus vs. Granholm, voters still didn't get a direct answer.

3
The 2002 Governor's Race

If you were forced to sum up the critical factors in the 2002 race for governor, they would be: charisma vs. experience; the Kwame ad; the porch ad; Jennifer, Jennifer, Jennifer, and reparations.

The outcome of the August 6, 2002 primary election went according to the script. It would be she vs. him. When I showed up at Dick Posthumus' post-election rally in Novi, one of the first guys I bumped into was Rusty Hills. He was on his last legs as state GOP chair, although there was no formal announcement that this was his last race for governor.

Hills nailed the contest in one simple sentence. "If we run this race on charisma, we lose. If we run it on issues, we win." The GOP did neither.

Posthumus showed up at the event with some great sound bites. He wanted voters to know he was the guy with experience and she was not. He went after her with, "We are not picking a senior class president here."

Republicans had long worried about what the media dubbed

Granholm magic—her uncanny ability to light up a crowd. It really didn't matter much what she said. The fact that she was there saying anything became the message. The GOP had not concocted the antidote.

I had first run into Granholm Magic more than a year earlier at a Michigan Education Association spring conference at the Lansing Center. Vice President Al Gore was speaking to about 1,500 rabid and politically hungry teachers. Union president Lu Battaglieri was warming up the crowd and went down the list of Democratic dignitaries in the audience. Each was greeted with politeness that barely budged the needle.

Congressman John Dingell . . . .yeah and clap.

Former Gov. Jim Blanchard . . . clap and yeah.

U.S. Senator Debbie Stabenow . . . clap, clap, yeah, yeah.

Michigan Attorney General Jennifer Granholm. Explosion. The place went nuts.

I remember standing next to my ole pal Hugh McDiarmid from the *Free Press*. We sort of looked knowingly at each other without saying a word. This was unbelievable. My first peek, but certainly not my last, at Granholm Magic.

Back to the day after the primary, Posthumus had a formidable opponent and was the media anointed underdog. He liked the label . . . at least that was his public take. He knew he could not out charisma the high school class president candidate but he would try to out experience her.

He had confided to me that he was well aware of her talents and her ability to use the tube to her advantage. I asked him about his own media savvy and he revealed that indeed he had taken one, count it, one media training course.

Mort Meisner had been the news director at TV 2 in Detroit and after he left, he set up his own consulting firm. Posthumus was a client but not for very long. As Meisner tells it, the west Michigan candidate had a lot of handlers, each of whom knew exactly what the Dickster was supposed to do. Meisner had his own ideas but didn't get more than three or four hours to share his thoughts. He concluded most of his tips were ignored by the know-it-alls surrounding Dick Posthumus

Posthumus dropped out of the course. "It was not me," he said. He figured he would be further ahead being himself. Usually that theory works, but when you are battling someone who has a wonderful image, maybe he should have enrolled for a few more media training credits.

Anyway he started his campaign with one of the craziest and lame brained ideas ever. He told voters that his opponent did not have Michigan values because she was not born here. The theme was completely factual, but completely ineffective, too. Granholm was born in Richmond, British Columbia and her family migrated south of the border to San Carlos, California where she grew up.

After trying her hand at becoming a Hollywood star, which included an appearance on the Dating Game, she decided that was not for her. By the way, the GOP never confirmed this but you know they looked far and wide to find a copy of that game show tape. Couldn't you see the resulting commercial if they had uncovered a copy? Bachelor number one: If I was an apple what would you do? Bachelor number two: complete this sentence: Love me with all your (blank). If the GOP wanted to recast her image, the appearance on that game show would have been great ammo. But alas the tape doesn't exist. Even Granholm doesn't have it. That was before VHS video taping at home.

Anyway, the Posthumus theme was: Here was a Berkley and Harvard graduate who didn't know squat about Michigan. Why would you want to elect her governor?

Reporters on *OTR* had a riot with this one. First of all, over half the population in Michigan were not born here. Secondly the other half were not as parochial as Posthumus thought. There were not many voters interested in a cultural war over who could best govern based on where they were born. In fact the only folks who liked the theme were already in the Posthumus camp. The strategy, at the very best, helped to solidify his GOP/conservative base, but he didn't have to worry about that. The voters he didn't have—independents, moderate GOP women, and conservative Democrats—were not moved by the attack.

Posthumus tested this approach on focus groups and apparently it worked with a room full of voters. But the fact was, at the outset of this campaign, very few voters even knew what a Dick Posthumus was. He took his first opportunity to tell them by attacking his female opponent because she was not born here.

In this race, voters first wanted to know who he was before he went after her, but in the GOP's misplaced blueprint, they went for the kill before the killer was even known to the citizens.

Campaign manager Packer says the intent was to play the "out of state" angle tongue-in-cheek. "Remember the wager we made about the Stanley Cup with her being from Canada?" Packer claims it was all supposed to be in fun. But she concedes some well meaning supporters "tainted our whole message."

Shortly after the August primary, Granholm staged a thank you rally for Lansing supporters on the capitol steps. Her backers were not the only ones on the evening news that night. Standing within shouting distance was a group of young Posthumus backers with protest signs and they were shouting: "Send Granholm back to Canada" and similar sayings that did not appear to be "tongue in cheek." Packer says, "We didn't orchestrate it. Posthumus had nothing to do with it. It was college kids acting on their own."

The story that night perpetuated the notion that the Posthumus camp was serious about the carpetbagger charge, and nobody in the Granholm camp or portions of the electorate, thought it were funny. Packer could do nothing. There were some things you just couldn't control and in this case, the unsanctioned event hurt.

That handed Granholm her first opportunity to paint the Posthumus image before he did. She responded saying Posthumus wanted to divide the state, while she wanted to bring it together. Which one of those themes had a more salutary impact on voters?

In addition to their chores of winning votes, the two candidates also had to assemble the rest of the ticket. Each needed a running mate, attorney general, and secretary of state candidates.

Posthumus had a laundry list of potential running mates. Some reporters thought Schwarz would be a good pick but that was never in the cards. Instead, Posthumus went into the senate chambers to pluck out a relatively unknown, who was on the ticket for one major reason; he was from vote rich Wayne County and a proven vote getter there.

I got wind of the decision one day before Posthumus was to make the announcement. I confirmed it by calling the wife of Senator Loren Bennett.

"Congratulations," I started out. "Have you signed off on your husband running with Dick Posthumus?"

When she answered yes and proceeded to explain how the two of them debated it back and forth, I had the story nailed. I thanked her for her help and wished her well. Within a half hour, I was on WWJ reporting the story. Posthumus told me afterward he was riding in the car that afternoon and heard the story and wondered how I got it. He soon found out because Mrs. Bennett called the campaign headquarters and notified them that, "I just got off the phone with Tim Skubick and he's got the story already."

As the campaign played out, Bennett who had a wealth of experience and a good political compass found himself on the outside looking in. Bennett alleged the Posthumus inner circle was not always inclusive. Katie Packer who ran the campaign denies the charge.

Granholm's camp set up a nicely orchestrated cattle call that the media followed. Names of potential candidates were freely leaked for two reasons: build up some suspense and provide an ego stroke to the interviewees—the vast majority of whom didn't have a snow ball's chance of getting the nod, but they got their name in print.

Turns out the man she eventually picked credits one of my columns for putting his name in play. Three or four months before the selection process began, I suggested that Genesee County Senator John Cherry would be a great pick. He had the legislative experience she lacked. He had respect on both sides of the aisle and was one who knew how to compromise. Remember Granholm ran on the theme of bringing us together and wanting to work with the GOP. Cherry had done just that for over twenty years, plus he had strong ties to organized labor compared to her shaky ties. He also had an entree to the gun lobby where she had upset some folks with her opposition to the state's concealed weapons permit bill. Further, and this was critical, he was not the kind of candidate to steal any of the limelight from her.

When you did the math, it all added up and four months later she picked him. Afterward, he said the column, 'clearly started the momentum' for me to get the nomination.

The two camps put together the rest of the ticket with Terri Lynn Land and Mike Cox as the GOP candidates for secretary of state and attorney general facing Butch Hollowell and Gary Peters for the same posts.

There was a quirky sidebar story that came out of the Granholm search process for an A.G. candidate. One of the names on the list was another female attorney. Marietta Robinson had run unsuccessfully for the state supreme court in 2000. She had lots of pop, was attractive, and had a good rapport with the media. She got in for the interview with Granholm, but one source explained, she never had a chance because Granholm did not want "Two Hollywood types on the ticket." In other words the candidate for governor did not want any competition from another savvy woman. The Granholm camp quickly denied the supposition, but I knew my source was on the inside and the quote was just too good to pass up, so I turned it into a newspaper column.

Several days after the column ran, the president of the state AFL-CIO held a meeting with fellow union leaders and in the front of the room was a blown up copy of the column. Mark Gaffney proceeded to lecture his labor brothers and sisters about making such utterances to reporters . . . .and I'm toning it down from what he really said. The intimidation did not work as my source continued to sing like a bird throughout the campaign and gave me lots of good inside material. Sorry Marky. Nice try.

The next GOP screw up that allowed Granholm to continue the same message of uniting the state, was the Posthumus ad involving the mayor of Detroit . . . the so called Kwame ad. Many felt the ad backfired. Packer claims it worked wonderfully.

Republicans, especially those from west Michigan, have always had an uncomfortable feeling about anybody who runs the city of Detroit. It's been reflected in legislative debate for years as the west Michigan delegation picks away at dollars headed for Detroit and redirects them to themselves.

The Posthumus ad sought to capitalize on that by hinting that a Democratic governor and a Democratic Mayor of Motown might connive to funnel more tax dollars to Detroit. The hook on the ad was a memo that somebody wrote suggesting that Kilpatrick would make those demands on Granholm if she was elected.

As a political theme, it was not bad. The relationship between a big city Democratic mayor and a governor of the same party is fair game. What turned out to be unfair, to some, was that the ad contained a huge picture of African American Mayor Kilpatrick dwarfing a diminutive picture of white candidate Jennifer Granholm.

The public and media discourse quickly shifted from the issue Posthumus wanted to raise on the relationship to the more volatile issue of race.

The *Detroit News* editorial page, in a surprising and internally controversial move, blasted Posthumus for playing the race card. Others piled on. The Posthumus camp was livid, and blamed Mark Silverman, who ran the paper, for allowing the statement into print.

Now there were two images of Posthumus on the public pallet . . . anti-out of stater and anti-black. In reality the GOP candidate was neither, but despite his attempts to clarify who he was, that impression took hold.

Once more, Granholm was handed a tailor made opportunity to depict him as "tearing us apart while I want to bring us together in one Michigan."

Given the outcry from the media and portions of the voting public, you would think the Posthumus camp might consider the Kwame ad as flop. Think again.

"Would we do it again? Absolutely," Packer answers her own question. "Without even thinking about it."

How's so?

She argues the ad worked with the constituency Posthumus needed to attract, namely union line workers, truck drivers, and those who were open to his message. In western Wayne and Macomb counties, the ad was a hit, despite the onslaught of negative press. Even though some believed the ad changed the focus of the campaign, she says the focus groups "gave us fantastic response."

Recall what Chairperson Hills said about running on issues. Posthumus tried to set the table with that ad but others unexpectedly overturned it. He also wanted to campaign on the experience thing, but that got lost in the cacophony of criticism over his early attacks on Granholm. Up to this point, a lot of what he was doing was playing into her hand.

There was one critical issue that never got much coverage. The state was facing a looming deficit. Whoever became governor, would be confronted with some nasty decisions about raising new revenue or whacking away at state services to balance the books.

It's not that the media didn't try, but you can only ask the question in so many ways. It became clear that the timid candidates were not going to take the bait. Granholm's standard and remarkably evasive answer was she couldn't give us an answer, because she needed to conduct an audit to document the size of the shortfall. Audit, shmaudit. The answer was a dodge. The audit, of course, would not be conducted until after she was elected. Isn't that special. So in the meantime she said, "I don't want to raise your taxes" but as the election got closer she was a tad more forthcoming. She added,as families are tightening their belts, she would do that to government. "The government has got to do the same. We will tighten up to 5 percent in all of the General Fund areas . . . holding education harmless." She never explained where all the cuts would come from.

Posthumus was not far behind in his unwillingness to confront the core issue. "If we have to face a budget deficit here," he promised not to raise taxes and hold schools harmless. Hello. Earth to Dick. Earth to Dick. Every think tank in town had numbers predicting a shortfall. There was no "if we have to" crap. It was only a question of how bad it was and how bad it might get. However, neither offered a solution you could get your arms around—for obvious reasons. Once they conceded a deficit number then the follow up question would be, what will you do about it and neither wanted to go there.

Once you start to discuss cutting this service or that, each special interest group that might be sliced and diced, would take a long hard look at that candidate. In other words, votes could be lost and who wants that in an election year? Certainly not the two candidates running for governor. (After Granholm was elected she never ordered that audit but proceeded with a budget cutting plan using the figures that had been there all along.)

While Posthumus was busy running commercials that didn't work, Granholm delivered perhaps one of the best spots of any campaign. It was affectionately dubbed the "porch" ad.

Sitting on a porch that was not her own but donated by a supporter, Granholm held a cup of coffee against a backdrop of flowers and sunshine. The only thing missing was the dog and the kids. She talked about something or other. It actually was about "any company that profits by selling your private medical records without your permission . . . . ," but to this day the only folks who remember the content were the ones who wrote it and the person who spoke it. In post election speeches around the state, I would ask audience members to recall the most memorable ad in the campaign and the porch thing won every time. Then I asked them to recall the content. What do you remember? I asked. It was a beautiful setting. She was on her porch and it just felt like she was one of us . . . talking to us . . . about something. It looked wonderful and so did she." But nobody could remember any of the content . . . not one word.

Granholm was running the race on charisma and image and the ad was proof. Recall when she closed the Marquette debate with, "I'm just somebody who is a regular person . . . ." Aw, shucks. The commercial was the personification of that message, and it worked. She didn't attack her opponent. She stayed on the high and neutral ground talking about an issue that affected everyone and with her coffee in hand, she was one of us. There's no way to catalog how many votes that ad produced, but suffice it to say, it didn't cost her any.

In my post election speeches, I conducted my own focus group on the Posthumus opening salvo regarding her lack of Michigan values. I would ask members of the audience who were not born in Michigan to stand. Large numbers would. Then I would tell them, "Dick Posthumus has asked me to ask you to please leave . . . and take your out of state values with you." The bit brought the house down everytime. It not only produced a good laugh but it confirmed how awful his strategy was.

As in any campaign for governor, the debates are what the media hankers to cover and in this race there would be only two although three were on the schedule. I was in there scrapping to get one of them for public TV. Since 1970, there were nine races for governor and public TV had landed seven debates. We never got a debate between Blanchard and Bill Lucas in 1986 and nobody got any debate in 1998 because John Engler stiffed Geoffrey Fieger. That year we interviewed both of them but at separate times. Of course, 2002 was an important year and filled with lots of firsts. It was the first open race in twelve years. With John Engler unable to run again, the contest featured two new faces. It marked the first time a woman was in the hunt making the race a historical event.

I had concerns about being shut out. The Posthumus camp had refused to give us a debate during the primary, even though I had lunch with his press guy Sage Eastman and came away thinking that it would happen. He says not so. Packer says *OTR* was ruled out because they didn't want to "legitimize" Schwarz by doing it. Back when she helped U.S. Senator Spencer Abraham get unelected in 2000, Packer was instrumental in making sure her guy and Democrat Debbie Stabenow didn't get within a hundred miles of our show either.

At the outset of the 2000 sweepstakes there was one actual encouraging debate sign that I didn't know about. Lansing attorney Peter Ellsworth had been asked to do the negotiations by the Posthumus team. The likable Ellsworth and I went back to the Milliken years, and had worked on numerous other debates.

During an early phone call before the two sides sat down to hammer out debate specifics, Ellsworth asked Granholm debate guru Mark Fox, "What about Skubick?" Ellsworth wanted to know if that would be OK. Fox, whom I also knew and respected from years of doing this stuff, did not rule it out. But as I was to discover there were concerns about another "Skubick" debate in the Granholm inner circle.

It is never good form to lobby the candidate directly because it puts him or her in an uncomfortable spot. All you really get from that is the comment, "It's not up to me" or "I can't make a commitment now." If you ask, you will get brushed off. But on one occasion, I broached Ms. Granholm in a joking manner knowing that it would not influence her one iota, but I still wanted her to know I was not going to go down without a fight.

"Man you're greedy," she laughed at my obtuse hint that she should agree to meet me on my turf.

"You're right," I laughed back. I was greedy.

While I had a friend in Ellsworth, he was of no use. He was eased out of the picture. It was never officially announced that he was out, but the Posthumus folks somehow managed to schedule talks with Fox and company without telling Ellsworth, or he would be notified about a meeting at the last moment. His other legal work usually prevented him from attending. Defacto, Ellsworth was out.

My other contact in the Posthumus camp was Dan Pero. He and I had worked on Engler debates over the years and he also helped steer two my way. But he was not in on all the talks either. I called him a couple of times to make sure somebody was making a pitch on my behalf, but without saying it, he left the impression it would not be his call this time around.

As each week of the fall campaign unfolded, I got less hopeful and finally all hope was dashed. Three debates were announced. One was at WOOD-TV in Grand Rapids, another at the Detroit Economic Club, and a third in Saginaw at station WNEM-TV. That one never happened because Posthumus would not agree to the date Granholm demanded.

After the debate schedule was announced, I waited a couple of days and then phoned Fox.

"So. Que pasa?" I inquired.

Fox explained the decision, 90 percent of which was based on not wanting to give the appearance that Granholm was playing favorites. I had that one debate in November and the one in August, and granting a third one would produce some jealousy and perhaps hard feelings among other reporters Fox explained. Plus, I learned well after the fact that having "proven" herself in the rough and tumble Marquette debate, there was no need to do that again. Besides she was perched on a pretty good lead over Posthumus, so why risk that by doing a risky Skubick debate.

I didn't like the answers, but I certainly understood. So my greed went unfulfilled. I had to settle for covering the three debates. I was not angry and since I would have to work with whomever got elected, I just sucked it in and put the debate setback aside. That also meant I would not be waking up in the middle of the night dreaming up debate questions. There is something to be said for that.

The first debate was in Grand Rapids. The station went a little overboard on the restrictions on reporters but it was their turf and they could do whatever they wanted. Reporters watched it live on the tube with the two main anchors for the station hosting the thing but not asking questions. WOOD TV's knowledgeable political reporter Rick Albin and the equally talented Detroit reporter Emery King from WDIV-TV provided the toss ups. Neither was a slouch.

The format was restrictive and designed to prevent any significant verbal crossfire between the two candidates. They stood at separate podiums. There were plenty of debate rules one of which was hotly debated just before the broadcast went on. The two sides had agreed that each candidate could have a three by five card.

Granholm showed up with writing on both sides, and Packer raised a stink. Her guy had not written down anything. She claimed her side was playing by the rules and Granholm was not.

Remember the scene here. Her candidate is minutes away from a live broadcast in his first and only TV face to face meeting with his opponent. He had a heck of a lot more riding on his performance than Granholm did, and here is his campaign manager losing it over a "rule violation."

"Nobody told me this," a flustered Posthumus addressed his manager. Instead of getting his game face on, he was left to worry about a relatively insignificant last minute dispute. If the incident rattled him, no one watching from the bull pen caught it. I didn't find out about it until long after the event was over.

Sitting here tonight writing this chapter I can't recall the lead out of the program. The only thing I really recall is when Posthumus responded to a Granholm statement by saying, "Jennifer, Jennifer, Jennifer." The line reminded you of the line Ronald Reagan laid on Walter Mondale, i.e. "There you go again." The reason it stands out is that it caused quite the stir in segments of the female voting population and to make matters worse, Posthumus was oblivious to the flap. After the program his team said, "The press is going to jump on that." They got that right.

Once more it underscored that having a woman in the race changed things. If Posthumus had been running against Blanchard and said, "Jim, Jim, Jim," nobody would have given two hoots. But here was a man saying it to a woman who was the attorney general of the state and the highest ranking Democrat in the state. The impression was he gave her no r-e-s-p-e-c-t as Aretha Franklin puts it.

Several days after the debate we did a TV 10 story on the react. I picked three women at random on the mall in back of the capitol and got an earful.

"He was disrespectful . He should have called her by her title . . . He was patronizing."

I went to Posthumus for a response and he seemed shocked by all the uproar. "None of the women I've talked to say that," he tried to alibi.

I came away from the incident thinking this guy wasn't a sexist, per se, he just didn't get it. Perhaps he traveled in a circle of women who were not offended, but it was pretty clear others were. He called her Jennifer eight times in the debate. She by the way called him "Dick" on occasion but also used his title as well.

Back to the debate itself, Posthumus waited until the end when she could not respond, to label her a flip flopper on her alleged support of legalized gay unions. "This is not leadership, folks. Who is the real Jennifer Granholm?" he asked the viewing audience.

Granholm earlier had made the same charge of him claiming he had switched positions on "corporate accountability, Blue Cross privatization, and directional drilling."

On slant drilling she had a point. Recall that Posthumus was the Al Gore of Michigan politics. Vice President Gore was running for president and trying to divorce himself from his boss, President Clinton. Posthumus on the state level had the same challenge: create his own persona minus the image of John Engler.

The evidence of that effort was clear. Engler appeared on the same stage with Posthumus at the state GOP convention in the fall of 2000 and was never seen with Posthumus again. Engler raised money for his friend but there were no ads saying, "Hi. I'm John Engler. Vote for Dick Posthumus." There were no joint appearances at rallies and Posthumus rarely if ever mentioned Engler's name in speeches.

One way to perform this separation was to select issues the two did not agree on and slant drilling in the Great Lakes was tailor made. During the campaign the issue was hot in the legislature as Engler argued for it and Posthumus against it. GOP leaders who had attended a meeting with Posthumus long before the campaign, contend that he was in favor of slant drilling then. He told them the party had trouble taking a stance on issues even when it was the right thing to do. No one in the meeting would confirm the statement because it would portray Posthumus as a flip flopper. I asked Senator Joanne Emmons about it. The usually talkative lawmaker gave me a "no comment" and walked away. She knew that I knew that she knew but she would not confirm it.

Posthumus during the TV meeting also picked up where Blanchard and Bonior left off on another issue. He tried to wrap her up in the "corrupt Wayne County environment." Instead of responding to the allegation per se, she told Posthumus to take it off the air.

"The fact that my opponent put ads on the TV that are actually lies and deceits are wrong," she said to avoid answering the charge. Calling the tone of the campaign "terrible" she offered to yank Democratic ads about him, if he stopped the spots against her. It made good debate fodder but provided very little insight for voters. He told her, "I appreciate you asking the Democratic Party to take the ads off the TV that are lies."

At one point Albin, bless his heart, was very blunt. He asked Posthumus if he was calling Granholm a liar regarding the Kilpatrick ad.

He said, "If it looks like a duck. It walks like a duck. It talks like a duck, it must be a duck . . . I think what I said speaks for itself."

She retorted, "Leadership is about bringing people together. The commercial that is running is deplorable . . . this is divisive politics. It is the oldest trick in the book" adding, "It's not worthy of a candidate for governor. It's not worthy of you, Dick Posthumus."

There were no knock out punches and afterward, pollster Ed Sarpolus observed that Posthumus should have told voters who he was. An old Posthumus senate colleague, former GOP lawmaker Phil Arthurhultz "sensed that he wasn't very comfortable with what he was doing and saying, i.e., attacking her.

During the post debate spin session, one of the Granholm daughters was there. Kate was twelve at the time and I asked her daddy for permission to interview her.

She of course thought her mom did well and then I asked if she had any political ambitions. "I'd rather play basketball and be an engineer." I asked if she wanted to host *Off the Record.* She laughed and said "probably not" but quickly added, "No offense." It was charming, sensitive, and just the right thing to say. Hum. Wonder where she got that from?

The debate in Grand Rapids was followed eight days later with the one in Detroit at the Economic Club. We arrived about an hour early. The first guy we found was Posthumus headed for his green room. We tagged along with camera rolling. Given the flap over the use of her first name in the last debate, I asked if he would call her Jennifer again.

"Her name is Jennifer and my name is Dick, "which indicated he would not change his tune. Liar, liar, pants on fire. Turns out the

name Jennifer never came off his lips. He substituted "my opponent," which he used nine times. Posthumus was in a comfortable
mood as we moved to this huge room that could have housed a 747.
Over in the corner was one tiny table where his wife and staffers
waited. He walked in, looking at the grandness of the Detroit facility and said, "This was part of my deal with Kwame." It was a not so
subtle reference to Mayor Kilpatrick's clumsy effort to solicit
Granholm's help if she was elected.

Next we searched for Granholm and got word that she would
arrive, via small bus, in front of Cobo hall within fifteen minutes.
We waited out front and she was right on time, as always. But as we
prepared to "ambush" her, this guy comes running out of nowhere
and motions the bus to keep rolling . . . right into an underground
parking garage where we could not go.

"Who the heck was that?" I asked cameraman Bassar. We'd never
seen him before, but I made it my duty to get his name, and register
my protest over the interference. I approached the mystery man in
the hallway and introduced myself and asked for his name which he
refused to give. Then I displayed my displeasure right in front of
him. He seemed unmoved. We left it at that. But now I was determined to get his name and I did. Moments later I walked up to
Jerome again. He smiled acknowledging that I had it right.

We set aside that little incident and Jerome Marks and I now
laugh at the silliness we had to go through . . . him as the advance
person for her and I assigned to get pictures that nobody else had.
He turned out to be an invaluable contact on the campaign trail. We
had no other "bus" problems after that.

I eventually caught up with Granholm in route to the hall, and
asked her if she was prepared to call him Dick, Dick, Dick? She
laughed, but didn't take the bait.

The Detroit session would be different from the rest: A panel of
reporters taking questions from the more than one thousand packed
in the room overlooking the Detroit River. WJR radio morning man
Paul W. Smith was the moderator, but he almost didn't get the honor.

Weeks before the event, the two campaigns met with representatives from the Detroit Economic Club and the Women's Economic
Club. They had a new suggestion for a moderator. "He's unconven-
tional" they warned and then popped the name of ABC-TV's

George Stephanopoulos on them . . . not to be confused with Snuffleupagus from *Sesame Street*.

The former Clinton advisor had turned on his former boss and was trying to turn into a TV journalist. ABC was putting plenty of heat on the two economic clubs to give him the starring role. The network saw the event as a way to establish their guy as a real journalist even though he would not get a chance to ask one question.

The Granholm team played it very low keyed to avoid any sense of enthusiasm. They were elated with the prospect of having "two stars" on the stage. "We figured Posthumus would get lost in the shuffle," with George and Jennifer up there.

Katie Packer from the Posthumus camp is told by Granholm's guys, "Let us think about it." But really, they are loving the idea.

Packer eventually put the kibosh on having Georgie Boy do it. The second choice was Mitch Albom from the *Detroit Free Press*, but they checked his schedule and he had a conflict so Smith got the assignment.

Word leaked out of the Granholm campaign that doing debate negotiations with Packer was a breeze. Because she had ditched Ellsworth and was pretty much doing it on her own, the other side claims it took advantage of her.

Example: The Granholm strategy was to devise a format for the Detroit gig that would permit as few questions as possible. She was in the lead and the more questions she got, the higher the risk of a screw up. The objective was to "Do no harm." One way to consume the question time is to have opening and closing statements. There's eight minutes down the drain right off the bat.

Granholm's advisors, as a ploy, balked at opening and closing statements and Packer immediately demanded them. Mission accomplished. "It was like taking candy from a baby," was one observation that made it to my ears.

The format, stage setting, and other details, fit right into the Granholm game plan. The candidates would be at podiums, miles apart from one another. Posthumus could have been in Toledo and she in Traverse City. The stage arrangement amounted to the same thing. The straight jacket format all but eliminated any personal interaction other than the hand shake at the outset. Reporters got one question and no follow ups. Furthermore, audience questions were generally very broad. That gave the candidates unbridled latitude to go wherever they wanted. They could flip a question on roads into a statement on apple pie and nobody could stop them. There were nine questions.

A good example was this softball on Medicaid. "How would your administration address the chronic under funding of the state Medicaid system and a rising uninsured population?" Mind you, there is nothing wrong with the subject. In fact it was high on the voters agenda. But the scope of the question was too broad. Pointed and specific questions are more revealing.

The show began with Paul W.'s very lengthy introductions. Posthumus tried to get off a funny line by asking the radio host, "What's the W. for?" The quip laid there.

Posthumus' best slam of the day came after an education question concerning his relationship, or lack there of, with the Michigan Education Association (MEA). Near the end of his response to the panel, he turned to Granholm and asked her how she voted on Proposal A. That was the granddaddy of all property tax relief ballot proposals in 1994.

"I'd like to know whether she voted yes or no on Proposal A?" he asked.

Granholm, as she had effectively done in other debates, ignored the direct question and took off on how wonderful it was to be embraced by the MEA. Once again the lousy format allowed her to duck. Those of us watching duly noted the dodge—nothing new there.

Later, on an issue dealing with a different ballot proposal on health care funding came up. Posthumus manipulated the format to repeat his earlier Proposal A question. He said he backed it and added, "You notice my opponent didn't answer whether she voted yes or no like my other Democratic friends." The format did not permit a response. Instead she got a different question which she was more than happy to address. Now the suspense is growing. She's evading "A."

During the closing statements, Posthumus takes one last bite out of the Proposal A apple and says, "My opponent won't even tell us whether she voted yes or no on Proposal A."

At this point, everyone figures he will knock this one out of the park and tell us why she won't answer. But he doesn't. Unbelievable!

He knew that she didn't vote on the plan. She missed the election, but he completely muffs the opportunity to drive home the point with the audience. He could have said something like, "My opponent, who I used to refer to as Jennifer, talks the talk about education. But when it came time for her to vote for Proposal A and bring badly needed property tax relief to every resident of our great state, she refused to walk to the polls. She did not vote. She did not think it was important enough to join you and thousands like you to stand up for tax relief and better schools! Is this the kind of leadership you want in the governor's office? I think not."

For the first time in the campaign, the rock star candidate was flustered and on the ropes. I was the first to corner her to ask about the vote. The exchange was a TV classic. I'm trying to grill her and she is slowly walking away, as her handlers guide her to a safe harbor . . . away from me.

"Did you vote on Proposal A?"

"I support Proposal A," came her first response.

"You're not answering the question madam attorney general?"

"I haven't gone back to look. I support Proposal A," as she continues to move away.

"But you don't remember voting on it?"

At this point she gives no answer. Instead she merely flips me a smile and that's that. Not quite.

She moved away from me, but next found herself in the middle of the gaggle of reporters waiting for her. They had the same question and I had a chance to jump in again.

"I saw the press release," from Posthumus she explains. "I've got to go back and look."

"You don't remember?" I continued.

"I don't remember specifically," she finally confessed.

She looked confused and flustered. It was her worst moment in the campaign and her handlers wanted to get her out of there pronto—which they did.

The Posthumus team was beaming. It had scored a great punch as he told reporters, "If you're unwilling to do that [vote] as a citizen, what are you going to do as a leader?" But as with other issues e.g., the

Detroit airport, and a host of others, Granholm emerged the Teflon candidate. None of it stuck and while the non-voting Prop A story dominated the news the next day, it disappeared soon after.

It was never explained at the time, but now, months after the fact, We know why Posthumus didn't close the deal at the end of the debate. It was a calculated move. He was hoping that she would say she had voted or make some other incriminating statement that he could then use against her. Plus he did not want to come off as too aggressive against her. To her credit, and you can't count on this with all politicians, she did not fib. However, her camp tried to avoid the obvious: She did not vote. That confession finally came out about thirty-six hours after the debate.

There would be no more debates, which is just the way her team wanted it. It was twenty-one days from the election. The rest of the battle was fought on the airwaves not on the stage. She would have total control of her message and if the polls were right she would win in a landslide. Democrats around the state talked up the Granholm coattail effect. There were dreams of taking over the House and Senate as she would surely drag lots of her fellow Democrats into office. So the theory went.

The contest actually ended for Posthumus on October 23, although it was never reported because nobody knew it. After the fact, Posthumus pointed to one event on that day that sent him back to the farm in Alto.

An EPIC-MRA statewide survey gave Granholm a commanding fourteen point lead. She had 51 percent. He had 37 percent, and those on the fence were 10 percent. When those numbers came out, Posthumus says his money started to dry up. Many of his backers put their checkbooks in cold storage. With the race apparently over, according to the polls, nobody wanted to throw good money out the window.

Posthumus tried to reverse the thinking, but perception became his reality. So, instead of having a ton of money to pour into more ads, Posthumus found himself begging for money and getting no real commitments.

His strategy was to run two sets of commercials. One blasted her, and another with a kinder and gentler message about him.

There were enough funds to put up that positive ad in which Posthumus talked about himself while ignoring her. The spot was good and positive—the kind voters like.

"Michigan needs a governor who can lead through any bad times," he started out hitting the experience button. "I talked about cutting property taxes and promising not to raise taxes." He concluded by going back to the values stuff." I share your Michigan values, and I'm ready to lead." Ironically his ending commercial should have been his first.

Over in the Granholm camp the countdown was on but there were concerns about her comments on reparations made at a Detroit NAACP gathering. The GOP had her on tape saying she favored that, and out state commercials were running showing her saying that. She was so concerned, that a spot was produced denouncing the GOP attack.

"Once more Dick Posthumus is distorting my record. He wants to divide us . . . I oppose any plan that calls for cash reparations . . . we don't right the wrongs of the past by writing checks." The Republican ad must have been moving voters or the Granholm team would never have responded.

Watching the election, for the first time in thirty-two years from the sidelines, was Gov. John Engler. After awarding some Golden Apple awards to school kids in late October, the press corps sought his analysis. True to form he minced no words on what he termed her "flower garden TV ad" (the porch spot).

"You sell what you have to sell. If you got image, you sell image. If you got substance, you sell that. Does image beat substance? It hasn't for a long time in Michigan," he concluded.

He was right. For the last twelve years voters evaluated John Engler, who had minus numbers on the charisma chart, based on his record and experience. Even though he was not warmly admired, citizens still liked the fact that he did what he said he would do. True, the Democrats never found a charismatic candidate to take him on. Nonetheless, he survived.

But Posthumus was viewed by many as Engler-Lite. Just because he worked with Engler didn't make him Engler and remember Posthumus was doing everything he could to divorce himself from the incumbent. Engler got in a good zinger when asked to comment on Geoffrey Fieger's public remarks that the negative commercials should end. "Geoffrey Fieger encouraging civility is like the arsonist speaking out against fires."

There's been a tradition in this state that days before the final vote, candidates take to the road for a last minute, last ditch effort to win. The Posthumus road show appeared on the capitol steps hours before the voters got into the act.

His buzz was that the race had narrowed and Posthumus was within striking distance as he had narrowed the lead to "single" figures. Mouthpiece Sage Eastman was making imaginary bets with reporters that his guy would pull it out. Not being privy to the inside tracking results, most dismissed it as an effort to put on a happy face for the statewide go around. Little did we know that Eastman was darn near right. It was no longer a fourteen point lead.

Granholm launched a grueling twenty-seven hour bus tour that made a stopover in East Lansing. She rallied the troops who were sardined into a tiny eatery on the border of the MSU campus. The speech was predictable and forgettable. She predicted victory. No news there.

Riding on the bus with her were her parents and as the rally ended, my cameraman and I were waiting at the bus entrance to get the good-bye shot. She said, "Come here. I want you to meet my parents." On the bus we go against the backdrop of cat calls from all the other riders. "Who let Skubick on?" "Hey, get him out of here!" She walked down the aisle to mom and dad who had stayed on the bus during the rally and cautioned them, "Now don't tell this guy anything, but this is Tim Skubick." Being from out of state they must have thought, So? But they were very gracious. They were also very low-keyed, which their daughter was not. We exchanged "hello's" and I asked them some question to see if they would follow her advice. They just laughed. Who says parents can not be trained?

I got off the bus and the Granholm express rolled along on its merry way. Afterward, I got reports that they were really rocking and rolling as the sleep starved contingency drove on to what it felt would be certain victory.

There was plenty of dancing in the aisle with Granholm joining in. As the bus headed from Grand Rapids to Detroit on election night, the driver developed a real lead foot. The bus roared along at ninety miles plus. A retired state cop, along for the ride and security, was convinced they would be stopped by one of his former colleagues, but they made it all the way without running into a smoky. When Granholm and husband arrived at the Marriott in Detroit, I was there with camera to greet her. It was five minutes before six and I had a live shot to do for TV-10, but I wanted that video and wanted a brief sound bite.

She said she was feeling good about the outcome and I asked, "did you make any mistakes?"

She said we would discuss that later on. We never did.

I just made it back for the live report as the crowd awaited the closing of the polls and the release of the exit results declaring the winner. There was little doubt in my mind that she would win. What I didn't anticipate was that it would not be by double digits. Turns out the Posthumus gang was right. The race had narrowed and she had a victory, but only by five lousy points, 52–47.

Posthumus would say well after the fact that if he had had another million dollars and if the campaign had gone another week, he would have won. Nice spin, but we'll never know.

With the release of the exit polling, Democrats in the room went nuts. Granholm watched on the tube from her suite upstairs. The media had one agenda, get her down there with them. But she would not do that until she got a concession call.

Posthumus, who was holed up in a downtown Lansing hotel, could have been mean. Knowing that she wanted to make a speech during the critical 11 P.M. newscasts statewide, he could have lost her phone number and called at 2 A.M. He did not. About ten minutes or so before 11 P.M., she got the call, and within minutes she was on her way to a victory celebration. It was the first one for Democrats since 1986.

Actually the audience got to see the Posthumus concession speech where he fought back the tears, as he said this race was not about one person, it was about the state. And as he spoke, the Detroit crowd started to sing that tune they sing at hockey games when the visiting team has lost. Na, na, na, na; na, na, na, na; ay, ay, ay; good bye. Over and over again. The pent up frustration over twelve years of Engler was finally assuaged.

And then she appeared. The stage was packed with campaign staff as she and the First Family-elect waded through the mass to the microphone. If you had gotten a dime for every hug and kiss on that platform that night, you could have tossed out your 401-K.

"This victory belongs to you," she shouted to the adoring legions.

"I am humbled and honored to stand before you as the next governor of the state of Michigan." Now the place erupts like no other state election I've seen in thirty-four years.

Near the end of her remarks, the last person she called to the microphone was David Katz, her campaign manager. I said to myself, "so that's what he looks like." Katz was totally "unavailable" during the entire campaign. Sure some reporters got some quotes from time to time, but he was a no show on the media circuit. I had never gone through an entire campaign not knowing the person in charge, so this was a first and it made you wonder if he had anything to hide. He acknowledged the applause but said not one word. Figures.

About an hour or so later she appeared in her first news conference as Governor-elect. She tossed the first question to me and I just asked, "How you doing?" I decided that this was not the time for tough questions. That would come later.

The only "news" we got was what she would now call her husband. The betting pool had an assortment of guesses from "First Hunk" to "First Squeeze." She went for something tame, "First Man."

Now with the campaign and the election finally over, it was time to sit back and relax. Wrong. There was more news to be had as we moved from the campaign phase to the transition phase—the passing of the baton from the JME to JMG.

The transition can go one of two ways, smooth or not. John Engler had ordered his troops to make sure it was the former. On the Granholm side it would be anything but smooth. In her defense, there were very few folks around her who'd been through this drill, including, of course, her.

The day before the election I had run a story that Granholm had decided on a transition director. Former state representative H. Lynn Jondahl was a premier selection that sent the correct message. Everyone liked him, but on the day prior to the election, he didn't like me.

Based on a great tip that I picked up at the East Lansing rally, I found Mr. J. and stuck a mike in his face wanting him to confirm my story.

"Whatever conversation I've had was with them," he moved into his evasive stance.

"So you have talked with them about this?" I went on hoping for some morsel of news.

"I'm not going to discuss this with you," his stonewall got a little higher.

"How about going off the record?" I suggested.

"I've never gone off the record with you," he shot back, and it was obvious he was not about to start.

He seemed testy, which was out of character for the former minister, banjo player and unsuccessful candidate for governor himself. I asked if it would look bad to have Granholm talking about a transition director when she had not won the election. He wouldn't bite on that either.

I had also reported that a Lansing barrister, John Pirich, was under consideration. He was a Republican and I found out after the story aired he was never in the mix, although it made a nice twist to the story. Within days Jondahl was formally announced and I showed up at the transition office within shouting distance of the capitol to see if he would now be more cooperative. He was.

A meeting of key advisors had just ended and I was standing in the room waiting for Jondahl to finish a conversation with an aide. We did an interview, and as I was leaving, I noticed a notebook on the conference table. "Granholm Transition" was the title. Oh, I wanted to read that. However somebody yanked the valuable book from my view but not before I could read one line. That sentence advised everyone on the team to adhere to one command, "No leaks!"

I took it as a personal challenge to turn the commandment into mush. Within days the inner workings of the transition team was leaking like a sieve as I was being tipped off about one appointment after another. About two weeks before the election, I got word that Granholm had settled on a chief of staff. Everyone felt it would be the invisible Mr. Katz. He was automatically ruled out, as were other Wayne County types, because the state police/FBI probe into the Metro Airport "problem" could eventually focus on Katz and others who had worked for Ed McNamara. It may have been a blessing for her in disguise.

The press corp was waiting to see how many Wayne County cronies would make the move from there to here. When the numbers were added up, there was only one and she was so remotely tied to the county that it didn't make a wave. With Katz out of the running by default, Granholm turned to Rick Wiener. They had known each other since the 1988 Mike Dukakis presidential effort. Wiener had been a Blanchard backer and state Democratic party chair. He would leave his lucrative lobbying job to join the Granholm cabinet.

I got wind of the Wiener move and reported it on *OTR* and the *MIRS* newsletter on November 18. Granholm waited almost a full month, until December 17, to make the announcement official. My source inside the transition office should have gotten a bonus check.

The next leak involved two key appointments—budget director and state treasurer. My inside source nailed it as Mary Lannoye and Jay Rising. Lannoye, had been Engler's budget director but left for the private sector before he left office. She was reluctant to return and Granholm had to make a hard sell to change her mind.

Engler's last Budget Director Don Gilmer, made a personal phone call urging Lannoye to come out of retirement. She had several issues. She was concerned about being a Republican working in a Democratic administration. She knew she would have to work with Sen. Shirley Johnson who would be installed as the new GOP chair of the Senate Appropriations Committee. The two had not had a warm and fuzzy relationship in previous years.

I got wind of the Lannoye move about a week before the announcement on December 19. There was a news conference in between during which Granholm announced some of her new staff and I asked her about the Lannoye decision which she, as expected, did not confirm. This is what she did say.

"Stay tuned, Tim."

"Was that a 'yes' to my question?" I couldn't resist.

Staying on message and not giving an inch she came back, "That's a stay tuned. We'll let you know. You probably won't be the first to know, but maybe you will be." Then she laughed and I got ready to report the story on December 16.

Two days later, I reported the Rising appointment. He and I went back a few years to the Blanchard administration where he served under the colorful State Treasurer Bob Bowman. Rising was the consummate straight shooter, great contact, but on the night before I ran the story, he was also tight lipped.

"Tim, I can't confirm that."

I knew that, but I wanted to give him a courtesy heads up the story was coming anyway. I have found over the years a technique that sometimes gets me around the "I can't tell you" roadblock.

I ask, "Look if I run this thing, will I make an ass out of myself?" There is usually laughter and then sometimes they bite and sometimes they don't. Rising didn't but I knew the story was correct without him. Granholm brought both of them in describing it as a great economic team. Interesting twist to the story was both of the nominees had ties to Wayne County government. They were the first two that she had tapped. So it was fair game to bring that up at their maiden news conference. Lannoye seemed annoyed by the inquiry. She had been budget director in Wayne and had nothing to do with the airport mess and said so. End of that cross examination.

Rising, from his position with the prestigious Miller Canfield law firm, he had done legal work for Ed McNamara for twelve years, mostly on setting up an indigent health care program. He did have a role in drafting the airport authority bill, but he revealed he had no role in any of the allegations surrounding the airport contracts that the feds and state were eyeballing. I was certain Granholm would never have selected them if there was even a hint of scandal. But the duo had to be asked anyway, just to get it on the record, in case anything to the contrary popped up at a later date.

The Lannoye appointment allowed the governor to prove that she would bring Republicans into her new fold. The combination of the two was an excellent move that got rave reviews in the media and legislative ranks.

As one scoop dripped out after another, the Granholm team began to wonder what happened to that "no leak" proviso in the transition book. During one closed door meeting, they half jokingly, half seriously suggested, "Either Skubick's got a mole in here, or he's just making educated guesses hoping that half the time he will be right." My source and I had a good chuckle about that.

To prove that I was not guessing, my leak delivered three more names for the state police director's post, the new head of the Department of Environmental Quality and a brand new cabinet slot for somebody I had covered for over twenty years—the soon to be former mayor of Lansing, David Hollister. Hollister resided in the

TV 10 market so it was important that I discover what role, if any, he might play in the new Granholm administration.

Earlier that previous summer, after Granholm got the nomination, I discovered Hollister was on the list for lt. governor. I stumbled into the story and found out he was being interviewed in Southfield that very day.

I got him on the car phone just after his one-on-one. He was flying high. It was an honor to be considered and he thought he was in the hunt. I needed an interview for the evening newscast, but he was on his way along I-94 to his mom's place on the west side of the state. She, by the way, advised him not to take the thing if offered. Hollister said afterward, "That's what mom's get paid to do."

He filled me in on his chat with Granholm, but I needed more than that. I suggested we meet somewhere along the freeway, but that wouldn't work. He graciously agreed to talk when he got back in the office at 4:30 that afternoon—a mere thirty minutes before air time.

He paid off on his promise and I was first in line to get his comments. I concluded from our conversation that he wanted the spot on the ticket although he took great pains to say he had not sought it or the interview. That was pretty standard stuff in the lt. governor game. Nobody ever campaigns for it because it's bad form. He had the reputation of working with Democrats and Republicans and I knew that had curb side appeal for Granholm. However, days after the interview, I learned Hollister was out. I ran the story. He got the obligatory phone call from her at his cottage up north, confirming the story. He lost that job, but after the general election, she still had her eye's on him for something else.

During the transition she asked him to draft a paper on combining the current Consumer and Industry Affairs Department with an economic development component. Hollister was no stranger on that. He had brought more General Motors' jobs to Michigan than anybody else in the country. When the giant automaker decided to build its first domestic auto plant in more than a decade, Hollister stood next to the GM big wigs when they turned over the first shovel at the Lansing plant site. Granholm wanted to see more shovels in the ground. Hollister worked on his paper and turned it over to her. He listed the attributes for the new department head. In a return phone call, she told him he fit the job description so she offered him the assignment. He did not take it, but said he would think it over.

That evening he and his wife, Chris, went for a long walk. She was not overjoyed with the prospects of her hubby trading the stress of being mayor for the greater stress of being a cabinet member. She was concerned about his health and the impact the new job would have on his degenerative Parkinson's disease. Up until now he had it under control, but she feared it could easily get out of control if he switched jobs.

They finally decided he would tell Granholm yes. Word leaked out hours before the formal announcement. I parked myself outside his office in City Hall. He would not come out. Now I knew the story was right because he had never stonewalled me before.

We scrawled the news across the TV screen at noon and Granholm confirmed it two hours later. Hollister confessed that he had been pressured into saying yes by "a very tenacious governor-elect." Granholm confirmed that, too.

The transition was not the only story developing after the election. On November 22, 2002, the U.S. Attorney's Office raided and pawed over the offices of Wayne County Executive Ed McNamara looking for evidence into possible wrongdoing associated with Detroit Metro Airport.

Remember legislative Republicans had launched a probe into the same matter with Democrats denouncing it as a witch hunt. Upon the news of the federal raid, the Senate Majority Leader Dan DeGrow said, "I guess it was not a witch hunt after all."

The timing of the federal action set GOP tongues wagging on a different front. What if the raid had come prior to Granholm's election? Had that occurred, maybe it would be Dick Posthumus in transition not her, the Republicans speculated.

The re-emergence of the airport mess triggered another round of speculation aimed at Granholm—none of it positive. The old " what did she know and when did she know it" stuff resurfaced just as it did during her primary and general election runs.

U.S. Attorney Jeffrey Collins, a Republican appointee, took the unusual step on December 9, of issuing a clean bill of health for Granholm.

"Jennifer Granholm, governor-elect, is not the focus of the federal and state investigation involving Wayne County government nor was she the focus of the search warrant we executed on November 22." Collins in the next breath cleared Mayor Kwame Kilpatrick, too.

The question of why Collins did that laid out there festering and unanswered until April 18th when he made his first statewide TV appearance on *Off the Record*. His first public comments, to some, raised more questions than he answered.

Collins explained that issuing the statement was consistent with department policy. He decided to do it after he read what he termed, "unfair inferences" surrounding the raid. In other words when Granholm's and Kilpatrick's names were linked to the probe, Collins decided to step in "in terms of setting the record straight."

But the critical question was, did anyone request the statement?

Did someone from Granholm's or Kilpatrick's offices put heat on him to act?

Collins would only say it was his office that made the decision, "That's all I can say regarding that." It was a non-answer.

"So was that a no to my question?" I continued.

"It's not a no . . . ah, I'm not going to confirm or deny" if anyone asked me to issue the comment.

It was a curious answer. If there was no pressure he could have easily said that, but leaving it unresolved only fed the suspicion that somebody did. So I tried again. "Can you tell me that wasn't the case?" Nobody intervened?

"I can tell you, ah . . . that there are no political, ah..reasons at all, ah." He seemed to be denying any outside political pressure, but he was not off the carpet yet. He was asked to explain the timing of the raid coming as it did well after the election for governor.

Collin's said he was not going to "politicize the U.S. Attorney's Office . . . the release was done in a way which would be consistent with our long standing history" of not playing politics with the office. That meant to me he was fully cognizant of the impact an earlier search might have had. In fact Republicans would have used the raid to beat up on Granholm just before the voters decided her fate. It could have changed the outcome.

With the Collins clean bill of health, Granholm got out from under the cloud hanging over her transition. However, it was duly noted on *Off the Record* that the statement covered the investigation up to the time of the announcement. That meant something else might happen in the future that would make his statement, as they use to say in the Nixon White House, inoperative.

As the hectic year 2002 came to a close, an interesting First Family story fell into my lap.

The three previous governors had all lived in the executive residence on the southwest side of Lansing. The home originally belonged to Howard Sober who had made his millions shipping cars. He wanted to unload the house to get a tax write off. His friend, the then Senate Majority Leader Emil Lockwood, brokered the transfer.

There was always enough room for the other governors. The Milliken's two children never lived there. Blanchard's son Jay took up residency in a loft that was constructed over the garage. The Engler triplets all slept in the same bedroom. But there were not enough bedrooms for the two Granholm girls and the one boy. Around Christmas time, one of my contacts revealed there was some chatter about adding onto the residence or buying a new one. There was also a third option, tear down the old house and start from scratch.

Any one of the options was a great story so I approached the governor-elect on what she favored. She was blunt.

She said the size of the home was "No problem . . . there are three bedrooms. We have three children, two of them will have to share the same room" momma Granholm decreed. Adding this, "It will be a bit of a tussle, but I think that happens across the state with many families." End of story.

Not quite.

Put all this in the context of events the new governor was confronting. There was that deficit that she had trouble addressing on the campaign trail. Now she had to get real about that and face a sea of red ink that was not conducive to constructing new digs for her family even if it was done with private contributions. Clearly the new governor was aware of the public relations bomb waiting to explode.

And the story refused to go away. Months after the initial report, I was tipped on a new twist. The spouse of Michigan's longest serving Congressperson, John Dingell, had quietly assumed the job of renovating the residence.

What about the governor's statements in December?

Debbie Dingell informed us in a news conference in March 2003 that she had gone to the governor and persuaded her to sign off on the project. Dingell said the house was in need of major repairs with a leaky roof, which was well documented. Engler, for example, had personally placed buckets under the leaks and was even recorded as climbing up on the flat roof to shovel snow to avoid more leaks. Some wag suggested he might have been mistaken for Santa Claus up there. The news conference was not one of Dingell's best performances. She could not attach a price tag to the project. Come on. How many of you decide to add on to your house, fix up the interior, and never get a ball park figure before you begin?

It was clear this puppy was going to run well over a million smackers. It was equally clear that the politically savvy Ms. Dingell did not want that number attached to the story and I bet you neither did the governor. (She was not at the news conference to explain her flip-flop.)

Dingell called me about the critical article I wrote about her stonewalling. She explained she would eventually come up with a cost for the new carpeting, new windows, new roof, 1,800 foot addition, a new kitchen, new plumbing, and heating. Later, she also revealed there would be an added cost for the removal of the black mold, mercury, PCBs, and asbestos they found in the old house. She emphasized again all this would be done without using your tax dollars.

The year 2002 went into the Michigan history books with John Engler leaving through one door and the state's first female governor coming in the other. It had been a long journey for her that started in 1998. I asked her if she was ready to write a book about her adventure. She declined saying she still had a lot to do before she got around to that.

4
Exclusive Interviews

A person conducts a ton of interviews in thirty plus years of journalism. Realizing that it's a guesstimate, I have done well over 12,000 radio reports for WWJ Newsradio 950 in Detroit. At this writing there have been about 1,500 *Off the Record* programs and probably another 8,000 commercial TV news stories. If you figure I talk to at least 50 news sources every week that would result in about 86,000 on and off camera/microphone interviews so far.

Not all of those have been state and local officials. While it is not an extensive list, a number of national figures have done our show or have been subjected to the Skubick interview style. Here's an alphabetic list.

1. Ralph Abernathy—Southern Christian Leadership Conference president.
2. Bella Abzug—feminist
3. Spiro Agnew—former vice president, Nixon administration
4. John Anderson—Independent party candidate for president
5. Joe Biden—former U.S. senator and candidate for president
6. Mike Blumenthal—former chair of Bendix Corporation and secretary for the treasury, Carter administration

7. Julian Bond—civil rights leader

8. Robert Bork—former U.S. solicitor general, Nixon administration

9. David Broder—*Washington Post* political correspondent

10. Patrick Buchanan—candidate for president

11. George Bush—former president

12. George W. Bush—current president

13. Laura Bush—first lady

14. Lt. William Calley—My-Lai Massacre soldier

15. Cesar Chavez—migrant farm worker union leader

16. Dick Cheney—current vice president

17. Lynn Cheney—wife to vice president

18. Charles Collingwood—former CBS news correspondent

19. John Norman Collins—convicted mass murderer

20. John Connally—former U.S. treasurer

21. Walter Cronkite—former anchor CBS Evening News

22. Dr. Walter DeVries—pollster who coined "Ticket Splitter" term

23. Robert Dole—former U.S. Senate leader—candidate for president

24. Robert Eaton—retired chairman Chrysler Corporation

25. Gerald Ford—former vice president

26. Doug Fraser—former president United Auto Workers union

27. Newt Gingrich—GOP speaker of the House of Representatives

28. Al Gore—former vice president

29. Jim Henson—creator of Muppets

30. Lee Iacocca—former chairman Chrysler Corporation

31. Jack Kemp—former congressman and candidate for vice president

32. Martin Luther King, Jr.—civil rights leader

33. H. Stuart Knight—former Secret Service director

34. Charles "On the Road" Kuralt—former CBS correspondent

35. Lester Maddox—former governor of Georgia and anti-civil rights leader

36. Mary Matalin –advisor to President George Bush

37. John McCain—U.S. senator

38. Pete McCloskey—former congressman and candidate for president

39. Paul McCracken—former chair of Council of Economic Advisors

40. Edwin Meese III—former U.S. attorney general, Reagan administration

41. Fritz Mondale—former vice president, Carter administration

42. Rogers Morton—Chairman of CREEP (Committee to Reelect the President)

43. Ralph Nader—consumer crusader

44. H. Ross Perot—former independent candidate for president

45. Colin Powell—former chairman Joint Chiefs of Staff, current U.S. secretary of state

46. Ronald Reagan—38th United States President

47. John Riccardo—former president of the Chrysler Corporation

48. Elliot Richardson—former U.S. attorney general, Nixon administration

49. John Rock—general manager of Oldsmobile

50. Mort Sahl—stand-up comic

51. Carl "Doc" Severinsen—trumpet player

52. Roger Smith—former chairman, General Motors

53. David Stockman—budget director, Reagan administration

54. Robert Teeter—GOP pollster

55. Mike Wallace—CBS *60 Minutes*

56. James Watt III—secretary of the interior, Reagan administration

57. Leonard Woodcock—former president UAW

58. Andrew Young—civil rights leader

George W. Bush

Michigan was a battleground state in the 2000 presidential sweepstakes. Gov. John Engler had hooked his wagon to the governor from Texas. In fact, Engler had been one of the first to visit the ranch in Crawford urging the chief ranch hand, George W. Bush, to run for president.

Engler and Bush were glued at the hip as the candidate and his number one Michigan cheerleader toured the state on their mission to win the primary here. One of the drills in these trips is to nail down as much free media as possible—that's air time the stations give without charge.

Engler's press minions were on the other end of my line with an offer.

"Skubick. You want to interview W. when he's in East Lansing next week?"

I told John Truscott I would be delighted.

"Only one restriction," he went on. "You can have two questions and that's all."

Two lousy questions. It was ludicrous. I figured if I asked Bush, "How are you?" They would count it as question one. So I protested.

J.T. would not budge. He was under strict orders . . . two questions. No more, no less.

We both knew he had me over the barrel. If I said no, they would just find some other reporter who would say yes, so I reluctantly said, "OK, you win."

I was used to drafting a lot of questions before a major interview but I wondered why bother this time. This thing will be over before it began. But the more I thought about it, I concluded this might be a chance to zing the Good Ole Texan with some goodies he had never been asked before.

I went to work and crafted more than a dozen inquiries.

The next day I headed to the Kellogg Center at MSU where Bush and Engler got off the campaign bus to a rousing welcome from the young college Republicans who were there chanting, "We love Bush."

Against the backdrop of all that shouting and cheering, Engler walks by and gives me a thumbs up. He was riding high soaking up all the national media attention. He was going to deliver Michigan for Bush and provide a so called "fire wall" to stop somebody else who wanted to win this state. A guy named McCain—John McCain.

Engler was cocky and as Bush slipped by me in the rope line I tossed a one liner at him, "Governor, if you lose in Michigan, will you support Senator McCain?"

Usually a national candidate is disciplined enough to ignore a question from the local media. If he or she stopped to answer every one, they would never get back on the bus.

But my question stopped Bush in his tracks. He smiled for the camera and suggested, "Won't be necessary, I'm going to win." That was the last I heard from him until after the rally.

Three local TV crews had been selected for the "honor" to ask two questions of this guy. I wanted to go last. My WKAR-TV crew, Dick Best, Nancy Kelly, and I waited in the hallway as one reporter went in. Five minutes later he was out. It doesn't take an eternity to ask two questions.

The second team went in. I cleared my throat and they were back out.

"OK Skubick. You're next," was the warm invite from Susan Schafer from the Engler press squad.

Bush was standing and looking taller in person making me look even shorter. He was surrounded by secret service guys—duded out in their sunglasses and suits. There were a couple of other folks I didn't recognize. They all looked bored as hell. I was the last freebie of the day and everyone wanted out of there to go eat some ribs and corn on the cob or whatever Texans chow down on.

Truscott was in there and made a little aside to Bush to "Watch out for this guy." Bush was shaking in his boots—at least I think he had on boots.

I was reminded of the two question limit as my cameraman got into place.

Ever wonder why they restrict the format to two questions? One reason is obvious, they want to get out of there. But the more important hidden reason is: It's darn near impossible to make anybody look bad with only two toss ups. Limiting the number of questions reduces the chances of a screw-up by the candidate. Even though it was a local interview, if he blew a question, you can bet it would end up on the national news given the state of modern technology.

I had no delusions about breaking into the big time by tripping up this guy, but I was pretty sure I had two questions he had not anticipated. I was right and then surprised . . . very surprised.

I started with my lie question again. The one where you ask the politician to promise to always tell the truth.

"That's a very interesting question," Mr. Bush commenced. He quickly suggested there was a difference between telling the truth on national security issues and his personal behavior and intentions. He said it could jeopardize the country to always tell the truth on "some deep intelligence" issue.

"I'm not going to fudge the truth but maybe I'm just not going to answer and tell you what I know." I thought to my self, where was Bush when Blanchard needed him!

One question left. I decided to use a state issue that had drawn plenty of public fire from the civil rights community. The legislature, at Governor Engler's urging, had abolished the duly elected school board in Detroit and replaced it with a so called "reform" board. It was a hot button issue with huge racial overtones, and Engler and company had been accused of being the Great White Fathers telling the blacks in Detroit what to do.

Bush didn't flinch when asked if the takeover amounted to a violation of local control. "In my judgment that is local control of schools, from the federal perspective," he took off. "The people of Michigan ought to be able to do what they think is right for their schools. This is a remedy the legislature put in place and I understand the conflict between local and state, but from the federal perspective, that is local control of schools." He suggested if Detroiters didn't like it, "They have remedies at the ballot box."

Bush was comfortable with this takeover because he had done exactly the same thing back in Texas. "I hear the same complaint. I understand the school board had fallen down on its duty, and we're going to help you right yourself and get up and run it again," he continued.

"End of interview, that's my two questions, right?" I asked.

"We are on a roll," he barked, continuing, "I appreciate this because we aren't on process questions that are often given me."

"You aren't going to get me in trouble here, asking more than my two questions?" I queried.

"I'm the boss!" We both were enjoying it.

"Should Michigan allow concealed weapons in schools?"

"It's not a bad idea to allow concealed weapons. That's my state law. Not only that, I think it's a bad idea to have juveniles carrying guns. If we catch you carrying a gun as a juvenile, you're automatically in detention."

"Do you vote the person or the party?" I continued in a rat-a-tat style.

"Person. Let me tell you something. It's not mutually exclusive because the person's philosophy often times will reflect the philosophy of the party. And that's what a leader does. A leader defines the philosophy of the party in many ways and that's why you're going to find the Republican Party will be one of compassionate conservatism when I win the nomination."

Darn. He finally was able to work in one of his standard campaign phrases, but so far it was only one.

"Have you voted for Democrats before?"

"On occasion."

"A weak moment?" I half teased, but with no smile.

"Naw. Because the person I felt was running on the Republican side wasn't qualified," he explained. I am now thinking he's a gamer!

He then went into his ability to attract voters from all sides, adding, "I wouldn't have been elected governor of Texas without conservative Democrats. He proceeded to explain how he got the support of this lt. governor, Bob Bullock, who was a Democrat. "Unheard of in Texas politics," he boasted. "He did it because he trusted me and I was doing a good job as governor."

"What do you think of the kids who went to Viet Nam?"

"I could understand that. I didn't choose that myself, but I was at that age."

"Did you think about it?"

"Not at all. Yeah, I didn't particularly respect the decision, but I could understand it. It was a very troubling period."

Bush joined the Air Force Reserves as a pilot and never flew a mission overseas. He also reveals that, like many Americans, his feeling on the war evolved.

"The war was not well defined. It was a political war and it cost us a lot of lives. I supported the administration for a while and then turned sour when I realized it was a war not being fought to win, but it was a political war. I think I reflect a lot of people in my generation that were disillusioned by the conduct of the war over time." He then went on to credit his dad with helping the country to reconcile its feelings for Viet Nam veterans, to the point that today they are held in honor.

"They should have been treated with respect the moment they came back," he went on.

"As for today, I am not suggesting kids ought to dodge the draft in times of war, but I can understand people making that kind of decision." It was a comprehensive answer and displayed some compassion for those who might have thought differently about the conflict. At this point, I handed him the list of my remaining questions, and sensing I was really pushing the time limit, asked, "Do you want to pick out one of these to finish?"

"I do, but I'm going to go. Great questions. You have obviously thought about them. You gave me a chance to show you why I want to be president. How about visiting me down at the ranch sometime?" He really surprised me.

"You don't want to do that," I advised.

"Come on. You'll like it down there—a man like you," he joked. I am not sure what he meant, but I didn't have time to ask for any clarification, as he was out the door to his next appointment.

Truscott gave me a smile and said, "He was on fire today."

He stayed that way until John McCain put it out with his upset win in Michigan days later.

I came away from the brief encounter with the next president of the United States with one overwhelming impression: I felt as if I had known this guy for twenty years. There was an instant rapport. He was down to earth. He had a good sense of humor. He seemed to connect with ease. And frankly I think that's why he won the squeaker of a presidential race. He had an intangible quality about him that made you like him, even if you didn't totally agree with his stance on the issues.

I don't think it was an act either. Maybe he was a real jerk in private. Maybe his public mask was a fake, but based on that one interview, I didn't think so. Engler told me afterward that what I saw was what I got.

About the interview itself, I was pleased to have broken the rules and squeezed in about a dozen questions instead of just two. And I found his responses to be quite good. I came home and told my wife about the exchange.

It struck me that he was like a school kid who had studied real hard for an exam and was finally given a chance to show what he knew. When he said he appreciated my questions because they were "not the process questions that are often given to me," what he meant was the media had a fixation on the horse race. Who was up?

Why were they up? What could you do to get them down? And what will it take to win?

None of those questions mean squat to a voter who is trying to choose between candidates based on issues. What I had done without really thinking about it was to ask him about stuff I thought the voters wanted to know. When he heard them, he decided it was worth the extra time to answer them.

It was a fun interview and about three weeks later when I covered Bush in Battle Creek I figured I could replicate the one on one. Silly me. He didn't remember me, nor the interview so he breezed by me as I got in two questions on casino gaming. Two questions. How prophetic.

John McCain

Everywhere he went on the campaign trail he was Johnny One Note: "I will never lie to the American people."

Lots of voters believed him. So did I. But I was wrong. McCain fudged. It was on statewide public TV, although nobody knew it at the time.

McCain was one, in an impressive line of maverick candidates, with whom Michigan voters have had a love affair. Those office seekers tell it like it is. The only "spin" they know is the one in their washing machine at home.

Most candidates are programmed by their handlers. Led around by the nose by their handlers, and if there is any ounce of spontaneity left in them, the handlers sap that out of them too. That's all done in the name of winning.

Mavericks like George Corley Wallace came into Michigan and showed there was another way of doing it. In his case he appealed to the baser instincts of white voters as he rode a school bus to victory in the 1972 presidential primary here. At the time suburban white voters were facing a possible cross district busing plan that could have delivered inner city students to integrate suburban schools. The former Alabama governor told voters he would oppose that and even though top labor leaders in Michigan told rank and file members to ignore Wallace, he won.

John Anderson was fighting an uphill battle. The Illinois congressman had the audacity to challenge the Nixon White House. Maverick Anderson had a populist platform, had appeal to moderate Republicans and Independents, and made inroads with the female vote. Michigan voters liked the gray haired guy. First Lady Helen Milliken not only liked him, she voted for him. And dollars to donuts, her hubby did too. For public consumption, though, Bill Milliken was for Nixon.

This brings us back to the McCain candidacy in 2000. His fledgling campaign, held together by bailing wire, limped into Michigan hoping to capitalize on McCain's growing appeal in other presidential primaries. He was getting plenty of national attention in his uphill battle against George W. Bush. The popular wisdom: His maverick candidacy didn't have a chance in the state that John Engler was going to deliver for "W."

My first peek at McCain was during his first visit to Lansing. A rally was slated for the Lansing Community College campus. McCain had demonstrated unusual support among younger voters who generally sit on their duffs rather than in an auditorium seat to hear a political speech. They packed the joint for him.

Standing in the wings as McCain paraded back and forth berating the political establishment, was another Viet Nam vet. State senator John Schwarz was there. He was the only recognizable Republican.

Anyone who even gave a hint of liking McCain or his independent message got Engler's evil eye. Problem was, Schwarz was politically blind and as fiercely independent as the guy he watched on the stage. As the crowd rose to its feet, McCain ended his monologue and walked off. Schwarz moved in. The two huddled for a moment and when McCain was engulfed by the press corps for the post speech news conference, he announced he had a Michigan campaign manager, John Schwarz.

Big deal. Schwarz had no organization; no access to the GOP party apparatus and whatever he did do, Engler would try to undo. That did not deter the McCain-Schwarz axis—as wobbly as it was.

They pasted together a donors list, staged a couple of measly fund-raisers, and actually got on the air with some commercials. But it was a waste. Engler told everyone, Michigan was going for Bush and most of us believed it.

It did all add up. Bush had more money, more organizational prowess, and Engler was opening doors everywhere for his friend from Texas. It was the tortoise vs. the hare.

That theory, however, left out one factor—the voters. In politics the media is often dazzled by all the sizzle that it sees daily on the campaign trail. The voters don't see it and don't hear much of the rhetoric either. Hence, they are not sucked in by the hype. By ignoring the voters, reporters missed a significant development, the tortoise was gaining on the hare.

I got a feeling of that as I covered a McCain rally in Livonia just before the presidential vote in February of 2000. It was an ugly and gloomy Sunday afternoon and the McCain bus, the Straight Talk Express, was cruising along I -275 headed for the Laurel Manor.

The joint was overflowing. There were balloons, little old ladies, and funny men with even funnier hats anxiously awaiting the arrival of their man. I was too. After the rally I was going to do a one on one interview on the back of the McCain bus. The twenty minute interview was part of a statewide Public TV program we were producing on the election.

I wanted to talk with McCain before the rally, to get something in the can just in case something happened with the extended interview. I headed for the empty front lobby and waited . . . and waited.

Up behind me comes Schwarz. "What are you doing?" he asks.

"I'm waiting to ambush McCain," I confess.

"You won't get him here," he discloses. "He's coming in the back entrance. Follow me."

Cameraman Paul Peritonzi and I elbow our way through the crowd until finally the senator deposits us in a back hallway where we resume our vigil for McCain.

Within minutes a side door swings open. Some of that gloomy Michigan light and a nasty wintry blast fill the hallway. And then there he is . . . McCain. All smiles. They've told him the place is filled to the brim. But before he gets to the crowd, I extend my hand and stop his forward momentum.

"Senator . . . a couple of quick questions before you run in there. Welcome to Michigan," the ambush begins.

"Thank you," he beams as he knows he's getting some badly needed free media exposure.

"You've said that you're never going to lie to the people." He says, "Yeah."

"But you know politics. Don't you sometimes have to lie in order to protect national security?"

He looks shocked, as if he'd never heard the question before. "Naw. I don't think so. Ah, I've never had to in seventeen years and twenty-two years in the military, so I don't think you have to do that. In fact I think the reason why young people are so skeptical is because they think we do that.

"Can you lie by omission and get away with it?"

"Oh, no. You always have to tell the truth and great presidents in history have done that."

With the clock ticking, I turn quickly to the draft dodger question. What did he think of the students who defected to Canada during Viet Nam?

"I didn't approve of it," he says, "because that meant somebody else went in their place." But then he adds a very compassionate response noting that he's put the issue behind him. "I've dedicated myself to reconciliation and healing over that issue, and it doesn't matter anymore who was for or against the war."

Now here's one really out of left field. "Would you encourage civil disobedience as president?"

"Of course not," he rejects the notion, but then he adds, people are free to practice it but he would not encourage it.

"Well what if it's for a good social cause?" I continue.

"Civil disobedience for a good social cause?" he repeats the question to buy some time to find an answer.

"I would hope that they would find satisfaction through their government and their president without having to resort to it." He smiles. He knows it's a great response.

I know I have only a few seconds left as he starts to shift toward the hall, "That means Rosa Parks could not ride in the front of the bus?"

"No, no," he protests. "What I'm saying is that was because there was an unresponsive government. I will have an unresponsive [wrong word] government so there won't be any need for it." He meant "responsive," but he is really flustered now, something most of the media had not seen.

And with that he is out of camera range. Walking behind him is

Mike Murphy his media advisor. Murphy and I go back to Engler's first run for governor. I figure I'm a shoe-in to get my other interview with him in my corner.

"You'll get me on the bus?" I smile confidently to ole Murph.

"I don't know. I'll try," he speaks over his shoulder as he follows McCain into the mob scene.

Schwarz whips up the troops and McCain grabs the mike and launches into his speech he's done a thousand times. He knocks Bush. Applause. He knocks Engler. More applause. He says, he'll win in Michigan. The crowd goes nuts. Those of us on the media platform smile knowingly as if to say, "What did you expect him to say—I'm gonna get trounced?"

As the event winds down, I look over my extensive list of questions I've been working on for a couple of days. I felt the first interview went well. He was fast on his feet and I was eager to have another give and take with him.

It came time to get on the bus for that extended interview. We boarded and look for a seat. There weren't any left. I guess that we'll stand on the ride back to East Lansing. Not so fast. A campaign aide tells us there was no room on the bus, not even to stand up. Bad luck or bad timing? No, there was a reason those seats were filled. I didn't realize it at the time, but during the interview, Mrs. McCain disintegrated from an adoring and smiling spouse to one upset lady. As we reviewed the tape in the studio afterward, with each of my pointed questions, the expression on her face moved down another notch until the end, she was whispering in his ear to stop the interview. She even motioned for one of the handlers to stop this inquisition now! After that, there was no way she would let me on the bus for another round of "Let's trip up John."

Of course, I was disappointed, but at the same time, if the truth be known, I was proud that I had done my job. I had come up with some questions that he had not tackled before. He did a grand job, but what I didn't know until three months later was, he had lied right there on the spot. It turned out that the day before the Michigan rally, McCain was in a debate in South Carolina. One of the cosmic issues of the day was whether it was OK to fly the Confederate flag over the state capitol. McCain, knowing that lots of viewers that night had roots that dated back to the Civil War, took a calculated risk. He said he didn't object. Turns out he did, but didn't reveal the lie until months later.

So there he was, hours after telling a lie down South, stretching the truth up North in front of our camera. I knew he was too good to be true and my instincts were proven correct.

Al Gore

Of course there was another guy in the presidential sweepstakes in 2000. Last name Gore. First name Al. Political party: Democrat.

It struck me in covering both Gore and Bush that voters really had a clear choice regarding experience. Whenever I ask groups who had the most experience to be president, Gore always gets the nod. For years he was the proverbial heartbeat away from the Oval Office. So then why did Bush win, although some Democrats still call him an unelected president.

Regardless of what transpired in the close Florida vote, if experience really counted, Gore would have won in a landslide. So what was going on?

First Gore really was a bore—at least he was when I met him in Grand Rapids on a cold October afternoon, before the November presidential election. He brought his campaign to downtown G.R. next to that piece of art I can never remember. Our crew showed up about 11 A.M. for a noon rally and then a one on one interview with the candidate afterward.

I was shocked when we drove up—the place was packed—maybe five thousand or more in a district that was supposed to be Republican. Remember the area around Grand Rapids was home to Jerry Ford, state senator Dick Posthumus and a whole host of other GOP notables, so on the surface Gore was coming into enemy territory.

What I found out later and should have figured out on my own was that the Michigan Gore folks felt they had a real shot at winning the city, otherwise they would have been somewhere else that day. Gore eventually arrived with former Governor Blanchard at his side, along with a blond woman named Granholm, the attorney general, and some other state Democratic hangers on.

Despite the blustery wind, the rally had an upbeat air to it as Gore railed on Bush and called for Democrats to keep the White House in their hands. With the rally out of the way the media was sent to a nearby hotel for the personal interviews slated to begin around 3 P.M.

Three o'clock came and went prompting one wag to opine, "Democrats couldn't run a one chair barbershop." It got to be 4 P.M. and I had to have this story back in Lansing for the 6 P.M. newscast. The clock was ticking; my stomach was churning and finally someone motioned me, "You're next—whatever your name is."

Cameraperson in tow we were led to room 238 to set up and before you knew it, there was Al Baby. He looked taller in person. We shook hands and assumed our respective chairs and the tape rolled.

Unlike the Bush interview there were no question restrictions or if there were, nobody had filled me in on them, so I just when until they said stop. Again trying to break some new ground and stay away from questions he had heard a thousand times, I began with what I thought was a pretty nifty opener.

"How are you different than Bill Clinton?"

Recall at the time, Gore was making a studied attempt to redefine himself apart from President Clinton, who brought with him some political baggage. So the question gave him a clear shot at putting some distance between himself and his boss.

But instead of that he said, "Everyone is different."

Wow. Thanks Al. Great sound bite and pretty deep thinking on your part, too.

I came back with, "For example: Do you have a temper?"

I had read enough books to know that Clinton was famous for his, but again Gore demurred, "Do you?" he asked me.

I wanted to say, "I asked your first" but didn't. After all he was the sitting vice president of the United States. The whole thing lasted about ten minutes. I thanked him and was out the door, into the car, hoping not to encounter any state police en route to the Lansing studios of WILX TV. In the car I had little time to reflect since I needed to bang out the copy, pick out the pithy sound bites and get ready for the live shot.

It was only later that night at home: There really was a world of difference between Bush and Gore based on my measly interviews with both. Bush was gregarious and friendly. Gore was not. You felt that instant rapport with Bush. Not with Gore. I figured if I felt that, perhaps voters would too. Bush connected better than Gore and in this media driven political environment, image often wins out over substance. This is exactly why the guy with the most experience never got into the White House. I can not back this up with any scientific evidence, but I firmly believe TV has changed the way we pick our leaders.

If you believe, as I do, that most voters are lazy about studying the candidates before they vote, and get most of their information from the tube, than image emerges as the predominant factor in many voting decisions.

"I just liked Bush," was a common refrain I heard on the campaign trail. Gore never got that kind of review and from the glimpse I got in that hotel room that day in October, I had a greater understanding of that opinion. It's not that Gore was bad—he just wasn't as good as Bush and I think that came across on the television for many voters.

Thirty years ago, experience meant a lot. Now it doesn't mean as much. If it did, we would not have term limits, which is the movement that denounces experience as anything but good.

Fast forward to the 2002 governor's race for Michigan, when Al Gore appeared once more. This time he was not a presidential contender, he was here to stump for Jennifer Granholm and test the waters to see if he would run in 2004.

While the rest of the press corps headed for the auditorium on the Michigan State University campus, cameraman Keith Basser and I headed to Capital City airport. I wanted to see if Gore remembered me. Ha.

(I always feel for candidates who have met thousands of persons when one of them comes up and blurts out, "Remember me? I shook your hand in Ironwood last July." The candidate doesn't know this Joe from a hole in the ground but must cover the situation with something like, "Help me remember, you're . . . . . . ?" It shows that common folks have no idea the drill these candidates go through. It can be to the point that they are lucky if they recall what day it is or what town they are in, let alone a reporter's name they met one time for three minutes. They call it life in the bubble.)

Anyway, we showed up at the private aviation hanger and saw lots of unfamiliar faces standing around. They looked at us like we had just stepped off another planet. I know they wanted to say, "Get the hell out of here and get back to MSU," but they didn't. I inquired as to his E.T.A. and was told 11 A.M. I was also told by one of the handlers that Gore was not granting any interviews.

We didn't budge. I asked if they could at least ask him if he might talk with me and someone said they would. The answer that came back was just fuzzy enough to make me want to try for the one on one.

Soon a sleek small jet—much smaller than Air Force Two, landed and onto the tarmac came my ole friend Al. He shook hands with the welcoming party—one mechanic whose job it was to put blocks under the wheels, and the guy who answers the phone inside the little hut. The brass band apparently had another gig.

Then we made eye contact, which was my signal to move in, which I did.

"Mr. Gore, welcome to Lansing." Without asking permission I just fired away. "What's more important in politics, experience or charisma?"

This was a question with a hidden agenda. During the governor's race, that very issue was on the radar screen vis-a-vis the candidacy of Ms. Granholm. She was the acknowledged frontrunner on the charisma scale but there were some serious doubts about her depth of experience. With my question I was leading Gore into playing a role in the governor's race without him knowing it.

Gore chuckled at the question and suggested, "Since I don't have much charisma, the answer must be experience." He laughed again, which was two more laughs than I heard in the previous encounter with him. I was immediately struck by the New Al Gore. He was relaxed and had a new air about him that actually made him approachable.

I fired off a couple more questions and thanked him for the time. He was off to the rally with us in pursuit.

He was quite good that afternoon. Repeating a joke he had used hundreds of times, he told the MSU crowd, he was now being introduced as "Al Gore, 'the former,' going to be next president of the United States." The kids loved it.

Just to give you a peek into crowd spin. The event had originally been slated for the big MSU auditorium but when ticket distribution lagged, Democrats moved it to the smaller Fairchild Theatre where it was a standing room only crowd, which presented a much nicer picture for the cameras.

Rally over, everyone retired back stage for a news conference with Granholm and Gore. Before it got started Granholm saw me and quickly nudged her buddy.

"Look out for him," she nudged the big guy standing next to her with her elbow.

"Oh yeah," he responded. "I already met him at the airport where he asked me about charisma and experience." He laughed. She did too, but she knew the implications of my question. To her credit, she never asked how I was going to play the story.

Bottom line, on the second Gore visit was much more positive. You felt a human connection. Laughter can do that and I'm surprised that more politicians don't use it to enhance their image, which continues to be more important than what's in their brain.

You'll note that there are not many business executives on this list of interviews. There's several reasons for that but the major one is they don't like the media!

Show me a CEO in trouble and I'll show you a CEO in the bunker with P.R. types all around him. Corporate America would prefer to reside on the seventy-sixth floor as far away from the media as possible. Accountability to the public isn't in their lexicon and granting interviews to explain anything is rare.

You can count on four fingers the number of business leaders on my list. I did about a five minute interview with Iacocca up in Traverse City while attending a conference. Bendix honcho Mike Blumenthal did our show and was quite good. But the hands down best of the bunch was John Rock. He was head of the Oldsmobile division. He came to Michigan via the Wild West. He owned a ranch, cattle, etc., and thus when he described himself as a cowboy, you knew he was the real McCoy. He was so down to earth he even ordered his employees to participate in cowboy day every Friday at his office. Every Friday. Yippe-kai-yo.

It was November 1992 and the *Washington Post* ran a piece that hinted the Olds nameplate was about to be eradicated. At the time it seemed far fetched but it's now a reality.

Instead of jumping out of view when the news hit, Rock jumped into full view. He bought up a nationwide satellite feed to hit the problem head on. He allowed his brain to be picked by me after the fact. The picking revealed a fascinating and rare peek into the head of a captain of industry who was extremely real.

Rock's first instinct was to ignore the story but when over half of the dealers around the country told him to do something, he listened and he did. After deciding to say something, the next question was, "what would he say?" He told the world, "I'm one pissed off cowboy . . . and by the way the story is wrong."

Next he wanted to develop a commercial to restore confidence in his product. His first gut reaction translated into "If you buy an Olds and we go out of business, GM will take over your payments." Talk about a bold statement, but he killed it himself. It sounded too much like a used car ad.

In lieu of that he settled on a factual pitch. Tell the world that Olds would always be around because it sells more cars than Mercedes, Infiniti, Acura, BMW, Volvo, and Lexus combined.

"Why would a company stop doing business that does this much business?" his ad would say.

Launching the commercial was a risk itself. His researchers told him only 14 percent of the public had even heard about the Post story and advertising the problem could lift the awareness level. Twenty-five percent of the Olds dealers knew about the story and here was the clincher, 35 percent of those in the market for a new car were aware of it, too. It was that number that made the Rock's heart skip a beat.

Rock was one part Ross Perot without the paranoia; one part Iacocca without the ego, and the rest of him was as common as the day is long.

He was at a fundraiser for the Humane Society in town one night and after it was over he invited about four couples back to his house. The joint was filled with animals. Three exotic cats, two Chesapeake dogs, a talking cockatoo and who knows what else. He and his wife Bonnie, gave a tour of the place and as one source said, "If you didn't know who he was, you never would have guessed it." And of course he was decked out in his cowboy get-up.

Rock departed Oldsmobile. And the Big Cheeses at GM started

to dismantle the division. The headquarters was shipped off to Detroit. And the next step, the end of the Oldsmobile line. Turns out the Post story was right. And Rock got out of Dodge, just before the movers came in.

Gerald R. Ford

Five years after serving as president of the United States, Gerald R. Ford was in Williamston, Michigan, just outside of Lansing to attend a GOP fundraiser at the home of John McGoff. McGoff was a media mogul who owned broadcast and print outlets and was well connected, otherwise, Mr. Ford might have been somewhere else the night of October 1, 1981.

Out of the blue and with zip advance work on my part, Mr. McGoff called to offer me a one-on-one with the ex-president. I gladly accepted.

We set up our cameras in a little room away from the main event and patiently waited for the guest to arrive. I had obviously seen him on the television, but since he had spent most of his adult life in the nation's capital, I never really covered him. He seemed taller in real life as he walked in and shook my hand—isn't that what they always say.

He was conservatively dressed in a watch plaid three-piece suit with a dark tie, and we began the exchange on one of the topics of the day back then—the religious right and more specifically the Moral Majority.

At the time, Rev. Jerry Falwell was making great inroads into the political system. To some he was not only crossing the scrimmage line between church and state, he was deep in the backfield picking and choosing candidates based on how well they did on his religious litmus test.

Ford was not amused. "I have some serious reservations about whether organized religion should get involved in organized government," he started out. The Moral Majority crowd was playing on the GOP side of the game and developing so called hit lists of candidates it wanted knocked out of office.

Ford was not amused over that either. "I've never thought a hit list approach by any organization, whether it's a business or union, is the best way to present candidates or issues for the electorate." He also observed the strategy could backfire, making a martyr out of the one targeted for extinction.

A religious person himself, he also objected to the notion that if you were not with the Moral Majority that somehow made you "not as dedicated to the religious principles they espoused."

I frankly expected him to pull his punches in this sensitive area. However, he waded right in and gave answers that put the M.M. gang on notice that he would not embrace many of their attitudes or their techniques.

In the early 1980s Michigan's number one industry was rockin' and reelin' from the continued onslaught of foreign competition. Ford, however, did not blast U.S. auto executives for mismanaging the industry even though those managers clearly misread the market's demand for smaller and more fuel efficient vehicles.

He did have an interesting take on the disconnect between union leaders and rank and file workers. It was a notion that began in the 1972 election when blue collar workers ignored their leaders and voted George Wallace the winner of the presidential primary here.

Ford said, "I used to get a lot of UAW votes. I got a great many over the thirteen years I ran for election" while the leaders "use to fight me all the time." He also pointed to the 1976 election for president, which Ford lost to a novice governor from Georgia named Carter.

The UAW leadership, however, could not deliver for Carter four years later because union members, "saw the high inflation and the unemployment under Carter. So I suspect that the union leadership went down one road . . . and many of the union members recalled how they were misleading in '76 and they couldn't buy that line again."

With little time left for the twenty minute exchange, we played the name game. I gave him a name. He was supposed to give a one word response. Apparently former presidents can not utter one word answers.

David Stockman . . . Reagan's embattled budget director.

Ford: "Very brilliant young man doing a tough job in a difficult situation."

California Governor Jerry Brown . . . Governor Moonbeam as he was affectionately called in the press corps.

Ford: "He's in trouble—made a big mess of the medfly problem."

James Watt . . . Reagan's interior secretary and poster boy for the anti-environmental crowd.

Ford: "Hard hitting. He's not always right but neither am I or you. He is probably his own worst enemy."

Richard Nixon.

Ford: "Well . . . it's a tragedy in American history."

And that was it.

In looking back at the tape I shouted out loud. "That's it, Skubick? Where was the hard hitting follow up? Where was the pursuit on why he pardoned Tricky Dick? How could you let him off the hook?" I muttered to myself.

I couldn't believe it looking at the video tape twelve years later. I accepted a seven word answer and said good night.

It was not my finest hour.

Maybe his reason for letting Tricky Dick go was old news. I still should have asked.

Ross Perot

The infamous, and paranoid newsmaker H. Ross Perot. The maverick presidential contender was a frequent flyer into our state, which was a battleground and MSU, of course, in 1992, played host to one of the national debates.

I got a tip that Perot was coming into Capital City Airport and I decided to be a greeting party that included my cameraman, Mr. Basser. Over the years, it's been a successful strategy to show up at the airport even if you were not invited. In fact, it was always more fun when you weren't. It was not fun for the Perot advance troops who didn't want us there. After lamely trying to get us off the story by sending us back to the auditorium where Perot was going to speak, we came to a truce of sorts. I told the media person that we wanted just a brief interview after he got off the plane. With the paranoia scale hitting record heights, I agreed to give him the questions. Generally that is a no-no, but I could tell I would get nothing if I didn't do it.

Perot's private jet landed and the greeting party went inside for what seemed like forever. Finally he emerged. This is the most worrisome part of the game because the reporter has no control. The pigeon can head for the limo and stiff you. You edge up as close as you can get, hoping they will walk your way. Perot walked toward me. He answered questions about the lay of the political landscape in Michigan and how well he was doing and off he went. He got his free bite on the evening news and I got a one-on-one that no one else got.

But who really cares or who really knew that we had the "exclusive A" other than the guys in the newsroom? Welcome to the world of TV news. It's all about image. Per chance that night, some viewer happened to be channel surfing and saw me with Perot and then saw the other station's coverage of Perot at the podium, do you think they think that "Skubick got the exclusive?"

Nope. But it's still fun to do and part of the thing that keeps you engaged—getting that something that none of your competitors have. Yeah, you're right, it's silly.

John Riccardo

In producing over 1,500 *Off the Records*, only once has an interviewee walked out. Say hello to the fiery Italian John Riccardo, former head of the sinking Chrysler Corporation.

I got wind that Riccardo was coming into town for some charity gig. I called his office and was lucky enough to nail him as a guest on the show. He showed up in his one thousand dollar tweed suit and we proceeded to the set, but we got only halfway there.

"So we're going to discuss the charity?" he said.

"Well yes sir, but we will also have some other questions as well," I informed him as he stopped in his tracks. Remember now at this time, the littlest of the Big Three automakers was on the ropes, just one losing quarter away from bankruptcy. It was my intent to throw him a softball on the charity but immediately get to the good stuff such as "Where are you working next week after the Chrysler board unloads your butt?"

Never got to ask it. He refused to take any questions on any other subject and I steadfastly refused to turn the program into a fifteen minute freebie for the charity. Having agreed to disagree, he walked out . . . never to be seen again.

Mike Wallace

The feisty Mr. Wallace with a firmly established reputation for taking no hostages, was in town to do a *60 Minutes* piece on the way Michigan had handled the multi-million dollar U.S. tobacco case settlement.

Instead of diverting most of the funds into smoking cessation and other health related programs, Governor John Engler and his lackeys in the GOP controlled legislature had decided to use most of it for a so called Merit Scholarship program. It was open to any student smart enough to pass the Michigan Education Assessment Program (MEAP) exam. For some it would mean a stipend of $2,500.

Wallace wanted to know why Engler had taken this tack and was in town ready to do a Wallace on the governor. But first he held court on the capitol lawn to interview state lawmakers who had approved the plan.

It was quite the sight. State politicians, sensing a chance to be on national TV as part of one of the most popular news shows on the tube, gathered around Wallace like the proverbial moths to a flame. They didn't seem afraid of his hard hitting reputation and they had no reason to be. It was pretty clear from his questions that Wallace was playing the "Good cop" with legislators to help lay the trap for Engler during which the "bad cop" Wallace would suddenly appear.

The seasoned journalist was getting sound bites from the likes of Representative Mike Murphy, a Democrat from Lansing, and his sidekick, Representative Kwame Kilpatrick, who was then the House Minority leader with his eyes set on being mayor of Detroit.

Murphy and Kilpatrick had managed to edge everybody else out of the picture as I stood next to Mr. Wallace as I began. "You aren't out to make the governor the bad guy in your piece, are you?"

From the opening bell Wallace amazingly stumbled, "If the governor's the bad guy then let," but then he stopped not wanting to complete that sentence and inserted a less accusatory comment instead, "I'd no, no, I'm not saying the governor's a bad guy. No. Not at all." A feeble attempt at maintaining his journalistic neutrality.

"Well, you just implied here [to the lawmakers in his interview] that the governor flip-flopped?"

Wallace continued, "He did flip-flop, did he not?" (Hey who is asking the questions here?)

"Does that make him a bad guy?" I asked.

"Depends upon, I guess, your point of view," he paused and then continued, "What you're trying to do, and I can understand it [with that Kilpatrick and Murphy break into laughter], you're trying to nail me in front of the state capitol suggesting that John Engler's a bad guy." Guilty. Skubick trying to pull a Wallace on Wallace. Believe me, as a reporter, when they don't level with you, that's when the trouble begins. That's when you pursue to see how far from the truth your subject will go.

Wallace was not finished. Now he looks down at the one newspaper clip he has in his hand from April 1999. He cites the *Free Press* article quoting a former employee of Engler. Ron David is an avid anti-smoker and anti-tobacco crusader. I was left with the impression that it was the only piece of "research" he may have seen on why Michigan diverted the tobacco bucks into scholarships.

"That was done with a majority of the legislature's support," I explained.

Wallace said "That's correct."

Anyway the interview had run out of steam and he asked, "Where are you from?" I declined to answer and just welcomed him to Lansing. "Are you from Lansing?" he tried again and I said, "Yes."

Now Kilpatrick picks up the conversation advising Wallace as he refers to me, "He is one of the toughest reporters we have [as he places his hand on Wallace's shoulder as if to console him]. He was going for the jugular with you. He does that with all of us."

At which point I turn the microphone to Kilpatrick with a wise crack comment, "Is it true you cannot be mayor of Detroit?"

With his undeniable chuckle and without missing a beat he shoots back, "I'll definitely be mayor of Detroit. There's no problem with that."

As for Mr. Wallace, his journey resulted in no story at all. The tobacco piece got yanked. And nobody from *60 Minutes* called to see if I wanted to pinch hit for the aging Mr. Wallace, which I did not want then or now.

Ronald Reagan

Democrat Jim Blanchard and Republican John Engler shared only about two things in common. They were both governors and both complained about the capital press corps unwillingness to travel to cover anything.

Blanchard once jokingly opined that reporters around these parts would only travel as far as the McDonalds in Portland and the Red Cedar Grill in Williamston. Both are about twenty miles outside of town going west and east respectively.

In my case they were right on the mark. Of all the wonderful trappings of this assignment, leaving for overnight or out of town gigs were my least favorite. When it came to covering the national GOP convention in which Ronald Reagan won the nomination, I had no choice but to cover it—it was in Detroit.

It marked the first of only two times that I "covered" Reagan. The second time was when we had lunch together at the White House.

The 1980 convention was the "New Beginning" conclave staged at the then new Joe Louis Arena home of the Red Wings. The right wings moved into town for the week long gala. Michigan Public TV undertook the ambitious task of grinding out a nightly half hour program on what the Michigan delegation was up to.

Governor Bill Milliken had been an ardent backer of George Bush, Sr. The two managed to beat Reagan in the Michigan presidential sweepstakes but Bush faltered later on and the former California governor had the nomination wrapped up when he flew into Motown for the coronation.

The only bit of excitement was the second spot on the ticket. Popular wisdom gave the initial nod to Bush but on the night the vice president was chosen, the convention floor was all abuzz with a juicy alternative.

As the night wore on and you circulated inside the Michigan delegation, the rumor mill was in full force. Reagan was considering

Gerald Ford for a running mate. The word was Ford had balked at being the second banana. He wanted a bigger piece of the action— a co-presidency!

Such a contrivance was unheard of in the annals of presidential politics yet the thing got legs as they say. When it got arms, hands, feet, and a head, I hit the airwaves on WWJ Newsradio 950 to announce to the free world that the deal had been sealed.

What a skoop for the skoop.

My sources were none other than Milliken and Max Fisher the multi-millionaire sugar daddy to the national GOP who was based in Detroit. Both "confirmed" the story so I was off to the phone to report same. With hands and voice both trembling I called the newsroom.

"Let's go live right now. I've got the Reagan-Ford story nailed."

Had I been working for a newspaper, there would have been a safety net. Somebody would have thrown up a yellow light, if not a red one, to say let's just wait and see. But radio news is a different beast. There were no caution lights, nobody to force you to double check, and so when I said I had it, we went with it.

Thank goodness the Newsradio 950 evening radio signal went only about as far as the hotel across the street from the studio on Nine Mile Road in Southfield because within minutes of that report a huge knot appeared in my stomach. The story was a dud. False. Wrong. Oh. Oh.

Where were Milliken and Maxie baby? Turns out they thought they were telling me the truth.

It was just a mistake and within minutes I was sheepishly back on the air undoing what had been done. That was enough convention work for me. I haven't been to one since.

I was invited to the White House for lunch with the president.

"Timmy," the familiar female voice on the other end of the phone started out. "How would you like to have lunch with the president in two weeks?"

It was my second cousin, Susie Engel, on the horn. After playing clarinet with me in the Fraser High School band, Susie had gone on to bigger and better things. She had landed in the Reagan White House media relations office and her invite was no joke.

The White House from time to time staged a so called regional news briefing. On that special day the regulars in the White House press corps step aside while their local yokel-cousins from the sticks get to eat with the president. Susie wanted to know if I wanted to join in.

I said "No."

I was sure that the tightwads at Detroit TV station WJBK would never pop for the plane fare and on my measly salary I was not going to do it even if it was a tax right off.

She insisted and we ended the conversation on a tentative note. I would check with the front office and if they had the bucks, I would fly in for the briefing.

She sealed the deal by promising to seat me right next to the president for lunch and even put me on his left side . . . that was the ear with the better hearing she secretly disclosed.

TV 2 seemed impressed with that. After all, a picture on the evening news with Skubick next to the president breaking bread must be worth something in the image dominated world of TV news. So on the appointed day I was off to D.C., which was about eight hundred miles south of the Red Cedar Grill as far as I could tell.

Anyway, it was a hoot, sure enough. Come lunch time, all the regional reporters, actually most of them were anchors [you could tell by the cloud of hairspray hanging over the East Room] were ushered in. Many made a dash for the table up front but were disappointed to discover it was assigned seating.

Way to go Susie.

As each one passed by the head table, there, next to the president's name plate, was this Skubick moniker. Five other lucky reporters got a seat near the president, but I got the best one.

Hey baby, it ain't what you know, it's who you know. Sitting right across from me with a wonderful warm smile was Cousin Susie. I can still recall the magic moment when I reached to shake Ronald Reagan's hand. In fact I can still look at it today. Never one to miss a detail, Susie had the White House photographer capture the moment for all our grandkids to see.

The picture showed up a week or so later with the inscription "To Tim Skubick. Best Wishes, Ronald Reagan." Never mind that some automatic signature machine printed his name. No one will ever know unless they read this book.

So you probably want to know what we . . . ya know me and the president, talked about. I was dying to ask him why he didn't save my radio career by taking the Ford co-presidency bait, but decided to tackle more delightful subjects, such as his disdain for the reporters in general and the White House press corps specifically.

He mildly complained about the press always hunting for bad news. I hinted that was part of our job. We agreed to disagree and for the life of me I can't remember one other tidbit from the thirty minutes we sat side by side. Had I known this book was going to materialize, I would have taken some notes, but then, I was a TV reporter and we never take notes.

Oh yeah, the gang at TV2 loved the video and within a year or so, I was fired. Seems they were getting increasingly disinterested in state capital political news. I knew I was toast when on the most important day of the legislative session, the last day, I was assigned to cover a more demanding story in Grand Rapids. Seems some woman had reported her Christmas tree had been stolen. I refused to go. The pink slip appeared soon thereafter, but the Reagan picture compliments of a dear departed relative, remains just across the room from this computer—for all the grandkids to see.

5

The Bumpy Romney-
Milliken Transition

In 1962, the state Republican Party was in ruins. The GOP had lost the governor's office for fourteen straight years. Then a guy who ran a car company formed Citizens for Michigan (C.F.M.). It was a classic grassroots effort aimed at rewriting the state's waterlogged and antiquated constitution. He propelled himself from that movement to win the GOP nomination for governor. When they counted the votes that year, George Romney departed American Motors Corporation (AMC) and headed for Lansing to run the state.

Romney was always ahead of his times. While at AMC he pioneered the small compact car platform that VW and others later copied. He predicted the future saying, "Who wants to have a gas-guzzler dinosaur in their garage . . . think of the gas bills."

AMC responded by dumping the small platform, and the U.S. auto industry ignored his warnings about gas-guzzlers continuing merrily on its way producing one right after another. That is until the flood of smaller Japanese cars in this country finally proved Romney was right. After he left, AMC went into the tank.

After the surprising Romney win in 1962, House Speaker Robert Waldron described it this way, "Romney was the Moses of the Republican Party leading us out of the wilderness." In those days the governor served for two years, not the current four, so when 1964 came around, Romney had to run again. This time there were problems at the top of the GOP ticket. Barry Goldwater was the nominee and that meant problems for Romney in Michigan.

The Romney team watched as Goldwater went into St. Petersburg, Florida, and called for the end to Social Security. There was one blunder after another and Romney knew if he didn't do something, his short reign in office would be over.

Led by a brilliant political scientist, Dr. Walter DeVries, a strategy was developed to divorce Romney from Goldwater. The party ran ads explaining to voters how they could vote for one party and then vote for the other. In effect they conceded that Democratic President Johnson would win, but if voters followed the GOP instructions, they could also vote for Romney.

They dubbed the strategy "ticket splitting" and called the voters who did it, "ticket splitters." The term is now used in every campaign and was coined in Michigan and acknowledges the importance of voting for the person and not the party. Remember back then one of the popular phrases was, "Make it Emphatic . . . Vote Straight Democratic." Persuading voters to vote for one party was a long standing tradition. Romney and company were trying to turn that notion on its ear and they did.

Romney withstood the million vote loss that Goldwater suffered in Michigan and won the governorship by 300,000 votes. All in all an impressive accomplishment given how poorly Goldwater did here.

Romney was also aided by a blunder state Democrats made. They ran Neil Staebler against Romney, which in and of itself was not bad. But when Staebler ran pictures of himself with a Hitler like mustache, the Romney folks were even more confident they would win. And win they did. Romney's coattails were so long that he dragged a whole slew of Republicans into office. The Democratic control of the Michigan House plummeted from a whopping 72 votes to a 55–55 tie. Republicans also forged a 20–18 edge in the Senate. The party swept all eight education seats on the statewide ballot and installed Republican Thomas Brennan as the newest member of the State Supreme Court.

It was that strong showing by Romney that propelled him into the national limelight and fostered his ill-fated bid for the presidency. That ended with his famous "brain washing" statement on the old Lou Gordon television show. His comment was in reference to the conflict in Viet Nam and his feeling that he was not getting the straight story from the military. The remark immediately damaged his credibility with voters who had not yet turned on the Johnson White House and its war strategy.

While popular wisdom suggests the brainwash thing cost Romney the election, he does not agree. The real deal breaker was Nelson Rockefeller getting into the race. Romney knew the only way he could topple Richard Nixon in 1968 was to keep it a two person contest. "I knew I had to get a clear understanding from Rockefeller that he would not run, and I got it," Romney wrote. Rockefeller later got in and Romney says that cost him the White House.

He felt Viet Nam was "the most tragic foreign policy mistake in the nation's history."

Of course years later Romney was vindicated as he was not the only one who was brainwashed. He never seemed bitter about his fate on the national level, but privately he must have felt he was a prophet that no one believed.

Before his presidential bid, there was still work to do at home. Romney wanted to institute a state income tax. He firmly believed the sales tax and property tax were unfair to the poor. The income tax he reasoned was fairer because if you earned more, you paid more. He knew it would be a tough sell but he was determined. He got the measure through the House but ran into a road block in the state Senate.

The new GOP leader there was an accountant Emil Lockwood. A master at bridge, Lockwood was also good at counting noses and he was two votes short on the income tax measure.

Lockwood came to Bob Danhof with the bad news. Danhof was Romney's arm twister in the legislature and when Lockwood explained that he needed two Democrats to join with eighteen Republicans to pass the tax, Danhof knew Lockwood was not kidding. The crafty Lockwood had done his homework and had developed two targets on the Democratic side and he wanted Danhof's help to nail them.

Danhof asked the critical question: What did Coleman Young and Stanley Novak want for their vote?

You are familiar with all the books about how a bill becomes law, but the books are wrong. The battle over the income tax gives you a peek into how it's really done.

The two Detroit Democrats had a price but it was very high. They wanted Sunday liquor sales across the state. Unheard of. Michigan had always been dry on Sunday and over-turning that tradition would be tough . . . especially with George Romney sitting in the governor's seat.

Romney was a Mormon, plus a non-drinker and non-smoker. Danhof knew if he went to his boss with the proposed vote trading deal, Romney would nix it. So Danhof decided to bypass his boss. Instead he went to Lockwood and told him to go forward. Young and "Stosh" Novak, as he was affectionately known, were told Danhof had signed off on the arrangement. That way the Democrats might conclude that Romney had agreed, but if the whole thing blew up, Lockwood could honestly say Romney never said that.

It came time for the income tax vote. Beryl Kenyon, the sometimes nasty and ill tempered secretary of the Senate called off the names. The count got to eighteen. Lockwood in a stage whisper tells Young and Novak it's time for them to vote yes and they did. Lockwood had his twenty votes. The governor had his income tax, and Danhof had a problem.

He goes to the governor and eases into the subject. He tells the governor sometimes in order to get something, you have to give something. Romney, not exactly a dummy, asks the going price for the two Democratic votes.

"Sunday liquor sales," Danhof says with fingers crossed. Romney doesn't flinch. Danhof is relieved. He knew that going around the governor as he did, could have gotten him fired, but Romney understood. He attached several conditions to the Sunday bill. Romney said there could be no sales until after 2 P.M. and the only places that could sell liquor would be those with more receipts from food than booze. And there was one more thing. Romney said he would not sign the measure. But fourteen days after it reached his desk, it would automatically become law without his John Hancock.

It was a classic example of how everyone got what they wanted. Young and Novak got their bill. Romney was able to say he didn't sign the legislation, which gave him political cover with the "drys," and Danhof lived to tell the story.

Romney with his trademark blue cardigan sweater ruled the GOP until he left for the nation's capital to join the Nixon administration as the secretary of Housing and Urban Development (HUD). That left his lt. governor, Bill Milliken, to run the state. Milliken was not Romney's first choice for the job. He really wanted state treasurer Allison Green, but that didn't work out. The Romney-Milliken relationship had never been very close. They were complete opposites. Romney could be bombastic. Milliken didn't know what that meant. Romney would grab lawmakers by the collar to muscle them for a vote. Milliken wouldn't even think of that, but he could get pushy if he had to.

With Romney in D.C. and Milliken trying to figure out how to operate the levers of the government and the party, the not so great relationship got measurably worse when the U.S. Senate election came up in 1970.

It was a comedy of errors and political pratfalls from the opening bell. Milliken did not have a favorite out of the twenty-five persons who initially indicated they might run. Among them was Romney himself. During a January 1970 news conference, long before the August primary, Milliken was asked about the "off again, in again, and out again" statements from Romney. The new governor could give no guidance on what was going on.

Supreme Court Justice Tom Brennan hinted he might get in. Then the rumor mill produced this dandy: If Mr. Romney did not run, his Mrs. might.

It was every governor's nightmare. You want to give the impression you are in charge and in control of your party but Milliken clearly was not. He kept telling reporters it was a healthy open process as the GOP fumbled its way to what they called a "consensus candidate." The intent was to find one person, unite behind him or her, and avoid a costly primary with a host of other candidates in the race.

Everyone knew that incumbent Phil Hart would be tough to unseat that year, but that didn't keep Flint congressman Don Riegle and state senator Bob Huber from sniffing out the nomination, too. In the end it came down to a showdown between those two and Mrs. Romney.

It took three meetings of the party's power brokers to resolve the conflict. The second session in the old Jack Tar Hotel was a total disaster for Milliken from the media's perspective. Even one member of his team confided, the governor looked out of control at the podium as Riegle, Huber, and Romney forces clashed. With the party in turmoil and no hope of resolving the internal bickering, the Milliken forces did the only thing they could do. They retreated and halted the proceedings. Another meeting was set for two weeks.

Milliken called a news conference on the Monday after the debacle and opened with this line, "My gosh, as I lookout on the press this morning, you look like you're in shambles." Then commenced one of the most belligerent news conferences Milliken ever had. The transcript had twelve pages of questions and answers, all focusing on his handling of this mess. His leadership was questioned. His judgment was questioned. It was like covering a train wreck.

"Have you lost control of your party?" I asked.

"I have not lost control of my party," he shot back.

There was a clear impression throughout the whole mess that Romney refused to let go of his power even though he was in Washington, which led veteran Booth Bureau Chief Bill Kulsea to inquire, "Is it possible for two politicians to run one party?"

"No, and two politicians are not," Milliken beat back the implication.

Tom Greene ended the conference with this dandy, "Governor, one more question since we're squelching rumors. We heard a rumor last night that you had been run over by a Rambler (Romney's old car company) by a little old lady. Would you turn around and let us see the tire marks?" Milliken said nothing and sought shelter with a question on drug abuse.

Eventually Milliken got Riegle to drop out. Huber would not budge and even asked me to be his press secretary. I graciously declined the offer. Thank you Lord. That set up a battle royal between Huber and Mrs. Romney. She did so poorly in the primary against him that on the day after the election Milliken could not even declare the winner.

"I think it's a closer race than many people expected . . . .when the Detroit figures come in, that'll give us the final picture we need to know, number one, who has won the race . . . ."

Mrs. Romney beat Huber but was damaged goods thanks to his unrelenting attacks and her own inability to transfer her immense popularity as First Lady into votes for the U.S. Senate.

We did a public TV debate with Romney and Hart. It was no contest. Hart went on to trounce the mild mannered Mrs. Romney by a commanding 67 percent to 33 percent margin. It was her first and last foray into elective politics. It was Milliken's first taste of hardball politics. He had learned a lot. He would need it down the road.

The hard feelings between the Romney camp and the Milliken squad were never healed. Mr. Romney felt Milliken should have done more to help Lenore. The Milliken folks did the best they could but that was not good enough for Romney.

While I never covered Romney as governor, we did numerous interviews over the years. I recall one Friday morning when the former governor was slated to be on *Off the Record.* I over slept and was thirty minutes late for the taping. He was kind enough to accept my apology. That never happened again. Years later prior to another taping, both Romney and I arrived early at the studio. We sat down in some chairs just off the set and talked politics. "You know, Tim," he began, "the thing that is wrong with politics today is we have lost our civility." He abhorred the bitter back and forth that the two parties waged against each other, not only during elections, but in off years as well. His analysis was dead on and pre-dated the even nastier years that were yet to come.

When John Engler was elected, Romney advised him to be "Bold," which is a story Engler tells over and over. Romney must have been proud of his protégée as Engler took the town by storm and never let go until he walked out twelve years later.

The final story I did on the man who saved the state GOP from extinction, was after he died. He was working out on a treadmill in the family home in Oakland County when he suffered a heart attack. The family got permission to bring the casket to the rotunda of the State Capitol. While the mourners paid their respects on the first floor, on the second floor, the family held an emotional news conference.

Days before that event Scott Romney went to his mom and suggested the family needed a P.R. person to handle the media calls that were flooding in from all over the country. He suggested Bob Berg. Mrs. Romney asked if that was the Bob Berg who had been press secretary to Milliken. Her son said yes and she said, who else is on the list? The hard feelings were still there, but on balance she was not vindictive.

At the family news conference, Mrs. Romney wore dark glasses, and sat next to Scott with brother Mitt next to him. Scott spoke first thanking Gov. Engler and the people of Michigan for allowing the family to use the Capitol. Then the questions began. I personally detest these kind of events, but I joined in along with everyone else and actually got the family to smile and laugh.

I asked Mrs. Romney about her race for the Senate and whether her husband tried to give her any advice.

She smiled, the family laughed, and Scott said, "I'll take that one."

Yes! And for one light hearted moment everyone reflected on how forceful the former governor could be. It was one of his trademarks. She then told us for the first time that her husband was forced by the media to stay out of the state while she was running for the senate.

"The hardest was that the media wouldn't let him come in the state when I was running because they said I couldn't do it on my own and I had to have him, so he stayed out completely. He just called and said, 'Carry on.' It was very sad cause I campaigned so hard for him all over the state when he ran for governor," she explained.

As the questions continued Mrs. Romney kept her composure but only by a thread as she joined in the praises of her departed spouse. Then, as if she could not withhold it anymore, she broke down into sobbing tears as she reflected on the depth of his love for her and her family. It was such a sad moment.

Months after the funeral, I called her just to see how she was doing. She seemed appreciative of the call. Often times in this rough and tumble political game, once you are no longer newsworthy you can feel abandoned. She explained that she was doing OK but then as I heard the tears well up, she reflected on what a wonderful husband he was.

"I really miss him, Tim," she tearfully revealed. They had been together some sixty-four years and were part of that generation that stayed together no matter what. They were high school sweethearts. We chatted about what a great governor he was and I told her about that conversation he and I had in the studio years earlier. I told her I would stay in touch. Three years later in the same month of July in which he died, a stroke took her life, too, at age eighty-nine.

But the Romney legacy lives on. Son Mitt was elected governor in Massachusetts and every time I see him on the tube, he looks so much like his dad, that it always gives me pause. I saw him on C-Span sometime ago as he used some of his father's phrasing and mannerisms. Son Scott Romney got on the Michigan State University Board of Trustees after an ill-fated effort to become state attorney general. He has his father's energy, personality, and desire to serve.

The former governor will be long remembered for ushering in a new state constitution, he practically invented the volunteerism movement, and his commitment to civil rights was second to none.

Before he died he reflected on what he didn't get done. He was sorry he did not convince the Constitutional Convention to allow governors to appoint judges. He also wanted an appointive State Board of Education and secretary of state. But on balance he concluded, "I have no regrets." The state should have none either regarding his stewardship that paved the way for the governors to follow.

There are plenty of common threads that run through the four governors I've been honored to cover, but the one that might surprise you the most is humor. The more you hang around these folks, and when they are not on stage, you see it. I think they need to laugh to survive the turmoil that sometimes surrounds their lives. Lose the ability to laugh, and you could end up in a home.

Between Milliken, Blanchard, Engler, and Granholm, William Grawn Milliken appears, on the surface, to be the most serious. Examine the following exhibits and see if you still feel that way.

Milliken was real good about scheduling regular news conferences, a practice the other three never continued. His office also provided transcripts of everyone that came in (handy for this section). During one such encounter with the capital press corps there was talk about expanding gambling.

Milliken was asked about dog racing. The reporter trying to catch him in an inconsistency asked, "What's the difference between adding dog racing and horse racing?" which the state already had.

Milliken's quick retort, "Well, the difference between horses and dogs, I suppose."

Theme and Variation. Question: The GOP leader has proposed an income tax hike for October first, but your House leader favors January first. What's the difference?

Milliken: "It's about four months, I'd say." Rim shot.

This next inquiry came in the midst of an ugly budget debate as the governor struggled with both the senate and house. He was frustrated, as governors often get, so when this question was asked he was ready.

"Do you support a one-house legislature?"

Milliken: "Today I would say a unicameral system in going only half as far as we ought to go . . . that's today," he told veteran Booth Bureau Chief Bill Kulsea.

UPI Bureau Chief Bob Berg dragged out an old quote that he sprang on WGM during a 1974 news conference regarding the sorry state of the Nixon presidency.

Berg: In 1971 at a leadership conference on Mackinac Island, you said, "I am convinced beyond doubt that future historians will rank President Nixon among the best presidents in this nation's history." Has anything happened since then to change your mind?" Berg closed the deal knowing what the answer was.

Milliken: "Bob, in answer to your question, yes. Next question," as he sought to cut his loses. But he did add, "By golly, you know, your words are going to come back to haunt you someday, too." But apparently not. That's because Berg eventually crossed over and became Milliken's press secretary. Maybe it was because Milliken was tired of his pointed questions?

Here's his playful side you seldom saw. In the midst of the 1970s energy crisis Milliken had urged everyone to shut off their holiday lights, conserve home heating fuel, and by all means cut down on your gas usage. He mentioned in the news conference something about using 10 gallons a week.

Some wise guy asked, "Your statement on ten gallons a week for gasoline . . . are you planning to go to Traverse City?" (It's a two hundred mile jaunt by the way.)

Without missing a beat Milliken does the math. "Yes, I am planning to go to Traverse City. Well, now let's see, I think we've done some computations. When we drive fifty miles an hour, which we do, (ha) we're getting close to thirteen miles per gallon. Closer to fifteen," he adds. "Now you make your computation and while I may be able to get there, if necessary I'll hitch hike back."

The guy from Traverse City was not only quick with the quip, but he could dance around tough questions with the best of them.

He was never a big fan of former Vice President Agnew who at the time was on a crusade against the news media. Reporters wanted Milliken to take a swipe at ole Spiro. They got this instead.

"I agree with the Vice President in many instances. I disagree with him in others. And you can draw your own conclusion about which is which." We did.

Because you didn't really anticipate his one-liners, he caught me off guard during the taping of one show at the executive residence. I was always a little nervous going into the taping and even more so as we headed into the program open. On the TV screen is the title: "Evening with the Governor." Just as I'm collecting my thoughts and getting ready to go he says under his breath, "You misspelled governor." I quickly looked at the screen. We had not, but he got me, which he acknowledged with just a hint of a smile as I said, "Good evening" to the TV audience.

Milliken seemed to have more run-ins with members of his own party than with the Democrats. Keith Molin who shepherded Milliken's agenda through the legislature reports he only heard Milliken swear twice and one of those times involved a heated dispute over raising the gasoline tax.

Jackson Republican Jim Fleming chaired the senate transportation panel where the fuel tax bill had been lodged for sometime. The measure was moving with all the speed of a receding glacier and Milliken was in deep negotiations with Fleming to change the speed.

The governor thought he had an arrangement but when a critical vote came, Fleming did not do what he promised to do.

Milliken said, "Damn." And later added this, "Some commitments were made that were not honored, and I don't like that . . . .if a man's word is not good, then what is worthwhile? What is good?"

Senator Fleming felt the sting of the rebuke and issued his own rejoinder, "It is regrettable that the governor of this state has blown his cool in resorting to name calling and innuendo in his efforts to saddle the taxpayers with a fat increase in the gasoline tax." Warm personal letter to follow.

One line of speculation hounded Milliken and later Blanchard and Engler. Are you running for vice president of the United States. This was the exchange with Milliken on repeated speculation by a Traverse City friend.

"Why does Senator Griffin keep mentioning your name for V.P.?" I innocently began my futile effort.

Milliken: "I dont know."

Question: "Have you talked with him about it?"

Milliken: "A long time, ago."

Question: "Is it unusual he keeps bringing it up?"

Milliken: "Well, he and I, no. I don't know why he keeps bringing it up. I would prefer that he not bring it up."

Question: "Have you told him that?"

Milliken: "Yes, we discussed it at one time."

Question: "Are you interested in the office?"

Milliken: "No, I'm not interested in that office. That's the last thing in the world I'm interested in is that office."

One of the things they teach you at governor school is never lose your cool or get angry in public. Milliken followed the rule very closely but there was one occasion when he let it all hang out.

Senator Joe Mack from the Upper Peninsula was about as crusty as they come and was not one who was sympathetic to the early stages of the so called women's movement. Milliken had a woman on his staff who was a trail blazer in that regard and when a private feud between Joyce Braithwaite and the senator became public, Milliken stepped in.

Here was the flap. The legislature was preparing to increase the pay checks of Milliken's personal staff but Mack had single handily blocked an increase for Braithwaite. He was getting even, according to her, for her decision to block one of the senator's friends to the board at Northern Michigan University. She says he blamed her and referred to her as "that secretary up there with all the authority."

Braithwaite who was shy and retiring in her early years on the job, had grown into a real b– buster and fired off a letter to the senator. In it she wrote that based on his comments she said it reinforced her observation that "There are more asses in the world than there are horses." She was still laughing the day she recounted the story for this book.

Milliken did not need to rescue this damsel in distress because she wasn't. But he waded in anyway. "I think the behavior of Joe Mack is outrageous. I think what he said during the last week . . . and I now learn what he also has said over a period of several year's time . . .

was crude and it was in very bad taste and it was inexcusable. I deplore that approach. I personally resent it, and I suggest that it is time for Senator Joe Mack to cease and desist in these tactics. Next question."

That was one of his favorite lines when he was upset . . . cease and desist. When you heard that, it was an instant code for, "He ain't messing around."

Shocked reporters refused to change the subject.

Would you expand a little bit on what he said over those years?

"I don't want to belabor the point . . . I don't like it."

He was then asked about the letter. Note that Braithwaite had skillfully avoided calling the senator a jackass although the inference was cleverly there. But reporters wanted to know Milliken's stance. Was Mack a jackass?

"I think Senator Mack may have met his match." There's an understatement of all times.

Every governor confronts basically the same issues. You have to cut the budget to balance the books, adapt to the state's roller coaster economy and pass a bill or two along the way to advance your agenda. While there is considerable heavy lifting for each item, the good news is, it's been done before and history can often guide you on how to do it again. That's why governors and former governors share their home phone numbers.

What every chief executive hates are those events for which there is no blue print. The ones that come out of nowhere can easily derail an otherwise successful administration. Bill Milliken faced such a threat with something no one could have predicted or prepared for . . . .a statewide contamination of the food chain.

The Velsicol Chemical Company in St. Louis, Michigan, just south of Mt. Pleasant made two successful products. One was a fire retardant. The other was cattle feed for the state's substantial farming industry.

The two products were made on parallel assembly lines, which ended with both the chemical and the feed on the same loading dock. The company used similar bags for each and as fate would have it, a load of the fire retardant, PBB, was shipped off to the farms. It was a mix up of huge proportions but nobody knew it right away.

The PBB was fed to the animals and soon some of them got sick. Some of those animals and even healthy ones produced offspring with birth defects. The Michigan Farm Bureau got involved and so did the state agriculture department which at the outset didn't inform the Milliken front office.

With dying cattle and deformed calves dotting the state it didn't take long for the news media to latch onto the startling story. I remember reading the first accounts not knowing a PBB from a DDT. I missed the significance of the mix up and its immediate and long range public health implications.

The chemical was slowly finding its way to the milk and meat shelves in grocery stores and eventually 90 percent of the population was exposed to low levels of the fire retardant. There was no scientific research on the effect of the chemicals on humans, but you didn't have to have a Ph.D. to worry about cancer implications.

That was only one of the governor's concerns. He needed to do everything he could to minimize the impact on the general population and on the second largest industry in the state, farming. What he wanted to do was lower the standards so that more cattle could be destroyed, but he could not do that unilaterally. He had to get approval from the State Agriculture Commission and he needed the help of his Agriculture Director B. Dale Ball to make the change.

Ball was a short and gray-haired bureaucrat who was elected by the independent commission and not the governor. That meant he appeared to be more loyal to the industry than to Milliken.

When Milliken pushed for the new PBB levels, Ball shoved. Ball stonewalled the governor's efforts, which not only created a public health dilemma but a huge political problem for Milliken was well.

For years the Democrats wanted to get the popular GOP governor out of office but they could not persuade the electorate to do it. Now the Democrats had an opening. If they could prove that Milliken was not up to the task of handling this threat, he could be history at the next election.

The governor was aware that much was at risk. During a June 6, 1974 news conference he was asked about his Department of Agriculture being aware of the contaminated feed being sold but doing nothing to stop it.

He chose his words very carefully. "I've been in very close touch with the department and its director and the Department of Health and its director, and I have called for a complete review of the internal procedures of the department as it related to this particular problem." It's a non-answer to the question.

His objective is to assure a weary public that he is on top of this thing but the follow-up question from UPI's Bob Berg is more pointed. "Are you satisfied that they acted in the best interest?"

Milliken evades a direct answer again. "I am in the process of asking for that review and when I get the departments' assessment and recommendations, I will better know what the problem is and how we should deal with it to avoid any possibility of this occurring again."

From a crass political standpoint, the Democrats could not be happier. They sense they have the governor on the ropes as he publicly struggles with Mr. Ball on lowering the standards while trying to assure the public that he has everything under control. It was a mixed message and the media reported it.

In the midst of this battle there was one moment of levity in an otherwise life threatening saga. One of the favorite indoor sports for reporters was to nab the governor for an interview as he moved from his second floor office to his black Lincoln four-door that was always parked in the back of the Capitol. (Now the governor's wheels are mostly parked in an underground garage with no media access at all.) With a few phone calls to the right insider, you could pretty much nail when he would run that gauntlet.

With the Milliken-Ball dispute festering, I had some questions for Milliken designed to ferret out his feelings.

Milliken had earlier indicated that canning Ball would not solve the problem so I asked if that meant he was 100 percent behind the embattled agriculture director.

The governor stopped in the tracks of this ambush interview and said, "Tim Skubick, I sometimes would like to throw you over the rail" as he set his eyes on the railing between the second and first floor with a convenient drop of about fifty feet.

I suggested, "How about now governor, I need a story." Handing his briefcase to his security guard Roger DeVolder, who was from my hometown of Fraser, he said, "Hold these, Roger. I need two hands." Now with both of us smiling I asked if that meant a "no comment" to my 100 percent inquiry. He changed the subject.

That was funny. Our next encounter on the PBB problem was anything but. In fact, it resulted in the governor becoming very angry with yours truly.

Democratic House Speaker Bobby Don Crim was a wirery self described hillbilly. He was short but as a former wrestler or razzler as he called it, he was tough in the clinches. Despite his outward charm he could be ruthless if he had to be. Up until PBB, he had worked well with the Republican governor over the years, but sensing blood in the water and a chance to set the governor up for a loss in 1974, Crim tried to put a choke hold on Milliken by exploiting the PBB story while at the same time trying to act responsible on it.

The cancer angle had been sitting out there for sometime and every time the media raised it, the governor did not have an answer because there was none. Crim took the lead from Milliken and sought the expertise of Dr. Irving Selicoff from the world famous Mt. Sinai Hospital in New York. Snatching the good doctor was a two-fer for Crim. One it was something Milliken should have done, but didn't and secondly it gave Crim more control of the human health aspect of the story . . . the angle that meant the most to voters.

While Milliken was struggling for answers from his own health department and its director Dr. Maurice Reizen and not getting much, Crim went outside the state for help leaving the impression that the state health department and the governor were not up to the task.

At the same time a documentary unit from the BBC in Great Britain had heard of the human-food chain contamination story and deployed a crew to Michigan to do its own investigation. Milliken's operative soon discovered that the documentary was not very flattering to the administration, and it was not about to allow a statewide showing of the film, "The Poisoning of Michigan" without some perspective from the governor.

The program was to air on all the state public TV stations, so Milliken's damage control experts asked for and got a half hour to respond after the documentary was broadcast. That segment of the show would be produced at WKAR TV in East Lansing and I drew the assignment to anchor what was to be a very controversial program.

Once the word got out that Milliken would get equal time, the Democrats went to work on me. Crim told me not to let Milliken off the hook. The message was echoed by his media types who let me know they would be watching. In retrospect I should have told them where to go, but instead I listened, and as it turned out, too intently.

Milliken and I sat in Studio B and watched the BBC production. It was a good thing the governor was not running for prime minister in England. The producers did a number on him and his lack of leadership on the compelling issue. It was a decidedly slanted piece of advocacy journalism.

The film portion of the program ended and the floor director cued me to begin the live segment with Milliken. I offered the governor his first chance to respond, then I proceeded to cross examine him over and over again. When the interview was over I said good night to the governor and TV audience. He walked out of the studio without saying a word. This was not the kind and gentle Bill Milliken that everyone admired. This was the angry governor I had never seen. I sensed I was in deep doo-doo.

I was right.

The first guy to check in on my performance was Bob Page, the station manager at the TV station. Normally he had a bedside manner that was similar to Milliken's but the six paragraph memo he hand delivered to me on October 5, 1977 was devoid of any such kindness.

"It appeared to me that you were more aggressive, more curt with the governor than with other participants," he laid into me in paragraph three. "Bobby Crim not withstanding, I really don't believe anyone is well served through such an overly aggressive approach, particularly on a program of this nature."

That was enough to cut me to the quick but he was not finished. "In sum, I guess I'm saying that we didn't do the job we are capable of doing from a conceptual standpoint. I also believe it is possible to be direct, incisive, and journalistically "pure" without being hostile and rude."

He finally ended with, "I'm disappointed."

He was not alone. The governor's office was more than disappointed. It was livid.

I was about eight years into my career and this was the deepest and hottest water I had ever been in. I had learned somewhere that the longer you allowed a disagreement to fester, the tougher it is to resolve. So within days I called the governor's office and requested a sit down with Mr. Milliken. I was going to do what needed to be done. I was prepared to apologize.

My request was granted. I showed up and was escorted to the sofa in the waiting area about thirty feet from the governor's office. Within moments the governor's personal secretary, the usually delightful Phyllis Dell, summoned me. She did not seem very delightful as she opened the big oak door to his office, and neither did he.

Gulp.

The governor was standing behind his desk but moved to the chairs alongside and motioned me to sit down next to him. (At this point I should have been thinking it would have been better had he tossed me over the railing several weeks earlier.)

I'm not sure how I began. We were breaking new ground here, but I think I said that I understood he was deeply upset with me and the manner in which I treated him.

He readily confirmed that.

I explained that I had misunderstood my role that night. I thought I was doing my usual *Off the Record* thing when the governor and my station management felt it was more of a chance for Milliken to speak rather than be grilled. I apologized for the misunderstanding and asked for his understanding.

Now it was his turn. He explained that I had not shown respect for the office and from that point on he warned me that he would be "wary" of me.

I thought he said "weary" and asked him to clarify. He did and in no uncertain terms he told me he would keep an eye on me in the future. It was clear that whatever bond of trust we had developed since 1969 was out the window.

He accepted my apology. We stood and shook hands and the five to seven minute meeting was over. I was wondering if my political journalism career was too.

Everyone saw me come out and nobody was there to hold my hand or ask me how it went. I returned to my Capitol cubby hole reflecting on the fact that he did not get angry but by the same token it was clear I was on his you know what list. Through the experience, I had learned a valuable lesson that would serve me well in the future.

You cannot allow yourself to be influenced by those who have a political agenda. Crim was not interested in my journalistic performance. He wanted Milliken to look bad and not restore his shaky standing in the public's mind. In a word I had been "used" to help him reach that political objective. I was saddened by the personal confession and vowed never to let it happen again.

The episode was never mentioned again by either the governor or me. He put it behind him in his own classy way and I became convinced that I had done the right thing by saying I was sorry. It would not be the last time I would do that with a sitting governor.

As Milliken moved into his reelection mode, PBB was still a hot item and his Democratic opponent sought to make it even hotter.

State senator Bill Fitzgerald from Wayne County could sense he had Milliken where he wanted him. The PBB standards eventually got lowered but the public was still up in arms. Now there was another problem. Dead cattle were piling up in barnyards all over the state. They needed to be buried someplace, but where? It was the governor's job to find a burial site. His Department of Natural Resources settled on tiny Kalkaska and Mio just east of Traverse City. Nobody at the agriculture department was asked to help out.

Local residents fought the move. Milliken bravely showed up at one burial pit in May of 1978. With the TV cameras grinding away the protesters surrounded Milliken. One of the signs shown in the book: *the Milliken Years: A Pictorial Reflection* read: "Come on folks. Join the picket. Tell the governor where to sticket." The expression on Milliken's face as the fifty demonstrators did their thing, showed concern. He knew those were not fifty votes for his reelection bid.

That was not the only demonstration he confronted. *Free Press* columnist Remer Tyson spent the day with Milliken during the 1978 campaign and recounted in his lead, "Almost everywhere Gov. Milliken campaigns for re-election, the issue of PBB haunts him in one form or another.

At the Potato Festival in Posen, Milliken walked by a Polish combo of singers who broke into a parody of the song, "You can have her, I don't want her, she's too fat for me."

Their version went, "I don't want it, you can have it, it's got PBB." Milliken did not join in on the second chorus.

When Milliken made his annual trek across the Mackinac Bridge on Labor Day, protesters threw meat in the water and jeered the governor.

Milliken was hanged in effigy in Mio and when he finally found shelter with some friendly real estate folks in Oakland County they wanted to know about the mess, too.

He confessed, "PBB represented one of the toughest issues I've had to deal with . . . PBB is not in the food chain of Michigan . . . but a lot of people don't believe that." Later it was confirmed that a ton of people had little bits of that stuff in their bodies. However, to this date a protracted tracking of those persons has not resulted in any documented evidence of health risks. Although lot of folks were clearly sick and their immunity systems were compromised by something, but was it the PBB?

At the end of the day with writer Tyson, Mrs. Milliken revealed just how pervasive the issue was. She asked him, "What's the big issue? PBB?" And then she added, "I shouldn't have told you until you had a chance to answer." It would not have made any difference.

The issue continued to dog Milliken. But one day, an unanticipated event moved the needle toward Milliken's side. That was the day the Democratic PBB commercial started airing. It suggested that babies were being born with birth defects. Not one scintilla of research could back that up, but hey, this was not a doctoral thesis it was a classic attack ad.

When she was told the spot was running, Joyce Braithwaite from the governor's staff declared the election over. She knew Fitz had crossed the line and instead of Milliken's credibility being scurried, it was Fitz who went down in the polls. She knew her guy would win and he did.

Attempting to capture the essence of a person in one sentence is not only impossible but unfair since each politician is an amalgamation of many complex elements. In reviewing his comments in various news conferences, this one popped out as truly representative of how Milliken approached his governing task.

"I work very hard for the things in which I believe, and I recognize that not everyone will agree with me at all times. And yet it's important for each one of us to do what he believes he should do."

His relationship with Detroit Mayor Coleman Young is living proof of that statement.

The two had been colleagues in the Senate but came from backgrounds that were poles apart. Young, the crusty inner city guy. Milliken, the refined son of a state senator from a decidedly outer city . . . Traverse City. Yet despite that, the two found a common ground for the good of Michigan and for the good of Detroit.

The Milliken-Young relationship was a work in progress. The road was sometimes bumpy. Milliken's able and likable lobbyist Keith Molin recounts one bump when the governor was trying to secure Young's vote but the senator would not take Milliken's phone calls.

Molin says things took a turn for the worse when Young made a speech over one weekend complaining about Milliken's tardiness on getting a bill done. "How many speeches does this M----- F----- have to give," Young was quoted as saying.

Molin says Milliken took it as a personal attack by a friend. Molin played go between and went to Young's office where he reported the governor was hurt by the M.F. remark.

"He immediately picked up the phone and called the governor," Molin retells the story. Young explains his use of the term is really a form of endearment, which had to be news to the startled governor.

That conversation broke the log jam on the bill and the two went on to pass it.

Their next joint assignment was more protracted but far more compelling. It had to do with saving Detroit from financial ruin.

One of the governor's pet phrases was, "As Detroit goes, so goes the state." Every time he used it, you could hear the groans from conservative outstate Republicans many of whom had no affection for the city or the mayor. Those lawmakers believed they could not win any votes back home by helping Motown. Milliken disagreed.

He and His Honor began work on a historic agreement that would be called the Detroit Equity Package. Mayor Young needed more state aid and the package was a way to get it. Over a period of time the two hammered it out and at a final meeting at the Kellogg Center on the MSU campus it fell into place.

But before it did, Milliken had to endure a whole slew of cuss words throughout the talks. In the end state aid was earmarked for Detroit services that everyone in the state could use. Money went to the Detroit Symphony, the Detroit Institute of Arts, the library, and a host of other areas. The equity package became a permanent fixture in the state budget until Milliken left town. Then the GOP systematically dismantled it sending many of the Detroit dollars to west Michigan where more Republicans reside.

The deal between the black mayor and the white governor was proof that when Milliken believed in something, he would not give up.

The Mayor reflected on his nine year bond this way, "Bill Milliken proved that you can appeal to people's best instincts and be a very successful politician. . . . A lot of people argued he was committing political suicide in dealing with Detroit's needs so effectively. Yet the last time he ran for re-election he piled up the biggest margin of any time . . . while being the first Republican to carry Wayne County since 1946." (Thanks to authors Joyce Braithwaite and George Weeks for digging out that quote.)

Milliken had a charm about him that people loved even though he was not fond of campaigning. He once whispered that he did not enjoy working a crowd, but he did it because he had to. He did turn on the charm when it moved him toward a political goal or around a hurdle.

Myra Wolfgang was head of one of the state employee unions that had a bone to pick with the governor. She was no tea and crumpets lady. She was hard-nosed and was more comfortable in the trenches than in the kitchen. She was ushered into the governor's office ready to display why her surname was so appropriate.

She was mad and wanted him to know it. She launched into her diatribe and about half-way through, as Milliken looks on seemingly unfazed by the attack, she blurts out, "And don't give me that warm smile before I get my message out."

She continues to rattle on and he continues to smile.

"Now damn it, governor, there you go again," she complained. Milliken's guys in the back of the room loved to see the byplay because in the end they knew he would win her over and he did. They eventually resolved their labor dispute with a handshake and the Milliken smile.

That willingness to listen and cooperate was reflected in his final words to the legislature during his last State of the State on January 14, 1982. He noted that for thirteen years he worked with a Democratic controlled house and for the last seven years the Democrats ran the Senate, too.

"But during those years our relationship has never broken down in bitterness or acrimony or petty partisanship," he told the hushed assemblage of lawmakers.

"To be sure, there have been moments . . . long moments . . . when we disagreed," he continued. "But we have never allowed those disagreements to degenerate to a personal level."

Then he quotes one of his favorite authors Judge Learned Hand: "The temper which does not press a partisan advantage to its bitter end, which can understand and respect the other side, which feels a unity between all citizens . . . which recognizes their common fate and their common aspirations; in a word, which has faith in the sacredness of the individual . . . this is what we have striven for," he told his soon to be former colleagues.

That conviction and many, many more were part of the reason why voters kept sending him back to the governor's chair. They would go out in a snow storm to vote for him, I always felt and even today on the speaking circuit, I raise the name Milliken as an example of how government should operate . . . without malice but with civility . . . without vengeance but with forgiveness and with an optimism that surpasses all challenges. I was fortunate enough to cut my political coverage teeth on his watch. To say I admire the man falls way short of how I really feel about him.

I have one personal regret however. I was not there when he and Mrs. Milliken got in the Lincoln for the last time on Inauguration Day 1983. Guys who were there tell me there wasn't a dry eye despite the bitter cold and the even more chilling feeling that a civil era of Michigan politics was walking out the door . . . never to return again in the same way.

6

The Even Bumpier Milliken-Blanchard Transition

The transition from a Milliken administration to the one operated by James Blanchard was, as they say on Monty Python, "Something completely different."

Milliken was white collar educated at Yale. Blanchard picked up a blue collar sheep skin from Michigan State University. Milliken was a non-smoker. Blanchard was known to whip out a huge stogie when the spirit moved him. You'd never cuss around Milliken. Blanchard didn't mind. Blanchard loved sports. Milliken thought a red wing was found on a cardinal and never on the ice. Milliken was out the door headed for Traverse City on most Thursdays. Blanchard was just getting warmed up near the end of his week.

In fact one of the first conversations we had after Blanchard was elected was on the elevator riding down from the governor's office on the second floor to the ground floor of the Capitol.

"Skubick you're going to be working a lot of weekends," the new chief executive warned. "Sorry Sir. You may be working weekends but I'll try not to," was my retort.

Blanchard was true to his word. It seemed he was on the go 24–7 and then some. If there was a room to work, count him in. A hand to shake, he'd extend his. A vote to secure, he was Jamie on the spot. Milliken loathed working a room and said so privately. He once confided that his idea of a good time was riding alone in a car at night to Chicago. Blanchard on the other hand was the first politician I had encountered who truly lived, breathed, and feasted on the political environment. (Another guy with the same M.O. was John Engler.)

Blanchard won the governor's office after surviving a hearty primary with lots of other Democrats. When Milliken was in office no Democrat in his or her right mind would run against him, but with him out of the way they came out of the woodwork. Blanchard beat them all as the anointed candidate of labor.

Since he was coming from Congress, Blanchard was pretty much an unknown quantity in the state Capital press corps. He called and suggested we break bread. It was a chance to get the measure of the man in private and, if the truth be known, he could size me up, too. The meeting took place at the old Stonehouse eatery in East Lansing down in the basement. I got there early not knowing that Blanchard was never on time. In fact once he got into office we coined the term "Blanchard time" to indicate he'd be at least twenty minutes late for any event.

He showed up by himself. That was a good sign. I always felt if a politician showed up with a press secretary or someone else, the conversation was not as candid and it reflected an unwillingness to take me into their confidence.

Frankly the dinner with Blanchard was a blast. He was easy to talk to. I liked him right away as he did not appear to be full of himself. It was clear that he wanted the job and loved the pursuit of it. He talked about the pluses and minuses of his opponents and gave a detailed analysis of how it would all shake out. He was pretty accurate. It was the beginning of numerous one-on-one exchanges we shared over his eight years in office. Most would come over the phone at his behest. He was the first governor to call me. There was one ground rule however: I never gave advice. I had heard of other more senior members of the press corps who fancied themselves close personal advisors to elected officials. Somehow I figured that was a bad idea. While it might have been an ego trip to do it, what if the advice turned out to be bad and taxpayers go hurt? That meant I was then part of the story instead of merely covering it.

Blanchard won the Democratic primary and went on to battle Richard Headlee. The GOP insurance executive was a stitch to cover. His most redeeming quality was he told the truth. If you wanted to know how he felt, you just asked and he told you. It also turned out to be one of his biggest political liabilities. Just ask his handlers who pleaded with Headlee to put a cap on his yap. He never did.

I requested and got to anchor one of the few TV debates in the contest. It was staged at the Wharton Center at MSU in front of a lively and unruly partisan audience. Despite the instructions that the audience was to be seen and not heard, the rule was violated more times than you can count. That's because both Blanchard and Headlee evoked strong passions from both sides. Conservatives tagged Jamie with being the handmaiden of organized labor, which turned out to be untrue. Democrats saw Headlee as a neo-nutso conservative who would move the state's social agenda back to the dark ages, which was only partially correct.

There were two memorable exchanges during the program that brought the house down. Headlee had taken the no tax pledge, which every GOP conservative took as soon as they came out of the womb. His promise was never to raise anybody's taxes no matter what. At the time the GOP president in Washington had supported a tax hike that led to this leading question:

"Do you support the president's tax hike?"

Headlee paused for just a second. It was a trap. If he said no, the president might be hacked, but if he said yes, Blanchard would be all over him for breaking his no tax hike promise. In other words it was a perfect no win inquiry. Headlee did what any self-respecting candidate would do. He pleaded ignorance.

"I don't know what I would have done. I wasn't there," he hoped to get off the hook.

The hoots and hollers erupted from the left side of the theater where all the Democrats were huddled together. I immediately swiveled my chair around and asked everyone to remain quiet and then I thought to myself, "Nice try Dickie but that won't float."

Then it was Blanchard's turn in the barrel. In doing these debates if you zinged one guy, you immediately went on a mission to even the score. It didn't take long to lure Blanchard into another no win trap.

One of the touch stones of his campaign was a statewide bonding program to pay off his campaign mantra of creating "Jobs. Jobs. Jobs." The intent was to sell bonds to create employment that gave rise to this question:

"How many jobs will your bonding program produce?"

"I have no idea," he suggested. "I don't want to over promise anything to the voters," was his slippery response.

"So under promise," I shot back.

Blanchard flinched and gave no answer. The audience, on the right side, applauded. I asked them to be quiet, too.

The score being even, we moved on to other issues and Blanchard moved on to beat Headlee. The most memorable Democratic bumper sticker during the campaign was: "Dick Headlee before he Dicks you."

The transition from Milliken to Blanchard was bouncier than a Michigan freeway after a bad spring thaw. One of his first acts of office was to board up the executive office to keep the media on the outside, unable even to look in.

During the Milliken years, there was a glass door that served as the main entrance to the waiting area of the executive office. To the right and down the short hallway was the governor's private office. Just to the left of that was his personal secretary. Down the hall in the other direction and off to the left was the governor's conference room with the clanging light fixtures that everyone bumped into as they moved to their seats around the giant table.

An enterprising reporter could make a career out of just sitting there watching who came in and out. You were free to interview whomever you wanted. It was accessible. It was wonderful. It was more than a reporter could ever hope for and it worked. Many a good story was generated by monitoring the ebb and flow in the front office.

The ebb and flow was promptly halted by the new governor. First thing to go was the glass door. It was replaced with one made out of oak. The only possible view was through the key hole. The elimination of the see through door was bad enough, but then the door was locked. The easy access was history. Blanchard blames his chief of staff Tim Lewand for making the changes. Security was the reason given. Nobody in the press corps bought that crap for a second. It was evident that Blanchard had a problem with the media . . . at least that was the popular wisdom among those of us who covered him. Reporters are a suspicious lot and when anyone infringes on our ability to get a story . . . well let's just say it was not the best way to start a new administration.

The openness enjoyed for fourteen years was gone in fourteen minutes. The only way you got into the inner sanctum anymore was with an invite and those were few and far between.

One of the elements you always ponder with a new governor in tow is, will this person make any news worthy reporting? About a month after the election we had our first peek at the answer.

The governor-elect had called a news conference at the Kellogg Center on the MSU campus to introduce the capital press corps to members of his new cabinet. That's always a revealing event in that you get a feel for what quality of actors you're going to be dealing with for the next four years.

There was one appointee in the new Blanchard administration that got everyone's attention. The post was welfare director. His nominee was a woman, a former Catholic nun. She was pro-choice on abortion. Stop the presses we have a story here: A catholic pro-choice former nun running the welfare department.

Almost from the moment Blanchard introduced Sister Agnes Mary Mansour this woman was making news. She was deeply devoted to the families she served. She had strong opinions and took no guff from anyone including legislators who were not used to being told off. She was not bashful about doing it and it was great to watch her take on the legislative power brokers as she blasted them for ignoring the needs of the needy.

She and Blanchard were sympathetic during the first year in office. He supported her during the annual budget battle over increased welfare spending. She won his backing for a 5 percent cost of living increase. That was the last time Blanchard sided with her on that. His non-support, she says, came after Blanchard took so much heat for hiking the income tax. She then observed, "A growing divergence in agendas" (with the governor). Translated: she was on one page and he on another.

Then the Pope got into the act. Word came out of the Vatican that the leader of the Catholic Church was upset. He delivered a public ultimatum to Sister Agnes: resign as welfare director or recant her religious vows to the sisterhood. Every time the media reported that a pro-choice Catholic nun was running the welfare department, the Pope's slow burn got even hotter. (I do not have that, however, based on first-hand knowledge.)

The Pope vs. Pro-Choice Nun . . . the kind of stuff a TV mini-series is made out of. To avoid the mounting publicity, Monsour adopted a new media strategy: Duck and hide. It got so ridiculous that on one day when I really needed to interview her, I got word that she was flying back from D.C. into Capital City Airport. You can imagine her joy as we greeted her with camera rolling as she came off the plane. There's an old saying in the press corps, you can run but you can't hide.

I can still hear her blurt out as she saw me, "Oh, Tim," as if she was saying, how could you do this to me? She gave me the interview but the story was clearly getting out of hand. Instead of her focusing on the needs of the poor, she was bombarded about her battle with the church.

One day in a private exchange she wondered, "Was I adding to the problem? Was I letting women and the poor down?" she went on.

To compound her difficulties around this same time, a report got into legislative hands documenting a rash of welfare errors and mis-management stories that were "wasting" tax dollars. The speaker of the house and pro-life lawmakers went after her in committee meet-ings on squandering tax dollars. My impression was they had been looking for an excuse to get even for all her attacks and now they had one. The governor's office watched in stony silence as Mansour was hung out to dry.

In the midst of that, she made an appearance on *Off the Record*. As we say in the business there are no tough questions only tough answers. She got a rat-a-tat-tat barrage of pointed ones.

"Dr. Mansour, welcome back to our program. It's always a plea-sure to do battle with you," I began.

"You and everybody else," she said reflecting her frustration she was feeling from all the controversy engulfing her life.

"Are you mismanaging the department?" the Q and A commenced. She says no.

"Do you rub people in the legislature the wrong way?"

"At times perhaps," she responded.

"You have said you will leave this post if you become ineffective. How close to being ineffective are you?"

"I'm not anywhere near being ineffective" she told me as Tom Greene picked up the inquisition.

"Are you satisfied with what Blanchard is doing?" (regarding welfare benefits) he asks.

"I think the governor is doing all he possibly can according to his best judgment," she tries to dodge. Greene will have none of it. That's why I loved him.

On a previous program he opined that Mansour "should be ashamed of herself for not telling the governor to stuff it." So he's not going to take a powder with her in front of him . . . even though he was a practicing Catholic.

"And are you satisfied with what Blanchard is doing?" he snaps back.

"He is the governor," she refuses to give an inch.

Greene tries again. This time his voice rising, "Are you satisfied? It's yes or no. It isn't that tough."

And so it went. *Detroit News* Bureau Chief Charlie Cain writing about the exchange noted, "Viewers watched Skubick and Greene tear into her like hungry lions." Later he suggests that "Faithful viewers of *Off the Record* have come to expect such spirited verbal volleys. Politicians know they won't get easy questions or much respect. That produces a show that can be alternately outrageous, informative, and entertaining." Charlie by the way has been part of the pack and the one with the most seniority doing the show.

Mansour bravely marched forward on her mission, but finally concluded it was time to do something. She resigned the sisterhood and stayed on as social services director. But the 1986 election cycle was drawing close and Blanchard would run again. Mansour could see the handwriting on the wall as she confronted another harsh reality closing in on her. There was speculation the governor would fire her. She thought otherwise because there was a chance she would do it for him by resigning. Blanchard asked her if they should talk and three months before the election they did.

The session was cordial. "It's best that I move on," she told him. He didn't ask her to stay and that was that. "I appreciated the opportunity the governor gave me, but it didn't seem right to me to stay if there was any sense they didn't want me," she explained.

Dumping somebody from your cabinet is one of the most distasteful things any leader has to do and each one I covered was forced to wade through it. Not only does it involve personal emotions but there's a political downside as well. It means the choice you made may have been a mistake. It brings into question a governor's loyalty and unless it is handled in a prompt way, it can blow up into a major story.

Long after I stopped chasing her in airports, we talked about her tenure and departure. She methodically outlined four reasons for moving on. (A) She was tired; (B) She may have overstayed her welcome; (C) She was always engaged in a legislative funding war on behalf of the poor; and (D) She became part of the problem and not the solution.

She was one gutsy woman and we always had a wonderful working relationship. I always got her blessing. Of course if the Pope knew she was blessing a Lutheran she might have been in even hotter water.

Blanchard had staged an earlier news conference in Detroit to announce two other key cabinet picks. He was appointing his two money men: Phil Jourdan as state budget director and Robert Bowman as state treasurer. Jourdan was a semi-known quantity and had been around the block a few times. Bowman was a complete stranger with no ties to Michigan. In fact the closest he had been to Michigan was when he flew over the state heading home to see his mom and dad in Milwaukee.

Who was this dude? Everyone in the media wanted to know.

He had worked for the Carter administration in the U.S. treasury and had played a pivotal role in the Chrysler bail out package that Blanchard had been instrumental in pushing through the Congress.

When Blanchard offered the state post, Bowman had two thoughts. One he really wanted to do it but two "I didn't know anybody in town. I didn't know Blanchard. It was frightening."

Most people would find someone to talk with to work it out. Bowman kept his own counsel. He couldn't say boo in his current post and his parents were staunch Republicans. He knew the wisdom he would get from them: "Why would you get to work in the government and even worse why for a Democrat?"

He took the job. He was first in and the last one out as he gutted out the full eight years with Blanchard.

But it got off to a rocky start. By just talking with him you could figure out this was no bumpkin from the other side of the lake. There was one potential liability: he was twenty-seven years old.

Hours before he was introduced to the media, he was called into a warm-up session with Blanchard stalwarts. They grilled him for hours on every question they could think of. Eventually someone brought up the age thing. Bowman's handlers hemmed and hawed about what to say. He demonstrated some maturity. He said let's just say I'm twenty-seven and leave it at that. After all that was the truth.

It came time for the news conference. No less than fifteen cameras were glaring at the podium as Blanchard, Jourdan, and this kid wearing glasses came into the room.

"I was so nervous," he reveals. The sweat is rolling all over him. "I've never been so scared in my whole life."

The first question goes to Blanchard. Then Jourdan gets a few. There are more for the governor and on and on it goes. Surprisingly the news conference is over and Bowman did not field one stinking question. Three hours of prep down the drain . . . well not quite. As everyone is walking out of the room somebody from the Associated Press corners Bowman.

"Mr. Bowman."

Bowman is taken aback. Maybe he didn't dodge the bullet after all. Nobody has ever called him Mr. but he's prepared for the worst.

"How old are you?" comes the innocent question.

"Twenty-seven."

End of interview . . . and the beginning of a stellar career in state government, but it almost ended before it got off the ground.

The Blanchard gang came into office with a huge barrel of red ink and quickly proposed a tax hike to erase it. The increase spawns a recall effort against Blanchard. The anti-tax cabal is not impressed with the new governor or his "whiz kid" treasurer.

Mike Kent was covering the capital for WILX-TV and got Bowman in an interview outside the senate chambers. After the camera was turned off Bowman tells Kent that the folks behind the recall are "anti-government kooks."

Kent reveals he has recorded the inflammatory remark, which is news to Bowman. He tells Bowman the story will run that night. Bowman protests claiming it was off the record. He says the camera was off. A bush league error. Camera off means interview is still on.

He leaves the interview and informs the Blanchard media folks of his comments. That results in a phone call to the station with the demand to kill the story. The station refuses. The "kooks" now want to kill Bowman after they hear his words on the tube. Blanchard's opponent Dick Headlee calls for Bowman's head. Oakland County Republican Brooks Patterson goes, "Ditto." As so often happens in this town, if you engage your mouth before your brain, it can get you into hot water. Bowman thinks about buying a one way ticket back to the City of Beer.

What worries him most is that one day goes by and the governor has not called. The story is everywhere but Bowman's phone sits there without a peep.

Finally the phone rings. It's Blanchard in a fake French accent. "Theesee is your Governor calling. I vant you to know that I agree with you that you didn't say those words. It would have been expletive deleted kooks had it really been you." That was the beginning of a beautiful relationship . . . almost like father and son.

Bowman was a reporter's dream come true. He was funny, he was on the inside, and more importantly he'd fill you in on what was coming down (making sure there were no hidden tape recorders). He was at times obnoxious, aggressive, and charming all in the same sentence; and he was a quick study, but not late at night. Here was the bachelor's routine. He'd work until seven or eight and then head home for his mandatory two Coors beers and two bags of popcorn. He discovered he couldn't go out, because "If I go out, everyone knows the next day where I was and how many beers I had." He was under a self-imposed house arrest.

Both of the B-Boys were night owls. So at midnight one evening, about three years into the term, Blanchard rings Bowman.

"Did you read that *New York Times* story today about Eugene Lang?" he was the guy who went into the Harlem schools and promised every student a free college education if they got a high school degree.

Bowman says he read it.

"I want to do that," Blanchard suggests.

"Great. We can get Lang in here and take it from there," Bowman responds. Obviously the Coors is having it's desired effect because Blanchard says, "You don't understand."

He tells Bowman he wants to create a program whereby kids can get a free college education here. "Can you come up with one?"

Bowman says, "yes" and within a month, just in time for the annual State of the State, the Michigan Education Trust (MET) program is hatched. The Michigan Education Trust is a savings account in which parents invest while their kids are young and on the other end, the state pays all the tuition when its time to hit the books.

Bowman recalls once writers got done sifting MET for any flaws or loopholes, they eventually called back on a more personal note. "Walk me through the numbers," the correspondents with college bound kids asked and Bowman did.

One other person also had some inquiries about the revolutionary program. An investment banker came into Bowman's office and said his company had a patent on the MET concept. Another more timid treasurer might have called the attorney general's office for guidance. Bowman didn't budge. He let the guy go on and when his monolog got to the final threat of a legal suit, Bowman struck back.

"You should have a lot of folks to sue, "Bowman reeled in his prey. I didn't know you had a patent on compound interest. The rube left the office and MET became one of the most popular Blanchard innovations ever.

Bowman did OTR ten times in eight years . . . the most appearances by anyone in the Blanchard shop. His rapport with reporters was above average with the exception of one *Detroit News* reporter.

"Dennis Mulqueen lived to get me," Bowman remembers and one day it appeared Mulqueen had gotten his wish.

The reporter wanted to know if Bowman accepted or made political phone calls on his state telephone? Did he use the copying machine to print political material and what about using the fax machine for the same stuff?

Bowman knew where this was going and could visualize the next day's headlines: Bowman Plays Politics on Your Dime. The story would go on to convict the treasurer of using taxpayer purchased equipment for partisan purposes . . . expenses that should be covered by his Democratic party.

Despite those fears, Bowman surprisingly pleads guilty. He says there is no way to control what mail he receives or incoming phone calls. Mulqueen must be thinking he's finally got Bowman's scalp.

Bowman strategically waits however until the end of the conversation to disclose one fact. "Dennis, you should know that each month I write a one hundred dollar check to the State of Michigan." He says that covers the cost of any accidental or other partisan use of the equipment. He strung Mulqueen along and then popped his balloon. Mulqueen left the beat and never got his prey.

Blanchard and Bowman got closer as the years wore on. Bowman recalls two memorable exchanges. One was on the porch of the governor's home on Mackinac Island and the other in a downtown Detroit hotel.

The governor was puffing his stogie on Mackinac. That was something he only did in private and from the isolated front porch of the island home there was no chance anyone would catch him. At the time there was a serious recall effort underway to bounce Blanchard and his buddies out of office for hiking the state income tax.

Since the two of them muscled the increase through the legislature, Bowman feels a certain ownership of the mess they are in. Blanchard seeks to reassure his young protégé that "if they recall us, we did the right thing. History may record it that way, but we stood tall."

Bowman says the brief exchange, "made me cry."

The recall drive floundered and flopped.

Their exchange seven years later on election night in the Pontchartrain Hotel was much more emotional. The two of them sat on Blanchard's bed. Below them hundreds of Democrats, who had come there for a celebration, were now lapsing into a deep funk. The election was close, but with each fleeting minute, it appeared Blanchard would lose to John Engler. The polls had predicted an Engler loss, but Blanchard always knew it would be close and now he and Bowman confronted what appeared to be the inevitable.

"There is an automatic recount," Blanchard began the talk. He feels they should do that because the margin is so close. Bowman who has matured well beyond his thirty-four years asks if Blanchard really wants four more years. Blanchard says "yes." And then for the next three to four minutes, nothing is said. Dead silence.

Blanchard finally reflects that they have had eight good years, and it may be time to move on, but he expresses concern for his supporters. They want to avoid the unemployment line and depend on the governor to keep them out of it.

Bowman turns the focus back on his friend and suggests that "If it doesn't work for you, it doesn't work." He's right and Blanchard knows it. At that point Blanchard says he will concede. There will be no recount no matter how close it is. Bowman returns to his room and tells his wife-to-be Lisa that "I've just been in bed with the governor." The line eases the tension and then he tells her what Blanchard has decided. She says it was the right thing to do.

The next morning, Blanchard delivers an eloquent concession speech as his reign comes to an unexpected end. To this day Bowman refuses to stay at the Ponch. Ironically had there been a recount, Blanchard now believes he could have won but for a reason he has never disclosed before . . . spoiled ballots.

Long before the voting snafu in Florida during the 2000 presidential race, Blanchard says there is evidence that upwards of 50,000 or more punch card votes in Detroit were never counted on election night. He says they were tossed out. Had they been tallied, Engler's slim margin of victory could have been erased.

So why didn't he recount them?

Because he didn't discover the "problem" until two years later. Blanchard was working on the Bill Clinton for president campaign and found himself in a discussion with Clinton operatives. They told him they were going to place special poll watchers at a number of Detroit voting places. Blanchard asked why. He was shocked to be told that the Clinton folks had heard about spoiled ballots in the 1990 race for governor. Blanchard called city election director Jacki Currie and she readily affirmed there was a problem.

"Had I known," Blanchard explains thirteen years after the fact, "I would have called for a recount and I'd like to think we would have won."

Those howls you hear are from Engler supporters who will see this new revelation as just one more attempt by Blanchard to redeem himself from an earth shattering loss.

You would think with covering governors, the stories that really stand out are the big moments when the entire political world is focused on something that the chief executive is doing. Turns out, I cherish the little things . . . those times when you get a glimpse of the man or woman behind the power. That's because the vast majority of the times you are covering someone they are "on." The word performing is appropriate and not meant to be disrespectful so when you catch a snippet of the "real" persona, it stands out. Such was the case with Blanchard.

He and I were on the same program one day . . . a memorial service for one of the state's top political figures. It was not a solemn event as the departed leader had produced many a hilarious moment during his elongated career. Everyone on the program had one funny story after another. There were more laughs than tears.

Blanchard did his thing and I did mine and we sat down with my wife between us. Everyone on the program had spoken and it looked like it was winding down. Then the master of ceremonies asked the audience: "Does anyone else want to say something about so and so?" Picture this. You have a place filled with 500 folks. Each one thinking he or she is a dynamic public speaker and the whole world is waiting for them to perform. Each one also believes they should have been on the formal program to begin with. Now they are given an opportunity to massage their egos by sharing their story about the departed person. The program was already into hour number two and with all those hands in the air it was clear, we'd all be there for hour number three.

With a slight grin on his face, Blanchard leaned over to Gayle and whispers, "Looks like we're in for a filibuster." It was not in poor taste but it reflected what everyone else in the room was thinking. Plus it was darn funny.

I also recall the phone calls from Blanchard. The first one came after he delivered his first State of the State. I remember I got home from anchoring the public TV broadcast around 10 P.M. when the phone rings. It's the governor.

"So. How did it go?" he asks.

For his first time out it actually went fairly well except for that line about the income tax increase for which only one legislator applauded. If there was one downside, it was Blanchard's desire to talk . . . and talk . . . and talk. It was not a malady reserved for him alone. Every governor gets up there and has so much to say that they sometimes forget the ole show biz adage, "leave 'em wanting for more."

In fact it got so bad one year Blanchard came up with a hybrid SOS format designed to give him even more time at the rostrum. His media handlers informed us that they wanted to do a mini SOS on our public TV network on the night before he gave the real address to the legislature. It was certainly a break with tradition, and there was no reason not to do it. Blanchard did his thing in our studio and even took some questions from the press corps. The whole thing lasted an hour.

The next morning we all showed up for his second SOS in as many days. He started speaking at 11 A.M. At about 12:30 . . . well into the time that lawmakers should have been scarfing down lunch with some high priced lobbyist, there was Blanchard still yakking away. Seems to me he finally finished around 12:45 setting a brand new record for long windedness . . . a record that, thankfully, no other governor has broken.

One of the mysteries of the Blanchard years was his on again and off again relationship with lawmakers. Blanchard loved to entertain them and many lawmakers got their fist peek at the executive residence when Blanchard took over from Milliken who was not a big party giver.

Many felt that Blanchard, coming from Congress, should have been more understanding of the legislators' role here in Lansing. But talk to some of the Democratic leaders and they tell horror stories about how Blanchard often abused lawmakers.

His most famous line was when he was in the middle of an intense budget fight. Blanchard like most governors wanted to hold down the spending and lawmakers then, as now, wanted to spend. Blanchard accused them of spending "like drunken sailors." It was an affront not only to sailors but more importantly to legislators. They let him know they didn't like it.

Former Lansing liberal Democrat representative David Hollister did not like another Blanchard broadside. He referred to Hollister as a "sick young man." On another occasion he referred to lawmakers as the "Don Knotts" of the government system. It was also my impression that most of the heavy lifting and negotiating aimed at advancing the Blanchard agenda was left to Bowman and not the governor. I'm sure he was in on the final deals but appeared to some lawmakers to be aloof and too good to get his hands dirty in the initial stages of discussions.

It was not always that way according to one influential Democrat who had a ring side seat. He says when Blanchard first came to town, House Speaker Gary Owen and Blanchard worked closely with Democrats. "We had lunch together but for some reason, he quit doing it," this source contends. After that and for many years, "he communicated poorly with legislators. He was very sensitive and took a lot of things personally."

There was one blow-up that sums it all up.

Two senior members of the Democratic caucus and members of the budget committee, according to this source, came to then House Speaker Lewis Dodak. It was 1990. Times were tough. The economy was sluggish and writing the budget was tough, too. Representative Dominic Jacobett, who chaired the panel and Representative Jimmy O'Neill were angry. They told Dodak that Blanchard was not listening to them about budget matters. They understood that he was the governor but, being veterans of the process, they also knew he was supposed to at least give them the time of day if he wanted to get anything done. After all they were all Democrats trying to advance his agenda.

Dodak reportedly takes their gripes to heart and tells the governor he needs to do some fence mending. He tells Blanchard, "They think you don't care what they say."

Before Blanchard agrees to the therapy session, Dodak advises him not to give a "sermon."

Comes time for the meeting, all the Democrats on the budget panel are there and Blanchard begins with . . . what else? A sermon. A twenty minute sermon. He goes on about how he brought the state back from the brink of default, etc.

Dodak wonders, according to a source that was in the room, if this was a listening session, since the governor was using his mouth more than his ears. The session was not working. Now the members take matters into their own hands. "Some of them went after the governor," one person recalls. Representative Charlie Harrison from Pontiac is especially vocal. But his stuff is tame compared to someone else who uses the M.F. label on Blanchard. After that Dodak reminds everyone that, "We are not here to fight." But that's exactly what's coming down. Blanchard backs off and permits his guests to talk some more. "He wasn't happy. He was less than pleased," one source recalls. The impression left by the meeting was that Blanchard thought he knew more about the appropriating process than the members. Obviously the feeling was not unanimous.

I talked with Dodak about all this twelve years after the fact. He would not confirm it for print, but he did say on balance, "Blanchard was good governor. He was talking with us 90 percent of the time on pending legislation. He cared, but even Dodak confesses in the end, "He had a problem with lawmakers."

Blanchard also had a problem with Dodak in 2002. The year before Mr. and Mrs. Dodak (Millie) told Jennifer Granholm that if she ran, they would back her. She ran and they did.

Dodak picked up the phone one day. Jim Blanchard was on the other end. He was not happy. He asked if the reports of Dodak's decision were correct. Dodak said they were and explained the earlier commitment he and his spouse had made.

Blanchard told him, "You are making a mistake."

Blanchard deeply believes Dodak made lots of other mistakes prior to that . . . miscues that complicated Blanchard's ability to advance his own agenda.

"Lou was a good man but he was afraid of his own caucus . . . he was a horribly weak speaker," the ex-governor observes. He says his working relationship with former Speaker Gary Owen was much better. They had a deal whereby the governor stayed out of legislative matters until Owen needed him to work on a handful of Democrats for various votes. Blanchard says the arrangement worked well and his personal relationship with Owen was even better. In fact, Blanchard asked Owen to be his running mate in 1990. Owen wanted out of politics and said no.

When Owen left, Blanchard says Dodak's goal was to please everyone in his caucus. Hence Blanchard says Dodak let the caucus run him rather than the other way around. And to make matters worse, the governor couldn't trust Dodak. "I couldn't have a conversation with Lou because everything I said got back to John Engler." It got so bad that Blanchard actually fed misleading information to Dodak.

"Engler thought he had a pipeline to me," Blanchard reports, so he fed disinformation into the pipeline to mislead the senate GOP leader.

Blanchard confesses that near the end "Democrats probably took me for granted and I probably took them for granted, too. I should have spent more time with them.

To this day, it is still fun talking with Blanchard. He has a keen eye for politics and his observations are often right on the money. It's fun picking his brain because he is still well connected to his beloved Democratic party. We go back a long ways and while we have disagreements from time to time (as referred to in the foreword) we can agree to disagree in a respectful manner. Maybe that's because we share at least one thing in common. We were both clarinet players.

7

Debates Are Where It's at

Covering the day-to-day comings and goings of state government and politics is a joy, but the real challenge and rewards come with candidate debates. In this day and age where the typical voter gets his or her candidate information from the tube, televised debates are essential to providing more than a thirty second glimpse at who these folks really are. Remember those commercials are controlled by the candidates and the image makers. What you learn from them is suspect. But sitting the candidates down in a studio for an hour of unedited back and forth is where voters can get a realistic impression of who is running.

Michigan Public TV has always had a strong commitment to providing these forums and I've been fortunate enough to be at the center of each one dating back to our first in 1970. It was the debate for governor that almost wasn't.

The Democrats thought they had a real shot at beating Bill Milliken who was running for the first time after becoming governor after George Romney went to Washington. They put up the affable Sander

"Sandy" Levin who chaired the Democratic party, and was the Democratic leader in the Senate. With that much power no other Democrat even considered getting in. The two sides agreed to a joint appearance, which our station would produce. Milliken declined to appear with Levin in a face-to-face matchup, which was my first choice.

The debate was divided into one-half hour for Milliken and a half hour for Levin. We were at a local high school with a live audience waiting inside the auditorium. Outside in the lobby the program was falling apart.

Milliken's crew showed up with a last minute request. He had another engagement and wanted to go first so he could get out of there. However, both sides had agreed to a coin toss to determine the appearance order. Milliken was adamant and Levin's team was equally committed to not giving him the first slot without a fight. Levin's handlers demanded the coin toss to resolve the impasse that was getting wider by the moment.

I first tried to convince Milliken to follow the original rules. He said no. I tried to convince Levin to give in. Wasted breath. Milliken imposed a time limit telling me that he was going to walk out the door if this mess was not resolved soon.

"Darn it," I thought to myself, "Here's my very first attempt at this thing and it was disintegrating right in front of my eyes." That's when fate stepped in. For the life of me I can't remember who suggested it. I know it wasn't me because my brain was frazzled and incapable of an original thought. The compromise was we would have a coin toss as scheduled and whoever won would be given the choice of being first or last. Regardless of the outcome of that, Milliken would still go first. We would merely edit the program to put the candidates in the right order based on the flip. It worked. My first debate was in the can.

The race itself was very close, but when Levin waffled on the state aid to non-public schools question, the Michigan Education Association yanked its endorsement and Levin lost.

The same evening we did the Milliken-Levin show, we also produced a U.S. Senate debate. Incumbent Phil Hart, rest his soul, had no problems with who would go first or last because he agreed to appear with his challenger, Lenore Romney, whose soul is also resting.

Romney, the spouse of former Governor George, was the so-called consensus choice of the state GOP as we discussed earlier.

The debate, such as it was, was a total bust. Every feeble attempt to produce some sparks between the two of them was quickly extinguished by Senator Hart. With a huge lead in the polls and being a gentle spirit in his own right, anytime we had Mrs. Romney on the ropes, Hart would throw her a life-line. And so it went for the full hour. It was a love in. No news. No hostages. No nothing. Mrs. Romney should have sent him a bouquet of flowers to express her gratitude. To no one's surprise she lost in her one and only foray into statewide elective politics.

During the early 1970s when we did debates they were usually with a panel of reporters. I soon learned that that was counterproductive. Put three correspondents on the dais and you end up with a mish mash of competing agendas. Just when reporter A got close to nailing a candidate on an issue, reporter B would jump in, change the subject, and a chance for the voters to really learn something was lost. After a couple of those productions, it struck me that going with one reporter was the superior format which we have used ever since.

The 1974 governor debate was a rehash of the 1970 race featuring Milliken and Levin. This time there was no battle over who went first. Instead we had a battle with a minority candidate who demanded to sit on the stage with Milliken and Levin, who had agreed to appear together.

Honestly, this has always been a troublesome point. On one hand the mission of public TV was to provide a forum for all points of view but from a journalistic standpoint including somebody who couldn't win, diluted the program. It made it more difficult for viewers to compare and contrast the majority contenders. Minority candidates, bless them, often provided comic relief. I mean when you ask a Socialist party guy what he would do to improve government and he says he would abolish it, well it's hard to do a follow up question on that.

Anyway the '74 debate had gotten a lot of attention because the Socialist Workers candidate, Mr. Robin Maisel, had figured out how to play the media. He issued a press release condemning the station for blocking him from sitting with Milliken and Levin. Darn, if the media didn't pick up on it giving him plenty of exposure. Frankly, it also helped us because the public discovered there was a debate. But the law was on our side. If Levin and Milliken got twenty minutes side-by-side, as long as we gave twenty minutes to Maisel during another segment, the station was in compliance with the law. So while the two candidates debated inside Studio B, the minority folks picketed outside the station before coming in to be interviewed.

The really big show of 1990 was the showdown between Jim Blanchard and John Engler. If you weren't around at the time suffice it to say there was no love lost between them.

Our public TV debate was the last of three, which is the position I wanted. I used to think being first was the best spot, but that usually meant those debates went unnoticed by the voters because they were too early in the campaign. Traditionally, citizens start to tune in a couple of weeks before the election. Blanchard knew that and would only agree to a program in early October, about a month before the balloting. That was standard operating procedure for most incumbents.

Our intent was to devise a format that had no rules. Most of the time, and somewhat amazingly, we usually got our way. This time, with so much at stake, the Blanchard camp demanded a more restrictive format. Under the rules, neither candidate could question the other, I was not given my usual unlimited ability to follow up, and time restraints were placed on each answer. It was like being tied up in chains, but if we wanted the debate, we had to agree to the rules and Engler was in the same boat. Blanchard held all the cards. Something was better than nothing.

Engler was thrilled when the night of the broadcast arrived. He knew he had been getting under Blanchard's skin with a series of commercials. One featured a nickel that Engler used to describe the Blanchard property tax relief plan . . . a lousy five cents a week for the typical family of four. He had coupled that with the so called airplane ad that told voters Blanchard was an imperial governor who flew all over the state on the taxpayers' dime of course.

Despite the ads, Blanchard still had a commanding lead but as I sat there waiting for my cue to begin, I sensed he wanted to be somewhere else. Conversely, Engler was loose as a goose.

Just after I asked him the first question, Engler didn't answer. Instead he turned to "Jim," as he impolitely addressed the sitting governor, and suggested that all the rules that had been delicately negotiated by both sides be tossed out right then and there.

"Let's have a real debate. Tim, I know you would like that [and of course inside my head I agreed but never said anything] and I know the viewers would enjoy it too. So, Jim, let's just have a real debate."

I paused for a second or two to see what Blanchard would do. He was staring at me and his lips weren't moving. A slight uncomfortable smile crept across his face but that was it. He wouldn't take the bait, so I concluded it was my turn to jump in. I sort of fumbled for words as I hoped Blanchard would say something but when he didn't, I suggested that since the rules had been established, unless Blanchard wanted to change them, we would proceed accordingly. Blanchard nodded approval and off we went.

That's the first and last time any candidate had tried that, and it was actually fun to be forced into thinking on my feet. I pulled it off that time but Engler wasn't done with his little surprises.

Another rule in the program was a prohibition against props. About twenty minutes in, Engler proceeded to break that rule, too. He brought out a nickel and held it up for the whole world to see as he launched into his spiel about Blanchard's cheap tax cut plan. Before he had two words out of his mouth, I interrupted Engler and reminded him, "No props," and ordered him to put it away.

He said he would but not before he held it up one more time for the camera as he continued his verbal criticism of the Blanchard tax relief plan. It was Engler being Engler. He didn't care if I called him on breaking the rules. He wanted to show that nickel.

Then came a senior moment for me. The two were discussing the tax increase that Blanchard engineered through the legislature to balance the budget. They disagreed on whether it was a temporary hike. Engler said it was not. Blanchard said it was, and then out of nowhere he asked me who was right.

And I bit. I sided with Blanchard.

Holy crap as the father on *Everyone Loves Raymond* would say. Engler lit after me. Suddenly I was the one being attacked, not his opponent.

"Tim, I'm surprised that you said that," Engler turned his heat on me. I was surprised, too, and disappointed.

For one mega second, I had gone off my game. I had allowed

myself to be drawn into the debate. I should have kept my big mouth shut. After all I wasn't running for governor, they were. I'd never been in this fix before and Engler had me dead to right.

The debate was finally over and I was mentally in a funk although I tried to keep my game face on. Engler and his handler Dan Pero rightfully objected to what I had done. They blamed me for defending Blanchard. By far that's the worst criticism of all. I was left with only one thing to do. I said I was sorry, but I knew that would not be enough.

Before everyone left the studio I told both sides that I recorded an apology that would air just before the debate began. I would tell the viewers to disregard my comments much like a judge admonishes the jury to disregard some prejudicial statement in a trial. It was the right thing to do and the only thing to do. Engler and Pero never let me forget it, and believe me I didn't. It never happened again. I was only sorry that it had happened once.

I remember sitting in the station parking lot in the dark after everyone had gone home talking to myself and admitting how I had blown it. I didn't think my career was over but my credibility had been damaged. It was the lowest I had ever felt after a debate.

In 1994 a public TV debate contributed to the end of one career and the beginning of another. In one corner was 82-year-old Richard Austin vs. Republican Candice Miller. Up for grabs, the secretary of state post that Democrat Austin had held for twenty-four years.

Before we get to the gory details of that contest, we have to go back to 1970 when Austin first ran for the post. Fresh from being Wayne County auditor, Austin was making a bid to become the highest elected African American official in state history.

It was a three person contest. Austin for the Democrats, Emil Lockwood for the GOP, and the third contender, Robert Miles. Miles had no previous elective experience unless you count being elected Grand Dragon of the Michigan Ku Klux Klan.

Lockwood had been the Senate majority leader. He and Austin were long time pals and Lockwood tells the story that he got into the contest to make sure Austin would win. The theory was Lockwood and Miles would divide the white vote and Austin would march into office.

The trio appeared on a debate we produced. Imagine the scene:

Austin sitting on the far left, Lockwood in the middle, and the KKK guy on the far right. I'm positively sure Austin had never shared the platform with a Klansman before and certainly never again.

The potential for sparks was obvious but none materialized. Miles did not look or act like a racist and there were no personal attacks. Austin, of course, went on to win. Lockwood went into the multi-client lobby business and Miles eventually went on to federal prison. He was convicted for fire bombing some school buses in Pontiac. A crime he claimed he never committed and he stuck to his story to his grave.

Over the years Austin had repelled every GOP challenger. The Republicans could never find anyone who even came close to knocking him off. Candice Miller was different. She had several things going in her favor as they came into the studio for the 1994 broadcast.

Austin was old. For years political columnists had speculated that he was losing it but there was never any hard proof, only "talk on the street." Nobody wanted to say in public that the king had no clothes. Miller came to the contest with strong experience in Macomb County one of the truly rough and tumble political battle-grounds in the state. She was running on a platform of change and all you had to do was look at the two of them and the visual contrast was apparent.

There was some debate within the Austin camp about even doing the program. By now, the *Off the Record* debate was firmly entrenched in the state's political landscape and to skirt it would surely send the signal that Austin was afraid. Not wanting to do that, he showed up for the only TV debate of the campaign. Little did he know it would be his last.

The program began innocently enough until I asked an unexpected question about abortion. It was not on abortion per se since that had nothing to do with the post they sought. Rather it had to do with Right to Life campaign contributions to Miller. I wanted to know how beholden she would be to that conservative group.

After she answered, out of fairness I felt compelled to ask Austin whether he was anti-abortion or pro-choice.

It was then that Austin had his own senior moment, as one of his aides described it.

"Pro-choice?" he said out loud. He couldn't recall what that meant. He turned to me for a lifeline and for a second I almost accidentally bailed him out by giving him the definition. Instead I look stoned faced and let him grapple with it on his own. The picture was devastating. He disintegrated on the air. He couldn't determine what his stance was but then he finally corrected himself and declared he was pro-choice.

I gave Miller a chance to respond to what she had just seen. Wisely she said nothing. She did not have to. The damage was done. The king indeed was naked.

The spin session afterward was a feeding frenzy. I remember Bob Kolt, Austin's handler, trying his very best to down play what everyone had seen. The press corps wasn't buying it. Here was visual proof that confirmed the "word on the street" about the kindly old man.

Nine years after that fateful day, Kolt and I discussed the historic program. Kolt said Austin walked out of the studio not realizing what had happened.

Kolt says, "I told him this would have an impact." Austin said he had corrected the abortion statement on the air but later told his handler, "I guess you're right."

Kolt remembers Austin had been "on his game" during the debate prep sessions before the show and as Kolt watched the program with reporters, he was feeling good.

"We were almost at the end. I'm counting down the minutes and feeling none of his answers have done any damage. I'm saying 'thank you' when the abortion issue comes up."

"I wasn't sure I heard what I heard. I was stunned," Kolt remembers.

In a way he was not shocked that the abortion issue did in his client. For years Austin had given a speech in which he said, "I want everyone to use their seat belts. I'm pro-life." Kolt says he told Austin that the phrase had a different meaning and he should expunge it from his patter. Kolt thinks when I asked the question, it triggered a confused response on what pro-life meant.

Kolt took some unjustified hits for allowing Austin to do the show in the first place. Up to that point, there was no evidence that the candidate was losing it. After the program Kolt says there was a "psychological effect." Austin started to slow down during other campaign stops. He looked old so finally seven days before the election, Kolt abruptly and correctly took Austin off the trail and put him back in the office out of public view.

"That program had a lasting impact," Kolt reports. Not only on Austin but on Kolt, too. "I loved Austin," he says, "but after that show, I distanced myself from other political clients so that if I had to be blunt with them, the friendship would not get in the way of doing that."

While most voters never saw the program, many more read about it in the newspaper. To make sure an even broader audience saw it, Miller had 150 VHS copies of the program sent out to key groups.

Needless to say, she won.

Austin and I had one conversation after the debate but we never discussed the program. From a personal standpoint, it was painful to see him come apart on the show. From a professional viewpoint, the debate had accomplished its objective: Show voters the candidates up close and let the chips fall where they may. I had done my job, but it still hurt inside to see such a great career public servant go out that way.

The Austin performance became a benchmark for other politicians. Attorney General Frank Kelley, in part, made his decision to retire, not wanting to go out on a stretcher. Ironically Kelley and union leaders had met privately with Austin and urged him to retire. He refused to do it, so the voters did it for him.

On the topic of Kelley and debates, he was always a gamer and provided some of the more entertaining moments during campaigns. Much like Austin, Republicans had a tough time fielding anybody to take on the "Eternal General" as he was labeled given his three decades in the office. Kelley devoured one sacrificial lamb after another.

The contest featuring Cliff Taylor was notable. Taylor was a long time John Engler crony and destined to do something in the GOP sooner or later, but before he got to that, he ran against Kelley. As successful as he was, Kelley couldn't possibly remember everything connected with his office so when he came into the studio with Taylor, he brought along a set of three by five cards filled with answers to possible questions, and he used them from time to time.

At one point, I can't remember what the question was, but it was apparent that Kelley was having trouble finding the right card. As the incumbent attorney general fumbled on camera, Taylor leaned in and motioned with his finger to the card Kelley was looking for. "It's that one, Frank," the gloating Taylor advised.

It was not quite the senior moment that Austin had but Taylor could have gotten some mileage out of it had he had a ton of money to send out his own video tapes. Alas, he had $800. And he lost. Taylor of course went on to win an appeal court seat and moved up to the Supreme Court thereafter. He still tells the Kelley story.

Doing debates with two candidates is a piece of cake. Doing it with six is not. That was the assignment as we dragged six contenders into the public TV studios during one Democratic primary for the U.S. Senate. The winner would face off against Republican Spencer Abraham who was well on his way to trouncing challenger Ronna Romney on the GOP side.

Here was the line up. Former congressman Bill Broadhead from Oakland County, U.S. Rep. Bob Carr, Lansing businessman Joel Ferguson, state senator John Kelly, Macomb County, Prosecutor Carl Marlinga and the lone female in the pack, state senator Lana Pollack from Ann Arbor. They were all in the hunt because the incumbent, Don Riegle, had decided to pack it in.

The challenge in these debates is to make sure everyone gets a chance to say his or her piece. These were all seasoned professionals and since it was the only televised encounter, each was ready to state their case while trying to undermine their opponents' case whenever they could.

As the broadcast unfolded, it turned out to be five against one. Everyone wanted a piece of the perceived front runner, Congressman Carr. The good looking, tall, and Kennedy-like Democrat began as a liberal from East Lansing in the 1970s, but over the years he had shuffled more to the right.

His opponents accused him of conducting a "Rose Garden" strategy of staying away from candidate forums. They hit him on using taxpayers' dough to send out campaign literature and he was blamed for turning his back on labor.

Carr claimed he "had a job to do for the people of Michigan and I've been doing it."

But he took the greatest heat from Pollack who sensed she had a shot at the nomination, but knew he would outspend her. So she tried to make up the difference with her words instead of money.

Carr, minus the tears, told the audience that his home in Washington was burgled recently, which allowed him to talk about locking up crooks. Pollack was unimpressed.

"It was a miserable feeling," Carr recounted. "I think anyone who is violated that way feels as violated as someone who is physically attacked."

Pollack would have nothing to do with that shooting back, "No way. Women who have been raped feel a lot more violated than a man who's lost his TV."

Carr, scrambling for a rejoinder called on an old Ronnie Reagan line, "There you go again."

Score: Pollack-one. Carr-nothing.

Carr did even the tally with a pretty good shot at her. "I have to say here . . . that state sen. Pollack's crime record is a miserable one . . . I believe she even voted against increasing the sentences for people who commit child torture."

All in all it was a lively and informed exchange. Dawson Bell the columnist for the *Free Press* said, "There were spirited exchanges but few sharp differences over major issues." The important thing was viewers got a chance to see them on TV and not in their commercials. Dawson's observations not withstanding there was one question that separated the candidates and gave those viewers some interesting answers to digest.

Crime is one of those issues that is easily exploited. The rhetoric can reach a fevered pitch as everyone suggests we lock 'em up and throw away the key. This question sought to cut through the clap trap and get to the heart of the matter.

What percentage of the crime fighting dollar should be allocated for prevention and/or prisons? The answers were all over the lot.

Kelly wanted to spend sixty-six cents of every dollar to buy more cops. The rest would go for prisons and not one red cent into prevention. He sheepishly conceded that prevention was needed but the government couldn't afford to spend on that until "citizens feel comfortable in their own homes."

Carr wanted eighty cents for prisons so that "everybody who doesn't play by the rules goes to jail." He would spend twenty cents on keeping them out of jail.

Pollack stayed true to her liberal upbringing noting that, "there's a lot of chest thumping going on in Washington" about crime. She thumped hers saying, "We ought to do better on the front end trying to prevent crime." But where do you put the crooks in the meantime?

"We have enough prisons," she argued.

Ferguson, a good friend of Jessie Jackson, took the civil rights leader line: "We have to spend money on the front side of life. That's where I'm headed."

Broadhead checked in by cutting the baby in half—fifty cents to prisons and fifty cents into prevention. He griped, "the wrong people are in prison." He wanted only violent lugs sent to the slammer, which brought this response from others, "That's too easy."

The only full time crime fighter in the bunch, prosecutor Marlinga checked in with twenty to forty cents for Headstart and other prevention measures and the rest to lock them up. It seemed to me as I wrote in a July 22, 1994 column about the debate that the right answer was, "If you elect me I won't solve the crime problem. I may not even make a dent in it." But politicians can't confess they are impotent when it comes to some issues. They perpetuate the myth that if elected they will solve every problem in the world. You know that's not true and so do they. They just can't bring themselves to say it.

Carr went on to capture the nomination. Pollack felt she could have won it had Ferguson not been in the race. According to her math, she would have done much better in Detroit, but Ferguson siphoned off much of the black vote and Carr scooted into the nomination with that unintended help from Fergy.

When it came time for the general election in '94, I found myself in court in front of Judge James Giddings.

The Libertarian party wanted a gun guy, John Coon, to run against Carr and Abraham. Coon had very little money but a pretty big mouth that often produced good sound bites. He was fun to have around even though he had zero chance of winning. There were two other minority candidates from the Socialist and Worker's World parties. Don't feel stupid if the names Bill Roundtree and Chris Wege don't ring a bell.

The public TV folks decided that since Coon had gotten at least 5 percent in the latest poll he would be invited to the debate but the other two would not. I went to the Abraham camp and told them the program had been expanded to three candidates.

His handlers said great, we won't be there!

We wanted this debate so we went to Plan B: Do Carr and Abraham together and give Coon the last twenty minutes of the show by himself.

"We'll see you in court," Coon's attorney notified us.

They filed suit against the station. I met behind closed doors with MSU lawyers and explained that if we allowed Coon to be on with the other two, we would not have a debate. We had a history of excluding minority candidates and had always prevailed. But nobody had ever challenged our thinking in court. On the day of the hearing, the legal eagles told me to stay home, which I gladly did.

The court date, in front of Giddings, was on a Friday afternoon. Proceedings started just after lunch. I awaited the outcome. When the phone rang around 3 P.M. I thought we had won, because the proceedings were rather quick.

Instead of a victory statement I was told, "Skubick, the judge wants to see you down here."

So much for hiding out.

I made the twenty minute drive to Giddings' court room not knowing what would happen. I quickly found myself raising my right hand and swearing to tell the whole truth and nothing but the truth. Being a reporter I was used to that.

The lawyer for Coon must have thought he'd died and gone to the *People's Court.* Instead of me firing off the questions, they were fired at me.

I tried to explain that if we let every so called candidate in off the street just because they declared themselves to be a contender, we'd have a hundred people in the debate. The audience would not be able to follow it and the purpose of the program, to inform the voters, would be lost in the mob scene.

The barrister hammered me on how unfair that was and frankly on the surface I pretty much agreed but I didn't volunteer that in open court. As he bore in on me seeking to hang me out to dry, I turned the tables on him and asked him some questions, too.

Then the classic line of the hearing. Judge Giddings, whom I had covered for years, turned to me with a grin and a glint in his eye, "Mr. Skubick, this is my show, not yours. Please answer the questions, don't ask them."

The joint was rocking with laughter.

Score: Giddings—one. TV journalist—goose egg.

My performance on the stand did nothing to advance our case. Giddings ruled that the station had two choices: include Coon with Carr and Abraham or do a twenty minute interview with each of the minority types, which would have expanded the one hour program into eighty minutes.

We again opted for interviewing all three together, but again Abraham shot that down. At that point the station said, let's do everyone at the same time. Which we did. Abraham's camp declared itself the defender of minority rights. By balking at each of our proposals, Spence's gang said it was really holding out for everyone to be there. Coon and Carr made the same claim.

In reality, Abraham was more afraid of a showdown with Coon and Carr than defending the rights of minority candidates. The two of them could have eaten the GOP candidate alive. So Abraham went for the "safety in numbers" strategy while denying that was the case. With five candidates around the table there was less time for Abraham to screw up and less time for either Carr or Coon to come after the GOP hopeful.

After everybody got out of court, we finally got into the studio to do the program with the gang of five. One classic moment unfolded between the two major party candidates. File this one under s-t-r-e-t-c-h-i-n-g for an issue.

Oliver North was running for the U.S. Senate at the same time as the two Michigan guys, and Carr tried to bring the controversial Iran-Contra fall guy into the debate. He did it by disclosing that North and Abraham shared the same media consultant.

Abraham had a quick comeback, "We use the same phone company, too."

Carr took it on the chin but fought back with the suggestion that North and Abraham "were out of the same cut of cloth."

"Are you accusing me of lying to the American people?" Abraham protested.

"Well, pretty much," Carr suggested with a straight face.

"Oh yeah," was the best Spence could do.

Abraham went on to beat Carr for the six-year term, which he turned around and lost to Debbie Stabenow. Abraham did not do any debates with us that cycle. Wonder why?

The 1998 race for governor started out with five Democrats slugging it out. They were Larry Owen, who had run in '94; Doug Ross, the former state senator and Blanchard appointee; Rep. Jim Agee from Muskegon; Jim Berryman, state senator from Adrian; and Ed Hamilton from Oakland County. He was never in the hunt and changed parties later on.

We lined the quintet up for our usual primary debate but quickly had to add another contender to the platform. Geoffrey Fieger filed papers with the state on July 9 to run, just about a month before the vote.

He explained in the debate that "I don't want to be governor. I don't want to run, but unless somebody comes out of this race with the ability to win, I'm going to do it."

That turned out to be the lead out of the program, but there was another exchange that revealed who the real politicians were in the pack. The question was, if former U.S. Senator Don Riegle ran for governor, would his involvement in the savings and loan scandal make him dead meat? Remember Riegle was implicated but he never got convicted of anything although his image was clearly smudged.

Owen and Ross, not wanting to offend their pal who might help turn on some money faucets down the road, punted. Ross whimped out offering this lame answer, "I don't know how the voters will respond." Real courage there, Dougy. Owen said the same thing and both of them suggested they had not really pondered the implications. Fieger went right to the point. He answered, "Yes, it would hurt Riegle."

After the debate in the customary spin session, it was a mob scene. Candidate Jim Berryman decided to get out of the race when he saw the entire press corps head for Fieger, leaving the other five to wait their turn. Berryman said it was amazing and only underscored Fieger's uncanny ability to work the media to his own advantage while leaving others cooling their heels.

With Berryman out, Agee and Hamilton followed, leaving a trio for the public TV debate that August.

Fieger picked up where he left off in the first debate by portraying himself as the outsider and non-politician while Ross and Owen showed they were polished officer seekers. The defining question that illustrated the point was the one I concocted just for Fieger. I was pretty sure he was so busy making money, defending Jack Kevorkian on the assisted suicide issue, and doing all the other things he did, that he would not know the answer to my revealing question.

"Mr. Fieger. Do you support MEGA?"

He had two choices: Tell the truth or wing an answer. I didn't have to wait long to find out which.

"I don't know what MEGA is," the wise guy attorney confessed in front of his opponents and TV audience.

Owen and Ross sure did and proceeded to show-up the Fieger man by explaining the Michigan Economic Growth Authority and how it helped create jobs. Not to be outdone, Fieger jumped back in and drove this point home by turning his ignorance into a plus. He reminded the audience that he was not a minutiae-type guy trapped in the inner workings of state government. No way. He was just like everybody out there in TV land who didn't know what MEGA was either. At that juncture it was game, set, and match for Fieger.

After the taping he accused me of setting him up. Here was the pot calling the kettle black. It was not a set up, I objected to his accusation. I was just trying to determine if he would lie or confess he didn't know. He didn't buy my defense. It didn't matter. Fieger got 300,000 votes with a ton of help from Detroit voters. He sent Owen and Ross to the showers where he would later join them after Engler clobbered him in November.

Four years earlier, in 1994, the Democrats really felt they had a shot at Engler. Four folks lined up for the right to take him on. They had all been friends for years, but when they appeared for the public TV debate, the friendships were placed on hold.

The perceived front runner was very coy from the outset about getting into the race. State senator Debbie Stabenow was on everyone's list as a potential candidate. Long before anybody had formally announced, Stabenow was slippery on the question.

During an October 1992 phone interview, the drill went like this: "Are you running for governor?"

Crank up the fog machine. "It's presumptuous to take the focus off the election [that year] to focus on something else," she insisted.

But then I hit her with, "In your mind are you running for governor?"

"I'm not going to answer that question." She didn't have to. She just did. By the time the 1994 race rolled around she was in with both feet.

She came into the debate loaded with lots of ammo aimed at John Engler. But Larry Owen and Howard Wolpe had her in their sights. The fourth candidate, Lynn Jondahl, the state representative from East Lansing, was the least aggressive but even he couldn't avoid going after Stabenow on the issue of property tax reform.

As you will read later on, Stabenow provided the amendment that led to the total repeal of the property taxes to fund education. Her opponents/friends had hardly settled into their *Off the Record* seats when she took her first hit.

Wolpe chided her for being "snookered by John Engler into implementing his agenda."

"Whether in fact the senator was snookered or not, it was bad judgment. It was still an irresponsible action to take," Jondahl chimed in.

Stabenow, now clearly under attack struggled to regain the stage. She denied all the snookering and suggested the bold move resulted in a better education system for everyone.

Owen was unimpressed. "Not true. There is nothing bold about taking away all of the funding for education and not having a backup plan in place," he lectured her as he parroted the company line from the MEA.

She told the audience her pals from Ingham County were playing politics in a vain attempt to undercut her standing in the polls. She had that right.

At a time when the term limit movement was getting up a good head of steam, three of the four Democrats suggested their experience was their main asset. Owen claimed mantle to the "outsider" title even though he was as experienced as the others. Between the four of them they had over one hundred years in the political trenches.

Wolpe won and earned the right to take on Engler. But Wolpe had stumbled before he got to our debate. His first ad had him walking the shores of Lake Michigan discussing the finer points of storing waste at a nuclear plant. Boring! Only nuclear scientists were talking about that. The general public was more interested in tax relief. John Engler ran an earlier spot painting Wolpe as a tax and spend liberal. The Wolpe campaign never responded to that, but kept running the silly nuclear waste stuff. Dumb.

Just after he secured the nomination, Wolpe went up north where he asked Helen Milliken to be his running mate. While she was turning him down, some inmates at the Ryan Road State Prison in Detroit decided to take any early out.

The escape was major news and a major embarrassment for the sitting governor Engler. But where was Wolpe? It took him three days after the breakout to resurface in this town with his criticism of the lapse in security. He should have high-tailed it down to Detroit the day of the escape to tape a commercial in front of the hole in the fence where he could have told voters, "See that hole? John Engler's failed prison policies not only produced that, but put the lives of innocent citizens at risk." Great spot that was never done.

Two missed opportunities. Privately it looked like Howie was not ready for prime time.

Engler and Wolpe showed up for our debate as the election got closer. Wolpe had raked in a ton of money from the trial lawyers and Engler arrived in the studio with a present for his opponent.

Just before the live debate, Engler pushes a coffee cup across the table. On it are the words, "Call Sam." Sam Bernstein was a well heeled trial lawyer and Engler was having some fun. Wolpe neither took the cup nor the joke. I kept my game face in place but was chuckling inside.

Wolpe had been instructed by his team to jump into the debate early with an attack on Engler regarding the abortion issue. In the green room, his handlers waited and waited. Finally near the end, he got to it, but it was too late. The idea was to throw Engler off his game early on, but that never happened. Although, uncharacteristically, Engler made two boo-boos of his own during the one hour live broadcast.

The first came when Engler left the door open to possibly backing state tax dollars for non-public schools. The issue had been around in one form or another since 1970 when voters turned it down. But Engler's answer was seen by some as backing state aid to those schools. It took the Engler camp ten days after the debate to indicate that he really opposed the concept. Asked why he had not given that response in the debate, the campaign dead panned, the answer had been "evolving."

Engler's manager Dan Pero conceded the governor could have answered it better.

Wolpe had his own deer in the headlights moment when asked a question he obviously had not anticipated. He fumbled on supporting health care to same sex partners. Instead of a response he called for more study . . . the standard life raft you head for when you don't want to give an answer.

But the best flip-flop of the night went to Engler. Just before the debate, Chris Christoff from the *Free Press* caught me in the hallway outside the studio. He told me that the head of the Michigan United Conservation Clubs (MUCC) was quietly pushing for more concealed weapons. The gun nuts would love that and the anti-gun nuts would not.

In my question to Engler, I kept the MUCC's Executive Director Tom Washington's name out of it at first. "Should citizens be able to carry a weapon without a concealed weapons permit?" I innocently asked.

Engler said no. It was as firm a response as you can get. One he quickly chucked when I indicated that Washington was looking at it. The governor did a back-flip and said he "would take a look at it." I bored in asking him if he was always so willing to change his mind if the gun lobby wanted something. He suggested he listened to everyone. Nice try, governor.

The debate was free-wheeling and covered a lot of ground. But the next morning on WJR, morning jock J. P. McCarthy objected to my aggressive style of questioning telling his listeners there were actually three persons in the debate last night.

This brings us to the GOP primary for governor in 1986. There was a splendid field that contained two firsts. The first African American man to run for governor. Bill Lucas had assembled an impressive resume as Wayne County executive and had brought the traditionally debt-ridden county back into the black. And the first female Republican to run for governor Colleen House-Engler was on the ballot. She was married to John Engler at the time. Then there was Oakland County Executive Dan Murphy. On paper he was the most qualified of the bunch. But paper doesn't run for governor, people do. His public persona however never moved the needle. Rounding out the field was Dick Chrysler who had made his millions tearing the roofs off cars and replacing them with rag tops.

He intended to parlay the moola he made in the CEO's chair at Cars and Concepts into a chair in the governor's office.

He leap-frogged over Lucas into the lead despite the fact that he was without a portfolio. When he wrote a check for $475,000 for a saturation TV ad blitz, he became a household name.

The four candidates were contending for the right to face Jim Blanchard in November but the Chrysler money machine could not stop the "crisis dejour" as media advisor Rusty Hills recollects. It was one bad story after another.

Capital correspondents David Waymire and Ed Petykiewicz at the Booth Newspapers discovered that Chrysler was so busy making money he never bothered to vote in a local school election. That revelation was a blip compared to the exclusive Roger Martin was working on.

Martin from the *Detroit News* Lansing bureau, got a tip from a former employee at Cars and Concepts about a scheme that seemed far-fetched at first blush. The allegation was that Mr. Chrylser had laid off some workers. However, he asked them to return to work but didn't pay them. But they did pocket their unemployment checks. Martin found an ex-employee in rural Indiana and drove there to nail the story. Turns out the source managed the whole scheme and spilled all the details of the unsavory affair. To some, Chrysler was just doing what aggressive and independent business folk do. Problem was it was against the law.

Hills called Martin when word reached the campaign that Chrysler was going to get hammered by the *News*. "If we are going to respond," Hills explained, "we have to know the story." Martin would not budge. Hills said if Martin didn't change his mind, the campaign would block the paper from any coverage of Chrysler's effort.

As the deadline approached for publishing the story Martin changed his tune. He called Hills to set up a clandestine meeting at the Denny's eatery in Southfield near Channel 7. Martin was willing to show them the story if they made Chrysler available for a response. Chrysler attended along with Hills and another aide. Martin was there with his editor Bill Giles and two other folks from the *News*.

Martin handed out copies of his proposed story and gave Chrysler and company time to read it. Hills says he finished first and was formulating a response along the lines of, "It's not true."

He kept waiting for the candidate to finish reading and finally Chrysler slowly put the paper down. Instead of denouncing the story he said, "If you print this, you will dictate the outcome of the election."

Chrysler never did deny the charge, even though the allegation was never proven. The state attorney general could not haul him into court because the Michigan Employment Security Commission did not have the paperwork for the employees in question.

The swirling controversy meant there might be some fireworks when the quartet met in an *Off the Record* debate. There was an air of anticipation as I arrived at the studio about 7:30 A.M. Soon Lucas, Murphy, and House came in. But no Chrysler. It got to be a little after eight o'clock when we were scheduled to begin taping and still no Dickie-poo.

When that happens your mind races through a variety of scenarios . . . he's caught in a traffic jam; he forgot and thinks it's on another date; or he's chickened out. When the phone rang at 8:05 I heard some chirping from the chicken on the other end of the line.

Former TV Detroit reporter Tom Greene was handling the media for the Chrysler team and had apparently drawn the short straw. "Timmy," he began in a business like tone, "Dick's in Washington D.C. He got called away to do some fundraiser and he won't be there for the debate."

Called away my foot!

This clown was 900 miles away because he did not want to face the music nor his opponents nor, for that matter, me. Greene apologized as I agonized in his ear to no avail. I told Tommy it would not look good to have this last minute withdrawal. He knew that, but it was a calculated risk they were willing to take. Better to take a hit for not being there than to be hit repeatedly during the telecast by his opponents and yours truly. The great debate was not to be.

We did the program with the other three and I told the audience why Chrysler was not there. He went on to lose as Lucas got the nomination and picked Ms. House for his running mate. In retrospect Chrysler did not demonstrate much class with his eleventh hour withdrawal. From a pure political standpoint I fully understood the move, but there was a better way to do it and he didn't.

A personal phone call the night before would have been a nice touch. A heads up would have taken the edge off the surprise call in the morning. At the very least a personal call after the fact to apologize would have been a gentlemanly thing to do. The call never came.

But Chrysler had good company in stiffing us. Before the November election in 1982, we lined up Dick Headlee's running mate, Tom Brennan the former chief justice of the State Supreme Court. It would be his only TV appearance with Martha Griffiths whom Jim Blanchard had selected as his lt. governor candidate.

That darn phone outside the studio in the hallway again brought bad news. It was somebody calling from Ms. Griffiths home announcing that the fog in Macomb County meant she could not fly up to East Lansing. When I suggested we would wait for the fog to lift . . . in effect the answer was, the fog ain't never going to lift stupid. Ms. Griffiths was not a morning person, but if that was the case, why did they agree to the session in the first place? She took that answer to her grave.

8

The Reluctant Governor:

Jennifer Who?

I can remember it as if it were yesterday. Back in 1998, the name Jennifer Granholm rocketed out of nowhere as a potential Democratic candidate for attorney general.

When the *Off the Record* panel discussed her potential candidacy I blurted out, "Jennifer who!?"

Back then she was known only to the likes of Ed McNamara, the Wayne County executive and his inner circle of seasoned political cronies who were grooming her to run. From the get-go it was a long shot.

For years the drill was you never ran for a statewide office until and unless you had paid some dues along the way. You had to be a "somebody" with some sort of political cache to even be considered. McNamara's band had the audacity to rewrite the rules and promote some woman who never wanted to be in politics in the first place. Originally she wanted to be a Hollywood star.

Within a few months Jennifer Who showed up on *OTR*. Her first statewide TV appearance was on June 19, 1998.

When she first walked in she had a bright smile, an outstretched hand eager to be shaken, and a quick one liner about finally making it to the big time by doing the show. "I watch you all the time," she confessed. Right.

There was one exchange out of that first encounter that she used time and time again on the campaign . . . thanks to me.

My question was on the minds of many voters, rightly or wrongly. Here was a candidate with three little kids at home. So what was she doing running for office? Personally I had no problem with that, but I was asking questions on behalf of common folk. I knew it was a 1950s question but felt it needed to be asked, however, I carefully worded my question to avoid being tagged as a sexist.

"As you run for this office, there will be some conservatives [there's my cover] who will wonder how you can do that, if you have three children at home?"

She knew it was coming and proceeded to hit it out of the park. "If John Engler was sitting here you wouldn't ask him that question," she lectured me. I expected that and got it, but I felt I had a job to do and I did it. That was enough for me! Problem was wherever she went after that, she was quick to recall her appearance on *OTR* and "that" question from Skubick. You live by the sword; you die by it too.

The next time she appeared on statewide public TV was October 31, 1998, just days before the election. She had secured the Democratic nomination for attorney general as she appeared in the final debate with the Republican candidate, a guy named John Smietanka. This was the second time around the track for the west Michigan attorney who got tanked four years earlier by Frank Kelley.

Smietanka was in the race over the strong objections of Governor John Engler. Engler had wanted Scott Romney to run for the post. Romney was the son of former Governor George Romney and had almost instant name identification. Even after running for the job once before, Smietanka's hard to pronounce surname was not on a par with Romney.

The Engler-Romney axis was rebuffed at the state party convention that Engler supposedly controlled. Engler butted heads with another west Michigan Republican, Chuck Yob, who favored his pal

Smietanka and when the dust settled, Romney was toast and Smietanka was the nominee. Democrats were delighted. They were actually concerned about a Romney-Granholm matchup because her name was not as familiar as his.

Smietanka was a huge fellow. Personable, but somewhat reserved. I had covered him during his last run against Kelley. Granholm took her seat to my left and he to my right on the *OTR* set. As with all our other debates there were no rules so it didn't take too long for them to get into it over their TV commercials.

The GOP had a spot claiming she was soft on crime. It wasn't an original theme but they trotted it out nonetheless. The Democrats, in a more personal vein, had gone negative against Smietanka with some family dirt. The spot suggested the divorced Smietanka had fallen behind in his child support. He denied the charge, just as she denied being a softy on crooks.

Granholm then offers a deal. (She would use the same tactic running for governor.) She promises to yank the ads running on her behalf, if he agrees to halt the ones against her. She reaches her hand across the table to shake hands.

"Come on John, let's do it," she eggs him on.

He took her hand and told her, "Every word I have put out about me and about you is true."

She quickly withdraws her hand as that was not what she wanted to hear.

"That is a lie. That is such a lie right there," she gets as indignant as she can get.

Bottom line on the ads, nobody withdraws anything.

Later in the debate, there's a development that became a part of political folklore in this town. Smietanka was making a point, and she again reached across to take his hand. As she reached, he recoiled. He flinched as if she had a bad case of the cooties. He spoke not a word, but his non-verbal message was, "Keep your hands off me."

Smietanka says he was surprised by her move. He meant no disrespect. He says he is a touchy feely guy, but at that moment he sure didn't look like it. After the hand business he got really animated about the child support allegation. The ad suggested that at the time he was in the arrears, he was loaning his campaign a ton of money. He denied the implication and lashed out at her.

"You're embarrassed by injecting my daughter in this race," he looked her right in the eye. "You ought to be ashamed of yourself."

"You ought to be ashamed," she fired back.

After the program everyone was talking about the hand rejection thing. Smietanka says to this day, nobody remembers it. But Granholm sure did when she appeared on the show two years later. She was part of a panel of four guests, grilling me for a change. At the top of the show, I shook everyone's hand.

"Thank you for shaking my hand," she blurted out. "I was beginning to wonder if it was me, or the show."

Granholm's come out of nowhere attorney general victory put to rest the theory that you needed lots of experience to run for statewide office. She had precious little but that didn't seem to matter. Voters liked her . . . liked her a lot. But oddly enough she never wanted to be attorney general in the first place.

You have to go back to around the time Frank Kelley announced he was going to hang it up. Speculation quickly turned to all the Democrats who had wanted to run for years but didn't because Kelley would not leave. On the first batch of names, Granholm was omitted. That's because from the outset she didn't want the job. Her Wayne County friends and her husband basically convinced her she needed to get in, and when she finally decided to do it, she did it with passion with her coming out party slated for Mackinac Island at the Detroit Chamber of Commerce leadership conference. The non-politician Granholm has her chatter down pat. She tells the power brokers and the press corps that, "Wayne County is the largest county. It's the county with the most votes. I've got the civil experience, plus I was a prosecutor for four years." The message is she's qualified. She adds for good measure, "If they want to have a woman in the slot, maybe they should look at me."

Pollster Eddie Sarpolus gets on the boat back to the mainland telling everyone, "What impressed me with Jennifer was how quickly the news media was willing to sit down, talk to her and cover her." In terms of generating media attention, Granholm was the female version of Geoffrey Fieger, without his mean streak.

Prior to Kelley's retirement announcement, Granholm was not on his short list. In fact he made a phone call to Kathy Fitzgerald, who was on his staff. He first told her he was going to leave and then encouraged her to run. Kelley also refused to huddle with

Granholm during her whirlwind island visit. However, somewhere between there and the Granholm candidacy, Kelley changed his mind. He became one of those inside advisors that Granholm heavily relied on. That's because she didn't know much about being attorney general.

To underscore that, one aide recalls a plane ride back from the Upper Peninsula during which she asks, "How much time does the attorney general get off?" Maybe she's thinking she'll have every other Tuesday off and her weekends free. The aide reveals the harsh truth. "You'll be on 24–7." Next question.

Knowing what we know now about her ability to work a crowd and capture the spotlight, it was not always that way. She would tell her team on the road that "Nobody knows who I am." She recounts how she goes to the local store, buys some bread and milk and gets out of there without a soul saying a thing. Her always attentive staff decided to do something about that. When she went into some store to make a personal purchase, they secretly commandeered the P.A. system and had her paged. She loved it.

The reluctant politician finds herself on the Capitol steps one wintry morning. She is not taping a campaign spot. She's preparing to be sworn in as the state's top law enforcement officer. She is the lone Democrat on the platform surrounded by John Engler and his cronies. Engler gives his last inaugural address. Because of term limits he's a goner in four years. She on the other hand, is just beginning and she kicks it off with a speech that makes headlines.

I watched her speech that chilly January morning from the warmth of our bedroom as Gayle and I packed for Grand Rapids to cover the Engler inaugural festivities. I was not impressed with her speech and said so in that week's column. Granted it was her first voyage, but it was still a sophomoric performance. I found out afterward the address was basically something she and her husband hammered out. She began with a reference to the "icy political indifference" in the electorate. OK, it was cold and the icy analogy was understandable, but not an additional seven times.

"How can I change anything with my one vote?" she asked the audience. "Isn't it better some say, to turn a cold shoulder and curse the politicians and candidates who created this icy climate of mistrust? My hope is that we will feed a shiver of involuntary cold and act before it's too late." Ugh.

Before that she said, "Today, right now America seems nearly frozen in political indifference." All right, enough already with the cold crap. The next line went in my ear and out the other but it was prophetic. She is talking about getting the citizenry involved in the process. "OK, you. You have many talents. Don't cheat the world by hiding them in an icy coat of indifference. Your playing cool does not serve the world."

Before her term was over, others might well have tossed those words back in her face as she had to be nudged to run for governor, but on that January day that was not in her heart or head. She just wanted to be the best attorney general she could be.

The headline in the Saturday *News* and *Free Press* shouted, "Granholm Steals the Show."

It seemed as though she had hardly lowered her right hand after taking the oath of office than the drum beat began: Will Granholm run for governor?

This had happened only once before, in 1994, just after Dennis Archer was sworn in as mayor of Detroit. The same question was asked and the same answer was given. It formed the basis for a newspaper column on January 7 of that year.

Archer was impressive. He had shown lots of guts by getting in the mayor's race before Coleman Young said he was getting out. He once got a standing ovation from the GOP legislature and showed signs of being able to work with all sides, ala Milliken. One of my columns suggested, "If Archer helps to turn his city around, if his statewide fence-mending pays off, and if he leaves the door open, don't rule him out" for governor.

Archer was asked about governor. "I'd like to be the very best mayor the City of Detroit has ever had."

It wasn't a yes or a no.

"So you don't want to be governor?"

"No, I have no intent to running for anything. . . . "

Fast forward to 1999. Granholm, still trying to learn the ropes, is peppered with the same stuff and she parrots the same type of response. Charlie Cain in a *Detroit News* piece reviewing her first one hundred days in office reported, "Her outgoing style and intelligence already spur talk that she could be a possible candidate for governor in 2002."

Granholm dismisses the growing speculation saying, "It's flatter-ing (but) I just want to be attorney general."

That's her story and she is sticking to it. She does huddle behind closed doors with her staff to discuss how to handle the seemingly unending speculation. She does not want to run. There is no ques-tion of that in her mind, but she is running all over the state as part of her attorney general duties. If there's a group to address, she is there. If there's an issue such as adults who peddle porn in chat rooms, she's there.

Near the end of the year she is onto another crusade, nabbing liquor companies that are using the Internet to sell liquor to under aged drinkers. After she does her thing on that, she does a little reflecting on the first year in office.

"Has it been fun?"

I always like to ask that question. It can be very revealing. All of the truly successful folks who work at this game answer it in the affirmative. If they don't, it signals they may be burned out, or look-ing for another job, or so frustrated that all the fun has been sapped out of them. If they are in that state of mind, it's a good story.

Granholm, not unexpectedly, was all smiles as she tackled the "fun" question.

"Well, it's been the greatest year of my life. It has been totally great," she gushed as my eyebrows went up.

"Better than having kids?" I asked.

"I was just going to say, all right, I take that back. Having kids was really great. Getting married was really [heavier emphasis] great. This has been third, how's that?" And now she's laughing.

"This has really been phenomenal." She explains the true legacy of Frank Kelley is the "great staff" she inherited.

"What's been the toughest to adjust to?" I go on.

"Probably this stuff," she reveals gesturing to the microphone and camera grinding behind me.

"What?" I am shocked given her naturalness on camera.

"Yeah," she doesn't change this answer.

"This was something I was never used to . . . the politics part of it has been difficult to adjust to. It's not something that I did before, and I've had to sort of hit the ground running and learn about that."

There, in two sentences, was why I believed she was not interested in the governor thing. If she's trying to figure out the politics and learning on the run, and winging it, she knows deep down inside, she is not ready.

There was another reason she had me convinced. Over the years I have found that when you turn the camera off and ask the same question, you sometimes get a slightly different answer. To the naked ear it might not be much, but you can tell if there is more to the story than you captured on tape. I tried that technique on her time and time again and each time, there was no equivocation. She was not interested. Period.

Turns out the Republicans were more worried about her running for governor than she was. Ironically, in the end, that attitude moved her from no to yes. As noted, the Granholm for governor stuff was all over town. Republicans monitor the media too and somebody decided something needed to be done. A handful of ill-advised GOP house members felt this was a great time to perform major surgery on the attorney general's powers. In a nutshell they wanted to wipe out some of her authority.

The story grew to epic proportions and finally came to a show down in a house committee room on the third floor of the house office building. The room was packed. There was some heavy tension in the air. At the front of the room was committee chair Rep. Mike Bishop, who ran the House Committee on Constitutional Law and Ethics. The panel was inundated with attorneys who knew as much about the law as she did, but didn't know squat about taking on a woman in public.

We had a camera in the hallway as Granholm came in accompanied by Frank Kelley. They both had their game faces on. She immediately went up to shake the chairperson's hand, which is what protocol demands. She then retired to a seat in the audience to await her summons. It didn't take long. As a silence engulfed the room, she took a few steps to the table at the apex of the horseshoe committee bench and opened her black notebook.

In her speech this time there were no "chilly" or "freezing" references but there could have been given the "icy" nature of the conflict between her and them.

The GOP had a dual agenda. Sure they wanted to dilute some of her powers, but the hidden motive was to cut her down a notch. They will deny that, but there isn't a member of the press corps that didn't believe it. They were preoccupied with her possible run for governor. Their agenda was to knock her off her game and give her some second thoughts about running for governor, even though she harbored none herself.

She had a delicate assignment. She had to be respectful of the committee process and the right of lawmakers to delve into this issue, but she also had to stand up for what she believed in and she believed these clowns were out in left field. (My words, not hers.)

"This is shameful. This [legislation] is . . . to dismember the office of the attorney general," she got in the first blow. Never one to mince words, she laid it on the line. The committee, which foolishly felt it would win this P.R. war, would not back down either.

Rep. Bishop (R-Oakland County) said, "You're an attorney, right?" It was disrespectful and arrogant. It played right into her hand. Rep. Andrew Richner (R-Grosse Pointe) claimed he couldn't find anything in state law that gave her the right to issue an opinion that was binding on the entire state until the courts ruled on it. He and state senator Bruce Patterson (R-Canton) argued she was acting like a court and a legislature all in one. And they didn't like it one bit.

"We're not making law, we're clarifying law," she lectured the law school graduates. Later she tossed in, just in case they missed it the first time, "I don't make the law. I interpret what you do."

At the outset of her testimony Chairperson Bishop, acting like a judge instructing the witness, told her to stick to the subject and not make political statements.

"I'm not the one here with the political agenda," she fired back. You couldn't hear it but her handlers must have gone under their breath, "YES!"

It was not a fair fight. It was all those guys against this new attorney general. She had been on the job ten months and the impression was, rightly or wrongly, that the guys were trying to take advantage of her. They had never tried to water down Frank Kelley's authority, but now that he was on the sidelines, they felt she would be easy picking's. Dumb.

Granholm's time on the stand was so long, that nobody else got a chance to testify. Kelley was especially livid. The committee let him stew. It certainly bruised his ego and worse yet, he never got in front of the cameras.

The hearing was a public relations nightmare for the GOP. Instead of dismantling this rising Democratic star, they managed to add more luster to it. She demonstrated for the first time that if she took a high hard one, she would stand in there and give it back. It was a skill she had learned in court and one she would apply against David Bonior, Jim Blanchard, and Dick Posthumus in 2002.

On *OTR* that week the GOP took a beating. It was pointed out that if the Republicans had actually thought about it, the best way to handle this legislation to realign her powers, which by the way had some merit, was to do it behind closed doors. Invite her to the table and negotiate the differences without the cameras and audience. She would not have had the public platform that they gave her. Maybe in the end, there would not have been a compromise, but the GOP would not have looked foolish either. In this town where perception is everything, that would have been a plus. As it turned out the GOP strategy was a bust. At the end of the year she summed up the confrontation this way, with a smile. "I learned that reasonable minds can prevail and eventually they would do the right thing which was not to dismantle the office that has stood for 160 years. They put it on the back burner." She was relieved, but the GOP wasn't finished.

The next time she appeared on *Off the Record*, she was not in the hot seat—I was!

Periodically, we do turn the tables around, a program where four officials get to grill me. If we did this every week and charged the participants, we could reduce the national debt. I asked Granholm to be on along with the Speaker of the House Chuck Perricone, the House Minority Leader Buzz Thomas and the acerbic comic from Oakland County, L. Brooks Patterson who ran county government.

She came loaded for bear. I let her start the questioning.

"Who did you vote for in the last attorney general's race?" she opened the festivities.

"I'm not going to tell you. It's none of your business," I tried to wiggle out.

Getting into her trial attorney role, she came back with "Who did you vote for president last time?"

"McGovern," I joked. Then I decided to be serious by saying, "Let me try to answer that question without answering it. You guys are used to that."

Laughter around the table.

I indicate that had I lived in Oakland County I probably would have voted for Republican Patterson, but if I lived in Detroit I probably would have voted for Democrat Thomas. My point was, I vote the person not the party, and suggested that anyone who voted a straight ticket was "irresponsible."

Granholm, who is as competitive as you can get, was not through.

In rapid fire succession she asks, "Ever have a bumper sticker on your car?"

I should have said, "Yes, I break for reporters." But my real answer was "No."

"Did you belong to any groups in college?"

"Nope. I was asocial."

"What was your major?"

"TV and radio, now everyone thinks I can now repair them."

"What magazines do you get at home?"

"None."

Brooks jumps in, "Have you ever had sex with Connie Binsfeld?"

The panel goes bonkers with that crass remark. I tell him we will edit that out. We don't.

But she is still not done.

"Did you file your taxes today?"

I had requested an extension.

And finally she wants to know, "How much did you give to charity?"

It was a fairly good amount and most of it went to our church.

"You go to church?" She seemed surprised. Hey in this business you need Divine help.

"Yes, working with you people, don't you think I should?"

Granholm is surprised to find out about my charitable contributions. About a week after the program, she sent a personal and hand-written note, commenting on my generosity. It filled both sides of the paper. It was a nice touch. Unfortunately it got lost and when I asked her if she had a copy, she suggested, "You probably made an origami hat out of it."

Back to Granholm grilling me on the program. It was clear that she was having the most fun. The others asked fairly inane questions. The speaker got on a trip about how I ambush lawmakers, i.e., run up to them with the camera running. I explain that I rarely do that, but I tell him that I respect his opinion and add that I really do like him. He won't let it go and hogs five minutes of the show to beat a dead horse. Granholm finally turns to him, "I just want you to know that you're really going down in terms of being his favorite guest."

One thing about her, she has a memory that won't quit, reflected by her next question.

"How many children do you have?"

"Four."

"Do you work full time?"

"Yes."

"Is it appropriate to work with children at home?"

That was the famous debate question I had asked her!

She concludes the segment by asking me about my dream job.

"I tell her I'm doing it."

"Which is why you've never moved on?"

"Exactly."

End of show.

In February of 2000, the GOP tried again to whittle away at her power as if they had forgotten the lesson of the previous October.

This time the powers of her office would be tested in the judicial arena. The GOP controlled Public Service Commission (PSC), which sets utility rates, launched a crusade to end the 167 year practice of the attorney general providing lawyers on both sides of a case. To the public that sounds odd, but Granholm claimed it was authorized by lawmakers, the Constitution and Common Law.

"It ain't broke. So what is it they're trying to fix?"

Granholm and Kelley both agreed this was just another attempt to do what they didn't do in the fall. Kelley told reporters in July, "This is like last fall when two junior house members introduced legislation and acted like they were running for sophomore class president." She noted again that they were after her adding, "The only thing that has changed is the sign over the door" in her office.

The PSC argued there was a conflict of interest. How could her office handle both sides of a case. Appearing on *OTR*, PSC Chair John Strand, an Engler appointee, said something Granholm quoted in her news conference. "He said on TV that the question of conflict is not even an issue in 99.9 percent of the cases." She told Strand if he found a conflict, she would appoint an outside lawyer.

There were several issues going on here. On the surface is the legal argument over who gets to appoint lawyers. What the public didn't know is that the power to select attorneys is a great way to reward your supporters.

The GOP knew Kelley had been doing that for years. He could farm out cases to lawyers outside of state government. It appeared Republicans wanted some of that action, too. Granholm concluded, "Anyone who doesn't think this is a raw power play is naive." After these two scrimmages, Granholm was more open to the run for governor. She certainly wasn't there, but on occasion she would now joke about it. Others behind the scenes, including her husband, were not joking. They were serious. Just as they had to persuade her to run for attorney general, the wheels were in motion to reprise the act, this time for the highest office in the state.

Ed McNamara said, "She did not want to run. We had to convince her to get in. Before discussing the decision to run for governor, Dan Mulhern [her husband] walked us through how he helped persuade her to seek elective office in the first place."

When Jennifer Granholm and hubby Dan moved to Michigan in 1987, there was plenty of talk about running for office, but all of it centered on him not her. He considered running for Detroit City Council. He did not.

Along the way the family moved from Detroit to be in the congressional district for Congressman Sandy Levin where Dan was employed. That was 1992. Dan still sort of had the bug for office and consulted with an old friend of Mayor Coleman Young.

"If you're me, what do you do?" he asks seeking wisdom and guidance.

He's told to stay out of local politics. It gets too messy, controversial, and "you get beat up more." He's told to look for higher office. During this entire time there is not one word about her running for anything save perhaps running the kids around town to soccer practice and the like. Fast forward to 1998 and Mulhern describes "rumblings" about Frank Kelley retiring. He is 100 percent behind nudging his spouse into the contest. The two of them leave for a Memorial Day weekend with law school chums in Chicago. Mulhern helps to kill time during the five hour trek by putting the hard sell on her but he gives her plenty of room to do what she wants.

The two are at somewhat of a disadvantage in that they are in the "Wayne County orbit." That means they have no direct ties inside the Lansing loop, but he is not deterred as he begins his pitch.

"If Kelley quits, this is a moment. With our young family it will be a short campaign. You have the gender thing on your side and the criminal and civil law experience. The stars are really aligned," he goes on.

She will have none of it and notes that, "I can't raise the money."

He will have none of that. "Politically this is the moment."

They do their thing in the Windy City including talking with those law school friends who seemed surprised at the prospect. Remember this woman has never even hinted at a political career. By the time they are back in the van headed back to Detroit she is asking him, "What do we do?"

They are off and running. The decision is made one week before Kelley makes his intentions known and once he says he is leaving, she is too. She leaves for Mackinac Island to get the word out that she is interested in becoming the state's first female attorney general.

The popular wisdom is there was never any discussion about Granholm running for governor until about two years before the 2002 election. Not true. Husband Dan says when she decided to go for attorney general, he also raised the point that she would be a natural to run for governor.

"Don't be ridiculous," she sternly replies. She doesn't want it, and frankly doesn't believe she is ready for it. The subject remains dormant between them, but the speculation begins to grow outside the family circle. It's now right around Thanksgiving 2001. He and she are again headed to Chicago to celebrate the holiday with his sister's family. This time the three kids are riding in the back without a clue that their lives are about to change without them knowing it.

It's now become a tradition that trips to Chicago include a discussion about her running for office.

"This time I am more forceful," Mulhern recounts. I told her, "she was the best person to do the job" of governor. She does not repeat her 1998 comments about not being ready and not wanting it. Over the two years as attorney general she had read the media accounts, allowed her ear to be bent by Wayne County operatives, and clearly the seed is there for her to run. He just needs to help it sprout.

The family does their Turkey Day thing and aims the van back to Michigan. Mulhern ends the trip convinced that she will run.

"I thought on the way back it was clear," he says.

He is so convinced that when he meets his mom for their annual Christmas lunch near the Twelve Oaks Mall he tells her, before his wife joins them, that Jennifer is running for governor. Mom Mulhern does not appear overjoyed by this sudden turn of events. She concludes that it is "pretty amazing" that she is getting in. When Granholm arrives at the eatery after meeting earlier with Rick Wiener, the former state Democratic party chair, she sits down and her mother in law says, "Congratulations!"

Granholm says, "For what?"

"I was stunned!" Mulhern reveals. On top of that he confesses, "I was befuddled and felt kind of betrayed. I thought we were both on the same page." He said it was like deciding with your spouse how to handle disciplining your children and when you get there, she says one thing and you say another. He couldn't explain it and was getting impatient for a very good reason.

Around this time former Gov. Jim Blanchard was making all the appropriate sounds and moves toward getting in too. And speculation surrounded Congressman David Bonior as well. Mulhern felt his wife could pre-empt the field. "You can still move these two out of the game," he whispered in her ear.

Even though he thought "all the cards were on the table," Mulhern in retrospect says his wife's hesitation allowed her to "get used to the idea." The stakes were much higher this time for the family. It would not be a short two month campaign as it was for attorney general. This would be a forced march for eighteen months and he knew it would get "ugly" if she did not force the other boys out. Turns out, Blanchard played a key role in her decision. He "forced her hand" Mulhern reflects and "pushed up the agenda." Asked if there was a specific moment when she finally said yes, he says, "I can't remember one."

But several things became apparent. The once reluctant candidate for governor was now in the race although she planned to hold off a formal announcement until Labor Day of 2001. And Mulhern made a mental note. If he wanted to persuade his wife to run for office, he needed to "head West" as he affectionately puts it. After all he was two for two on trips to Chi-town.

The folklore surrounding Granholm's rise to political prominence credits Mike Duggan of Ed McNamara's office with being the first to notice her ability to communicate via the tube.

As the story goes, Granholm went to dinner at a Detroit restaurant with her friend Butch Hollowell and his wife. The trio could not get seated and concluded it was because two of the party were African Americans. They decided to press the issue and Granholm was tapped to do the media stuff. The first time Duggan saw her on the tube he concluded if she ever ran for anything, she would kill'em dead.

Columnist Hugh McDiarmid was among the first to put the Granholm for governor speculation in print. His June 19, 1999 column quoted commentator Bill Ballenger. He tells Mac that Granholm "will probably be pushed into it." He gave her the edge in capturing the nomination. Remember this is long before she made any decision to even think about it. That shows you how far ahead the rest of the political world was in regard to her future plans.

Speaking of future plans, how about a Granholm for president campaign?

To add even more pixy dust to this fairy tale story of the reluctant governor, there is talk of running her for president of the United States. She is even more reluctant to do that and has at least one thing going in her favor. She can't run.

The Constitution bans foreign born naturalized citizens from seeking the highest office in the land. But now, a growing list of influential politicians in and around Washington, D.C., is talking about changing the law, so that Canadian born Granholm could run. She herself favors the alteration.

The first person to embrace the concept was syndicated and conservative columnist George Will, and he did it in front of the whole nation. A few days after Granholm was sworn into office, Will went on ABC's *This Week* and called for what he labeled, the "Granholm Amendment." Then he proceeded to explain how she could not run for president unless the law was altered. Many in this town, including yours truly, thought he was joking. But a few phone calls later, it was clear he was dead serious. The fledgling staffers for the new governor who were still trying to find the washrooms were pressed into service to debunk the Will suggestion.

Here was history repeating itself. The day after she was sworn in as attorney general, the chatter started about running her for governor. Now that she was governor, it was her running for president. Granholm magic.

That same week Granholm was asked by the national Democratic Party to deliver a radio address in response to President Bush's weekly radio message. And of course, she did it and got high marks for doing it which meant her presidential thing went up another notch.

The spec story sort of faded into the woodwork only to surface in the midst of the 2004 race for president. During one of the Democratic debates U.S. Senator Bob Graham was asked his position on changing the law. Without missing a beat he said he was behind the effort because "There was a woman Democrat in Michigan who would make a fine president."

Clearly the Granholm magic had captured the imagination of a nationwide audience and the Will thing in January of 2003 and Granholm's endorsement were only the tip of the iceberg. Granholm's Lansing office was inundated with requests from *Meet the Press*, *Face the Nation*, and a host of cable shows too numerous to mention.

The print folks got into the act, too. Eleanor Clift flew into Michigan to depose the new governor. Clift penned a glowing review in *Newsweek* magazine that had nothing but wonderful things to say about the state's first female governor.

And the requests have not fallen off. The U.S. senate minority leader has joined the parade, too. During a news conference featuring Dan, the First Man, Mulhern, I started chatting with one of the Granholm media types.

"What's the one thing that has surprised you about working with her?"

"All the national attention," came back the not so surprising response. And then this source pointed to Senator Tom Daschle, who calls "weekly" trying to secure more Granholm appearances on the national stage. To her credit, Granholm has for the most part turned a deaf ear to the siren song out of Washington. It would be so tempting to succumb, but she knows she must tend to the home fires less she be criticized for playing with the Big Boys and Girls in D.C. (That was a common knock on Governor Engler in the last few years of his term in office.)

The Granholm for president stuff again went into remission only to be resuscitated with the recall election in California in the fall of 2003. The whole nation was engrossed . . . emphasis on the word "gross" . . . in the election of Austrian-born Arnold Schwarzenegger. With the elevation of him to the statehouse, the Granholm presidential story went back in the news.

Noted Michigan GOP pollster Steve Mitchell can connect the dots. "With the election of Arnold, now even the Republicans can vote to change the law so that by 2012 we could have a Granholm vs. Schwarzenegger race for president."

The Terminator vs. Wonder Woman. If we sold seats to those debates, the national debt could be wiped out.

You're laughing, right?

That's what Governor Granholm was doing when we confronted her with the issue days after the California recall. She explained that changing the law was a good idea, even though three fourths of the states would have to ratify it. "Because we are a land of immigrants . . . that is who we are as a nation, and if you put enough restraints on how long you had to live here or have been a citizen, I think it is perfectly appropriate to change the Constitution."

Such a statement only pours more grease on the fire which is why she quickly added with a chuckle, "But let me make it very clear, I am not interested in running . . . " (and here instead of completing the statement with a clear comment, she fumbles around for words that don't make any sense) "to, to make sure I suppose what you were going to ask me next."

What?

Then she does add in clear terms, "I'm not interested."

Which is exactly what she said about running for governor.

9

First Ladies

The role of the first lady in this state has been a work in progress over the last thirty-four years. The state has been blessed with four women who occupied that unelected office during my time as a capital correspondent: Helen Milliken, Paula Blanchard, Janet Fox, and Michelle Engler. Mrs. Milliken was the pioneer in an arena where men sometimes had no use for the title or the role.

The 1982 GOP primary for governor was a wide open affair. Milliken had decided to retire making it an open field for Dick Headlee, Brooks Patterson, John "Jack" Welborn, and Jim Brickley who was Milliken's choice.

The quartet appeared in one of our primary debates on *OTR* and the question was, "What role would your wife play in your administration?"

Remember this was over twenty years ago and conservative state senator John Welborn was direct, " My wife is a housewife, and that's where she wants to remain and that's where she will remain . . . she will not be out carrying on special programs. The governor is the one that's being elected . . . "

Next was insurance executive Dick Headlee who had a delightful wife Mary. But if Headlee had his way, none of the citizens in Michigan would ever see that side of her. "Well I don't think there is a role for the wife to play. We are electing a governor to manage the state like a business and bring jobs to Michigan. My wife is very supportive. She's a great team player, and obviously she'll do whatever is necessary to bring credit to the position of first lady of the state."

Patterson from Oakland County pretty much fell in line although he at least acknowledged that his wife had some talents, but not for governing the state thank you very much. "My wife and I have an understanding that, should I be the governor of the state, I'd make the decisions that affect the state. She would like to play a part as a team . . . for instance, my wife is a fantastic artist. She would like to donate art to charity and raise funds for special projects and things of that type. But actually in the government process? No."

Candidate four, Jim Brickley who was the most moderate of the group, had an easy out to the question. "I don't know because I'm not married and I haven't thought about it, so I don't see any need to answer it."

All in all a rather unusual answer for Jim Brickley who had been married the first time he served with Milliken and then divorced when he went to E.M.U. At the time of the debate his love interest was Milliken's inner circle advisor Joyce Braithwaite. The two would eventually marry, but as you have already read, he lost to Headlee in the August 10 balloting.

But back to Mrs. Milliken who came into office with her husband. She stood at his side as he took the oath of office in the tiny executive office on the second floor of the capitol. And after that you never saw much of her. That's the way she wanted it. Braithwaite reports that Mrs. Milliken was shy. "When she was introduced to a crowd she had all she could do to get up and say thank you."

Mrs. Milliken was more than content to work on her landscape architecture degree at Michigan State University and apply her vast talents to the yard at the executive residence and at the Milliken home in Traverse City. In reality this was a woman of great political substance and aplomb. It's just that nobody had really seen it until her maiden voyage on *Off the Record*. That was six years after becoming first lady.

In this modern political era where spouses are fair game and very out in front on a variety of issues, Mrs. Milliken never did an extensive TV interview on her own for six years. It took a hard sell from

Braithwaite to get the first lady to take the plunge. Braithwaite says,when Mrs. Milliken married her husband, "She didn't have a clue that there would be a public role for her."

I had been asking for quite some time to interview her and finally Braithwaite convinced the first lady that "You will be fabulous." It took a couple of days, but in the end Mrs. Milliken said, "If you go with me, I'll do it." Braithwaite knew *OTR* was a hardball forum but she believed Mrs. Milliken "would not get the rudeness that men on the show got." Her instincts were correct.

The first lady's answers were living testimony to her honesty coupled with a sharp respect for what her words could do to her husband. At one point she was asked about her voting record and possible support for non-Republican candidates. She confessed that she did not vote the straight GOP ticket but declined to name names. Asked if that was to avoid political embarrassment for her husband she said, "You're absolutely right on the point."

The relationship between the elected governor and an unelected spouse was always interesting to explore and she was a gamer. She revealed what she termed a " low-key but substantial influence" mainly because the governor listened to what she had to say. The environment was near and dear to her heart and when there was talk of drilling in the pristine Pigeon River Basin, lots of folks heard from the first lady on that.

What about family disagreements, the nosey panelists wanted to know. She remembered very few "along the way" with the exception of a 1970 vote on the controversial plan to funnel state tax dollars in religious schools, the so-called parochiaid question. She was against it. He was for it.

Throughout his fourteen year tenure, Governor Milliken was tagged with the Mr. Nice Guy label, but the Mrs. had a different take. "I don't find that to be at all the case. As I see my husband operating, I feel he is very definite and very aggressive . . . "

As for living with him in the fishbowl town of Lansing, she suggested that news stories on "private lives" sometimes obscure more important issues. At the time of the interview U.S. Senator Don Riegle was embroiled in a smarmy story concerning another woman. Mrs. Milliken did not shy away.

"On the other hand, it seems to me a very difficult thing to just draw a curtain and say this side of the person is totally private and it doesn't affect at all his public life. I think if you are going into public life you've got to assume the risk that whatever you do privately is up for public perusal."

The far-reaching exchange touched on national politics and the reign of then Governor Ronald Reagan. "I frankly do not see him as a person of substance." And she added her husband agreed!

I can recall sitting on the set and looking into the control booth, there was Braithwaite watching intently. Now, some twenty some years after the fact, she says Mrs. Milliken went home saying she had done all right. It was an important first step that moved her down the road toward a more public persona. She would never hide in the flower bed again. In fact she became co-chair of the Equal Rights Amendment movement in Michigan.

After that *OTR* appearance, Mrs. Milliken was invited to join in on the *Evening with the Governor* series for the last fifteen to twenty minutes of the broadcast. It was always fun to see them interact and on the eve of them leaving office, they were asked to reflect on the race for governor that ended with the GOP candidate Headlee losing to Democrat Jim Blanchard.

Governor Milliken on a previous occasion said that Headlee "puts me in mind of an ass." The first lady did not go there but since she personally had become an on again, off again issue in the race, she did venture in.

Headlee had taken her to task for her very visible stature in the women's movement. She was a vocal and avid backer of the Equal Rights Amendment. For many conservative men that meant women would be using the urinals in the men's bathroom. I pressed and pressed the Millikens in a valiant yet vain attempt to disclose for whom they voted. Former *Free Press* columnist Hugh McDiarmid summed it up best when he wrote, "the only awkward parts of the interview involved repeated refusals by the Milliken's to say for whom they voted in November . . . Republican Headlee or Democrat Jim Blanchard.

That's private they said.

"And obvious," Mac correctly concluded.

Speaking of innocent remarks, to show you how far she had advanced after her maiden appearance on *OTR*, Mrs. Milliken agreed to appear in a roast of yours truly to celebrate the fifteenth anniversary of the program. She was in great form and delivered some biting lines that still ring in my ears.

Attorney General Frank Kelley introduced her to a packed house of Lansing insiders and other hangers-on who were there to see the grilling. There were fourteen roasters on the dais and she got the biggest and warmest hand of all.

She shook my hand as she approached the microphone and began in a gentle way characteristic of her image. "Well Poopsie. I hope we're still friends when this is done," she said as she looked me in the eye with a warm smile. The "Poopsie" reference got lots of laughs that night as the audience found out for the first time that in my disc jockey days, I used the nickname when I was Jeff "Poopsie" Stevens at an R and B station in Flint. She seemed delighted to zing me with that and went on to do it again and again. "When I told my husband I was coming here tonight to honor Tim Skubick, he said, 'Who?'"

The crowd loved it and went even crazier when she talked about the executive residence on Mackinac Island. "We loved going there," she told the audience "and the secret of the appeal of the island is that you can't get *Off the Record* on the island." Bam. Pow.

Now she had them eating out of her hand as she referenced the many years I had covered the Capital. "I'm sure he has enough information for a book [little did I know then that I would write one] but I'm sure as a broadcaster he never learned to write." That actually brought a sympathetic oooh from the crowd. At this point in her stand up routine, I was wishing she had never done our show.

On a roll she finished with a one-two punch. "Tim's been spat at, maligned, sworn at . . . .and rightfully so. And if ignorance is truly bliss, Tim is one of the happiest people in the world!" Shouts, applause, and laughter erupted as she returned to her seat, giving me a brief kiss on the cheek as she passed by me.

She was great. The rest of the roast was as off-color as it comes as the likes of Speaker Gary Owen, State Treasurer Bob Bowman, Senate Majority Leader John Engler, L. Brooks Patterson, and others carved me up pretty good. Mrs. Milliken sat through it all and a few days after the broadcast I wrote her a note apologizing for the rough and tumble humor she was forced to sit through. She never complained. I was honored that she would drive all the way from Traverse City to tell the audience "When Tim was little he wanted to be on television in the worst way . . . and that's just the way he did it."

Now years out of the public eye, the Millikens still reside in their home on Grand Traverse Bay and occasionally I see them both. One day Mrs. Milliken invited me into her front yard, where she has a wonderful garden. She was composting and shared with me the finer points of burying rubbish, which she advised me to do. Always one with a great sense of humor, I think she appreciated my line, "I only cover garbage. I don't bury it."

Paula Blanchard

Jim and Paula Blanchard's only teenage son is sitting in the principal's office at Okemos High School . . . a very upscale school just outside of Lansing. Mom and dad are with him. Jay has done nothing wrong. He's there with his parents to discuss going to Okemos when he enters the ninth grade.

When the principal asks Jay if he has any questions, the first thing he asks is, "Do you have fights at this school?"

First Lady Paula Blanchard finds it to be an odd question and afterward she belatedly discovers its origins. Her son finally discloses that during his years at a Lansing junior high school his lunch money was stolen, he had been picked on, and he had a personal bodyguard, fellow student Bobby Richardson, to protect him from the taunts of the other students who knew he was the first son.

Mrs. Blanchard is shocked as any mom would be on discovering that not only had those events occurred, but that her son had never revealed it before this time. This was only the beginning of a news story that refused to go away until Paula Blanchard made it go away.

The Blanchard family was at Okemos because the state police security details, according to the former first lady, had "great concerns" about sending Jay to Sexton High School also in the Lansing district.

"They told us there were weapons around that school and they strongly suggested finding another high school for Jay to attend," she recalls.

She said they considered sending him to Cranbrook, an expensive and very high-end private school in Oakland County. Mrs. Blanchard refused to sign off saying, "He was my only child and I didn't want him to leave the nest." Her husband felt the same way.

The Blanchards liked the treatment they got from the Okemos school officials and the decision was made to send Jay there. It was a decision with political implications that Jim and Paula weighed before they said yes.

They both knew that once it got out, there would be criticism that they were abandoning an urban school for a rich one in the suburbs. They stated, "We made the best decision for our child and were willing to ride out the criticism for the good of the kid," she says.

The news eventually got out and Detroit TV reporter Tom Greene got on the story, and like a dog with a bone, he refused to let go. Greene showed up at the high school trying to get pictures of the first son. The principal stood in the school house door and kept the tenacious Greene at bay.

One day Mrs. Blanchard got a phone call from the principal explaining that, "This is becoming a real problem." Mrs. B. decided to take matters into her own hands and without asking her husband she called the station manager at WDIV-TV where Greene worked.

"It was 11 P.M. at night and I had her number," Mrs. Blanchard recounts. "I told her I really want you to think about the price of this story." By that she meant she wanted Greene's boss to weigh the impact on Jay. Here was a kid, she explained, in a new school with no friends, the governor's son, students talking about him behind his back and having to confront this burly reporter who refused to go away.

The conversation lasted five minutes. Amy McCombs gave no promises but did say she would look into it. Blanchard hung up the phone not knowing what would be next.

Greene stopped pursuing the story for one thing and sometime after that he wasn't chasing any stories. He was no longer an employee. He proceeded to sue and Paula Blanchard ended up as a witness in the case. She was grilled on the stand but stood by her son explaining to the jury that she was not responsible for Greene's loss of job.

Dealing with Jay's problems was just one of the challenges this first lady tackled. The other major one was, "my whole life was consumed by my husband's job. There was so little time or emotional energy for me. I got the crumbs of his time and attention emotionally."

Being governor is a full-time job and the duties are not confined to the eight-to-five time frame. Jim Blanchard was a hands-on governor who was everywhere and that often meant the first lady finished second on his schedule.

But it was not always that way.

Before they came to Lansing it was Paula and trusted Blanchard advisor Ron Thayer who always talked about the "Big Picture," which was code for running Jim for governor. Blanchard served with distinction in Congress but when Ronald Reagan was elected in 1980, the Big Picture suddenly got clearer.

"The prospects of eight years of Reagan and being a Democrat in a Ronald Reagan town was very frustrating," says Mrs. Blanchard. "Ron and I wanted him to run for governor." He did and won.

She played a very active role in the campaign and while sitting in their Pleasant Ridge living room one night surrounded by campaign staffers, they were going over the A and B list of possible running mates. It was Mrs. Blanchard's suggestion that her husband pick Martha Griffiths.

The immediate reaction from the group was negative. They figured the former congresswoman would never come out of retirement plus she was making too much money. Paula did not give in asserting, "I think she would listen because she has a special place in her heart for Jim."

Indeed when he was first elected to Congress Blanchard treated Griffiths with respect and often asked her how to navigate the waters in D.C. Paula says Griffiths "took him under her wing and developed a soft spot for him."

The more Paula talked the more the group backed away from its original prognosis. Finally, "Jim got up on the spot and called her." He suggested that Martha and husband Hicks join the Blanchards for dinner, and he let her pick the spot. She chose Chuck Joseph's in Berkley.

The quartet had a wonderful time but the subject of running mate was left for dessert. "Jim finally popped the question and she said yes. I was surprised," Paula says as she watched her idea come to life. The Blanchard-Griffiths ticket was a winner. Jim Blanchard recalls it allowed him to make an even stronger appeal to female voters many of whom were turned off by his GOP opponent Dick Headlee. He also maintains he didn't select her because she was a woman. It was because "She was Martha," he says.

After they won the election, it was time for the transition and the current first lady Helen Milliken invited the first lady-in-waiting for lunch at the governor's residence. Paula was accompanied by her son Jay and when they walked into the living room for the first time, she vividly remembers what she saw.

"All your technicians were setting up cameras for your *Evening with the Governor* program to be taped that night. I should have recognized right then and there that this living room was a public place not a family place."

Mrs. Milliken apologized for the mess. It should have been an omen, Ms. Blanchard remembers.

Indeed each first lady over the years has observed that it's not the kind of room you can casually walk through to get to the kitchen for a snack.

"I felt every time I walked in there I had to have on a dress, a hat and gloves and a purse," Ms. Blanchard complains.

In the four years that followed, that living room was in constant motion. It was not uncommon for the governor to host three parties every week starting on Tuesday and ending on Thursday. It was the first lady's duty to be there too. Many times she would cover for her husband who often arrived late.

"It was hard work," she says. "It was emotionally, physically, and mentally draining and demanding." First of all she says you had to be in a pleasant mood even when you weren't. Secondly, you were on your feet for two hours at a stretch, and while you were enduring all that, you had to be on your toes mentally. You had to search your mind for the name of the person you were talking to and then try to remember what they did.

It never ended. My husband "was generous at using both the residences." That meant receptions in Lansing and then the whole shebang relocated for weekend gatherings at the stately home on Mackinac Island.

Those chores were in addition to her duties as an unpaid cheerleader for the State of Michigan. She established an office in the Commerce Department where she peddled the four P's: people, places, products, and pride. This was the fun part of her life. "It may sound corny but it was fun to meet extraordinary people and attend events."

Without knowing it, she was honing skills that would help her as a divorced single mom. She learned how to cultivate relationships, to tell a story, and learned the art and science of public relations.

By the end of the first term in office, Paula Blanchard had come to a quiet decision on her own. She would leave her husband and marriage. She told no one but kept it locked inside . . . until after her husband's reelection effort.

"I owed that to him," she now says years after the fact. She knew if she made any public comment before the election "It would make the reelection very difficult. I didn't want to do that."

As Paula Blanchard assumed a different role as her soon to be ex-husband took on GOP candidate Bill Lucas in 1986. Actually Blanchard didn't need much help from anybody as the Lucas effort was lackluster and seemed doomed from the opening bell. Blanchard won the election, but was on the verge of losing his wife. In June of 1987, the couple issued a joint statement announcing that there were "long-standing irreconcilable differences," which was the only grounds you needed for a no-fault divorce in Michigan. They also pledged to "continue an amicable relationship both personally and professionally." The announcement came within days of their twenty-first wedding anniversary.

"We hoped it would be a one day story . . . or at least short term," she says.

I have made it a practice to stay away from the personal lives of politicians. But this was one story I could not ignore especially when it was handed to me on a silver platter. Imagine my shock when a house Democratic lawmaker pulled me aside in front of the chambers on that fateful morning and said, "Skubick, the governor and his wife are filing for divorce today. I was told that at a breakfast this morning." Then this source proceeded to tip me off that the two attorneys for the plaintiff and the defendant would be in the Ingham County clerks office at noon. It was about 10:30A.M. I told no one and counted the minutes before I walked across the street from the Capitol to Lansing City Hall. I recall walking down the hallway to the clerks office not knowing who would be there and then suddenly I recognized both lawyers. There was Tom Lewand, Blanchard's

personal friend and former chief of staff. He was signing and handing papers to Camille Abood, a prominent Lansing barrister. They
turned around as I walked in the room. They were shocked to see
me. I can't remember my exact words, but I apologized for being
there, but they knew I was just doing my job. They asked if I would
wait in the hallway until they finished their business then they
would consent to a radio interview. I mentally did a double-check to
make sure there was no other way out of that office and then agreed
to their request.

The papers were filed and I was sitting on the biggest story of the
day. They each gave me a brief comment and I was off to the phone
booth on the same floor to go live on WWJ at 12:30 P.M. Somebody
picked up the phone in the newsroom. I'm sure they could hear the
excitement in my voice since it was higher than normal. "Get me on
the air now. The Blanchard's are getting divorced." For just the second there was silence on the other end. There's a huge rush for all
the players involved in a breaking story that no one else has.

The anchor that day was John Delmonache, a veteran broadcaster, who came immediately out of the station identification with
this lead in "There's a breaking news story out of our Lansing
bureau where our capital correspondent, Tim Skubick has learned
the governor is getting divorced."

"That's right John," I began, and since I do all my radio pieces
unscripted, I have no idea exactly what I said after that. I know I did
lay out the specifics and recounted that I had talked with the two
lawyers so everyone knew the story was legitimate. The obvious
question from John was, did we know this was coming? Good question. There had been talk in town about some "problems" but I felt
everyone, except perhaps only their closest friends, were as surprised as I was.

That night at 6 P.M., I was doing the story live from the empty
executive residence for WJBK-TV 2 in Detroit. Since neither of the
Blanchard's had been available that day, I was lucky to have some
archive stuff of them when I interviewed them in 1983. I ran that
clip and then did some MOS . . . man and woman on the street reaction and fielded numerous questions from the two anchors. It may
have been a hot story, but it was very sad. It was an all too common
story in the political and journalistic world where three out of four
correspondents are divorced.

I still have that videotape from that broadcast in which I speculated on the political fallout and how it might affect the governor
just into his second term. "In the end, I think the media will come
out looking worse than Governor Blanchard," I told the Detroit TV
audience. "That's because a couple of non-political types I spoke to
today in effect said, "Why don't you leave them alone." If that turns
out to be the prevailing attitude, the governor wins and we (the
media) lose," I suggested.

Over the years it's fair to say the media and the public are out of
sync on these personal stories. The media paws over all the details
while many in the audience believe, and correctly so, it's overkill.
That's why they put an on-off switch on radios and televisions.

The Blanchard divorce was not messy, but it was not a one-day
story either, as the Blanchard's had hoped. As the story wore on,
more and more people were telling their version of what happened.
It got to the point that Ms. Blanchard was tired of hearing all of the
wrong accounts, so she decided to take matters into her own hands,
just like she did with Jay going to Okemos High School.

She wrote a book. "Our divorce was a public story," she reflects
"and I wanted to tell my own story."

"Jim tried to talk me out of it. He asked me to think about it
before I did it. Then he suggested I write a magazine article
instead." She rejected his suggestions and wrote the book.

After that she took the lessons she learned by promoting the Four
P's and parlayed it into a public relations job with Casey Communications in Detroit. She then formed her own company and remains
active in the Lansing area. She and her former husband remain
friends and when Paula decided to remarry she called Jim to tell
him. Being the classy guy he is, he wished her well.

Paula Blanchard closed that chapter in her life and Janet Fox
picked up the pen and began where the former Mrs. Blanchard left
off.

Janet Fox

Within weeks after the final divorce settlement was announced it
was time for another in the yearly edition of *Evening with the Governor*. Without his spouse this time, Blanchard and I sat down in the

executive residence living room and tackled the usual stuff, but I couldn't resist tossing in a final inquiry regarding his personal life.

I came at the obvious question through the back door. "Is there a political advantage to you being married going into 1990?"

"I don't know (chuckle) . . . Do you have any ideas?" he tries to bounce the ball into my court. But I remain silent.

So he goes on, "I don't know, I haven't thought about it (more chuckling) . . . I, um, you got me." Viewers saw him moving around in his seat which is one of the best nonverbal cues that I was onto something.

"Think about it right here," I refuse to retreat.

"Well I don't know that this is the place to think about that," he demurs again.

For my part I don't want to take the hit for prying into his personal life, so I frame the next $64,000 question putting the blame on others. "Your staff is the one that had me ask . . . are you going to be engaged soon, governor?"

(The speculation had been rampant for sometime about Ms. Fox and the governor so the question was legitimate. His response was a hoot.)

"Aw, c'mon (laughing)."

"I'm serious," I explain.

(More laughter followed by a patented Blanchard deep breath.) "I'm nowhere near that situation, and I'm not planning to make any social announcements here. I trust you aren't either," he smiles. Remember this is the guy who in 2002 promised not to fudge the truth.

The engagement announcements went in the mail exactly one month after the interview: "Governor James J. Blanchard and Ms. Janet Fox, are pleased to announce their engagement to be married in the Fall of 1989."

The two made their first appearance at the Mackinac Island residence two days after the mailing. In attendance were staffers and close friends who got a sneak peek at the new First Family to be. The soon-to-be former Ms. Fox had been Blanchard's personal secretary and as such had not been in the media limelight. Persons in those critical posts have an ironclad rule: Don't talk to the media. It took her awhile to figure out she could now not avoid it.

In a September first column, I suggested the bride-to-be had drawn a "schizophrenic line that not many reporters have crossed. Her press policy has been bumpy at best and unrealistic at worst."

While Blanchard-ites complained about reporters hounding the two and turning the story into an *Entertainment Tonight* segment, Ms. Fox granted two extensive interviews to newspapers. When a capital correspondent asked for equal time the response came back, "She is talking but not to political reporters."

The ruling was appealed to the press office and a few days later a delightful, contrite, and congenial Ms. Fox phoned me. She said she was not one to "put people off," but she was concerned about politicizing the impending marriage."

Nonetheless, she agreed to take my questions but just in case, she tape recorded it. Smart woman. She suggested, "Reporters have been fair, courteous, and good to me. I was not uncomfortable (being interviewed) to my surprise," she shared.

The two were married in a private and family only ceremony with no media cameras permitted.

Political writers are always sifting every angle on a story and on this one; some suggested Blanchard was getting hitched to enhance his own reelection prospects. In this game any far-fetched notion is fair game. There was no evidence of that, but in this town, that kind of thing is not uncommon. The two of them addressed it head on. Blanchard went first, "I would be a fool to politicize my marriage . . . our marriage. It wasn't a political decision."

She added, "He is the most wonderful person I know. He's sensitive. He's funny. He's so caring." That's about as apolitical as you can get. It was true love.

That tender sentiment came through loud and clear years later in Blanchard's own book, *Behind the Embassy Door*, which chronicled his years as ambassador to Canada. He had thirty-eight references to his wife often referring to them as "a team." In his final pages he added that he hoped it was clear the "debt I owed to the work, support, and love of my wife, Janet . . . she and I were free to share the joys and the burdens of the job, from the constant entertaining to the extensive traveling to the late night meetings . . . She was unofficially dubbed the "Ambassadrina" in recognition of her contribution."

Before the two left for Canada as part of the new Clinton administration, they consented to one last interview on *Off the Record*.

Over time, Mrs. Blanchard had wonderfully honed her media skills much like Mrs. Milliken had done before her.

The program came at a bittersweet time for the First Couple. Christmas was just a few days away. He had lost an election but both expressed optimism about the future.

Very much at ease she revealed that he had not wanted to run again, which he confirmed. "I probably was the least in my circle to advocate running for a third term," He confessed.

She told him, "You have all of these wonderful programs, why leave now?" As for the loss, she was asked what would you have done differently and wisely she noted, "When you're that far ahead until the very end, why would you do anything different." That was true. Blanchard had a hefty lead going into the final week but he and she saw it go poof.

The two of them talked about the pressures of being governor, which some contends works against a relationship. They didn't find it that way at all.

"We had a lot of time together . . . I can not complain about the last year and a half. I've enjoyed my role as first lady. We made an effort to be together, "she reflected and he concurred suggesting that he had seen other careers/marriages that were harder to manage.

"The governor's office and the two residences encourage the first couple to be together. It's easier to do than most careers."

"I think so," she adds.

Blanchard suggests high-powered attorneys and congressmen have a tougher job because there are no provisions for family within the confines of those professions.

She said even in a crowd of a thousand people, you can be intimate. "You can grab each others hands. It's the emotions that you have that are important."

He suggests that those with a good relationship can be intimate anyplace or anytime but "if you have a bad relationship you can be home every night and feel a thousand . . . miles . . . away (as his voice gets lower.) Anyone with an intimate relationship understands that."

One issue that each loving first lady has had to resolve is how to handle all the negative comments they hear about their spouses.

Mrs. Blanchard takes a page from her hubby's playbook. She basically ignored most of it.

"You might read the papers in the morning, but then you schedule helps you to forget about it," she explained.

What about that harsh criticism from Martha Griffiths when she was removed from the ticket? Surely the new wife was upset over that I inquired.

"We know Martha. We love Martha and we invited her to our Christmas party and she came last week."

That was some pretty rough stuff she said, I reminded her. But Janet sought no revenge adding, "Other people say bad things about him and I don't like that."

Concerning the decision to run for a third time, the governor reveals that if there had been anybody standing in the wings "ready and wanting to run for governor, I would not have run, probably."

Somewhat surprisingly he confessed, "If I thought the Republican was more in my mold than John (Engler), I probably wouldn't have run either."

He tells the audience he is not trying to rationalize his stunning loss. He says it was the right decision to run, "but I didn't have any choice if you think about it."

They both did think about it but quickly moved on. She suggested, "We had a highly visible political career and now we will have a highly visible business career."

It was clear they had their dance worked out as they left town for new adventures . . . together and clearly in love.

Michelle Engler

John Engler's first wife was Colleen House-Engler. The two met when they both served in the Michigan House. After their divorce she wrote a book about her life with John Engler. The word on the street was it was a tell all and let it all hang out dissertation—which was never published. Rumor suggests it's locked in some vault somewhere and likely never to see the light of day.

It's unlikely Michelle DeMunbrun of Texas was asked to sign a pre-nuptial agreeing never to write a book when she first met Engler in July of 1989. What she did agree to do was work with

Engler to keep her name out of the media while he ran for governor even though they were deeply in love.

Engler who had a penchant for protecting his privacy pulled it off even though the striking blond Ms. DeMunbrum did show up in the state and was even there on the night her husband defeated Blanchard. But nobody in the press had even a hint of the long distance romance and impending marriage.

Theirs was a quiet courtship that began in Florida in April of 1990 over Easter break. Engler was vacationing with good friends Dan and Colleen Pero who had planned their get-a-way to include their friend Michelle. She tells author Gleaves Whitney in his book *"John Engler: The Man, the Leader, the Legacy"*, "I had mixed feelings. Colleen and Dan had no intention of setting us up that weekend, they really didn't, but I just wanted to be with close friends."

She confessed to know nothing about politics so when John arrived, the two of them stayed up until the wee hours of the morning talking about "all kinds of interesting things."

Afterward she told Colleen, "I really like him. I really do like him."

To show you how myopic the arrogant media can be, at the state GOP convention in Cobo Hall where Engler got the party nomination for governor, his bride-to-be was literally waiting in the wings as he introduced his parents to the 3,000 screaming Engler lovers.

The *Detroit News* quoted Engler's running mate Dick Posthumus who had a ring-side seat for the rare display of Engler emotion and tears. "I'll never forget that state convention when John cried as he introduced his parents. There was a warmth there. I had never seen that John in public. I think it was all connected to his engagement to Michelle. His life was becoming whole again. . . . It helped that the warmth came across," Posthumus observed.

Engler and she decided to get married regardless of the election outcome. They talked on the phone each night and she noted, "He had such an inner drive that he kept himself going. I'd like to think that I helped him keep going, too," she told the *News*.

The rest as they say is history as the two were married after the November election in Texas and thus Michigan had another first lady.

Even though she suggested she had no political savvy, one of the first things she did was unload her foreign made car . . . a fancy blue BMW convertible. Her hubby probably filled her in on the political facts of life that one could not flit around Lansing, which was GM country, driving a foreign car.

After her introduction to the media the headlines the next day read: Engler is marrying a pro-choice, BMW-driving Democrat." She told Whitney, "I was in tears feeling I'm not going to be good for his career."

Nothing could have been further from the truth.

Three days after he delivered his knock out punch to Blanchard, Engler graciously agreed to do *Off the Record* and half-way through Hugh McDiarmid tried to get under the governor-elect's skin with some pointed inquiries about the soon to be first lady.

The *Free Press* columnist started out innocently enough. "I'm sure we're all glad you will have company in the governor's residence."

Engler smiled and said, "I know I am."

But McDiarmid wanted to know, "Will it mellow you at all that your prospective bride is not only pro-choice but a Democrat?"

"I've always attracted ticket splitters," Engler chuckled as he tried to weasel away from the cross-examination.

What about that? Mac continued. Engler suggested, "I'm a mellow guy. Mr. Affable in your paper."

"Will you answer that? Is this awkward for you?" Mac continued.

Engler never really did take the bait, but as it turned out her differing views had no impact on Engler's solid standing with Right to Life. Those who are familiar with the two suggest she did mellow out the man she married.

The mellowing went even deeper when it was announced Mrs. Engler would present her hubby with not one, not two, but three beautiful daughters. The arrival of the triplets came after arduous attempts and several failures by the couple to have children.

Mark Hornbeck was the first Capital reporter to nail the story and he did it by using an old trick. He called Mrs. Agnes Engler and started the conversation by saying, "Congratulations on becoming a grandmother." When she said thank you, he had his story. It was plastered all over the front page of the *Detroit News* the next day.

For awhile Hornbeck was persona non grata in the Engler

administration. The governor was not happy that his mom had been duped into confirming the story. That did not take away from the joy he expressed on Sunday, November 13, 1994.

"I am proud to announce the birth of Margaret Rose, Hannah Michelle, and Madeleine Jenny. Michelle is healthy and all are doing fine." As he described the birth experience, John Engler could not fight back the tears. Clearly his heart had been touched and many observers in this town believe the combination of a wife, whom he loved deeply, and three little babies allowed the public to see a John Engler who was anything but the aggressive-take-no hostages kind of politician.

Mrs. Engler was never shy about sharing her thoughts if you gave her a chance. I recall being at the Ionia Free Fair the day after the August primary election in which Democrats selected Geoffrey Fieger to take on Engler. It was a cold and somewhat rainy day and her mood matched the weather.

Fieger had earlier made a reference to the governor being the byproduct of bestiality and the only thing missing from the triplets was curly tails.

Mrs. Engler was not too pleased and she took after Fieger on camera suggesting that the people of Michigan did not want to deal with a candidate such as that.

"Anyone who will go after children is someone who I think the people of Michigan are not going to be real crazy about," she offered.

Her appearance at the fair was a complete 180 degrees from where she had been four months earlier when she and I talked about Engler's future.

There was some event at the Lansing Center that March and Mrs. Engler was there. I wasn't interested in the event per se but wanted to quiz her on whether she wanted the governor to run again in 1998. While the question would be direct, I expected her to waffle, turn on the fog machine and head for the nearest exit. Instead she surprisingly disclosed, " I'm not sure I'm ready to share him anymore.

"You're ready for a normal life aren't you?" I inquired trying to get more out of her.

"I think so and our children are getting to the point where we need to think about more than just John and Michelle . . . we need to think about our children." Spoken like a great mom who knew as her children got older the political fishbowl they were in would get more uncomfortable.

Based on those remarks, even a cub reporter could have connected those dots . . . . Engler was not going to run again, which is what I began to tell groups on the rubber chicken circuit around the state.

But a funny thing happened. She changed her mind and so did he. Engler broke a campaign promise he made on *OTR* in 1990 to serve two terms. Instead the Engler family went after a third term.

As first lady, one of the more trying aspects of her life was to confront a number of rumors about the strength of her marriage to the governor.

I can't tell you how many times I took anonymous phone calls at home with the same storyline: "Did you know Michelle has left with the kids for Texas?" They suggested the marriage was kaput!

Strangers would also approach me on the streets with the same stuff and other reporters were inundated with it as well. The intensity of the rumors would ebb and flow like the morning tide but they never went away. That is until the first lady took matters into her own hands.

In the Engler book, it's reported that the *Detroit News* was ready to run a story about the speculation and the Engler's were not happy about it. During a phone conversation with the first lady on the island with the governor in his office, it was decided they would try to produce a better story that would top the *News*. Mrs. Engler would come home and tell the *Detroit Free Press* that her husband was running for re-election and that all the rumor mongering was false.

The Dawson Bell article the next day trumpeted: "Engler Will Run Again. First Lady Puts Rumors to Rest, Says Governor Will Seek 3rd Term.

The first family had planned on delaying the reelection announcement but the intensity of the marital problem story, which the governor privately called "bullshit," forced them to move quickly. They did and it worked.

Unlike other first ladies who did not get directly involved in partisan politics, Mrs. Engler changed all that. In 1994 when she was flat on her back and under doctor's orders to stay there because she was carrying three tiny babies, she found the energy to record a thirty second radio spot for Dick Chrysler who was making a run for Congress.

He got elected and when his reelection came up two years later, he was knocking on Mrs. Engler's door again. And she answered. "Whatever the campaign asks me to do, I'll be happy to help."

Since Chrysler was running against Democrat Debbie Stabenow, Michelle seemed more than eager to take the opportunity in front of 1,000 rabid Chrysler stalwarts to take a poke at Stabenow.

She claimed the Democrat "had led a deceptive and malicious campaign against my husband [when Stabenow ran with Howard Wolpe for governor in 1994] all the while oozing sincerity and smiling sweetly."

The crowd loved the swipe even though most seemed stunned to hear it coming out of Mrs. Engler's mouth.

Afterward Engler was asked, "Weren't you a little nasty up there?"

"I don't think so," as she smiled sweetly adding, "I think truth is an absolute defense."

Reporters wanted to know if she would debate Stabenow. "Oh, I'm not the candidate." Maybe she should have, because this time Chrysler lost.

The bottom line on all these first ladies is that each brought her own dignity and style to the posts. Each got involved in a variety of projects from advancing the rights of women to putting food in the cupboards of the needy. They didn't seek the attention, but they got plenty of it. The political world today is a lot different than it was when Mrs. Milliken came to Lansing. She went seven years before the media noticed her. Those days are long gone. Just ask Paula, Janet, and Michelle.

10

The Great Tax Debate

Governor Bill Milliken was staging one of his regular news conferences on March 23, 1972. He was embroiled in a Byzantine
debate over getting rid of the property tax to fund education and not
having much luck.

Jerry Blocker from WWJ-TV in Detroit says he's talked to a
Democrat who wants to know, "What happens if the property tax cut
goes into effect and there's no other tax or source of revenue to make
up for that loss?"

That was the central question in the debate that Milliken and
others had not solved. It was exactly the same issue some twenty-two
years later when a different governor and a different legislature was
still trying to solve the same issue. They lecture in civics class about
the legislative process being deliberative, but the tax cut/school funding debate was more than that. It took state government nearly a quarter of a century to get its arms around the school financing monkey
that refused to get off the backs of well meaning politicians.

One of the first things Milliken did when he became governor was
to form his much heralded Education Reform Commission. Out of
that came a call for changing the way schools are funded. During a
broadcast in November 1969 with reporters at WILX-TV, Milliken

was asked about the need to move cautiously as he called for testing school kids, evaluating teachers, eliminating the State Board of Education, and changing the property tax funding system.

"To approach this question of education reform in such a cautious and restrained way would, I think, leave us ten years from now where I think we are today or where we have been ten years gone by."

The new governor boldly proclaimed in April 1971 that, "if the governor's plans were adopted, 1971 would be the last year in which property taxes will be used to finance regular school operating costs." 1971 came and went. No deal.

At that time some school districts were rolling in the dough, while others scraped here and there to make ends meet. The governor argued, "We must end the inequities among our school districts so that every child in the state receives an equal education." It sounded so good. So much was at stake. But a quick fix was not in the books. Not by a long shot. It's a textbook example of how the legislative process does not work.

However, Milliken came out of the legislative ranks and held the legislative process in high esteem. He was working with a divided body. Democrats called the shots in the house and Milliken's Republican buddies ran the senate. That meant some bipartisan compromise would be needed. He did not have the votes to jam through his blueprint in the house and had an even rougher go of it with his own party in the more conservative senate.

In pawing over his news conference transcripts for 1971–72, you can literally feel the frustration emerge in his words as each opportunity to resolve the question produced nothing. On July 1 1971 he was hopeful. "I feel, I continue to feel, very strongly that we must have some decision from this legislature on the reduction of property taxes." On August 12, there was only one senate Republican willing to vote yes with fourteen firm no votes. Milliken won't give up. "I don't think anyone yet knows how many votes there are or are not in the senate," he tells a doubting capital press corps. By the time Labor Day rolls around, Milliken is no longer in denial. He's all but given up hope on the legislature and intends to launch a statewide petition drive to get what he wants.

"I continue strongly to believe that the only effective approach to this problem is to see that we have a constitutional amendment which . . . will mandate a sharp reduction in property taxes for school operating purposes."

As good as he is, he cannot craft a compromise on ballot language because the Democrats want to roll a graduated income tax issue into the amendment. Democrats lusted for the graduated tax rather than the flat rate.

The flat rate applies the same percentage take to every income level no matter how much you make. Putting on a sliding scale would mean the rich would pay more and the poor would pay less. Democrats loved it. Republicans did not. Milliken sided with his party, which produced a stalemate on getting a solution apart from the legislature.

The one positive development for the increasingly impatient governor was the court system. In California and Minnesota, the courts had declared the property tax illegal for funding schools because it did not produce an equal amount of money for each district. Milliken warned the same thing would happen here if nothing was done. But still nothing was done.

He eventually launched his own petition drive. It sputtered as the names he needed were not rolling in. Some felt his language was illegal and as 1972 unfolded, he had to scrap that drive, redraft the verbiage, and start all over again.

In the midst of that, the cross district busing controversy burst into full bloom. Federal Judge Roth had declared the Detroit school system was illegally segregated and made noises about busing black and white kids to desegregate suburban classrooms. Milliken opposed that, saying, "Simply put, children, black or white, don't learn by riding buses." However he was against a movement to ban busing with a federal constitutional amendment. All the fury over that issue overshadowed the school finance reform issue, but the governor tried to link the two in an attempt to get tax relief back on the front burner.

For the first time in his young administration he decided to use the power of the tube to communicate an urgent message. The governor's advisors called and asked if WKAR-TV would produce a special televised message on the busing issue and school financing. We jumped at the opportunity.

Milliken arrived a half hour or so before the 7P.M. air time. Usually the Milliken crew was jovial and worth a few laughs. But not this time. From my front row seat that night, I recall a more somber tone. The governor looked determined. This speech came against the backdrop of the most emotional civil rights issue he and this state had faced.

The busing controversy was ripping at the very fabric of civility in the state. You had to be color blind to miss the fact that many whites were on one side and many blacks were on the other. The governor's goal was to bridge that divide and somehow find some common ground. His task was to get both races nodding in agreement, and not pointing their fingers at each other. It was a balancing act of severe importance if he was to avoid a race war.

He began in a slow and reassuring tone. "My purpose in coming before you tonight is to make two major announcements and to place in proper perspective the issues of inter-district busing, school financing, property tax relief, and other questions that go to the heart of elementary and secondary education in Michigan."

Since busing was dominating the news and was on everyone's mind, he tackled that first. "I will, at the earliest possible legal opportunity, appeal the Federal District Court ruling in the Detroit school case."

In his briefing with black state lawmakers earlier in the day—a smart move by the way—that message was not well received. Generally Milliken worked well with the black caucus, but this was not some run of the mill legislative issue he was facing. Emotions were high and anything that sounded as if Milliken was siding with the anti-busing crowd was greeted with suspicion among black lawmakers. He tried to address that in his speech.

"I believe it is absolutely imperative that Michigan move forward in a logical, systematic approach through what is presently an emotionally charged atmosphere."

He tried to reassure the audience that busing was not a done deal. He emphasized it may be an appropriate remedy but quickly added, "The Court has not suggested that cross-busing must be or will be the remedy."

With each paragraph you could feel him carefully weaving a message to lower the anxiety level in both races. He says he is appealing the ruling "not to evade the law and the facts, but to clarify the law and the facts." It sounded like a reasonable course.

But just in case there were some who doubted his motives, he added with emphasis, "No governor more clearly recognizes the moral injustice of inequity; and no governor feels more strongly a moral obligation to remove it—not only to correct an injustice, but also to preserve the very fabric of our social order."

He didn't reveal it too often, but when it was needed, he displayed his passion. It was clear from his words that he was serious about dealing with this racial crisis. He then turned to a discussion of how to address the inequity issue. And of course that meant education finance reform.

"The next question I want to discuss goes to the very heart of the equality in education, much more so than does busing. . . . The rulings of courts in California and Minnesota reflect for those two states what I have been saying about Michigan for the past two years . . . that our present system of financing primary and secondary education is inequitable."

He warns that court opinions are "rolling towards us. We would be irresponsible to sit idly by waiting for them to hit."

Despite his urgent language, that's exactly what was happening in Michigan. Nothing was getting done, which is why he and the attorney general took the unusual step of asking the state supreme court to rule on the legality of the state's school funding system.

If 148 lawmakers could not get the job done, Milliken and Frank Kelley hoped seven justices could help.

The last three paragraphs of that address captured the essence of Milliken the man, the leader, and problem solver. "There is no problem, including education, that people and their government can't solve together. . . . Frankly there is no job I would rather have than governor of this state. . . . I hope each of us, as we approach the problems in the months ahead, will speak to each other with calm voices, listen to each other with respect, and work together with enthusiasm. That's how we've done our best work in the past, and it's our only hope for the future."

The speech was over. It was a masterful job. He must have been pleased. And tonight as I read it again for the first time in thirty-three years, I realize even more the wisdom of this governor. Another might have been tempted to use flamboyant ruffles and flourishes to confront the crisis. Not Milliken. It was steady as she goes. One measure of understanding. One measure of confidence and determination. One measure of togetherness and a final one of optimism. That in a nutshell was Bill Milliken.

Fast forward to March 1972. Milliken got the first good news he had in a long time. The Michigan Education Association was endorsing his petition drive. But the organization was also supporting a companion drive to lift the ban on the graduated income tax.

"I very strongly commend them for providing this kind of leadership," an emboldened Milliken told the media.

It was a hybrid beast, but at this juncture Milliken would jump at anything. He said he supported the idea of letting voters decide both issues, but he would not back the graduated tax.

Hope was in the air—ill placed as it was.

The petition drive got off to a bumpy start and with one month to go before signatures had to be filed to secure the statewide vote, there were 150,000 of the 300,000 needed.

"It is no easy effort, no easy battle, but, in my judgment, it's the single most important thing we can do for the future of this state," Milliken said in words Governors Blanchard and Engler would echo years later.

Eight days before the deadline, they were 100,000 names short. The press corps figured Milliken would suffer another loss.

On July 11, however, three days after the deadline, Milliken called us in. The first question was, "are you a candidate for vice president?"

"I am not. Next question," he moved on.

He announced they had gotten enough names and singled out reporters Walt Sorg from a local radio station and Gary Schuster from the *Detroit News*.

"You figured we were not going to make it. Do you want to make any statement now? You'll have to admit we're on the way, wouldn't you have to say that? Or are you still predicting doom and gloom?"

That's the first and only time I can recall him gloating in front of the media. He dodged the bullet and criticism that he couldn't get the job done. But now he needed voter support to pass the thing. He was encouraged by a poll in September, but that was before the big boys went to work on the amendment.

Proposal C was targeted first by the giant AFL-CIO. The union was telling its members that a yes vote on C would mean a tax break for business on the back of the working class. Milliken called the charge "factually incorrect." He refused to call it a lie.

Near the end of October a citizen lawsuit was filed to remove the issue from the ballot, with critics saying it was "a disguised tax increase." Milliken called it an 11th hour scare tactic.

Then two days later, the United Auto Workers piled on, claiming "working families are going to be harder hit under Proposal C."

Milliken rushed in with a chart talk to explain away the charge. He had to concede that if you made over $20,000 you "will be paying somewhat more and families under it will be paying somewhat less."

Well you can guess the outcome on election day.

"Have you formulated any plans yet to overcome the defeat of the tax measures?" was the first question the day after the defeat.

"No, I think a great deal of discussion has now got to take place."

Wow. There was an understatement. The great deal of discussion would take another twenty years as there were plenty of other ill fated efforts in between. Democrats in the house who had worked well with Milliken on the issue wanted to go back to the ballot with another plan. Whacked once Milliken would not be whacked again. "The public itself has rendered its decision as of the last election. I don't approve of that approach."

In December of 1972, the state supreme court checked in with the ruling Milliken and Kelley requested. On a razor thin margin of 4–3, it declared that "Our present system of distributing financial resources based upon the wealth of local school districts violates the Michigan Constitution."

Now what?

Milliken in a "Report to the People" in February of 1973 retraced his steps back to the legislative arena and embraced the so called "equal yield" formula.

This plan meant that regardless of where you lived, the school millage raised in your area would produce the same money for every school. The state would make up the difference between the rich districts and the disadvantaged.

"For too long, we have tolerated an inequitable system of distributing money for education. We can tolerate it no longer." You've got to give him credit for not giving up.

Not everybody loved "equal yield." In fact Milliken's own lobbyist Keith Molin told the boss he could not in good conscience work on it. Milliken assigned somebody else to the chore, and it was adopted.

Milliken in October 1973 congratulated lawmakers. "We have this year adopted a milestone in school finance reform . . . an historic step forward in achieving equity in educational finance and equality in educational opportunity."

Notice he said, "step forward." The operative word is "step" which meant the problem was still there. Meanwhile winds were blowing on another front that would propel this issue to a more confrontational level.

In 1976 an initiatory petition led by anti-taxers asked the voters to approve a tax limitation amendment. It said state spending would be tied to 8.3 percent of the state's personal income. The outsiders were no more successful than the Lansing insiders. The plan went down in flames with 1.8 million saying no and 1.4 million saying yes. The next attempt came after some startling events about 1,500 miles from Lansing.

In 1978 the number thirteen became very newsworthy on the West Coast. More specifically Proposition 13, authored by a political unknown named Howard Jarvis. The ballot plan in California sought to cut property taxes. It slapped restraints on government spending and was promptly blasted by the governor and Los Angeles mayor. Governor Edmund "Pat" Brown told the citizenry, "If I were a communist I would vote for Prop 13." L.A. Mayor Tom Bradley chimed in, "This will hit the city like a neutron bomb."

Voters turned a deaf ear to both and Proposal 13 became law. The anti-tax crowd in Michigan was watching and tried to pick up where Jarvis left off.

An insurance executive named Dick Headlee became Michigan's Howard Jarvis. As a Mormon, he was close to former Governor Romney. The fact that he was an outsider made him instantly attractive to a suspicious electorate that was fed up with Milliken's feeble attempts to stuff some cash in their hands.

Headlee was also an instant hit with the news media. He gave great quotes. He often engaged his mouth before he engaged his brain but he also spoke the truth as he saw it. Often his advisors cringed and wanted to sanitize his remarks. Headlee would not play along.

He led a statewide petition drive for the Headlee Amendment. It sought to stop the legislature from creating new programs for local government and then sticking the locals for the cost . . . the so called unfunded mandate concept. It also limited the growth of state spending by cementing it to personal income growth. And it slapped a limit on taxes at the state and local levels.

Bingo. In November 1978, 1.4 million citizens said yes while 1.3 million said no. This was a step forward but it was not the huge property tax slice everyone wanted.

Yet another amendment appeared on the 1978 ballot to accomplish that. Voters said no to eliminating the property tax for schools and the creation of a voucher plan to funnel state tax dollars into private and other non-public schools. The linking of vouchers to the tax relief probably did it in. The vote was not even close. 2.1 million against and only 718,000 for.

This story is now in its ninth year when a crafty drain commissioner from out of nowhere appears with his own plan to change the way we fund schools.

If the well dressed Dick Headlee was polished and refined with an uncontrollable mouth, the blue jeaned Bob Tisch was unpolished, unrefined, with an even greater tendency to pop off. The media loved him too.

The Shiawassee Drain Commissioner quickly became a household word as he drove around the state in his "Tischmobile," which looked like the Flub-a-dub character on the old Howdy Doody kids show. Tisch himself was a gangly, six foot something cusser from the back forty. He knew he was onto something when he collected enough signatures to put his Tisch Amendment D on the statewide ballot.

Nobody in the Lansing crowd thought he could do it, but he showed them. When he got the required signatures he also woke up the Lansing crowd, which went to work to discredit both the messenger and his message. It worked. Tisch's Proposal D went in the dumper by a substantial 1.7 million to 1.0 million margin. Official

Lansing breathed a collective sigh of relief. They thought they were done with Tisch.

1980 was a watershed year for ballot proposals. There were three for voters to decide. The first was funded by the Michigan Education Association (MEA) under the title the Smith-Bullard plan named after GOP liberal Rep. Roy Smith and an even more liberal Democrat Perry Bullard. Originally they were going to call it the Bullard-Smith plan but they figured someone would tag it the B.S. amendment and that would be that.

Also out in the field was Tisch who reprised his 1978 performance with a different image. This time, instead of wearing his blue jeans with suspenders and looking like he hadn't shaved in months, the new Bob Tisch appeared with a big black DeSoto and a brand new city slicker suit.

His Son of Tisch plan this time would have cut the property tax, required a 60 percent vote of the citizens to hike any new state taxes, and forced the state to replace any revenue the locals lost under the plan. Tisch was getting advice from Headlee, and Tisch II got some momentum.

Noting his change in image, Al Short, the lobbyist from the MEA who'd been working on tax relief since they coined the term, took after Tisch claiming he was just using his crusade to run for governor. Tisch denied the charge, "Oh, I would never do that." Fact is he did in 1982, which put him right in there with all the other mainstream politicians who had trouble uttering the truth too.

Watching all this was the rest of the legislature, which crafted Resolution "X." This baby cut property taxes, added a sales tax, and fashioned a state Rainy Day fund. The real intent however was not to bring tax relief, but to confuse the voter. With three plans in front of them, the backers of "X" hoped to defeat everything. Their hopes were met.

The B.S . . . .oops..the Smith-Bullard thing got 746,000 yes votes. Tisch II got 1.6 million yes votes and "X" received 894,000. Problem was, over 2 million voters didn't like any of them. Now we are 11 years into the story and property tax relief is as illusive as ever.

In May 1981, yet another legislative scheme is advanced. Sponsors of this one think they have a sure bet because it contains language that earmarks all the lottery profits for education. Since 1972 when voters created the lottery, every time a lawmaker was on the stump, you just waited for this question to come up: Where does all the lottery money go? At the time it went into the general fund for all state services, even though there was a public misconception in 1972 that the money was supposed to go only to education. That was never in the lottery plan but citizens believed that it was. So lawmakers in 1981 felt this Resolution "G" would carry the day. It did not.

Tisch and Headlee both run for governor in 1982 and both lose. Bill Milliken heads back to Traverse City where he continues to pay the same property taxes on his Peninsula Drive estate that he paid when he became governor. Jim Blanchard comes into office promising to do what nobody has been able to do . . . cut property taxes.

But the anti-tax gang out of Macomb County led by Mike Sessa and Oakland County's Bill McMaster are unwilling to wait for the new governor. They formulate a hodgepodge amendment that has so many elements in it, you can't determine which side is up. It was a plan by committee that doomed it from the start. This thing was so bad that even Dick Headlee denounced it on *Off the Record*.

Patrick Anderson who worked for Headlee says he remembers watching the program with Tom Ritter, another Headlee advisor. When Headlee proclaimed that this plan "stunk" Anderson says that sealed the measure's fate. "We never recovered in the polls after that," Anderson now laughs. "Never have I seen one TV appearance turn an election like that one," he recalls. The 1984 plan got 1.3 million yes votes and 2.1 million no votes.

We now move to 1989. Blanchard has been in office for six years. The unresolved property tax debate is in year number twenty. Incredible, and to top it off there is still no consensus. Blanchard and legislative leaders give it the ole college try but cannot find a middle ground. So they do the next best thing—put competing plans before the voters who by this time must be getting weary, don't ya think?

Both plans propose tax relief with a hike in the sales tax. Both are rejected. That was Blanchard's last shot at paying off on his promise and forces him to go into the 1990 reelection cycle at a distinct disadvantage. John Engler is fixing to run against him, and can tell the voters that he will get it done.

Blanchard's point person on this issue says failing to adopt tax relief was "our biggest disappointment." Bob Bowman shoulders the blame, saying "We blew it . . . we refused to be the heavy by centralizing state spending for the schools." The administration focused too much on preserving local control over funding and thus we "never figured a way out of it."

All of the previous ballot plans had two flaws. The richer school districts fought the change because they did not want to give up dollars to poorer schools. The so called "equal yield" notion crafted years ago tried to do that. None of the subsequent ballot plans erased the "robbing Peter to pay Paul" fears.

The other flaw was giving the voters a choice without any negative consequences. That was corrected in 1994 when voters were told, if you don't vote to increase the sales tax for schools, we will impose an income tax on you. But it was still four years before that would happen.

Blanchard leaves office and Engler comes in. If anybody can get this done, he says he can. His first effort put him in the same sinking boat as his two predecessors.

Legislative Resolution "H" placed a cap on how high your property taxes could increase each year. This was designed to bring relief to senior citizens on a fixed income. While their Social Security check crawled up a percent or two each year, the bill on their home skyrocketed. But the MEA opposed the plan and so did 2.3 million voters.

1993 arrives and Engler has not delivered one cent of tax relief, making the nickel a week that Blanchard offered in 1990 look pretty good. But Big John is not one to give in, especially with his own reelection bid just around the corner in 1994.

Finally the stars appeared to be aligned with Legislative Resolution "G." Every special interest group you can think of is on board. You have the CEO of the Michigan Chamber of Commerce standing next to the head of the MEA teacher's union. You have former State School Superintendent Phil Runkel fronting the effort to give it some legitimacy. And the polling suggests this one might fly. Until a fly appeared in the ointment.

Messing around with local property tax revenue raised some deep concerns in the police and fire communities. Their paychecks were tied to that tax and it didn't take them long to launch a counterattack.

They tell the nervous voters they might not get an answer when they phoned the police or fire departments. While it was close, 1.1 million listened to the first line responders and 1 million listened to Engler et al. Another plan, number thirteen, is rejected.

About one month later, the beginning of the end begins. The governor and lawmakers, rebuffed by the voters in June, commence a protracted debate on property taxes on July 20, 1993. As the night wears on, Lansing senator Debbie Stabenow proposes an amendment to eliminate the property tax as the basis for funding schools.

On the surface it is an outrageous idea that no one, to this point, had even joked about. If approved, it would mean all the schools would have no revenue stream. How would you find a new one?

The two sides differ on what happened next. Democrats contend that Engler's senate floor leader Dick Posthumus saw the stupidity of the proposal and rejected it out of hand. Lansing folklore has John Engler calling in Posthumus and telling him to take the deal. Posthumus claims he was always on board, but either way Engler was willing to roll the dice where Blanchard and Bowman were not.

The elimination of the property tax over the strenuous objections of the MEA was adopted. Now what?

I am not proud to report this but on the eve of this historic vote, I was home watching TV. I did get a phone call on what was happening, but I missed an eyewitness account of one of the biggest stories of the last twenty-five years. (Had I known I'd be writing about it in a book, I might have shown up.)

Job one was to find a method to replace the lost property tax cash if the voters eventually adopted the ballot plan. After both houses passed it, both sides staked out their funding positions: Income tax for Democrats. Engler and cronies go for the sales tax increase.

Democrats have always felt the sales tax was unfair to the poor, since everyone pays the same rate regardless of income. Democrats argued the income tax at least captured more money from those who made more.

The governor conceded that, "there was a fundamental difference of opinion here between the two parties." So voters were given two options. If the people said no to the sales tax, then the income tax would go up. If they said yes to the sales tax, schools would not be funded with the income tax.

"Let's give the public a choice," Engler said. "You think you're right and we think we're right." The dye was cast.

In October 1993, Engler delivers what he terms a critical message to lawmakers on the education funding issue and after that he takes to the campaign trail to sell it, but he had to sell the GOP on the income tax alternative. "I had to talk Republican lawmakers into voting for a higher income tax rate," he explained in an exit interview in 2002. It was not an easy sell, but he did it.

Engler himself was not up for reelection when he went on the road, but he knew that if he didn't deliver on Proposal A, it would damage his chances of winning when he did run later in 1994.

Charts in hand and his best spin on the plan, Engler did one town hall after another and did a statewide TV appearance for public TV in the midst of the sell job. He took phone calls, fielded questions from a live studio audience and I jumped in with follow-ups.

At one point I tried to pin him down on the importance of winning this fight vis-à-vis his own reelection hopes. I suggested he needed to pay off on a campaign promise that was made four years ago and remained unfulfilled.

"Tim, sometimes fulfilling a campaign promise is a good thing," he lectured me with a smirk.

Meanwhile in the legislature fourteen members worked on the funding issue in anticipation of the March vote. There were hundreds of years of experience in those closed door meetings as the top guns in the house grappled with the nuances of paying for education. I can't help but wonder if term limits had been the issue what the end product would have looked like or if they would have even drafted one.

The March vote was held. They counted the votes and it was not even close. 1.6 million-plus said yes in virtually every county in the state. The no votes totaled just over 750,000. The longest debate in legislative history was now history.

That vote "deserves a place of honor on the mantle piece," Engler told me in 2002. "It unlocked the Gregorian knot of education financing that had been around for decades."

I asked if he ever sent a thank you note to Senator Stabenow for undoing the first knot, and in typical Engler fashion he opined, "Her role was pretty minimal."

"What? She sponsored the amendment," I reminded him.

Backing off ever so slightly, he conceded that, "I guess technically she was the sponsor."

So what's the grand lesson in all this? Sometimes the Democratic system is messy, incomplete, and frustrating. It would have been quicker if some dictator had come up with a plan and imposed it on the masses, but delay is the price for a representative form of government. When everyone wants input, it can take forever.

Milliken and Blanchard tried their best but came up empty because the voters and special interest groups could not agree. Engler succeeded in part, I believe, because he learned from the miscues of everyone else. So in a way the protracted debate really led to the passage of Proposal A. Each failure provided some guidance that slowly laid the groundwork for a plan that was eventually ratified. The mission impossible was done without riots in the streets or an overthrow of the government. It just took time and in the legislative process, everyone has plenty of that. This one just took a little longer than normal.

Next time you look at your property tax bill, know that it's lower now because of this twenty-five year struggle—the Longest Story Ever Told.

11
Pop Quiz

Here's a little game you can play with your friends. Have them answer this question: In the last thirty-four years what's been the most important political story that changed Michigan politics for better or worse?

These are the multiple choice answers:

(a) The recall of two Democratic state senators in 1984

(b) Milliken fails to turn reigns of power over to Jim Brickley

(c) Former Speaker Ryan redraws voting district so John Engler can win

(d) Blanchard raises the income tax

(e) Republicans control all three branches of government.

The answer is not a slam dunk.

The typical person would pick "B": Blanchard raising the income tax. True it was a monster story. It set into motion a wholesale redesign of the political landscape in the state, but answer "C" is the correct answer to the quiz.

I can hear the boos right now as you either scratch your head or nod your head in disapproval. Stick with me here.

I never knew it but in 1972, then Democratic Speaker William Ryan actually helped John Engler get elected. There was no way that Ryan could know that Engler would emerge as one of the most powerful governors in state history. What he did know at the time was that Engler was pro-life and his potential opponent, Rep. Dick Allen, was pro-choice. Ryan and his pals at the Michigan Catholic Conference wanted to send Allen to the showers because he was not pro-life. So Ryan went to work to make sure Allen would lose in the next election.

All of this is disclosed in the book *John Engler: The Man, The Leader, the Legacy* by Gleaves Whitney. Democrats controlled the redistricting process whereby voting districts are reconfigured every ten years to reflect shifts in population. The ability to set the lines meant that Ryan could give Engler a huge leg up in the primary against Allen. As Dennis Cawthorne recalls "The district was redrawn so that Dick Allen's house on one side of the road was in one district and his mailbox on the other side of the road was in another district." In other words Allen lost his original voter base that had earlier elected him. He was forced to run in a new district where the voters didn't know him but they knew Engler. It was not a fair fight and Ryan knew it. Allen lost. Engler won.

In a fair fight, it's possible that the younger Engler could have been wiped out by the more popular Allen. Engler's political career could have ended at two years. Instead he went on to last thirty-two years in this town and ended his career as one of the most influential and powerful chief executives of all time . . . all thanks, in part to an unsuspecting Democrat, Speaker Ryan.

Having argued that "C" was the most important story, let's look at the other answers in our little quiz.

Let's take the Milliken-Brickley thing first. Theirs was a wonderful relationship. The two were consummate gentlemen out of the same mold, although from different parts of the state. Milliken came from Traverse City lineage with a father who served in the senate. Brickley had urban roots in Detroit. Anyway, they made a good looking ticket both physically and politically and were able to squeak out a 44,409 vote victory over the Democratic team of Sandy Levin and Ed McNamara.

The next time Milliken ran in 1974, Brickley wanted off the ticket because of family concerns and his need to earn more money.

Milliken turned to another Jim to fill the slot. Jim Damman was an Oakland County representative who came into office with John Engler in 1970. He had a strong business background in the hardware store game and the Milliken-Damman combine was victorious over Sandy Levin and his new running mate Paul Brown. This time the win was by 114,618 votes more than double the 1970 margin.

As the next election cycle in 1978 rolled around, there were deep concerns in the Milliken camp about some alleged unethical conduct by Damman. *Free Press* political writer Remer Tyson wrote, "newspaper stories and an attorney general's investigation into Damman's role in a secret land company while he was a member of the Troy city council make him too much of a liability." To make a long story short, Milliken stopped communicating with Damman and quietly and surgically removed him from consideration.

That gave rise to one of the biggest guessing games in town. The capital press corps thrives on the little cat and mouse contest with the candidate. Can the candidate keep his running mate secret? Can the media find it out before it's announced?

In this case the thirty-five news hounds, including me, could not uncover the nominee. So when it came time for Milliken to reveal his choice, he milked it as much as he could.

The usual drill when a ticket is announced is for the two candidates to walk in together. It makes a good picture and that's what we expected. Instead, Governor Milliken walked in alone. He couldn't contain his grin as he knew he had us right where he wanted us . . . still guessing who his choice would be.

Milliken announced that he would leave the room and return with his running mate. Out the door he goes. He stayed out in the hallway for what seemed like five minutes. Back inside the news conference room, reporters are going bonkers, names are still flying through the room when Milliken returns with . . . Jim Brickley.

"I wish I would have had a camera to get the expression on your face, Tim," Milliken would reveal years after the fact. He had pulled it off. He called it one of the most rewarding moments of his political life. He had beaten us at our game. Nobody had guessed Brickley but there he was back for another shot at being lt. governor.

Everyone assumed the two had made a deal. Milliken would retire and Brickley would run for governor. But that was not the real reason, which is disclosed in chapter fourteen.

There's no debate that Milliken thought Brickley would make a good governor. All the very popular Governor Milliken had to do was tell voters, if you liked me, you'll surely love Brickley.

In the campaign of 1980 that's what they tried. Milliken decided to retire and Brickley ran. But conservative Republicans, in part lead by John Engler, who was now an emerging political force, had ideas of their own and it didn't include electing Brickley governor.

Engler took on Milliken's buddy Brickley by tossing an Oakland County insurance executive at him. Dick Headlee got in the primary along with Senator Jack Welborn and L. Brooks Patterson, also of Oakland County.

The popular wisdom was that it was Brickley's primary to lose which he promptly did.

I recall spending one day with the Brick on the campaign trail just before the August voting. "I've seen a lot of Headlee signs out there," he told me in the car as we whizzed by one. Turns out in addition to the signs there were a lot of Headlee voters out there too. When it was over Headlee had 220,378 votes to Brickley's 194,000 and some loose change. In other words, it wasn't even close.

The end of the Milliken era came sooner than Milliken expected.

Indirectly the John Engler era commenced.

While Headlee was cleaning out what was left of the Milliken wing of the state GOP, over on the Democratic side a field of eight contenders were slugging it out.

With Milliken leaving town, that meant the governor's chair was an open seat. That seldom happens, so all the governor wannabes in the world suddenly realized it's now or never, which is why so many of the Democrats ran.

The Harold Stassen of Michigan politics, the lovable and extremely liberal Zolton Ferency was in the hunt. It wasn't a race for governor unless "Z," as he was affectionately known, was there to keep everyone honest. His compatriots included Senator Kerry Kammer of Oakland County, Ann Arbor's state senator Ed Pierce, Wayne County's state senator David Plawecki, Detroit senator Bill Fitzgerald, whom Milliken had devoured four years earlier, Senator Gary Corbin from Genesee County and a virtual unknown John Safran from who knows where? And there was Jim Blanchard.

Blanchard almost didn't run. As this race started to unfold, the congressperson was sending mixed signals about his desire to trade a cushy seat in D.C. for the hot seat in Lansing. *Off the Record* played an unreported role in his final decision.

Blanchard was booked for the show and on the morning of the taping this is how Ron Thayer, Blanchard's bag man, puts it. The two were walking up the sidewalk to the studio and Thayer tells his pal that reporters are obviously going to ask him about running for governor. No duh.

Thayer is well aware of Blanchard's ambivalent feelings and says, "Just keep the door open. Don't close it all the way."

Blanchard does just that. He gives an answer that gives him wiggle room to stay out or get in. After the show aired, Blanchard reports the outpouring from would be supporters convinced him to do the latter and not the former.

Billy Fitzgerald had run an awful campaign against Milliken in 1978. He would probably disagree with that assessment but the proof is in the vote totals. Milliken by 391,000 votes.

Senators Kerry Kammer and David Plawecki had labored long and hard in the Democratic vineyards, but they were never in the hunt although they thought they were. Most candidates for statewide office assume they can win. Most don't.

Senator Gary Corbin was an interesting study. A low-keyed, moderate Democrat who was much like Milliken in style and approach, thought he could parlay his Genesse County labor support into grabbing the nomination. He was a Baptist minister by trade and was well respected in the highly partisan state senate. He was also the first one to drop out.

I had gotten wind of the fact that Corbin was going to withdraw within days. I called his home and got daughter Susan. I told her I was running that story and she broke down into tears. Now on the staff of Governor Granholm, Corbin recalls the call. "I was working on a paper that was due and just didn't want to deal with the story." The family was deeply supportive of daddy and equally disappointed that he never got any traction. Labor was going for Blanchard and within days of our story, Corbin packed it in.

The former mayor of Ann Arbor turned state senator Ed Pierce turned out to be the darling of the *Detroit Free Press*, which endorsed him in the seven-person race. Pierce was a little gruff around the edges and had that Ann Arbor air of arrogance about him, compounded by the fact that he was also a physician. But you liked Big Ed because he told it like it was, never played footsie with the facts, and had the touch of a prize fighter in him. He had a temper too and when you got a story wrong he'd let you know it in forceful terms. "Come on Skubick. You've got the whole thing wrong." And then after venting, he'd return to being the nice Mr. Ed.

This was a great time for the capital press corps. We had eleven candidates running all over the state trying to engage the voters who traditionally during the summer are more interested in going up north. Nonetheless the election was held, and Blanchard won the Democratic primary and Headlee secured the GOP nod.

It was on to November with the Headlee vs. Blanchard matchup, providing a striking contrast for voters to decide. It was a fun campaign to cover, made more interesting by Headlee's inability to keep his foot out of his mouth.

A good illustration came on the day Headlee was making a number of media calls to get some free radio air time. On the list was the student station in Mt. Pleasant. Headlee proceeded to use the name of First Lady Helen Milliken and the term lesbian in the same sentence as it related to the Women's Assembly that Mrs. Milliken had attended.

Moments after the taping, the student called Headlee's headquarters to see if it was OK to run the story. That is unheard of in the real world. Had it been a commercial station, the sound bite would have been aired first with no questions asked later. As a result of the phone call the campaign went into deep spin control trying to take the harsh edge off the Milliken/lesbian crack. One aide suggested to the student that Headlee was tired from doing so many interviews. Nice try. Finally, Headlee's anxious handlers, sensing a loss of more female voters whom they badly needed, conferred with the candidate and suggested a strategy to nip the controversy in the bud. Headlee would not play. True to his convictions he said, "I'm not apologizing for anything I said about Helen Milliken."

So it went until after his defeat when the Millikens finally checked in on the issue. The venue was the public TV "*Evening with the Governor*" series, which was an hour long sit down with the governor and his wife at the executive residence.

Free Press political columnist Hugh McDiarmid described the show: "This one was exceptional because Skubick invited Milliken to expound at length on his version of real politics in the Michigan GOP—particularly with regard to Headlee."

"I found that Mr. Headlee, beginning with the primary campaign, focused almost solely on the Milliken administration, attacking many of the things in which I deeply believe, creating a situation which . . . did divide the Republican party," the soon-to-be ex-governor confided.

Milliken was right, of course. Headlee simultaneously was running against Blanchard and the Millikens, which led the first lady to opine: "Frankly, I think Mr. Headlee shot himself in the foot. We didn't."

In another interview, Gov. Milliken was asked to sum up his feelings about Headlee and in vintage Milliken form he said, "He reminds me of an ass."

Any other politician might have connected the word "jack" to the a-s-s moniker, but not Milliken. "He reminds me of an ass" has to go down in political history as one of the all time great, yet sensitive, put downs.

At this same time the Millikens were drawn into another battle as the anti-Milliken forces stormed the Bastille. At the front of the line was Peter Secchia who made post-election remarks that stuck in the Milliken craw.

The tart-mouthed Secchia suggested that anyone who deserted Headlee, and surely the first family had without announcing it, should be shot.

Milliken's one word reaction: "Gross."

Asked to expand on the provocative statement, the ex-governor demurred. "Let that word in my response stand for itself." It did. Milliken concluded, "There's nothing, really, that I could have done to save Mr. Headlee from himself."

Those Milliken remarks signaled the end of that era, and as he rode out of town on Inauguration Day, there were tears in the eyes of reporters and supporters alike. This town would never be the same without William Grawn Milliken at the helm.

Next let's examine answer "D" which most observers believe was the event that shaped modern day Michigan politics the most: The Blanchard income tax hike.

During the campaign for governor, Blanchard called a tax increase his last resort, but his critics say he lowered his right hand after taking the oath and immediately moved to raise taxes. Before he did that Blanchard first commissioned a blue ribbon panel to advise him on how to lower the deficit. Budget cuts were in the plan, but when State of the State (SOS) time rolled around, Blanchard endorsed a 38 percent income tax increase.

During that first SOS Blanchard announced he wanted a tax hike and in the dead silence was the sound of one senator clapping. It was Highland Park Democratic state senator Basil Brown. Blanchard acknowledged him saying, "No, don't hear a lot of applause."

Also in the audience that night was a senator named Engler, as in John. He must have thought he had died and gone to heaven. Blanchard was setting the table for a huge struggle over boosting the income tax. Engler would give no ground. Compromise was not in his playbook. He would, however, squeeze out of the debate all the political advantages he could rack up.

Blanchard, himself no political dummy, knew he had to pass the tax with Republican support to give the public the impression that it was a bipartisan package. The governor's point man on the tax fight was his new treasurer Robert Bowman. For a time, Bowman and Blanchard were making some progress at wooing what was left of the moderate wing of the senate GOP. One senator was key to that effort—William Sederburg from East Lansing. Sederburg was not averse to a compromise. He was from a university town where voters understood you couldn't cut your way out of a deficit. Some new revenue would be needed.

There were others who were possible yes votes, but Engler sat on them to make sure they couldn't reach the green yes button. In the end Sederburg's demands were not met and when the vote came the tax hike passed with strong Democratic support and one lousy Republican vote. Battle Creek maverick Harry DeMaso, whom Engler could not control, bolted and Blanchard was more than grateful. The governor may have won the battle, but the war was just beginning.

The tax increase produced the recall of two state senators, both Democrats and both of whom were yes votes on the tax. John Engler contends he had nothing to do with it, but there aren't many pundits in this town who believe him, including me. The two senators were David Serotkin from Macomb County and Phil Mastin, representing neighboring Oakland County.

Both had ridden into office without much effort because they were popular back home. But soon they realized they were in for the battle of their political lives. Recall petition signatures were easily gathered as the anti-tax crowd went to work. Next there was an election and the media attention was riveting. We had never seen anything like this before. The stakes were high as both sides dug in.

The outcome should have been predicted. When the votes came in, Mastin and his pal Serotkin would win a place in our political lore but lose their place in the state senate. They were recalled.

But the story was not over. Next there had to be an election to fill those now empty seats. Republicans fielded Kirby Holmes from Utica and Rudy Nichols from Oakland County. It didn't matter who the Democrats ran—they were destined to lose. What kind of campaign could they run? They certainly couldn't embrace the governor and his income tax hike so the election was over before it began.

Holmes and Nichols came to the senate and with those two votes, the GOP took control away from the Democrats. Engler became the majority leader moving overnight from a non-descript political nobody from Beal City, to the man who would use his new leadership post to make Blanchard wish he had stayed in Washington.

Blanchard critics claim that after the recalls he never took another controversial stand, and governed with his finger in the wind, testing the political currents before taking any stance on anything. Engler objected to almost everything Blanchard did, but in the next election, Blanchard became the Come Back Kid. He won 68 percent of the popular vote sending GOP challenger Bill Lucas to the showers.

Engler took the loss in stride and plotted his next move: To defeat Blanchard in four more years in what would turn out to be the upset victory of all times.

12

The John Engler
You Never Knew

Governor John Engler was the proud new papa of three beautiful young babies when I encountered him Christmas shopping in a nearby mall. The crowds went rushing by, oblivious to the head of state standing in the local bookstore. He was trying to check items off his list like all the common folk buzzing around him. Beanie Babies were all the rage back then so it seemed only natural to ask if he was purchasing some for the triplets.

He didn't know what a Beanie Baby was!

That is retold here not to embarrass Daddy John or to cast aspersions on his fatherhood skills. Rather it underscores what some politicians give up in order to serve the voters. John Engler was so engrossed in being governor that he missed out on a worldwide fad. I thought to myself . . . how sad. What a price to pay.

But the essence of the Engler years was just that. He paid the personal price and so immersed himself in the job in which he had no choice but to succeed.

It might seem strange doing a chapter, "The Engler You Never Knew" in that everybody knew John Engler. They knew what he was like. He was bullheaded. His supporters would call him focused. He was a true policy wonk. He knew more about that state budget than anyone else in the room. His skin was as thick as a hundred elephants and while others would wilt under the heat of public criticism, he seemed to thrive on it as he redoubled his resolve to do what he thought was right.

But there was, believe it or not, a private John Engler. In fact the issue of privacy was very much on his mind as he prepared to become governor in 1991.

Three days after he was elected, Engler was the guest on *Off the Record*. He was still basking in the joy of his upset victory but he turned serious when asked this final question, "What scares you about this job?"

His answer came very quickly as if it was something that he carried with him every day. "I am not going to enjoy the complete loss of privacy that seems to be looming for me. I value that. That will be the most difficult," he reflected.

Ironically days before he finished his third term as governor, the issue came up again, this time during an exit interview when I probed the "emotional wall" he had so successfully constructed to keep the media and public out. He confirmed there was such a wall to preserve what privacy he did have, adding, "I never felt that I owed that, that I had to give that much. I wanted to save something for myself and family." And so in this chapter, we try to get on the other side of the fortress to reveal aspects of the total man who dominated this state for so long.

Carol Viventi was the first staffer Engler hired when he surprisingly won a house seat from a long time incumbent in 1972. He did it by implementing a battle plan he crafted while at Michigan State University. Helping him at the time was a fellow farmer named Dick Posthumus.

Viventi recalls Engler's attention to detail. When most lawmakers were out at night attending fundraisers or what-not, Engler was embedded in his office reading bills. He also applied that attention to detail later on when he was governor.

He was attuned to personal details, too. One aid recalls being with him on one of his overseas sojourns when there was free time to shop. Engler would find this gift or that saying, "So-and-so will really love this. And he bought it." So-and-so was always delighted.

Former Governor Milliken issued a weekly list of his public events. Engler got rid of that in short order. He wanted control of his agenda and if he wanted the media there, the front office told us and if he didn't, you were on your own to find out. That's why one story I did was so satisfying and sent the Engler squad scrambling for some answers.

One of my sources handed me a copy of the governor's personal schedule from May to December 1995. Can you imagine my delight? It had everything in there . . . trips to D.C., vacation time on the island, critical meetings with business leaders and the like, out of state trips for this and that, and on-and-on. I couldn't believe it and couldn't wait to write about it the following Friday in the *State Journal* column.

Engler's office went bananas and slammed into high gear to ascertain how such private information had fallen into my public hands. That evening at home, the phone rang. It was the head of the governor's state police security detail. He apologized for having to call. He and I both knew it was a fruitless effort, but he had to do it, and I respectfully took the call but gave him nada. We both had a good laugh as I told him I would see him in Jackson prison as I expected to be arrested for not telling him my source.

Rusty Hills, the communications guy, was high on the suspect list. Here and now for the first time it can be said . . . he was not the leak. To this day they still don't have a clue. Of course, another print out of the schedule never got out again. But once was sure a treat.

When Engler was in the legislature and Milliken was in the front office, the governor could never be sure Engler would be a help or a hindrance. Once when the governor wanted Bill McLaughlin to continue as state party chair, Engler launched a counter candidate, F. Bob Edwards, from Flint. The Milliken folks had to scramble to win the fight. Some on the Milliken team to this day complain that "Engler would lie right to your face." Keith Molin who carried the water for Milliken as his lobbyist had a different take on Engler.

Molin says when he would talk to Engler about a pending bill, he went away from the conversation thinking Engler was on board, but when the vote came he went the other way. Molin upon reflection retraced Engler's words and concluded he never really did say he would vote with us. "He had an uncanny ability of leading you to believe he said one thing but he didn't do what you thought he would do. He was very clever," Molin reflects. Molin describes Engler as a political animal while Milliken was bipartisan and politically ecumenical, which explains why they did not always see eye-to-eye.

I was also the beneficiary of an Engler gift late in his term. He was not trying to influence my coverage, since the exchange came literally days before he ended his term. It was the day of his final news conference. I had been in Traverse City and returned early because I could not miss this one.

Engler was especially upbeat—no gloom and doom and no hint that, in his heart, he probably knew this would be a melancholy event. He made no news and after he gave the last question to Jerry Crandall, who had worked for Engler years before, it was over. Engler slowly walked to the door chatting with this and that reporter as he made his way out. I waited for him at the door as he approached.

"You know in all these years you've never taken me to your office," I reported. True I had been in there once on an election night, but sort of uninvited.

Engler advised me to meet him on the second floor. With my cameraman, Keith, alongside, we went in and I asked the receptionist to inform him that I was there. Moments later the governor opened the door and motioned me to the next room.

Boxes. That's all I could see. Boxes. I asked Keith to get some shots as it would make a nice sign-off to our story that night. The governor had been up at all hours packing things. His wife describes him as the consummate "pack rat" and the assemblage of boxes seem to bare that out. Some were marked for the archives, some were personal, and he gave me a running commentary on how hard he had labored to make sure he was out of there in time for the new governor to move in. A security guard whispered to me that he had not gotten any sleep the previous night—Engler had been there at 3 A.M. finishing the job.

The governor stood leaning against the doorway into his private office and I was leaning on the other side. We chatted about all the crap he had accumulated over the years as he showed me this and that. Then it was time to go, but just as we were moving toward the door, he said, "Wait a second."

He disappeared for a few moments and returned with two tiny boxes. I asked if they were ticking?

With the hint of redness in his eyes, and to be truthful in mine too, he handed me and Keith a pair of cuff links. "Here, you can have these," he said as he handed them over. The jewelry had the State of Michigan seal on it with the name Governor John Engler encircling the seal. There's no telling how many of these he had handed out over the years, but at this moment he was probably giving out his last two.

I thought for a second that it might be inappropriate to accept them and muttered something about, "Are you sure we can have these?" He said, "Yes."

Fact is he didn't have to do that, but he wanted to. It was not planned. It was spontaneous. It was not part of a hidden agenda to advance his career. It was that private John Engler being the real John Engler. It was a touching moment. I expressed my appreciation and was out the door.

About a week before that, there was another glimpse at this private man only this time it was on statewide public TV for everyone to see. I had been asked to produce an hour long documentary on the Engler years. It was a monumental assignment in that there was so much to cover.

I wanted to end the program with a one-on-one exchange . . . one last chance to go mano a mano with the man who had ruled this town with an iron fist for twelve years. The front office agreed.

In pawing over hours of video, I came across the swearing in ceremony on a very cold January day back in 1990. I thought the scene would be useful, but in reviewing it, I stopped the tape. I wasn't sure what I had just seen was real so I rolled the tape back. Chief Justice Dorothy Comstock Riley was administrating the oath and when she came to the governor of the State of Michigan, I noticed an unusual catch in Engler's voice when he repeated it. Reviewing it for a second and third time, I was convinced he had almost cried while choking on the word "governor" and the phrase "so help me God."

The exit interview began with, "Do you remember almost choking on the word "governor" when you took the oath of office?"

"A little bit," he volunteered.

(You could always tell when he didn't want to talk about something. His usually expansive answers got very short. His wall was up, but I knew there was something on the other side.)

"What was going on in your mind?" I went on.

Again a brief but provocative response, "Well, it was one of those overpowering moments."

Now I'm surprised to see his eyes turning red as he ended his response. I merely added, "In that . . . ."

His eyes looked up for just a moment as if he was thinking whether to unlock this door, and when he again established eye contact, the answer finally came out.

"I think back," he started cautiously, "and I was standing there with Michelle, my father was there . . . there was a lot of pride being able to accomplish that," he revealed.

It was the end of a twenty year legislative journey and the beginning of a new adventure as the top elected official in the state. That would be a very "overpowering moment."

The governor did not shed a tear, but I found him shortly after that wiping his left eye. His staffers who were in the room at the time, and those in the TV audience who saw it on tape, remarked about that rare display of Engler tenderness and deep emotion that lived within. He also exposed that during his final State of the State message in January of 2002.

Over the years the final SOS of any governor has always been a bittersweet affair. As SOSs go the vast majority are noteworthy for not being noteworthy, but the last one always has a sentimental touch. The touch that Engler used that night was delicate, warm, loving, and for many in the audience, completely out of character.

He began the address in his usual upbeat style recounting all of the accomplishments during the Engler years and there was no hint that he would touch any hearts that night.

As I sat in Studio C at WKAR TV from which I was anchoring the broadcast for public TV, I had a copy of the address and I knew as he moved into the reflective portion of the speech, there would be dead silence in the Michigan house. I wasn't sure the usually "in control" governor could get through it without shedding a tear. Frankly, I was not sure I could either just watching it.

"I see my mother, my family . . . brothers and sisters. This family has been through a lot," he began the last segment of the speech.

He tapped his finger quietly on the podium before he continued.

"Campaigns, the ups and downs, the loss of their privacy [now his voice is cracking as the TV camera reveals his wife sitting with the three children. She is nodding her head in agreement on the loss of privacy line.] Their support has never wavered [a trembling in his voice and again a shot of Michelle moving her head up and down].

"I love them and I'm very proud of them." With that he asks them to stand and he joins in the applause for his family.

In those few moments, the whole state saw John Engler the man and what they saw was real.

One trait about Engler repeated itself time and again in the legislative process and when he was in the front office. If he felt he was right, there was not getting around it. Ask a former state representative from west Michigan.

Representative Mike Nye was a six-foot something, 270-pound Republican from Niles. His trademark was his cowboy boots and a straight shootin' attitude about what he wanted to do. On the issue of property tax relief, Nye and his sidekick Glenn Oxender concocted the Nye-Oxender school funding scheme. Frankly, they were quite proud of it. John Engler was not.

The scene is Engler's senate majority leader's office on the ground floor of the Capitol. The two house members are there with their leader Paul Hillegonds and his aide Jack Mowat. Their agenda is to brief Engler on the plan, but minutes into the meeting it became clear to Nye, as he retells the story, that Engler didn't like it.

"John was reading some papers," Nye says. He let the staffers do the dirty work as they dismissed Nye-Oxender as "junk." Nye felt the governor ought to be paying attention and as the brief ten minute encounter drew to a close, Nye got up and started moving toward Engler's desk. "A lot of people thought I was going to go at it with him," Nye recounts, "but I never hit anyone."

Hillegonds suggested, "Mike, it's time for you to leave."

Ironically, the plan used the sales tax to replace lost revenue from the property tax, which is exactly what the final Proposal A plan used, but by that time Nye-Oxender got zero credit for coming up with that first.

Another element of Engler's life you never saw: his work ethic was over the edge. I remember a state trooper assigned to the security detail confessed to me that one night he thought he was going to get home at a reasonable time. But just when the event at the Lansing City Club was ending around 7 P.M., Engler jumps in the car and announces, "Hey, there's another reception down at the Radisson. Let's go there." It was not on the schedule but the cop couldn't say that. So they went, and the trooper did not get home early that night . . . or most nights, for that matter.

Engler's track record on presidential campaigns had to be a low point in his career. He was a politician who effectively called the shots in the state, but when he was playing with the big shots on the national level, there was often a disconnect.

The Bob Dole campaign for president in 1996 is a fine example. You can never criticize Engler for not trying. He did everything he could to deliver Michigan to the aging former Senate majority leader, including riding around the state in a bus just before the election. Engler privately knew it was a losing cause but he never let on in public.

On the day after the election, it was clear Michigan had gone to Clinton. Engler was once more on the losing end. He was gracious enough to hold a post-election news conference that got me into hot water.

Reporters banged the governor pretty hard on how he had failed and not once did he say anything about making a mistake or shouldering part of the blame. You could feel the frustration level rise in the press corps with each bob-and-weave on his part.

Finally I phrased a question that brought a hush to the room filled with Englerites.

"Governor is there anything about yesterday's loss that you are proud about?"

It was a smarmy question and everyone in the room sensed it . . . accept me. The governor gave some answer and the news conference ended. As I was walking out, I noticed that many of the Engler folks, who usually have some smart aleck remark aimed at me, were silent. I sensed there was a problem.

I think I called Rusty Hills, the communication director with whom I had worked with for years, and asked if there was anything wrong. He quickly identified the problem. He suggested my question was over the edge. He didn't say offensive, but I could read between the lines even though I had slept only three hours the night before. I hung up the phone and immediately called Sharon Rothwell, the governor's chief of staff. I told her I needed to talk to the governor. She asked why? I said I wanted to apologize.

I wasn't in her office at the time, but I assume she did not fall to the floor since there was no boom, but I'm sure she was surprised. I was darn serious. The more I thought about it, I had to agree it was a lousy question and I wanted to tell him so.

Within the hour, he and I connected on the phone. "Governor, I just wanted to apologize for that last question. It was over the line and disrespectful and I am sorry for saying that. I hope you will please accept my apology." He did. We chatted for a few more minutes and ended the conversation. He was not bitter. He did not gloat. He did not threaten to get even. And we left it at that. But I was not finished.

I went on *Off the Record* that week and repeated my apology to the TV audience. After the taping some wondered why I had done that. I felt then, as I do now, that when we screw up we should fess up. It's the same standard we hold politicians to, and in the long run I believe it enhances our credibility with a suspicious public. The public holds journalists in about as much public esteem as used car salespersons and convicted felons.

Whenever there was a national election, Engler for vice president (V.P.), Engler for the cabinet, or Engler for something on the national level always popped up. It has happened with every governor I have covered. Milliken was always V.P. material, and Blanchard was also on the cabinet list, especially when his buddy Bill Clinton arrived in Washington. None of that stuff ever came true, but that never stopped the speculators from speculating. After Blanchard lost, he did join Clinton.

I remember one July morning when Engler was revisiting his roots at the Ag-Expo at Michigan State University. This yearly event was a farmer's carnival without the rides . . . unless you count combines, tractors and hay bailers as rides. It was muggy. Engler was in his shirt sleeves working the crowd as he always did if he had the time. The farm hands wanted to know about the weather and the price of corn. I had other things on my mind . . . not to diminish the importance of corn prices. With the huge musty tent nearly empty and the wooden floor creaking beneath us, we found ourselves standing next to the stage and since I didn't get a story out of the speech, we went around the mulberry bush on Engler joining another Bush in Washington.

Engler was always a challenging interview. He gave no comfort and volunteered very little, but on this occasion, I saw a side of him that most had never seen. He laid it directly on the line.

"Why would I want to go to Washington and schlep around there," he confessed, to my shock.

"Schlep" is more often heard coming from some hip cat on the Lower East side so coming from a guy from Beal City left me no choice but to ask what that meant.

It meant joining a bureaucracy in some cabinet post where he would have no power. Sure he'd be in the cabinet but so what? Back home in Michigan, he explained, he had the power to get things done. He was convinced a life in D.C. would be filled with one frustration after another.

"Frankly," he candidly continued, "I can have more access to a President Bush from the outside than if I was in the White House competing with everyone else for the president's ear." Engler was scheduled to become the chair of the National Governor's Association within the year and he knew Bush, being a former governor, would seek advice from Engler and the rest of the nation's governors. Once more his analysis was right on.

Engler was quick to suggest that he could handle a Washington job. He just didn't want it and there was somebody in the family who agreed. Mrs. Engler was not excited about a stint in D.C. She was happy with the girls being in Michigan and was opposed to packing them up and moving away.

Of course that never happened. The interview showed a different side of Engler. He was not lusting for power at any cost. He was a hands-on politician who wanted to get things done, not just to see his name on some fancy smancy door for the thrill of it all. For him there was no thrill in D.C. at all.

If you asked the general public to slap together a list of Engler traits, warm and fuzzy would not be among them. There truly was a human side to this man and not surprisingly it came out on the day after his father died.

Most sons would have stayed home. John Engler went to work.

He attended a rally in Ypsilanti where General Motors was closing down the Willow Run plant in March of 1992. Nobody in the audience, including the union protesters who greeted him, knew the grief he carried in his heart.

As recounted in Engler's book, after the speech, reporter Hugh McDiarmid found himself backstage with the governor. After Hugh said, "I'm very sorry to hear about your father," Engler finally broke down in tears.

As we learned in our exit interview, Engler said his father was tenacious. Like father, like son. He credited his dad with being well-read and a leader in his own right as he helped create the Michigan Cattlemen's Association. His dad was a survivor in a business where many perished. The governor had the same traits.

Remember that Engler was not very generous in feeding stories to the media and in fact made a studied attempt to stiff us whenever he could, but I saw a different side when it came to the book that was written about him.

Writer Gleaves Whitney had asked me to make a contribution before it hits the bookstands. He called to tell me the governor was going to the print shop to see the first books come off the line. Did I want to tag along? I said sure. Gleaves said he would check with the boss. Engler said it was OK.

It gave me a chance to quiz the governor on one great story that I thought captured Engler's doggedness, which was the hallmark of his political career. His mom told the story about her son being in grade school and his teacher telling him to change seats. Little John liked where he was sitting and rebuffed the teacher's request saying, "Why don't you change everybody else's seat. I like where I am."

Engler in our interview said he had talked to his mom and claimed she was suffering from a little memory loss. He protested that it never happened. Put your money on Agnes Engler's version.

Well before I arrived on the scene, it was common practice for governors to seek advice from reporters and some reporters gladly gave it. I always felt uncomfortable. It was inappropriate. I recall Senate Leader Robert Davis, a former undertaker, came to me one day with a news release.

"Skubick read this before I send it out and let me know what you think."

"Senator with all due respect, that is not my job. Why don't you release it, and then I'd be happy to tell you what I think."

Giving advice may be a power trip but that's why a governor has his own paid advisors.

I did, however, violate the rule one time with Engler. It was in December during his last month in office and the annual media gathering was on the agenda. The holiday reception at the executive residence was for many folks the highlight of the year, but Engler had been called to Washington to consult with President-elect Bush. Let's see? Go to D.C. and rub elbows with the new president or stay in Lansing and rub elbows with a bunch of free-loading reporters? It was not a tough choice, but Engler did ask, "Hey, you're the senior capital correspondent. Should we cancel the party and reschedule it or have it without me?"

"Governor, we can't have the party without you." Who would we pick on? I should have added. Anyway, the party was postponed and for some funny reason, was never rescheduled. He owes us one.

After Jennifer Granholm was elected I was often asked on the rubber chicken circuit if I missed John Engler. Since everyone assumes reporters are die-hard liberals, they expect the answer to be "Heck no. Good riddance. Glad he's out of here."

Not true. If you thrive on controversy, then John Engler is the full employment bill for working stiffs like me. I do miss him. He was a hoot to cover. I clearly did not agree with everything he did, nor how he did it and I'm sure the feeling was mutual. But he did what he said he would do. I think voters respected that.

Engler may have been the last governor to get elected based on his experience. He certainly was not elected on charisma. I often wondered what it would have been like if he had allowed his human side to be seen more often. He did that in private with his family, but for those around him who had known him for years, the common take is, "We really didn't know him."

Engler was serious about the business of government but he did have a great sense of humor. I was getting ready to do an interview with Engler and asked my longtime colleague and friend, Rob Baykian, if he had any unusual zingers I could ask.

Rob recounted a taped interview he had done with Engler and afterward, somehow, the subject of the Three Stooges came up. At the mere mention of the comedy team's name, Engler burst into a chorus of one of their famous bits.

That's the one where Larry begins singing, "Hello; Moe follows with another "Hello" and Curly finishes the harmony with another one. Engler sings all three parts for Baykian. It cracked Baykian up and it was just what I was looking for to spring on the governor.

We finished our discussion of some pressing business of state when out of the blue I asked him, "Why do you like Larry, Moe, and Curly?"

I can guarantee you in thirty-two years in this town, nobody had ever asked him that, and his laughter in response to the question still rings in my ears.

"You do watch 'em, don't you?" I pressed on for more.

"No, not anymore," he said trying to act grown-up, but his continuing little boy laughter gave that away.

"Well, you did 'Hello, Hello, Hello,' so you must have watched them?"

"Oh, I have watched them. You bet," he confessed with the camera still rolling.

Which brought me to the closer, "Which one are you like?"

Now both of us are in stitches at the absurdity of the question. Here's the governor of the entire state being asked to compare himself to one of the Three Stooges. Barbara Walters eat your heart out. Instead of punting as a more reserved governor might have done, Engler wades in with this dandy, "The smart one!"

The whole room of technicians, staffers, Engler, and I are on the floor. He refused to explain which one that was, but I took it to mean, Moe. What's your take?

He really got a chance to display his biting humor as the lead off roaster before an audience of Lansing insiders at a free dinner to celebrate the fifteenth year of *Off the Record*.

Engler began his stand-up routine: "Tim's real motto is "Getting the Inside Out." That's also the motto off Ex-Lax . . . but really what's the difference?" Encouraged by the laughs he got on the first joke, he ventured on for more.

"Tim's routine in front of the mirror every night, as he washes the mascara out of his mustache [not true by the way]: Mirror, Mirror on the wall who is the fairest star of all? Just answer the question, yes or no!"

By now he's beginning to feel like the Michigan version of Shecky Green as the audience sees a side of JME he never shows on the senate floor. He calls me the Geraldo Rivera of Michigan, claims I'm the only guy who can get away with calling someone, baby, sweetie, doll, and poopsie. . . . "I think the name still fits."

But then he says, "Seriously." (When you hear that line you know you're in for another zinger) "We're having fun at Tim's expense tonight but I want to tell a story that I think all of us can agree on. Former Speaker Bobby Crim once said from the rostrum, "Will the sergeant at arms please escort Mr. Skubick from the chamber . . . and have him shot!" Spontaneous applause when Crim said it and when John boy repeated it.

Engler never lost his cool in public, but in private, he was not afraid to go after somebody if that somebody was standing in the way of the Engler agenda. Ask Senator John Schwarz. He and Engler went back a long way and while Engler managed to intimidate many an opponent into submission, it never worked on the Battle Creek lawmaker.

"We used to have knock down, dragout battles," laughs Schwarz, and it was usually over higher education spending. It was a cause Schwarz often championed.

When there was a disagreement, "We would clear the room," Schwarz recalls. That meant Engler's Chief of Staff Sharon Rothwell would exit giving the two combatants plenty of room.

"Go to hell," Schwarz remembers shouting on numerous occasions. And he recalls hearing back, "You go to hell." Unfortunately for Democrats neither of them did.

"You don't understand the f–in issue," they would say to each other. When it was over Schwarz says, "We would shake hands. He loved it, and so did I."

In fact a number of lawmakers who possessed the "you know whats" to stand up to Engler came away saying he would respect you more if you took him on.

"He was loyal to his friends. He was always sending notes or making phone calls when someone in the family was ill," Schwarz says.

Clearly the guy had a heart. He just kept it hidden from public view.

Senator Dan DeGrow's little daughter back in 1989 learned about that first hand. While Engler was on the campaign trail running for governor he saved money by staying at the homes of supporters. It was DeGrow's turn one night and Engler, the nondaddy, got into a conversation with DeGrow's daughter. She asked Engler to throw her a tea party on Mackinac Island if he got elected.

Engler got out a card and wrote, "One tea party for Allison DeGrow." Then he advised her to "Save this. It'll be worth something." He signed it, boldly enough, "Governor John Engler."

Engler was a detail man to a fault. In a special report by the fine capital bureau staff of the *Detroit News* headed by talented Bureau Chief Charlie Cain, they uncovered a clear example.

Several days after Jim Blanchard was elected, Engler tapped John Kost to keep track of everything Blanchard did or had done in Congress. It was opposition research in anticipation of Engler's bid to unseat the sitting governor. The next election was four years away but Engler wanted the file started now.

He also formed the so-called Saturday Morning Group of his closest advisors. Tom Shields from Marketing Resource Group, Jerry Crandall, Engler's chief of staff, LeAnne Redick who worked on organizing groups, Gail Torreano, Engler's chief senate assistant, and David Doyle, who was great at political strategy.

The group knew one thing for sure, Engler had a lousy image. They knew he was a poor public speaker; was known as an insider whose main playing card was making back-room deals and obstructing anything he didn't like and that was everything Blanchard touched. Plus they concluded he was unknown beyond the capitol loop.

In reality, however, that was a plus because it gave the team a chance to define Engler with voters who had never heard of him and his less-than-sparkling image with Lansing know-it-alls.

They confronted one other sticky problem: the battle of the bulge. Engler had tried and failed at every diet under the sun from popcorn to liquid and planned menus. His exercise bike in his East Lansing bachelor's pad had become a clothes rack. He was told to restore it to its original intention and, by golly, by the time the race rolled around, Engler was not rolling around as much as he had before. He actually looked svelte.

Engler had a 192 page playbook on how to beat Blanchard and a key component was hard work. Engler was used to that down on the farm and rolled up his sleeves. As Cain and crew outlined in their report on October 25, days before the showdown at the polls, Engler made twenty-one separate campaign stops in southwest Michigan. The state GOP also helped extend his message via the airwaves with a whopping $1.1 million TV and radio buy one week out.

The ad that capped it all showed a side of Engler that lots of folks in town had seen. He would do anything to win, including doing a spot with his own mother. My own mother wouldn't vote for me if "half of what Jim Blanchard says about me was true," he tells the voting public as he looks into the camera. The next shot is of Agnes Engler who chimes in, "Oh, I was voting for you all along, John."

She later told a friend, "That ad seemed silly when we were doing it, but I guess it turned out OK." Sure did, it got Agnes and Matt Engler a front row seat at their son's swearing in the next January.

Up to this point, all of these behind the scene looks at Engler have been snippets or snapshots. Those can be misleading. To really get the measure of anyone, you want to look at the long-term. There are two gentlemen who have experienced John Engler in that regard. Their stories are worth retelling because they add another dimension to the Engler most didn't know.

The two are former Rep. Bill Martin and former attorney general candidate John Smietanka. Martin told his story over lunch at the Lansing County Club one day. He began by suggesting he didn't have any good Engler stories and then proceeded for the next ninety minutes to recount one after another. The pattern of a benevolent Engler emerges.

Engler was a master at moving the pawns on the chess board of political life. For a time Martin wanted to be a major player by securing the GOP nomination for secretary of state. The former state trooper turned state representative knew it was time to change jobs. Term limits were engulfing the Lansing scene and breaking up his old gang of semi-moderate Republicans.

Martin met with party chair Betsy DeVos and got a "lukewarm" response. He was pro-choice. She was not. Enough said.

Martin stepped up his speaking engagements at GOP events and was quite serious about his efforts. Then he heard that a woman from Macomb County was also interested in the same post. Her name was Candice Miller. Just learning that he might have competition was not enough to jolt him out of the contest, but he knew they'd have to talk, and they did. "She did not commit to running," he says, "but it was clear she was likely to run." He says he told her he was running. This was in August, almost a year before the election.

By the time the annual State GOP Leadership Conference was staged on Mackinac Island a month later, Martin saw Miller handing out candy. He concluded her campaign was in "full bloom." To make matters worse, he concluded Engler was in her corner.

Martin called Jeff McAlvey, the governor's lobbyist, to find out what was going on. "I want to know," the soon to be ex-lawmaker said.

A session with the governor and his aide Rusty Hills was set. It lasted one hour. Engler sat through the whole thing without muttering even a grunt. Hills did all the heavy lifting. He blabbed on about "balancing the ticket" and getting a candidate from "a different side of the state," which was code for Billy Baby, you ain't going to get the nomination. Martin asserted that he felt he could win and did not want to retreat. It was wasted breath. He walked out "relaxed" but disappointed. Without saying a word, Engler let Martin know Miller was in and he was out.

Martin figured the governor kept his mouth shut for a reason. If Engler never said anything and Martin was quizzed by the media on the governor's stance, Martin could honestly say, he didn't know. Although he certainly did know because Engler's "words" were spoken by somebody else. Of course, Engler also avoided the tough assignment of telling a friend he was going to get stiffed. That's why governor's have handlers.

After that, McAlvey calls Martin. This conversation centers on a different job offer. Would Martin like to run the lottery? Martin is not sure. He quickly consults with Patti Woodworth the governor's bean counter. She tells him lottery is a loser. "There is no way you would want that," is her free advise. Next Martin meets with Jerry Crandall the current lottery czar. He says it's a great gig and a week later Martin tells the governor yes. He stays there for four years and boosts the take from $1.2 billion a year to a respectable $1.6 billion when he left.

Question: Did Martin get the lottery thing because he stepped aside for Miller? That linkage was never discussed he says. A lot of what goes on in politics never is. Sometimes it is just understood. Martin was a team player and landed a cushy job. In the middle of all this, Martin remembers a great story on how Engler gets what he wants through deception.

During the debate over finding a new method of school financing, Martin had cobbled together enough votes to use the income tax to replace lost property tax revenue. Engler was opposed to that so he summoned Martin to the office.

Martin sits there as he and Engler chew the fat about the issue and after about two hours of chewing, Martin finally figures out what's going on behind his back. While Engler lured the unsuspecting lawmaker far away from the debate, the governor's lobbyist was on the floor methodically dismantling Martin's income tax coalition. What you see with Engler is not what's really going on. Martin of course lost that round of the tax debate.

Back to the story line. Martin is happy at lottery, but Engler has a vacancy to fill. Long time prison director Ken McGinnis is retiring. Engler, his chief of staff and legal advisor call in Martin to offer him the post.

This time he checks with no one and just says yes on the spot.

The governor pauses long enough to say congratulations and then asks Martin about a replacement at lottery. Martin says his pal from the legislature, Don Gilmer, is busy lining up clients for his post term limit career. Engler asks Martin to call Gilmer about the job. Gilmer eventually takes it.

Engler moves quickly when he knows what he wants. Otherwise he can be methodical as he plots his every move.

Martin tells one revealing story about his days riding herd on 50,000 inmates in and out of prison. There is a lawsuit concerning the use of female corrections officers in a male dominated prison. Martin is on his way to federal court in Detroit to testify in the suit and he spies a camera crew ahead of him. He thinks to himself there must be something big going on. Moments later as the microphone held by Geraldo Rivera is shoved in his mug, he discovers he's the big news.

"I just kept on walking," Martin now laughs as he tried to outrun the ambush interview. "I looked like a Medicaid fraud doctor walking away," Martin suggests. After his testimony and back in the office, Martin concludes he doesn't want that run and gun interview to hit the airwaves. He calls Rivera's office and agrees to a sit down interview with Rivera but in exchange the incriminating tape can not be aired. A deal is struck.

The interview lasted two hours. He prepared for it but confesses, "I prepped more for *Off the Record* than I did for Geraldo. With him I knew what I would get, but with your show you never knew what was going to happen."

Martin also digresses to tell me his first appearance on *Off the Record* produced some grumbling at home. His wife felt I was unkind to her husband and she still felt that way on the morning of our lunch.

"When I told my wife this morning I was having lunch with you, she said, 'Why? He was so unkind to you.' "

As it turned out our lunch was on of their twenty-fifth wedding anniversary and when I found out Mrs. Martin was still in a funk, I sent a nice letter to her saying I was sorry about treating her hubby so poorly.

Now we come to John Smietanka's story. If the Martin relationship with Engler reveals one side, Smietanka's run-in with the Big Guy shows another, and it ain't pretty.

My first contact with the west Michigan lawyer was in 1998 on his maiden campaign for state attorney general. What I didn't know then is that he had been on a twenty-year mission to run for that post.

In 1978, Governor Milliken's right hand woman Joyce Braithwaite and GOP party chair Bill McLaughlin asked him to run. Smietanka wanted a pledge of financial support before he said yes. He didn't get it so he didn't say yes.

In 1986 he was asked again. He wanted Bill Lucas, who was running for governor, to commit $300,000 for the attorney general's contest. Once again the pledge was not given, and he stayed on the sidelines, but forces led by John Engler almost drafted Smietanka nonetheless.

By 1990, Engler was calling all the shots and now there is talk of Smietanka for lt. governor. Engler's guy Spence Abraham talks about giving more power to the office, which appears to be the standard ploy for persuading someone to take a do-nothing job. But that doesn't pan out and neither does the A.G. thing.

Engler turns up the charm, however, in 1994 and Smietanka is now ready, after obtaining clearance to run from his then 9-year-old daughter. "You've got to do what makes you happy," she tells daddy during a Florida vacation. With that nudge he decides to take the plunge.

Smietanka feels he had Engler's support until April 1994 and suddenly for no reason, that backing turns neutral and the heretofore cordial relationship begins to go south.

Smietanka senses he is in trouble when he sees Engler at the podium with his Democratic opponent Frank Kelley at a news conference on child support payments. Then the two are seen together at yet another news conference on air pollution. And to cap off these developments Engler gets angry at Smietanka concerning his appearance on *Off the Record* with Kelley.

In the debate prep prior to the broadcast Engler gives Smietanka a line to use on Kelley. It was something about, "It's time, after about forty years, that we get a new attorney general."

"I never got a chance to work it in," Smietanka recounts, and I found out afterward that Engler was "livid."

On election night when the 11 P.M. news came on Smietanka was told he had knocked off Kelley. "I was not declaring victory," he says because he had this sixth sense it was not true, and it was not. Despite spending $390,000, he lost to Kelley.

Six months later Engler summons Smietanka to talk about the defeated candidate's future. They talk about becoming the state's drug czar. Smietanka is interested and describes the talks as "friendly." Then he gets a call that the czar thing won't work out. Engler's chief of staff makes the phone call so that Engler avoids that messy task again.

Life goes on to February 1997 and Smietanka still wants the A.G. thing. He and Engler meet in Macomb County where the issue is discussed again.

"If he had said he didn't want me to run, I wouldn't have run," Smietanka reveals. This confession comes during a three hour lunch in Grand Rapids during which he lays out for the first time his side of this story. That breaks a five-year self-imposed silence on the issue of his crumbling relationship with Engler.

Smietanka continues to travel the state lining up delegate support. State rep. Frank Fitzgerald is in hot pursuit of the nomination too. Smietanka wears out his Ford Probe with a whopping 235, 000 miles on it. Next he takes his brother's car and logs another 50,000 before he buys a van and slaps 50,000 on that. It's obvious he is serious, but he also knows the governor is "cool toward me."

Engler moves very quietly behind the scenes which is one of his trademarks. Smietanka gets word that the governor is interested in Scott Romney for A.G. So Smietanka calls Romney. Romney makes no commitment on running, but says if he does, he wants Smietanka's support. Smietanka tells Romney he can't do that because, "I'm going to beat you!"

From the beginning of election year 1998, Smietanka wants an audience with the governor but keeps drilling dry holes. Finally they meet and the press corps speculated that Engler offered Smietanka the moon to get him out of the race.

"That's not accurate," the lawyer says. "I'm asked about a seat on the State Supreme Court or Court of Appeals." He indicates interest in the former but not the latter. Turns out Engler says he could run for the seat, then held by Democratic incumbent Justice Mike Cavanagh. Smietanka sees the folly in that because no one knocks off a sitting justice. He rejects Engler's overtures and redoubles his efforts to win the A.G. fight.

In the meeting with Engler, Smietanka learns what he's known for sometime: Engler wants Romney. There is no shouting match. They agree to disagree. But one thing you learn about Engler, even though it appears things are over, they never are.

Romney gets in and soon thereafter he raises a charge that Smietanka had fallen behind in his child support payments. The story gets legs since Smietanka is running for the top law enforcement job in the state. Being from the southside of Chicago, Smietanka recognizes "gutter" politics when he sees or smells it. Both of his senses nailed this one. He gives an adequate explanation but the seeds are planted and later on Democrats will try to cultivate the child support issue again.

Fitzgerald drops out of the race and later gets appointed state insurance commissioner by the governor. Smietanka goes after Romney on "qualifications" and publishes a brochure suggesting he has the right kind and Romney does not.

The whole thing comes to a head at the state party convention where the delegates will pick between the two. On the first ballot, Smietanka surprises the political world by winning with eighty-nine votes to spare. Romney is gracious and moves for a unanimous vote to nominate his opponent. That's where the niceties end. Engler avoids the traditional hands held high victory pose with Smietanka until Secretary of State Candice Miller makes him do it. Smietanka says he and Engler don't speak.

The headlines the next day were not what Engler wanted to read. He loathed any suggestion that he was not in control of his own party and the Smietanka win over Romney proved just that.

Smietanka up until our lunch had never commented on the notion that he was the reason Jennifer Granholm became governor. Engler and others promoted the theory that had Romney gotten the A.G. nomination, Granholm would have lost to him and never would have run for another office, let alone governor.

For five years Smietanka never responded but on this day he argued, "If John Engler had supported me as enthusiastically as I supported him, I probably would have won." In other words, Smietanka contends Engler is the one to blame for the meteoric rise of one J. Granholm.

Smietanka says what bothered him most was that "people who backed me got pushed around after the election." Asked if Engler pushed him around, he made his only real punt of the lunch, "I'm not ready to answer that question."

The whole episode, revealing another side of Engler from Smietanka's perspective, still bothered Smietanka five years after the fact, but he adds, "I do not want to dredge this up anymore. There are things I would have done differently, but I can't re-run the election."

Given all that, I asked why he agreed to talk about it.

He explained that his supporters over the years have asked him to do it, and as it turns out he added, "You were the first one to ask."

One postscript to the Martin-Smietanka sagas. As Engler finished his final days in office, he appointed Martin, who was now a lobbyist, to the Western Michigan University governing board. Engler gave nothing to Smietanka who continues in his private law practice from Grandville, Michigan . . . with a host of memories, not all of them fond, especially of one John Mathias Engler.

My last encounter with Engler was on Inauguration Day 2003. With camera in tow we were prowling around on the first floor of the Capitol where the platform party was forming to go out in the

January chills where the new governor would be sworn in while the old governor looked on.

It wasn't long before Governor Engler and his wife came in. He was wearing a giant ten gallon hat that President Bush had given him. He did not have on the cowboy boots to match. Oh shucks.

We chatted for a second and Mrs. Engler talked about how long it took for her husband to pack up all his office stuff.

Then I asked him if he was going to pull a Milliken on us. By that I meant, when Milliken left office he almost never returned to town. Engler, sarcastic to the bitter end, said he would not be like Milliken because the former governor always seemed to reappear on the eve of an election by endorsing someone usually a Democrat. Engler got in one last dig at his old "friend."

The soon-to-be ex-governor then moved next to Democrat U.S. Senator Debbie Stabenow and lobbied her on some GOP appointments that were on hold in D.C. He was working right up to the last minute. They both stepped aside as Jennifer Granholm emerged from the holding room to lead the procession onto the platform outside.

I returned to the high rise media risers where a phalanx of cameras recorded this little bit of history in the making . . . the out with the old and in with the first female governor.

When it came time for the oath of office, Ms. Granholm did not choke on the word "governor." Instead, as one of her mentors, Federal Judge Damon Keith said each line, her voice got higher on each phrase and so did his, so that by the very end they were both gleefully shouting in unison "So help me God."

The ceremony ended with the new governor and her husband riding in a convertible down Michigan Avenue to the Lansing Center where she would deliver her speech. As she made her way to the car, I watched Engler and his wife. They formed an informal receiving line on the platform and one-by-one everyone on the platform came by to shake their hands and exchange one last hug. When there were no more hands to shake, they took each other's hand and walked slowly up the capitol steps for the last time. They walked through the big doors and disappeared inside. The doors closed and so did a most unique chapter in Michigan history.

13

Lieutenant Governor

It really never dawned on me until I sat down to write this chapter that of all the political infighting over the years in this state, a lot of it has revolved around governors and their running mates or would-be ticket mates.

Milliken had ethical problems with Jim Damman. Engler had difficulties with Connie Binsfeld before he picked her. Blanchard had a rough and tumble brawl with Martha Griffiths. Dick Posthumus was privately criticized by Loren Bennett backers, and Howard Wolpe's camp reports he got in a shouting match in 1994 with his mate Debbie Stabenow—a charge she denies.

The Democratic primary for governor in 1994 started out on the right note with the quartet of candidates pledging to stay on the high road. The unison sounded so good. There was Wolpe, Stabenow, Lynn Jondahl and Larry Owen all smiles, all on the same page, and all committed to a positive campaign.

For a time they pulled it off. That is until the election got closer and the polls did too. It turned into a dog fight between Wolpe and Stabenow as each had internal polling showing the race tightening. I recall listening to a radio debate in Detroit days before the August primary. The fur was flying. It was difficult to decipher what they were

saying with everyone shouting at the same time at each other. Everyone except the mild mannered former minister Mr. Jondahl. He
bemoaned the bitterness as another example of why voters are so cyn-
ical about politics. Stabenow and Wolpe turned a deaf ear to that.

Prior to the debate Stabenow created an issue by going negative,
i.e., running a commercial that was a direct attack on Wolpe's
integrity. The thing that made it even worse was the fact that these
two competing politicians had been friends for years. They served
in the legislature and worshiped the same moderate to liberal philosophy, but she was on TV questioning Wolpe's role in the infamous house Post Office scandal.

Congressmen and women had abused the postal system in D.C.
using the house mailing office like a bank to bounce checks, and
Wolpe had eight checks with insufficient funds. He was by far the
least guilty of the bunch but that didn't figure into Stabenow's ad.
She used a broad brush and painted Wolpe along with all the other
"crooks" in D.C. It was a hard-hitting spot and it moved votes to her
column.

During the WJR radio mud wrestling match, Wolpe said the ad
was the "same old sleazy politics." Stabenow countered the ad was
accurate and technically she was correct. However, she left out some
facts that would have taken the edge off her broadside aimed at
Wolpe. Hey, don't let the facts get in the way of a great attack ad.

The Wolpe camp was furious, and after a lengthy internal debate it
decided to strike back. But with what? Wolpe did not want to lower
himself to her level, but he needed something to silence her blast.

In the midst of these "what the hell do we do?" discussions, came
a phone call from Steve Gools a long-time Democratic activist and
former Wolpe drone. He remembered when Wolpe was running
for congress that Stabenow had done an ad for her friend. Gools
said if they could find the thing, it might help out.

A Sherlock Holmes search was launched as Election Day drew
closer. The consultant who produced the spot looked everywhere to
no avail. Then as if by divine intervention they found it. When they
played it, they could not believe it. Here was Stabenow on camera
praising Wolpe for his long standing integrity . . . the very thing she
was now impugning in her ad.

Wolpe's handlers crafted his commercial, suggesting that
Stabenow would say anything to get elected including talking out of

both sides of her mouth. The commercial worked. Wolpe won and the search for a running mate commenced in earnest. Stabenow was not on the short list.

Detroit Police Chief Ike McKinnon, the African American law and order type, was perfect to counter balance Wolpe's more liberal image. Wolpe went to Traverse City to huddle with McKinnon, who was attending a conference at the resort up there. Wolpe made the offer; the chief said no.

Plan B: Find another cop willing to run. They turned to former State Police Director Ritchie Davis. He had run the state cop shop during the Blanchard administration. He got caught selling fund raising tickets for the governor, which was not illegal, but it smudged his record a little but not enough to exclude him from the Wolpe ticket. Had he been offered the post, it was clear to Wolpe's gang, Davis would have said yes.

But he never got the chance. During this time, Stabenow forces were putting the heat on Wolpe to pick her. Former Rep. Maxine Berman, an avid and cut throat women's movement mover and shaker, implied that if Wolpe didn't select Stabenow the female vote might stay home on election day. Other female groups got into the act and turned up the pressure another notch to the point that Wolpe caved. As a result, his campaign manager Ken Brock almost resigned.

There was plenty of bad blood between the two candidates. The primary had been brutal and some lost respect for Stabenow. One of the takes on her is that she would walk on her grandmother's grave to get elected. A harsh commentary but it serves to underscore the depth of animosity between the two camps. There were other stumbling blocks. Wolpe had campaigned against Proposal A, the property tax relief plan. Stabenow got that ball rolling in the senate that led the way for "A." So there were deep philosophical as well as personal hard feelings to iron out.

Against that backdrop then, imagine yourself in the room as these two warriors and enemies try to patch up their relationship so that she can run with him. Talk about an emotionally charged situation.

Not surprisingly the "peace accord" was not reached in one session. It took about three or four "Come to Jesus" meetings and then when they did shake hands, it was an uneasy truce.

Every good politician tries to figure out how the media will respond to a story and Wolpe knew the first question out of the box would be, Why did you pick someone who has attacked you? The tougher question would be for Stabenow: If you believed all those things you said about him, how could you join his ticket? Either you didn't mean it, or you are a hypocrite! Pick one.

The two of them grappled with her answer. The Wolpe camp claims she agreed to admit she was wrong. Asking a politician to do that is like asking the president of the United States to admit he had an affair.

With that agreement in place it was time to go public. The Wolpe campaign bought satellite time so he and Stabenow could be interviewed by every TV station in the state. The drill was a standard one. The two candidates would sit in a studio in Detroit and through the magic of uplink technology they could get into every major media market in the state without driving a mile.

As one Wolpe aide commented, even the dumbest anchor could come up with the right question to ask about her attacks. Hence it was no surprise when it came up during the first uplink.

What turned out to be a surprise was her answer . . . . She refused to say "I'm sorry." Instead, she couched her answer in the terms of "I said those things in the heat of the moment." That's the Wolpe camp version.

"Howard was getting furious," recounts Brock. And after the cameras were off, the fury turned into a shouting match while embarrassed technicians and others looked on. Brock says, "She wouldn't walk the plank." The bitter disagreement carried over to the taping of a TV commercial in a classroom at Lansing Community College where the two went at it again. This time Brock says they went "nose to nose."

Amazingly Stabenow has a completely different take on what happened. First of all she contends she did not want the job. "I had to be talked into it . . . I was not pushing for it," she recalls. She concedes that others were working hard to get her the nomination. Given the "blood bath" in the primary and for the sake of party unity, she was urged to go on the ticket.

Stabenow was no dummy. She knew the battle against Engler would be a "tough campaign," which is code for he was going to win. She had a career to consider down the road, but finally she took the leap.

Once that happened she confirms there were several meetings to work out their differences. She had a list of her own. Stabenow says during the campaign Wolpe's folks "did a lot of stuff" that was objectionable including raising the issue of Stabenow's divorce "and there were other things," which she now refuses to recount. Suffice it to say she says, "There were hard feelings on both sides . . . and she was disappointed with Wolpe for permitting the 'undercurrent' to exist."

As for shouting matches, Stabenow scratches her head and recalls none. "He did pull me aside once," she does remember, "and asked me to say something differently . . . but there was no blow-up." She says if it did occur, it happened at the staff level where tensions were running high between the two sides.

Stabenow has an interesting take on all the acrimony in the primary that created the tension. She says she was the first woman who had a serious chance to tie down the nomination and all the men didn't know how to handle that.

For example, she argues, if a man had done the post office commercial, nothing would have been said about it, but because it was a woman who was being aggressive, it created a stir.

Stabenow believes, and Jennifer Granholm does too, that Stabenow "laid the groundwork" for Granholm, although neither knew it at the time. In a way Stabenow was bucking the United Auto Workers union, which wanted to control the party and deliver the nomination for Wolpe.

Granholm, ironically, ran into the same thing. The UAW backed David Bonior. But she won. Stabenow did not.

Now long after the fact, Stabenow says she has no hard feelings and found her run with Wolpe to be a blessing. It opened doors for future fund raising, she developed more statewide contacts, and because nobody blamed her for the loss, she came out a winner. It was Wolpe who headed to Africa to lick his wounds. Stabenow parlayed the effort into a seat in Congress and eventually the U.S. Senate.

Isn't it astounding that no one can agree on what happened? However as the campaign moved along word came from Mike Duggan, out of Wayne County, that the Wolpe folks were "screwing up on how they were using Debbie" as Brock recalls. Brock says it became apparent that she began to "distance herself because she knew we were going to lose." In other words, if she was going to go down with the ship, she did not want to get blamed just in case she wanted to run for another office. And Debbie Stabenow did.

Well, the Wolpe-Stabenow ship did sink. The two of them made a concession statement on election night but Wolpe walked off the stage refusing to take any questions. The day after the election, my assignment was to find Howard and get him to talk. Even in defeat, the losing campaign usually makes the candidate available, but this time the word was, "Skubick get lost."

I contacted everyone I knew in the campaign as I refused to go away. Finally, I found out Wolpe was packing his bags to move from a condo in East Lansing. I told Brock or somebody that we could do this one of two ways. Howard could talk to me or I could ambush him. I was prepared to do either. Frankly, I was ticked that this guy was ducking the media.

In his defense, any political loss is hard to swallow. When you put in countless hours, shaking hands, running all over the state, making speeches, answering stupid questions, and trying to give the appearance that you and your running mate are one big happy family, you are going to be exhausted and not eager to concede any mistakes. From a personal standpoint I deeply understood that, but from a professional standpoint, I still needed that interview.

Wolpe was not happy to see me when our TV truck pulled up to him loading the trunk of his car. I told my cameraman to stand back while I approached him.

"Howard I'm sorry, but I really need to talk with you. I promise to be brief, but I need something." He relented but I could tell he was upset.

In a somber tone, he said he was feeling very good, "because I'm looking forward to new challenges and a new direction. In political terms I'm obviously disappointed at the outcome of the election." His sharpest remarks were aimed at the new Speaker of the U.S. House Newt Gingrich, who won the night before. "That scares me," Wolpe began. " . . . he is one of the most frankly amoral politicians I've ever met. I don't think he stands for anything other than whatever he thinks works at the moment."

I said thanks. He and wife, Judy, left. I haven't seen him since.

Connie Binsfeld was elected to the Michigan house in 1975, where she served as the assistant minority leader. The Maple City former Mother of the Year had the image to match. She was approachable, very likable, good sense of humor with a ready smile, and she learned the political ropes quite well.

When she was elected to the senate, she wanted to move into a leadership role. She had her sights on the floor leader's job of directing the daily flow of floor debate—a glorified traffic cop.

The only impediment to her getting the post was John Engler and his former MSU buddy Dick Posthumus. Neither of those guys bothered to tell her that she would have competition. Finally, the weekend before the vote, Posthumus called her to say he was running. "I was surprised," she says. It turned out, when the votes were counted, Connie was out. Dick was in. She was disappointed.

She says there were no hard feelings and no need to kiss and make up. She moved on, putting the defeat and dispute with Engler behind her. Four years later Binsfeld and Engler moved into the next election cycle with him running for governor and her ready to retire from the senate. But with him in the race, she thought she would stay around, too, in that, "it would be good for John to have me in the senate."

She went on to secure the primary nomination for her seat and he continued to call her to run names by her of potential candidates for the various statewide offices.

Then one night she got home and the family told her, Engler wanted to talk with her. She usually stayed up to watch the 11 o'clock news and just before that, he called. The topic was lt. governor but he gave no hint that she was under consideration.

"I advised him," she says, that since both he and Blanchard were young, the ticket needed "a little gray hair." John agreed. She also thought a woman should be on the ticket and recommended Loret Ruppe, a long time GOP activist.

Engler told Binsfeld you have just given me a job description, "So will you?" he asks out of left field.

"Will you what?" she wants to know.

"Will you be my lt. governor?" he requests.

Binsfeld says she was surprised again. She had no idea he'd asked.

She pointed out that having two candidates from the state senate might be a problem. Engler said he had thought about that and felt it would not be. But what about her senate seat, she wondered? Somebody would have to fill that vacancy and Engler had that figured out, too.

This illustrates how foxy Engler was. He knew that the Democrats had not fielded a very strong candidate to face Binsfeld, because she was so popular. Since it was past the filing deadline, they couldn't change candidates. Republicans, however, could legally select a replacement, and Rep. John Pridnia was the pick. That meant that someone would have to run for his house seat and Beverly Bodem was selected for that. Engler had this all figured out. So the only thing left for her to do was to discuss it with her loyal and loving advisor, husband John.

Engler said he would call her back in the morning and she hung up the phone. "My husband was standing over there and as I put the phone down he said, "He just asked you to be his lt. governor."

"I was shocked," she says with her husband adding, "I always thought he was a smart fellow and now I know it."

When Engler called the next morning, she said yes and never wavered on her decision.

When it was time for them to meet the press in a capitol room packed with supporters, a grinning Engler and Binsfeld entered the room. She joked with reporters about their bets on who the choice would be and then Engler took the microphone.

"I'm honored that my partner in our campaign to make Michigan a better place to live and work will be my good friend, my hard working colleague, a woman I respect and admire so very much . . . the next lt. governor of the State of Michigan, Senator Connie Binsfeld."

Forty-five seconds of thunderous applause. The announcement comes sixty-eight days before the election and both he and she predict victory. Engler is quizzed about his decision. Many names were considered and some persons who might have taken the job declined. He wanted to leave the impression that she was his only choice. Read his answer carefully as he answered the question, "When did you decide?"

"Prior to today," was his smarty pants answer. The crowd loved it when he'd zing a reporter.

"Was she your first choice?"

"Connie was the choice that I made first," as he turned the question inside out, "and by that I mean Senator Binsfeld is the only choice that I put in this process and took through the process."

So was she the first and only? Probably not.

Blanchard's much publicized problems with Martha Griffiths came up. Binsfeld punted. "I have always admired Martha Griffiths. She was a leader in the women's movement before there was a women's movement," she went on. On the critical question of the Democratic wrangling she said, "I don't wish to comment on any internal happenings in the Democratic party."

Engler was asked if he was trying to take advantage of the "disarray in the Democratic party."

With a straight face he suggests, "I've certainly never been one to take advantage of someone else's problem." Profound laughter engulfs the room since everyone knows it's a bold face . . . . mistruth.

The issue of their disagreement four years earlier over the senate majority leader's post: Engler says it is "water over the dam" and she agrees. Then she gets a round of applause for her next comments. "You know if you think about it, the way I handled that situation, today puts me in a situation to be a candidate for lt. governor." In other words because she didn't seek revenge for losing that race, she proved she was worthy of being on the ticket. The crowd loved it, and so did Engler.

With that out of the way, she was prepared to give it her all as Engler's first running mate and she did, right up to election night.

"I stayed up," she tells with a beaming smile. "Governor John [he wasn't governor yet] went to bed." He told everyone, "I know we have won, just wake me when you know the margin."

At about 6 or 6:30 in the morning, Engler got the wake-up call and emerged from his slumber as the governor-elect. Ms. Binsfeld was on his arm when they approached the cheering, yet sleep deprived crowd in the downtown Radisson Hotel in Lansing. I was up all night too. "You didn't think we would win, did you, Tim?"

If there were anymore spats between Engler and her, it was never reported. She served two terms with him and then quietly retired to Glen Lake to allow Posthumus to be Engler's running mate in 1998.

In 1974, Jim Brickley had just completed four years as the second in command to his good friend Bill Milliken, but as you read earlier, he had family problems, and that $27,000 salary was chump change. He made no reference to that in his five paragraph statement. "In making this decision, I considered that the office is by nature a transitional one. It holds no ultimate political or administrative responsibilities. . . . It has not been an easy decision to bow out." Milliken in his statement was prophetic, "I still believe Jim Brickley can have a promising future in public life." Milliken then went into the legislative ranks and plucked out an Oakland County moderate Republican/hardware store owner named Jim Damman.

Damman was a low-keyed kind of guy with very little bravado and almost a perfect personality match with Milliken. They were elected in 1974 and spent four years together but when it came time for the 1978 election, word surfaced that Damman had an ethical, if not legal, problem.

To this day one of Milliken's closest advisors still doesn't completely understand all the twists and turns in the allegations, but that was beside the point. As one insider recalls, "Remer (Tyson) did a great piece that gave the story legs. The *Free Press* editorial folks also applied pressure on Damman."

Milliken had his own problems. He was in the middle of the PBB contamination mess and facing a formidable Democratic opponent Senator Bill Fitzgerald. Milliken didn't need a Damman albatross hanging around his neck, too.

He still had to face the media and on February 7 1975 a reporter wanted to know if Milliken would ask Damman to step down. Milliken's carefully worded answer gave no hint that Damman would be cut lose. "I have seen nothing up to this point which would lead me to making such a request of Mr. Damman. I do not anticipate that that would happen . . . I basically trust him. I believe that he's going to do an outstanding job as lieutenant governor." Wrong.

Milliken met Damman and removed him.

Earlier Braithwaite and her sidekick George Weeks had done the customary examination of Damman's personal history. "Is there anything in your background that looks like a skeleton in your closet?" they asked with the answer being no. It turns out the answer was yes.

Damman was deeply disappointed he got the boot. One of his aides told me years ago that he felt his boss had gotten a bum wrap from the Milliken folks. But Damman never said that publicly and he quietly disappeared. Milliken won re-election with Jim Brickley back on the ticket in 1978.

There is a ton more to that story. For years in this town it was assumed that Brickley returned to the ticket after sealing a deal with

Milliken. The legend goes like this: The two of them meet. Milliken promises Brickley that if he returns to the ticket, Milliken will either retire early and turn over the keys to Brickley, or Milliken will retire in 1982 and help Brickley run for the job himself that year.

The theory had so much credence that Oakland County Republican L. Brooks Patterson accused the Milliken bunch of crafting the deal without input from the rest of the party. Virtually ever member of the capital press corps agreed with Brooks. Why else would Brickley leave a cushy job as head of Eastern Michigan University to get back in the trenches in Lansing? There must have been a deal.

Wrong.

Not only wasn't there a deal, the two never really talked about it, according to Braithwaite. She acted as the go between. Plus, she contends Brickley had a "distaste for doing all the things you have to do to be governor."

So if that was not the reason, why did he come back? My source tells me it was for personal reasons. Let's just say cupid played a dominant role in his decision and six years later from his post at the State Supreme Court he wrote his colleagues to announce he and Ms. Braithwaite had been married. "From this point on," he wrote, "all single women should be referred to Charles." Charles Levin was unmarried at the time.

When Dick Posthumus ran for governor all sorts of names were floated for the second spot on the ticket. One prominent name was that of Oakland County Sheriff Mike Bouchard, but there were problems according to one Republican who watched that story unfold. There is something about being second banana that carries with it potential dangers. I am referring to the Wolpe-Stabenow mess. She lowered her profile before the ship sank. Bouchard's inner circle concluded it didn't want him to even get on the boat for fear it would go under. The feelers from Posthumus to Bouchard quickly disappeared. "We knew he would not take it. Mike had all the spine of a tadpole," was the caustic take from a noted GOP insider. The sheriff had his own political ambitions that went well beyond nabbing drunk drivers in Oakland County. Bouchard denies the spineless allegation and urges that person to, "tell that to my face."

Eventually Loren Bennett was selected, but he could not weasel himself into the Posthumus inner circle. He had plenty of solid advice to give, he just couldn't give it. A Bennett source reveals there was an understanding from the moment Bennett agreed to be on the ticket that he would work almost exclusively in the Wayne, Oakland and Macomb county region. Posthumus reportedly made the pledge while the two discussed Bennett's role at the Posthumus kitchen table after the primary.

But Bennett found himself criss crossing the state and hitting podunk towns where voters were few and media coverage even fewer. At one noon time stop at a township hall there were supposed to be three people working. When Bennett arrived to shake hands, only one set of hands was there. The others were at lunch.

There were signals early on that Bennett might be left out in the cold . . . at least from his side's perspective. On the day Posthumus was going to introduce his running mate, he and Bennett and their wives were standing in the Green Room waiting to go out. This source explains a decision was made by the group about handling some aspect of the event. Everyone was on the same page but the page got turned when Katie Packer came in. The campaign manager quickly reversed the decision and Bennett is described as wondering who was really in charge.

Yet another gripe. Bennett backers say he was frozen out and couldn't get past the palace gate and the inner circle to voice his concerns and offer advice. Campaign manager Packer finds all this to be, in a word, wrong. From a big picture standpoint she says Bennett's team was disappointed he did not get the secretary of state nomination and "there was some bitterness toward Terri Lynn Land" who did get the nod.

"They wanted a floor fight . . . it was personal . . . and they never got over the fact that they lost," Packer observes.

Next she says Bennett had Posthumus' cell phone number and "not all the calls go through me" so if he really wanted to voice his concerns he could have, she contends. Next she says Bennett's closest aides, Bill Sullivan and Wendy Anderson, attended weekly meetings with the campaign, so they knew what was going on. Besides, she adds, "Bennett had ample opportunity to go wherever he wanted to go." In fact she says he wanted to spend a lot of time in Detroit churches and we let him go even though we were sure we couldn't win that battle for votes there.

As for those sparse crowds greeting Bennett, she adds with just a hint of sarcasm, "I'm sorry they didn't have presidential size crowds" for him. She added "Dick had that happen to him, too."

"I never heard the complaint that he was not being used correctly," she recalls and as for the screw up on election night, she has her take on that, too.

After the polls closed that night, Bennett was in his Lansing hotel room with his wife and staffers. At 11 o'clock he turns on the news and sees his running mate standing at the podium downstairs in the hotel conceding the race to Granholm. Bennett was personally hurt. Some of his supporters were angry he was not invited.

It is pretty standard stuff that when the ship is going down on election night all hands are on deck even though they'd rather be somewhere else. Bennett did not want to be in his room.

Later Posthumus press secretary Sage Eastman tried to explain it away saying, "We sent a runner to get Bennett but he never got there."

Packer has her version. Just prior to the 11 P.M. newscast, Posthumus assembled his team and said he wanted to go on the air before the news, so that Granholm could be the lead story off the top of the local news. Not everyone in the room was so generous. "What do we owe her?" was just one of the dissenting remarks. But Posthumus was firm. "She is our governor" he explained. So the wheels were quickly put into motion to meet his desires. In the shuffle Bennett got left out. Packer says her job was to do what her boss wanted her to do and she did it.

"I feel bad this is being dredged up. Dick never regretted the decision to pick Bennett," she contends. "There are no hard feelings. Dick would not treat a guy like that."

There are some folks who admire Bennett who are not so sure.

Welcome to the word of running for lt. governor.

Bennett's woes pale in comparison to this next tale. In fact you can take all the other lt. governor sob stories, roll them into one, and it will still not reach the critical mass of the Blanchard-Griffiths civil war.

The former congresswoman had been on the ticket with Blanchard in 1982 and 1986. In 1990 she first sent signals about hanging it up but then she reversed herself, which is where the fun began.

She was getting up in years and the speculation in town was that Blanchard did not want her running even though he held her in the highest of esteem. It was delicate to say the least. Blanchard needed the female vote and didn't want anything to jeopardize that. The odds makers in town had Griffiths out and Blanchard putting State Treasurer Bob Bowman in. That became a running story, too.

Bowman was thirty something compared to Griffiths eighty something. The contrast was obvious, but Bowman did everything humanly possible to distance himself from the story, which reporters refused to let him do. In 1989 he came on *OTR* and got a good going over as the panel did a tag team assault on whether he was running for lt. governor.

"Had I lived before General Sherman," he began his rehearsed answer to the anticipated question, "the denial I'm about to give you would be Bowanesque not Shermanesque. No, in no way will I be a candidate. I hope Martha will be."

Unwilling to take no for an answer Hugh McDiarmid chimed in, "Could you be drafted?"

"No, Hugh, I couldn't be drafted. Thank you but no thank you."

Unable to nail him down on that, somebody asked him about running for governor in 1994. Bowman who was quick on his feet and a great quote machine responded, "Listen, the only thing I want to do is play shortstop for a major league baseball team. That's a dream I've had and that's probably just as unlikely," he laughed and the panel joined in. (Ironically among the many things he did after his stint as Blanchard's chief bean counter was the head to Major League Baseball Owners Association . . . where he probably played shortstop for some team, but not during the regular season.)

Anyway, while he worked hard to keep his name out of the press, privately Griffiths concluded that he was Blanchard's choice.

"I think it's Bob Bowman," she confided to me during a personal phone conversation from her farm home in Armada. But she quickly observed that Bowman had "some real drawbacks." It didn't take much prodding to get those out of her. First, she said that he had turned down the steelworkers union at McClouth Steel in Michigan when it sought a state bail-out to save the failing factory. "They were madder than hell," she explained.

Next, "people think he is so arrogant," but she quickly tacked on, "he never acted that way around me." Bowman was arrogant but in a lovable way. Who in this business isn't? There was one theory in town: One of the ways to move her out of the way was to move her over to another job. There was an opening on the University of Michigan board so would she run for that?

"Hell no," was her terse two word response. She did offer that she heard Blanchard and company were trying to recruit Erwin "Magic" Johnson to run for the Michigan State University board. It never happened either. The easy way out of this mess for Blanchard was for her to quietly bow out. She was in no mood to do that. I asked anyway "Will you take him off the hook?"

"No, I'm not!" she shot back. End of phone conversation. She had been helpful, candid, delightful to chat with and crusty as always. It was Griffiths being Griffiths.

Blanchard didn't help himself either when he told the media that Griffiths "is ready and able to be part of the team. That's great news. As to what the team will be, and the ticket will be, that's going to happen late in the summer." The statement was a smoke screen and misleading as all heck. He wanted her out, but there he was leaving the door open, which meant the story got legs and turned into a Chinese water torture as it drip- drip- dripped Blanchard right into a corner.

With her unwilling to take a powder and when backwater attempts to move her out failed, the governor had no choice. He made his decision. She was off the ticket. Another younger woman, former State Democratic Party Chair Libby Maynard, was on. But he waited to reveal it. What happened to Bowman? Turns out he was on the list all along, but Blanchard called him on the phone and told him he was out. Under different circumstances Bowman might have gotten it, but he did not wear a dress, so he was toast. Blanchard needed a female running mate. Bowman might have done anything to get the job, except have a sex change.

The story dragged on when finally Blanchard called a news conference to announce his decision. As I listened to the tape some thirteen years after the fact, it was a darn good performance by Blanchard, under very trying circumstances. The story had matured into soap opera proportions but he did everything he could to respect his soon-to-be former running mate.

He thanked us all for being there on a Friday afternoon. Normally on a Friday nobody would have been there, but on this story, the Friday golf games were put on hold. He began in a somber tone, "This decision I've had to make today is one of the most personally trying and agonizing that I could possible make and that is to ask Lt. Governor Martha Griffiths to step aside as my running mate for lt. governor."

Almost in unison the press corps asked why?

Here it got very delicate. The real answer was that he had concluded she was not healthy enough to takeover if something happened to him, but he deftly masked his answer. "The lt. governor must be ready on a moment's notice to step in to take over the heavy responsibility of being governor should anything in the future happen to me. I base my decision solely on what's best for Michigan."

No matter how the question about her failing health was asked, he would not go there. He stayed on message refusing to reveal that she had been sick, on and off, for sometime and that the administration had actually withheld that information. He wanted to protect her privacy.

He was asked about her age.

"That was not a factor," he said.

What about her health?

"I refer you to the statement out of respect for her privacy," he repeated.

Blanchard conceded "politically, this is not helpful to me. . . . If the decision was based on wanting to win, I'd pick her . . . she's been a wonderful friend and ally."

Prior to this announcement Griffiths had rattled off a great one liner suggesting that Blanchard "might need psychiatric help if he picked someone else."

So as Blanchard left the history making news conference, somebody reminded him of the quote and asked if he was going to see one?

"After you get through with me that may be true," he chuckled as he walked out the door hoping this story was over.

Over? Ha.

Shortly after Blanchard's announcement, we got a call from Griffith's office. She was staging a news conference at the MSU University Club. If they had sold tickets to this event, the national debt could have been retired twice over.

The club was packed with cameras, microphones, and reporters.

What's that old saying about hell knowing no fury like a woman scorned? The scorned lady showed up with her beloved husband, Hicks, at her side. There was some tension and anticipation in the air because none of us had ever seen a scene like this before. That's because all the other flaps with running mates had been pretty much handled behind closed doors. This was war and very public.

Hicks took to the microphone first. He laid out the ground rules. "Identify who you are and who you work for" he lectured the gaggle of reporters chomping at the bit to get at his wife. He rambled on for awhile and finally turned things over to her.

One of the lines floating around town was that she had called Blanchard a "son-of-a-bitch." Since none of the broadcast media types had that on tape, we tried to get her to repeat it. Instead of repeating it, she clarified it.

Her quote was, "The biggest problem in politics is you help some SOB get what he wants and then he throws you off the train. I didn't say the governor was an SOB."

Was she implying that? "You judge," she said.

She explained that she would vote for Blanchard and as for taking him off her Christmas card list she explained, "I can assure you we don't have a Christmas card list so he won't be taken off anything."

Blanchard says to understand this story, you must go to the heart of the relationship between Ms. Griffiths and her husband, whom Blanchard paints as the manipulator behind the scenes goading his wife to do what he wants.

"Martha was considered an ugly duckling," Blanchard said and recounts that her mother once said she would be lucky to find a man. She did find the handsome, up and coming, attorney, Hicks, and they were married while going through the University of Michigan Law School. Ms. Griffiths wanted to attend Harvard, but women were not admitted in those early pre-caveman days.

Blanchard says she was always afraid of 'losing' her husband, which gave him extensive control over her decisions and behaviors. "He often used the silent treatment on her," Blanchard recounts, as he fingers Hicks for causing the flap over her place on the ticket. "He took over her life." He also says that Griffiths had several strokes which were deliberately covered up as the media was told she had a cold. Blanchard says as a result of those strokes, "Martha changed."

Blanchard also says when he picked her in the first place, she told him she did not want to finish out the four year term, but she changed her mind and stayed eight years. "Frank Garrison and Owen Bieber asked me to replace her for the second term," he goes on. Garrison ran the state AFL-CIO and Bieber was head of the UAW. I ignored their request and kept her on the ticket in '86. Four years later when he went to her and asked her to step down, he claims "she agreed to get off the ticket." But then, he says, Hicks went to work and got her to change her mind. As for why he let this thing drag out in the media, Blanchard was convinced that over time he could "talk her back into her senses." He didn't.

The relationship between Blanchard and the two Griffiths was so sour, he stopped telling them when he was going out of state. Blanchard was afraid Hicks would convince his wife to make pending judicial appointments in the governor's absence.

After her news conference the Blanchard team breathed a sigh of relief, as it felt the story was finally over, but the woman scorned was not done. Blanchard went to the state Democratic convention to piece the party back together. He wanted the theme to be unity, so the party offered to give her a tribute. She unceremoniously, through an impersonal press release, told them to shove it. She complained she did not like listening to "hypocrites."

To make matters worse, the story got national attention. Blanchard blamed Engler's campaign manager, as well as political newsletter editor and former GOP state lawmaker Bill Ballenger, of peddling the story to the *New York Times*. Soon there was Griffiths being interviewed by Connie Chung of CBS News. So Blanchard was dumped on all over again, in front of millions of viewers all across the country.

The Blanchard-Maynard ticket was defeated and some quickly speculated that the Affaire-Griffiths was a major factor. I think not. Blanchard pretty much lost that election on his own and Ms. Griffiths could not have saved him from himself even if she wanted to. She did vote for him, by the way.

Were there some women voters who were angry with the way he handled it? Clearly. His major mistake was taking so long to move. When she said she would step aside and then changed her mind, that was the time to jump in, but I'm sure he kept hoping hope against hope that she would "do the right thing." But like she said in the phone conversation she would not take him off the hook.

So he dangled on the hook for weeks until he took himself off by making the decision.

When Martha Griffiths died in 2003, Jim Blanchard was there. The hard feelings of the past were only a memory. When Blanchard spoke he could not have been more warm and respectful of his departed comrade.

Martha Griffiths, the woman who blazed the trail for other women in politics, was laid to rest, but nobody in this town will ever lay to rest her battle with the guy who "throws you off the train."

Democratic candidate for governor, the acerbic Geoffrey Fieger is taking a lunch break with his running mate Jim Agee. The two are reviewing the campaign when an older gentleman with a thick foreign accent approaches the pair. Even though he speaks in broken English, Fieger can surmise this man is not a supporter. He lambastes Fieger up one side and down the other. When the man finishes, Fieger says with a straight face, "May a camel pee on your shoe."

Agee tells the story and says it is one of his favorite Fieger tales. Another one involves a rather large woman who sees Fieger and Agee at a downtown Detroit outdoor barbecue. Even though she has four blocks to go before her bus stop, she gets off where the two men are and runs over to Fieger. "I love you. I love you," she jubilantly embraces Fieger. She goes on an on and finally Fieger has to get back on the bus. Following up is Agee who thanks the woman. Not many folks really loved Fieger, so when one was found, Agee figured he'd make sure she didn't defect. She explains that she needs a ride to her house. Agee, being the wise politician that he is, gets on the bus and sees Fieger sitting in the back. He goes back and suggests they give the woman a lift. Fieger won't bite.

"She got a free hot dog and another bus will be along in a minute." He orders his bus to drive off leaving his "lover" at curb side.

Agee tells that story to underscore the fact that Fieger was no ordinary and image conscious candidate. "In fact he dislikes politicians and distrusts them, too," Agee remembers.

So how did the former member of the Michigan house from

Muskegon end up as Fieger's running mate? Agee says because "we had a comfort level and there was trust. He felt I would not jump off the train" when things went wrong.

When Fieger won the 1998 Democratic nomination for governor they were not exactly lining up to run with him. Agee says the two had several meetings and seemed to hit it off.

Agee knows whoever the nominee is for "lt. governor doesn't make any difference . . . it doesn't turn anything," but he says he accepted because he was on a mission. Everyone asked him about his hidden agenda, such as laying the groundwork to run for another office.

He had none, other than to beat John Engler.

Agee got the Fieger offer about 10 P.M. on a Thursday. Agee was staying in a Lansing hotel because the next morning, he's was a guest on *OTR*. Fieger asks him to join the ticket and Agee says yes.

The next morning, because he has promised Fieger not to say anything, he waffles all over the place when the questioning turns to being on the ticket. After the show, he pulls me aside, and confirms what I suspected.

"Yeah. I'm running," he confides in me.

"Can I put that on the radio?"

"Just don't use my name," was his only request. "What is your name?" I asked.

I honored his request and had the story on WWJ within minutes.

Fieger had an absolutely awful relationship with State Democratic Party Chair Mark Brewer, Agee says. "The tension was really bad." Fieger was also having problems with the United Auto Workers union, which didn't lift a finger to help him out or give him any money. The money didn't matter, Fieger had a ton of his own, but the votes would have.

Despite Fieger's troubles with the union bosses, he got along with Agee. The two had a candid conversation after the funeral for former Detroit Rep. Morris Hood, Jr. Agee and his friends retired to the Locker Room bar, one of Hood's favorite haunts. Pretty soon the waitress motions Agee to the phone. It was Fieger time.

"I want to put a luxury tax on fur coats and yachts," the millionaire Fieger tells his running mate. Agee tells him he is nuts. "If you want to sink to the bottom and get your ass kicked, do it," Agee lectures his pal. They go back and forth and Fieger "blows up," but in the end he follows Agee's advice.

That would be a surprise to former Attorney General Frank Kelley, who once said he liked Fieger, but described him as the kind of guy who would take your advice inside the room, leave, and do something different.

Agee and Fieger, of course, lost. Agee wonderfully sums it up, "It was not one of the wisest things I ever did, but one of the best things I ever did. . . . I did it for the right reason." Sounds like no regrets there.

14
Upset Victories

In those grand pre-term limit days, if a person got elected two terms in a row, unless you did something obscene on the Capitol steps with a goat, chances were you had a job for life. Beating an incumbent is tough and nearly impossible which is why in 1974 nobody in this town thought the chair of the house appropriations panel would eat his lunch.

Representative William Copeland was a permanent fixture in the Capitol. He had been elected eleven times, had spent twenty-two years in town, and ran the most important committee in the house. With control of the purse strings, Copeland was every lawmakers' pal . . . not because they necessarily liked him but because he had the means (money) to help them reach their end (reelection).

Copeland may have had a D for Democrat after his name but he was conservative. When a bunch of college kids came to visit trying to persuade him to support lowering the Age of Majority from twenty-one to eighteen, he scoffed at them. "None of them vote," he shoved them out of the office.

Nonetheless Copeland was also a character. I remember sitting on the back steps of the Capitol one sunny summer morning picking his brain about politics when I suggested it must be pretty heady to be running the budget panel.

"Skubick, that and ten cents, you can buy a cup of coffee," he suggested.

It was the first time I had heard that line and while the ten cent figure has gone up a bit, everytime I hear it, I think of the ole chairman.

The twenty-two year veteran entered the 1974 election cycle expecting to win without having to lift a finger.

A twenty-three year old fellow, who was a baby when Copeland was first elected, thought he could do the impossible so Jeffrey Padden, playing the part of David, plotted to unseat the chairman playing the part of Goliath.

Padden had returned to Wyandotte after spending 482 days playing second chair trombone in the Clyde Beatty circus band. He had done two shows a day, seven days a week with only one day off and that was when the semi truck hauling the big top center pole broke down. Unfortunately for Padden he was not in New York but rather in some backwater berg in Arkansas.

Anyway, he finally gets off that grueling gig and wonders what he's going to do with the rest of his life. His family had been very active politically and before he blew his brains out in the Beatty band, Padden himself had worked on some local campaigns.

He looked briefly at the state senate from his area but that was held by the husband of his first grade teacher. Padden did not want to run against Sen. Jack McCauley. Then he looked at the Copeland house seat.

"I went to three people I knew and if anyone of them had said don't do it, I would not have run," Padden recalls some 30 years later. His mom said, "Do it." His best friend at the University of Michigan agreed, and his on again, off again girlfriend Kathy made it unanimous.

His pal at the U of M suggested Padden get in touch with a newly elected representative from Ann Arbor. Padden drove to the Capitol not knowing where to find Representative Perry Bullard. The two finally connected by phone.

"I want to run for Copeland's seat," Padden announced.

"You're going to take on ole shit head?" Bullard barked back in his best liberal Democratic voice. Bullard and other liberals in the house, and there were lots back in those early '70s, would have done anything to get rid of "ole shit head."

"Bullard gave me three pieces of advice," Padden remembers.

One was to read the book *Campaign Craftsmanship*, get in touch with a guy named Jim Bollam at the U of M, and cut your hair and shave your beard. The first and third items were easy. Finding Bollman was a challenge because his name was really Vollman, but the two finally connected.

Bullard's hair suggestion seemed two-faced since he donned a full beard, mutton chops and a full rag mop on top. When Padden questioned the hypocrisy of Bullard's suggestion, Bullard opined, "Yeah, but I'm not running in Wyandotte." Off went the hair.

One of the book suggestions was to contact everyone Padden knew. He touched base with all fifteen of them in a short period of time. One of them was a teacher in Trenton. He loathed the dastardly Copeland who, at the time, was sitting on a teacher retirement bill. This teacher agreed to hold a coffee for Padden and forty folks showed up. They proceeded to grill him on the issues and he proceeded to display his twenty-three years of ignorance right in front of them. Had they asked him to play a circus march, he would have done better.

"I didn't know bullshit back then," he recalls, "but I was honest. When I didn't know the answer, I said so and when I did I responded." The gang of forty formed the foundation of his infant campaign and "gave us a sense of reality," he says.

1974 was the worst year of Watergate. Distrust of incumbent politicians from the White House to the state house was off the charts. Padden ran on the slogan "He Wins. We Win." He swiped it from the book. He raised an almost unbelievable $3000, one third of which was his own.

Money was not the key to victory, but some masterful political strategy was. Padden and Vollman checked and re-checked the vote totals for previous Copeland victories. They discovered that while Copeland was winning all the time, he was not turning many voters out. In one race there were just 3,200 votes and that was against a weak challenger. The outcome was always predictable but the low level of support suggested the old man was vulnerable, or at least that's what the team of Padden and Vollman hoped.

Padden and Vollman targeted districts where Copeland had not done very well. Those turned out to be higher socio-economic families with more education. They ignored the areas where Copeland did well, which meant Copeland didn't know he was facing a formidable opponent because he never saw many voters.

"He believed he was invincible . . . that was his blind side and it gave us a huge advantage," Padden says.

Padden became more brazen about being able to unseat the incumbent based on two meetings. The first was when Copeland showed up in Padden's government class wearing a three-piece suit complete with pocket watch and pot belly. "I heard the first three minutes and literally fell asleep right there in the front row as he spoke."

The second time was during the aforementioned Age of Majority meeting in Copeland's office where Padden reminded the lawmaker that those eighteen year olds would soon be voting.

On primary election day Copeland got whacked by a double whammy. Padden was able to increase the voter turnout in the districts he targeted while Copeland saw fewer of his supporters show up since everyone assumed he would win anyway.

When they did the vote count, Copeland had fifty-four fewer votes than Padden. I recall going on the radio the next day announcing that a twenty-three year old trombone player had done the impossible, ousted a twenty-two year veteran of the Michigan House.

Copeland ordered a recount but to no avail.

Not willing to concede defeat, he then launched a write-in campaign against Padden in the November balloting. "They got real aggressive on election day with poll workers everywhere. Some were telling voters I was a homosexual," Padden laughs declaring he was a confirmed heterosexual. Copeland's gang handed out stickers with his name on it, but voters could not figure out where they went and the instructions on the voting machines confused them even more. Some of the stickers ended up on Padden's part of the ballot and some on the outside of the machine, which meant Copeland lost more votes.

Padden won again.

Copeland tried again two years later and lost again.

For ten years, Copeland and company tried to find somebody to unseat the trombone player.

"He never got over it," Padden says.

Then in 1984, conservative Democrats recruited a guy named Joe

Palamara whose daddy had been on the city council. By this time Right to Life was an active ingredient in local house races and Padden remained pro-choice. There was also an anti-tax fever engulfing the community in the aftermath of the Jim Blanchard 38 percent tax hike which Padden voted for.

This time when they counted the votes in Padden's parent's basement, he was one hundred votes short. His legislative career was history.

"I originally ran for office because people were telling the younger generation to work within the system rather than trying to tear it down." Padden took that to heart and says he got the best graduate education a college drop out could ever get.

He did not run for office again, choosing instead to finish his undergraduate degree and get a master's degree to boot. Along the way, he also married that off again, on again girlfriend, Kathy. Padden continues to monitor the Lansing political scene from an outside consultants seat rather than from one on the house floor.

It's one thing to knock off the chair of the budget committee, but it was quite another insurmountable task to unseat a sitting speaker of the Michigan house. Mike Goschka can lay claim to that feat.

The year was 1992. House Speaker Lew Dodak was a shoe in to win back his seat. The popular wisdom in town was Louie was unbeatable. Somebody forgot to tell his challenger that. Novice Republican Mike Goschka, who was a UAW fork lift operator, turned the popular wisdom on its ear.

It was an unusual year for the Democrats. They had failed to field candidates in 14 of the 110 house seats, in effect conceding those seats to the GOP. One of the conceded seats belong to Representative Paul Hillegonds from Holland. Since the GOP minority leader had no opponent he refocused his time on other districts where Republicans might pick up a seat or two. Dodak fell into that category.

Dodak was so sure of his reelection that he did his first two days of campaigning with a bow and arrow in the back woods. Too bad deer don't vote. Back home Goschka was taking advantage of several factors.

1992 was the year of Ross Perot. He made it fashionable to oust incumbents. He motivated a whole new crop of voters to show up at the polls to do just that.

"We never saw the Perot vote coming," Dodak reflects long after the fact. Since the Democrats didn't know they were out there, those folks never got a mailing or anything else to persuade them to pick Dodak.

"In every house district where Perot got more than 25 percent of the total vote, an incumbent lost," Dodak reflects.

1992 was also the first year of the new house voting districts and Dodak had lost 50 percent of his old seat. While he won where he was known, he lost were he wasn't.

One week before the final vote, Dodak reports having a ten point lead, but Goschka was cutting into that with a decidedly misleading campaign commercial. In the previous two years the Michigan house had been renovated as part of a mammoth state Capitol restoration project. As part of that a new speaker's chair, costing $10,000, was purchased. The ceremonial chair sits in back of the podium on the rostrum in the house.

Goschka's ad conveniently left out that detail and only told voters that Dodak had purchased a $10,000 speaker's chair. Well you can imagine the uproar in this blue collar district. Couple that with a tactical mistake by the incumbent, and the ten point lead was fading fast. Because he thought he was ahead, Dodak refunneled money from his campaign into other house races, which meant he did not run any counter ads to rebut the Goschka spot.

Election day: Dodak out. Goschka in.

"He was lucky," Dodak now laughs as he lobbies Goschka and other lawmakers for his own Dodak and Associates lobby firm.

Goschka has a different take. He says hard work, including a massive door-to-door campaign, turned the day. But don't kid yourself. Dodak made enough miscues to help the process along, and Mr. Perot helped, too.

For years Macomb County state senator Gil DiNello served as the "full employment bill" for former *Free Press* columnist Hugh McDiarmid. Whenever Hughy had writer's block, the conservative and sometimes volatile conservative Democrat would do something that produced an instant column. But little did DiNello know that McDiarmid indirectly cost the senator his seat, in a race he should never have lost.

DiNello had always enjoyed a close working relationship with senate Republicans because his philosophy was more aligned with them than with the Democrats. So it was no surprise when he switched parties and found himself running against Democrat Ken DeBeaussaert.

The Senate GOP obviously wanted to hang onto the seat and was prepared to spend mega bucks, about half a mil, to keep Gil Baby in the senate. It was also hoping to give him a free ride in the primary election that year, i.e., no opponent to contend with.

But Nancy Dedenbach had a different idea. She will go down in state history as something less than a footnote, but her entrance into the GOP primary forced DiNello and company to shell out a cool $80,000 to win . . . that was money he could have hoarded for the general election. Dedenbach got in, according to then Macomb County Democratic party chair Leo LaLonde because, "she hated DiNello."

The Republican woman of course lost but in a small way helped the Democrats. They went into the election knowing it was an uphill fight and next to impossible to unseat Mr. Macomb County. But the impossible became the doable after a fateful radio interview DiNello did in February of 1994.

Columnist McDiarmid had been pounding DiNello for years with special emphasis on DiNello's ardent support for the death penalty. In 1990 DiNello led a petition drive to put the issue on the ballot. After a while the lawmaker conceded he couldn't collect enough signatures and McDiarmid opined that the "Blustery Cro-Magnon had thrown in the towel." Mac wrote that on one of his nicer days.

His relentless criticism included calling DiNello the "Clown Prince of the legislature." And when the senator launched the petition drive, Mac sarcastically ended his column saying, "It's a comfort to know DiNello is leading it." (If you haven't figured it out, Mac was dead set against capital punishment.)

In July 1992, long before the senate race, DiNello wrote an op-ed piece for the *Free Press* in which he claimed McDiarmid was full of "hot air" and accused him of being an "idiot." But that was nothing like his tirade on WJR radio two years later.

Get a load of this quote, which eventually led to DiNello's come-up-ence. The senator was complaining about the verbal abuse from the *Free Press* writer and suggested on the air that, "You throw acid in his eyes. You pull his brain out of his head. You cut off his hands so he can't write. You pull his tongue out of his mouth and if that's not enough you put this guy in an electric chair and execute him."

Astounding. The worst verbal attack on a political journalist in state history. I dare you to find anything more vile.

Senate Democratic photographer Gary Shewsberry was listening that day and immediately called Democratic headquarters. They scrambled to get a copy of the remarks.

A week later DiNello appeared on *Off the Record* and was singing a different tune on February 26, 1994.

He apologized, confessing the remarks were "Totally, totally inappropriate." But he did not extend the apology to the writer. DiNello's damage control seemed to work, but this was months before his reelection bid.

As November got closer, the Democrats produced a radio ad featuring DiNello's own words, which came back to haunt him big time.

LaLonde remembers "playing the commercial constantly." It started to resonate all over southeastern lower Michigan. "We started getting phone calls about the ad and people talked about it when we went door-to-door" for DeBeaussaert, LaLonde remembers.

"We knew we now had a shot at winning," he goes on.

And they won.

GOP senator Dan DeGrow summed up DiNello's defeat perfectly: "His big mouth got him in trouble." DeGrow credits the ad with producing the defeat and Democrats agree.

Almost ten years after the fact a retired McDiarmid reflects, "It never bothered me much." For his part DiNello died of a heart attack riding an escalator at the Somerset Mall during the Christmas shopping season. It's a safe bet he was not looking for a McDiarmid gift.

1990 was the election for governor that will go down in the history books as the grand-daddy of races the incumbent should not have lost, but Jim Blanchard did.

For years John Engler had his sights on being governor and when he began his lonely bid in 1990 to do it, he was probably the only one who truly believed he could. Along the way he made some converts, one of whom was his campaign manager and a virtual unknown Dan Pero.

Over lunch, thirteen years after the fact, Pero was still smiling over the upset win which he attributes to four main factors, foremost of which was Engler's dogged determination. Then there was the nickel ad. The fact that many Democrats didn't like Blanchard and were willing to take Engler around the state to various Democratic events that Blanchard had never attended during his eight years in office. The final elements were the refusal of then Detroit Mayor Coleman Young to lift a finger for the incumbent, and Blanchard's assumption that he would win.

The media played Engler as the underdog because the polls continuously said he was. Even though Engler was the senate majority leader there weren't many folks beyond the capital loop that knew him. He slowly turned that around by riding around in his famous Oldsmobile, while Blanchard flew from event to event in his infamous jet copter.

Pero recalls Engler and Blanchard happened to show up at the same event one day and after it was over, "John got into the car and Blanchard got into the helicopter. We found out afterward that Blanchard flew over the car making some less than complimentary remarks about the GOP challenger." Blanchard says not true.

Pero's take on Blanchard is blunt. "There was no passion for him in the electorate after eight years. The focus groups we ran revealed that citizens couldn't recall one positive thing Blanchard had done." Couple that with the reports that Blanchard's reelect numbers in the polls were low and Engler was able to convince others he was really a contender. Nonetheless there were still the naysayers, even in the Engler camp.

Pero recalls being on the road and Engler would call the headquarters to hype everyone when the polls suggested he could not win.

"We also had a bible of events," Pero recalls. It listed every festival between here and Ironwood and whenever there was a free moment, he would head off to an event that was not on the schedule. Noted for his lead foot, Engler arrived a little late at one such gathering and explained that he was a little late "because I was just meeting with some of your local law enforcement officials." Of course the "meeting" was the result of being stopped for speeding, but the crowd was none the wiser.

TV commercials played a major role in the battle. Blanchard

started his air war with a divisive ad that put him on the defensive right away. The spot dealt with crime but the ad showed a Caucasian drill sergeant type shouting orders at a group of African American boot camp detainees as they were running by the camera. The message was not lost on black voters, many of whom were offended by the image of white man domination.

Engler, on the other hand, devised a spot that addressed the tax revolt issue, which Pero says Blanchard did not connect on. "He was out of touch," he claims. For years, politicians had been trying to sell property tax relief, and Blanchard had such a plan.

John Kost was an advisor to the Engler effort, and one day he figured out that Blanchard's scheme produced a whopping tax savings of five cents a week. Within days, the nickel ad was hatched. It poked fun at the Blanchard tax relief plan by showing a coke and a hamburger and telling voters that's about all you could buy with the governor's cash windfall.

Then Engler ordered a bunch of nickels that he carried with him and he proudly handed them out reminding voters that's what they would get if they voted for Blanchard. If the incumbent had a counter strategy I don't recall it.

Engler was also aware that the relationship between Detroit Mayor Coleman Young and Blanchard was rocky, which is why Engler made it a point to meet with Young and promise to help the mayor down the road. Engler said he would not take Young for granted.

Neutralizing His Honor hurt Blanchard who needed the Detroit vote to win. Pero says near the end of the race, Blanchard was going to ask the mayor to do some radio ads, but "they went to Isiah Thomas instead." Thomas, the famous basketball player, was prepared to do the spot but his agent convinced him to stay out of the contest Pero says. "Then they went back to the mayor and he said no," Pero adds.

As both sides moved into the final week, Engler was feeling what Pero described as, "overwhelming crowd support. At one session a voter told John that Blanchard was so arrogant." Pero says they had a mole inside the opposition campaign and got word that the race was within two points, not the wider margin being reported by the regular press.

But when did you know you had it wrapped up?

"It was days before the election and John and I were speeding down a Detroit freeway when two motorcycle cops pulled us over. Engler was driving. They came up to the car and said, "We just stopped you to say hello and to tell you we're going to vote for you." They didn't get a ticket and got two votes to boot. Turns out they needed them.

That weekend, the Blanchard camp got word that he was in trouble. They tried to beef up the Detroit vote with radio spots, but no air time was available. This was turning into a horse race with a photo finish in the works.

On election day, the first exit poll revealed to Engler that the race was even. Engler phoned headquarters and told everyone not to give up. By this time I was at the Engler election night headquarters in the Radisson ballroom in downtown Lansing. On the Friday before doing the *Off the Record* taping, each reporter was asked to predict the outcome. Three said Blanchard, the fourth, me, predicted Engler. Truth is, my guess was just that, and done in part because there was nothing to lose. If I was wrong, no one would remember. If I was right and Engler won, someone might remember.

On most election nights you can figure on being home sometime around 1 A.M. with the outcome settled anywhere from 8:05 to 11 P.M. depending on how fast the returns come in. This night would be different. Oh yeah.

The 11 P.M. newscasts came and went and it was still too close to call. Around 2 A.M., Engler went to bed telling folks to "wake me when we've won." At about 6 A.M. that's exactly what they did.

I was standing outside the vote counting room just off the main ballroom floor and could hear some shouting inside. According to Connie Binsfeld, who was in there, Spencer Abraham had just gotten the vote count out of Detroit. The margin of victory was razor thin . . . about 17,000 votes, but a win was a win.

Engler appeared and declared victory. It was an election he should not have won.

Having interviewed Pero on his perspective, I asked Blanchard to offer his version. He never responded.

Nothing can top the Blanchard-Engler upset, but the Democratic contest for governor in 1998 did produce some shock waves that caught many of the so called political experts by surprise.

Engler ran unopposed on the GOP side and a trio of Democrats wanted the right to do to him what he had done to Blanchard eight years earlier. Larry Owen had run for governor in 1994 and had the endorsement of the Michigan Education Association, but he lost the nomination to Howard Wolpe. Doug Ross had been commerce director during the Blanchard years and had always flirted with higher office ever since his early days as head of a consumer coalition that got the sales tax on food and drugs wiped out. The third contender was a novice at running for statewide office. What he lacked in experience, Geoffrey Fieger made up with his brash rhetoric that captivated the press corps, and elevated him to the edge of celebrity status, even though many voters couldn't stand the man.

Prior to Fieger jumping in, Owen was leading in the race he should not have lost. However, as 1997 turned into 1998, the East Lansing politician, who had also served with Bill Milliken and was a member of the Blanchard cabinet, kept hearing rumors about Fieger. Owen wanted to know, so he arranged a lunch with the flamboyant barrister at the Town Center in Southfield. It was the first time the two had met.

Fieger wasted little time putting his analysis of the race on the table. Owen recalls Fieger saying, "You can't win. I'm the only guy who can beat Engler. It will take a terrorist to take him out."

Then Fieger somewhat surprised Owen by explaining, "I don't want to be governor." Then he laid out a scenario Owen was not anticipating. Fieger asked Owen to run as his lt. governor, and after a year, Fieger would resign turning the show over to Owen. Owen says he laughed. The deal was never struck and eventually Fieger, after playing cat and mouse with the media, got in.

Owen suspected that Fieger would be strong in Detroit and had hoped to counteract that with an endorsement from Wayne County Executive Ed McNamara. Owen says, "I had a deal in December 1997 with McNamara, but then he got into a dispute with the UAW over a privatization issue." Owen says McNamara came to Owen and asked him to intervene to get the giant union to back off. Owen did not and McNamara withdrew his endorsement.

Owen also failed to secure the MEA endorsement again. The teachers' union took a huge hit from its membership for embracing Owen in 1994 and the new president, Julius Maddox, did not want to go there again. The union remained neutral.

Owen figures had it been a mano-a-mano fight with Fieger, Owen could have won. Having Ross in the race set up the potential for him to siphon votes from Owen. As the campaign went on, the bad blood between Owen and Ross was visible and reached a new low when Ross took off the gloves. He came after Owen on an ethical issue. Owen's stepson had gotten involved in a Las Vegas deal that went sour and Owen ended up sending off a cool $500,000 to help the lad out. "I foolishly helped settle the case," Owen reflects. Ross made an issue out of it, which didn't help Owen one bit.

By the time the three showed up at our studios in July for a debate just before the August vote, the steaminess between the trio was everywhere. Fieger and Owen were seen standing together, laughing, carrying on, and completely ignoring Ross who looked like the outcasts in *Animal House* who were banished to the corner of the room by the frat boys.

When the votes were tabulated, Fieger shocked the experts with a 41–38 win. Owen points to a variety of factors why he went 0–2 running for governor. (1) Money. Fieger spent about $4 million. Owen didn't even come close to that. (2) Ross divided the vote, which Owen figures cost him 10–15 percent. (3) There was a casino issue on the Detroit ballot that drove up the voter turnout by an extra 30–40,000 votes, and Fieger got the lion's share. And (4) the angry young voter went to the polls plunking for their poster boy Fieger, who appeared to be anti-everything.

15

Tough Decisions and
Bad Choices

Dorothy Comstock Riley was the newest and lone female member of the seven person State Supreme Court. After her day at work, she returned to her hotel room at the old Capitol Park hotel, which was within shouting distance of the state capitol. She told her driver before dinner that the "guys [on the court] were a little different today." The date was February 15, 1983.

After she got back from dinner she discovered her woman's intuition was right. The clerk at the desk told her there was somebody from the court waiting for her in the lobby. She walked over and was handed an envelope, the contents of which put into motion, one of the most notorious and politically charged chapters in State Supreme Court history.

"I've just been voted off the court," she told her driver.

The state court system is the least covered by the capital press corps, but that doesn't mean there is no news over there. On the contrary, over the years, the Supreme Court and the honored justices have produced plenty of headlines . . . many of which they didn't want to make. Those headlines often produced controversy that effected the image of the court. If there is one thing this court wants to protect, it is the public perception of that august body.

In the court's defense, it has labored under a Rube Goldberg system that by definition, calls into question the very integrity the court wants to foster. Under the 1963 state constitution, justices for the court are nominated at a political convention. They are forced to ditch their black robes of impartiality and get down in the trenches to grovel for delegate support, just like some slob running for a university governing board. It's very un-judicial and hypocritical.

That's because the day after these contenders are forced to play the partisan game, they emerge, presto-change-o, as non-partisan candidates. One day they are knee deep in the partisan arena and the next they are not. Go figure. What the constitutional framers were drinking at the time of that idiotic decision has never been disclosed.

To make matters worse, the Supreme Court races have seldom been run on judicial philosophy because the candidates are prevented, by judicial rules, from telling voters how they would vote on this case or that. So the contest has degenerated into the 'name game.'

One could make the convincing argument that if you attended a Catholic Church and your relatives came over from Ireland, you've got a darn good shot at sitting on either the appeals court or Supreme Court bench. The roster of court bench sitters includes the likes of Thomas G. Kavanagh, Thomas M. Kavanagh, Mike Cavanagh, Harry Kelly, Marilyn Jean Kelly, Michael J. Kelly, Vincent Brennan, Tom Brennan, Tom Fitzgerald, John W. Fitzgerald, and Jim Ryan.

Even if your lineage was not linked to the church and Ireland, if you had a name of a former court member, your chances of getting elected went up. That's in part why we had Otis Smith and Talbot Smith, Clark Adams and Paul Adams and Robert Burns and Thomas M. Burns on the bench. Voters often couldn't tell one Smith, Adams, or Burns from another.

You get the picture here? The ridiculous system of electing judges has created the impression that all you need to win is a good name. Sure each one of those folks was and is a fine lawyer in his or own right, but very few voters actually knew that. Because of that, many often vote based on name and gender. A female candidate, by the mere fact that she is on the ballot, can automatically count on at least 7 percent of the vote without lifting a finger.

If a candidate was not blessed with a great surname, the high court manipulated the legislature to create an even greater advantage. Whenever a justice runs for re-election, next to his or her name on the ballot is the title, Justice of the Supreme Court.

Talk about a huge advantage. If the electorate knows nothing about the candidates and they see that designation, chances are they'll plunk for the incumbent. History has shown very few incumbents get sent to the showers . . . . save one, and that one grew out of the Riley ouster we talked about earlier. Her removal from the court begins with the death of Supreme Court Justice, Blair Moody, Jr. He was just elected to another term, but two months before his old term expired, he did too.

Governor Milliken appointed Riley to that vacancy. She had just run for the court against Mike Cavanagh and lost. She got a seat by appointment when she couldn't get it at the ballot box. Democrats were furious.

Milliken tapped Riley as he was preparing to leave office and Jim Blanchard was preparing to come in. Blanchard's pal and former employer state attorney general Frank Kelley filed suit with the Supreme Court. In a nutshell he argued Milliken, could not make the appointment, but Blanchard could. Riley was caught in the legal cross fire.

The six male members of the court, minus Ms. Riley, met on a Friday to discuss the case filed by Kelley. Eventually there was a three to three vote. The tie meant Riley would keep her seat and the Chief Justice G. Mennen "Soapy" Williams, duly informed her in a phone call that night.

Riley of course was elated and felt the matter was over.

What she found out afterward is that Democratic Justice Thomas Giles Kavanagh, who had joined two other Democrats to bounce her, told Republican court member Jim Brickley, in the bathroom that, "We're going to bring this back for a vote. We're going to work on Chuck over the weekend." [Chuck was Justice Charles Levin who voted with the two GOP members.]

Brickley said, "Chuck can't change his vote." And Kavanagh told Brickley, "He's got to."

Over that weekend, Levin changed his mind. When the court

reassembled on the following Monday, another vote was taken after Riley left her office. "There was heavy tension in the room before the decision," one of the participants remembers. "I remember Justice Ryan was more upset with Chuck," after the 4–2 vote was taken.

Even though the court is supposed to be non-partisan, the media did not play it that way. Instead we reported that the two Republicans, Brickley and Jim Ryan, were out voted by the Democrats Williams, Kavanagh, Mike Cavanagh, and the former Democrat Levin. The story was Democrats oust a Republican from the high court. It doesn't get more partisan than that.

After she read the terse letter she was handed in the hotel lobby, Riley left Lansing for her home in Grosse Pointe. She wanted to get to her husband, Wallace Riley, before the media got to him. At M-52 just miles away from Lansing, the former Justice Riley heard the story on the radio. By the time she got home, the TV satellite trucks were parked in her front yard. The headlines the next day read: Riley Ousted as Justice Levin Changes His Mind."

The story does not end with that. In fact it was only the beginning.

Levin was forced to attend a rare news conference in which he said he regretted the appearance that the high court was in disarray. He added all the justices, "Must assume responsibility for conveying that impression." He explained that he erred by not voting to remove Riley four days earlier.

Milliken issued his less than flattering assessment of the historic ruling. "There is the fact that the process itself was absurd. The people deserve better. It appears what they got was a response to outside pressure. This strange process serves neither the ends of justice, nor the credibility of the court."

The governor-elect was more sanguine. "I am surprised by the decision. I will have no further comment," as Blanchard distanced himself from the firestorm.

While the fallout from the ouster festered, Blanchard put the heat on federal court Judge Patti Boyle to leave her lifetime appointment to join the Supremes. It is not an easy decision but she said yes.

By now the Republicans are having a field day playing up the partisan aspect of the decision. It does nothing to enhance the image of the court. The GOP bangs the drum so loudly that many citizens conclude the decision had nothing to do with the law, but everything to do with giving the Democrats another seat, and control of the bench.

"It was a pure legal decision," reports Justice Mike Cavanagh who was there. There was no pressure from Blanchard or anyone else. "I never got lobbied."

As for the Levin change of heart and vote Cavanagh added "I thought, Oh my God, why couldn't he have done that out of the gate"?" Regardless, he felt "an anvil was off our heads."

Clearly the pivotal man in all this was Justice Levin. He did attend that news conference, but over the years I always felt there was more to his story.

I was right. Justice Levin graciously agreed to fill in the gaps as we met at an Oakland County restaurant shortly before publication of this book. He had a tuna fish sandwich. I ate potato soup. And there in this deserted eatery with only the waitress to check on us, he unfolded his side of this historic story for the first time.

To put his remarks in the proper context, you need to understand how he got on the court in the first place. Even though he had been a Democrat all his life, and his relatives Carl and Sandy were well-known Democratic office-holders, Levin served on the Court of Appeals as a nonpartisan.

He was fiercely independent, so when he raised his sights on the state's highest court he researched the possibility of running as an independent, thus bypassing the very partisan convention process discussed earlier. He was told by party bigwigs that there was no way he could get the Democratic nomination anyway. It was already ordained that Horace Gilmore and Robert Evans would get the nod to run for the two open seats in 1972.

Levin's legal study revealed there was no state law either permitting or banning an independent candidate from running. To make a long story short, he filed 15,000 petition signatures and staged his own nominating convention at the Olds Plaza Hotel.

His name was placed in nomination by a law school professor at Wayne State University. Levin gave about a two-minute acceptance speech, everyone had dinner, and that was that. The Non Partisan Judicial Party was born, and Levin was the standard-bearer.

He pumped $100,000 into TV ads where he stressed his independence, and got elected. "I would not have run had there not been two openings on the court," he reflects. And running with the Levin name was a plus, too. "That's what counts is the name," he chuckled, taking another bite from his sandwich.

So he wins and arrives on the high court as one of the most cerebral members with no allegiance to either political party. Little did he know that he would be shoved into the middle of the Riley ouster story ten years later.

As the lunch went on, he quickly dispelled one of the popular notions that has dogged this story for years. Given the remarks of Justice Tom Kavanagh to Justice Brickley in the bathroom after the 3-3 vote, everyone assumed tremendous pressure was brought to bear on Levin from Friday night to the next Tuesday.

There was none.

"I didn't take one phone call from anyone over the weekend," he debunks the popular wisdom.

On the day the court ruled 3-3, Levin recalls he was putting the finishing touches on his opinion when Justices Williams and Ryan showed up in his office. It's Friday afternoon, everyone wants to get out of there, and they want to know the status of Levin's opinion.

"I was surprised," Levin recounts. They told me Dorothy would be staying, since there was a 3-3 tie. There was never a formal vote by the bench. Everyone filed their opinions and took off for the weekend.

Levin was troubled by the deadlock. He firmly believed that the court did not have the right to rule on who should get the seat.

It's a thought that returned to him in 2000 when the U.S. Supreme Court picked the President of the United States. Levin believes that was wrong, too.

Nonetheless his "we should not decide" opinion was in the minority on the state court. He gave himself the day off on Saturday to clear his thoughts and then got into the matter again on Sunday. He mulls several options: Do nothing and allow the 3-3 tie to stand or expand the court to eight seats, allowing Milliken to fill one seat and Blanchard another. He was pretty sure there were no takers among his colleagues for such an unusual arrangement, even though the court had done that before.

Eventually, after his due diligence is done, he decides he will change his vote.

On Monday he calls Justice Kavanagh and shares his thinking.

The two then drive to Lansing together on Tuesday. That afternoon, after the regular court business, Riley goes to dinner. The six men stay behind.

Levin is ready to formally change his vote. GOP Justice Jim Ryan comes unglued. He was angry and demanded there be, at the very least, a court hearing on the matter before a final decision is made. Ryan says something about the court giving more due process to somebody who files a motion on the back of an envelope than they are giving a sitting justice of the court.

Levin listens intently. He knows the three Democrats are not persuaded by Ryan's impassioned appeal. Levin knows they want to "get this monkey off their backs." He also concludes that Brickley, while seemingly supportive of Ryan, is not chiming in to buttress Ryan's case. Levin quietly concludes there are not enough votes to hold a hearing.

In one of his best asides of the luncheon that day, Levin notes that the only thing you need to know on the high court is "how to count to four." And he laughs. Without four votes you can't do anything, he explains to this non math major.

There are now four votes to remove Riley as a result of Levin's new decision.

"It was the right and principled thing to do at the time," he explains.

"At the time. . . ." stuck in my mind at the moment he said it to me. Did that mean that long after the fact, he has some doubts?

Indeed he did. Looking down, he quietly reveals, "I never really knew what was the right thing to do. . . . We should have had a hearing . . . I still have doubts," although he repeats at the time it was the right ruling on his part.

What an honest man. What a principled jurist. Someone else might have ended the interview without such a revelation, but not Justice Levin.

To this day, Justice Levin and former Justice Riley have never discussed this story, even though they have been together on several social occasions, including a group tour to Russia with their spouses and friends.

Levin tells me that once Riley returned to the court via the ballot box, he provided another pivotal fourth vote . . . this one to elect her Chief Justice of the court. That's the highest honor to be bestowed on a judge, and it came from a court that once told her to talk a hike. Irony of ironies.

Levin contends the court never did decide which governor had the power to appoint. That might be left to a future court to decide.

Some urged Riley to appeal the new 4-2 ruling. And when she refused, as the 1984 election cycle began, she was urged to run for her old seat and get revenge once and for all.

The 4 foot 11 inch woman, who had to purchase her clothing in the children's department, was not a vindictive jurist. She had served with distinction on the state Court of Appeals and was more interested in deciding cases than fighting political wars.

She practiced law for fifteen years before getting married at the age of thirty-nine. She faced rough sledding in the Wayne State University law school, where she was encouraged to go to business school. When she went to an interview she was often told law firms did not hire females and was encouraged to apply for a secretary's post instead.

"They would look at me and say, "Why aren't you married?" She said she didn't know how to answer that. "I think it's such a stupid, stupid, question," she told the Associated Press.

In 1963, she did marry the former president of the American Bar Association, Wallace Riley. They began their own practice, and when son Peter came along, the two continued to work seven days a week while a grandmother cared for the baby. In 1972, Riley became the first woman on the state Appeals Court.

Now twelve years later she was willing to discuss another bid for the Supreme Court. She dined one night with John Engler and his wife Colleen, at Jim's, a Lansing watering hole. The Engler's wanted Riley to run against Boyle who had to run for the seat after Blanchard appointed her.

The Engler's liked the match-up of a woman against a woman. Besides he told her if she ran against Thomas Giles Kavanagh, who was also up for re-election, she would lose. Engler said, "No Kavanagh has been beaten in a statewide race whether it's a 'C' or a 'K.'

The GOP state party chair, Spencer Abraham, concurred with his buddy Engler. "He wanted to ram the partisan thing down their [Democrats] throats," recounts Gary Mitchell, who handled the media chores for Ms. Riley. Riley, who weighed only 100 pounds, was a heavyweight when it came to her own political career. She boldly told Engler and Abraham, "I've got no quarrel with Patti." She rejected their advice and set her sights on Kavanagh. Now the media had a grudge match . . . the ousted woman tackles the man who ousted her!

On March 7, 1984, Riley read from a five paragraph statement as she tossed her robe into the ring. "I believe that I can bring to our court a measure of balance, fairness and independence that is required for a sound legal system. Thus, today, I announce that I shall be a candidate for nomination to the Michigan Supreme Court." She made reference to the ouster, but not in critical sense. She indicated that she did not appeal the ruling at the time "to spare the court further embarrassment and because I believed that it was necessary to take my appeal to the people of our state . . . "

She and her closest advisor, husband Wally, decided to downplay the removal question. They knew the ouster issue would be raised by others. Wally told her, "You can't raise it," Mitchell recalls. It would have looked self-serving and she did not want to play the role of the abused damsel in distress. Instead her TV ads stressed her judicial independence, which she demonstrated by rejecting the party's plea to exploit the law and order theme.

In reality, however, the media wanted to run the campaign on her removal from the bench. Everywhere she went the topic came up. "Every editorial board we visited brought it up. They did the work for us," Mitchell smiles. On the night before Riley was to appear on *OTR* with Justice Kavanagh in a historic meeting of the two combatants, Riley and company reaffirmed that game plan: If the panel brings it up, we'll discuss it. If not, we won't.

Getting the two candidates together on the set was not as tough as you might expect. Kavanagh, when he was Chief Justice, had done the show and made headlines when he called for the decriminalization of pot, pornography, and prostitution. It was a startling pronouncement that made statewide news and set tongues wagging in the legal community. No other sitting justice in state history had ever been so bold and candid.

Kavanagh was a treat to cover. He was approachable, down to earth, had a wry sense of humor and didn't balk when I suggested he appear with her in what was to be their only joint TV appearance of the campaign. The reporters on the panel were Hugh McDiarmid from the *Free Press*, Ed Petykiewicz from the Booth Newspapers and Tom Greene from WDIV-TV Detroit. None of us really knew what to expect. Riley and Kavanagh were cordial, but no hugs were exchanged. There was an air of anticipation as this was the first time they had met since the removal vote.

Going into these things you never know how they will come out. Based on the first ten minutes of the broadcast, nothing was coming out. It was a dud.

The opening line of questioning centered on whether the current court was too liberal. "I'm persuaded it does not serve the court well to engage in personalities," opined Kavanagh. I could hear the TV knobs all over the state turning to Dallas. [I don't think we had remote controls back in those dark ages.]

Having had enough of that stuff, I turned to the removal issue.

Riley took the bait. She suggested the 4–2 court decision had "impugned the integrity of the court." She then challenged her former colleague to explain how the court could change its mind when "There was no lawsuit. So how did the court act to remove her?" she asked him, and the legal cross-examination was underway.

Kavanagh: "That case involved a ruling, a determination on the constitutional limitations on the governor's powers to appoint . . .

Riley interrupts. "Justice Kavanagh, there was never any, that case was dismissed with a 3–3 decision. There is no definitive determination of that constitutional issue."

Kavanagh: "Well, I suggest," he continued in a slow and deliberate tone, "if you read the opinion . . . .

She jumps in mid-sentence with a direct question, "Well Justice Kavanagh, was the case dismissed or wasn't it."

Now slightly perturbed, but yet totally in judicial character, Kavanagh firmly tells her, "It was not." With a decisive emphasis on the *not*.

In watching this video tape again, it strikes me that viewers were seeing something they had never seen before. Two former colleagues of the state's highest judicial body hashing out their differences, not behind closed doors, as is the usual drill, but for all of us to witness. It was riveting.

Riley continues to press her view that since the court voted 3–3, that settled the matter. Then she amplifies on her charge that the court action demonstrated its "arrogance and rejection of the rule of law."

She tells him, "There was no case pending, no motion to reinstate the case, I was never notified nor were my attorneys that the case was going to be reviewed. Now that's fact," she closed her argument with a strong emphasis on the word fact."

"Is it fact?" I asked her opponent.

Instead of a yes or no answer, he told her that as a good attorney, she knows the courts "speaks through its orders . . . and when the order of ouster was issued, the matter was before the court when that order was entered."

"How?" she incredulously questioned his opinion.

Suffice it to say the two would never agree on that legal point and went onto other matters.

Setting the legal arguments aside, I wanted to hear her comment on the "charge that she was trying to get a sympathy vote and using the ouster for political gain."

She was well rehearsed. Long after the fact, Democratic Justice Mike Cavanagh suggested "she played the issue like a violin."

"That charge is completely incorrect!" she told the panel.

Then to buttress the point she says she never raises it in her stump speech, but I was with her at the Cooley Law School in Lansing and reminded her "you raised it in your speech a week ago."

"I did not raise it in my speech, Tim. You were there." I corrected myself and said, "You responded to a question."

Innocently she responds, "You know I get specific questions and when I get specific questions, I give the answer to the question." That's just they way she planned it. She didn't have to bring it up, it naturally came up and what was she to do, ignore it? Hardly. It was winning her votes.

Kavanagh was asked about her allegedly using the removal to win votes. His remarks revealed his passion for the court's image.

He says it's futile for him to comment on that. But what about her criticism of the court, "do you enjoy sitting here defending these kind of remarks?" I asked.

"Well . . . . [there's a little chuckle under his breath] I don't enjoy defending these kinds of remarks because I think it does a great disservice to the court . . . the institution, hopefully, we both respect."

Greene cuts to the chase, and now Kavanagh really rises to the occasion. "Was there any political pressure brought to you" to remove her from the bench?

"Of course not . . . of course not," he protests.

"Was it a coincidence that four Democrats voted to throw her out?" Greene follows up. That was the core question we had been waiting for all night. Taking a breath he begins, "I think the suggestion, Tom, that this was a partisan, politically inspired decision is not only, ah, unfair and improper, but I think it's ah, ah, um, *extremely* unfortunate because it brings the court as an institution into disrepute."

He continues speaking from his head and his heart. "The idea," [Greene tries to stop him but Kavanagh will have no part of that] "Let me finish please. The suggestion that my Republican colleagues voted because they had been Milliken appointees . . . I find absolutely reprehensible. I don't believe it. And [his voice is now going up] it's just as wrong to say that the Democrats voted from some pressure on account of Democrats. [Pause] It's ridiculous. It . . . is . . . not . . . true!" he says in a staccato tone. Greene ain't buyin' it and offers a sarcastic comeback, "Mere coincidence, right?"

Nonetheless, it was a passionate defense of the high court by Kavanagh. It may have been one of his finest moments. You could not help but be moved by it, but Riley was not. She had a rebuttal. She says the focus has shifted in this debate "as it always seems to do" to play up the fact that she was upset over losing. She says that is irrelevant. "If I had lost the lawsuit . . . I've been in the legal profession for thirty-four years, Giles Kavanagh. I would have accepted it. But . . . " she revisits her main point again, ". . . that's not what I object to."

Riley again accuses the four members of the court of making a decision without notifying her. "It was an arrogant abuse of power."

Was it political? someone asked. "It was worse than partisanship. It was a disrespect for the Rule of Law . . . it went beyond the partisanship," she concluded.

As the program wound down, Petykiewicz asks Riley if she is elected, how can she serve on a court that in effect kicked her out?

She describes that potential "as a very difficult situation" but advises she and the court will make it work.

Kavanagh wants to answer the questions too. He praises her by name for her work on the Court of Appeals and Supreme Court and breaks the tension with the laugh line of the night.

If you are elected, he says, "You and I are not going to have that problem." That's because Kavanagh would not be there anymore.

As is often the case, the debate continued after the red lights went off in the studio. Riley blamed him for being part of a rigid Democratic court majority that was determined not to grant due process to a "Republican lady."

Kavanagh took the bait. "Dorothy, dear, we had a Republican lady on that court once and thought enough of her to maker her Chief Justice." A reference to former jurist Mary Coleman.

Riley would not let go of her assertion that "I didn't lose the case." Kavanagh retorted, "She lost the case." And so it went.

Kavanagh, who spent the entire program on the defensive, missed a golden opportunity to portray her as a hypocrite. While Riley cut herself off from the GOP and cast herself as an independent, there was one damaging quote that she delivered during a very partisan GOP conclave on Mackinac Island. Having lost her place on the bench, she told the shouting crowd, "That is our seat." Kavanagh never brought it up, but frankly somebody on the panel should have.

The program got wide coverage. The day after Eric Freedman for the *Detroit News* wrote under a banner headline: *Race for Supreme Court Turns into a Brawl.* "The battle is beginning to resemble an old-fashioned political brawl instead of the traditionally polite judicial race," he informed his readers. He went on to recount that Riley continued to call the court a "joke" and her opponent suggested, "I'm sorry to hear that assessment."

McDiarmid got a column out of the broadcast, telling his avid readers about the ouster: "Riley talks about it with great passion. Kavanagh talks about it with great resignation. And the high court, which can't talk, just bleeds."

When the votes came in, it was not even close. She got an impressive 56 percent while he got 38 percent.

On a normal election night nobody bothers with the outcome of Supreme Court races. You just assumed that all the Kelly's, Brennans, and Kavanaghs (with a C or K) were victorious. However, this was not a normal night, and Riley made it even more unusual. She refused to talk about it.

She told Mitchell that she would be unavailable. He decried the decision, advising her she had to say something. He wanted to know where she would be. She refused to tell him.

So instead of oncamera interviews, the media had to settle for a two paragraph statement that began, "In the closing hours of this campaign, I would like to thank the people of the State of Michigan, etc, etc, etc." Ending with, "What I sought to do [focus attention on the court and force a dialogue] I have done. Thus, whatever the results of this election, I shall have no further statement to make."

Riley was sworn in and picked up where she left off after serving a scant sixty-nine days on the court. Thomas Giles Kavanagh watched from afar, as the voters, for once, paid attention to a court race and settled the score.

"I hope everybody is going to roll up their sleeves and get to work," suggested Democrat Soapy Williams who remained. Justice Brickley chimed in, "Everybody here's been in the political wars in the past." Justice Boyle, who replaced Riley added, "I think we'll work it out professionally."

Riley later went on to be elected Chief Justice and served on the court until she contracted Parkinson's disease and once more our paths crossed.

A court source told me she was ill. I notified Mitchell, who was still her media advisor. I wanted to talk with her about it. On one hand the story was a private medical story. I was very sensitive to that, as I explained to Mitchell. But on the other hand, the disease could have an impact on her court decisions. I concluded the public had a right to be advised on that potential.

Mitchell conveyed my thoughts to her and it was agreed that I would interview her prior to the State of the State speech, which the justices always attend.

I approached her, with camera, near the senate chambers. Before the interview began I expressed my concerns over her contracting the disease. Then we chatted briefly about the line of questioning I would take. Normally I would never do that, but this was an extremely delicate story and I wanted to walk the extra mile to treat her with dignity and respect, while still fulfilling my journalistic duties. I also thanked her for agreeing to talk.

She spoke on camera saying that "I feel just great, Tim. Just great."

She conceded that her balance was sometimes shaky as was her voice from time to time. It was clear she had told her colleagues she was not leaving.

"I told them that I intended to keep working because I love my work, and I feel just perfect, except for the slight problem with my balance and with my voice on occasion."

Was she up to staying on the bench?

"I certainly am and I intend to stay 'til the end of my term," she firmly suggested.

I reminded her that she always was "a scrapper."

"I have been," she smiled. And the interview was over.

I ran the story that night. Days later Mitchell phoned to report that Justice Riley was deeply appreciative of the manner in which I handled the report. She was very gracious to give me the interview. She did not have to do it. I think she granted the interview because we did have a long term and successful professional relationship.

As the disease progressed, the she finally concluded that she should leave the court before her term was ended. She told Mitchell that she wanted to leave while she was still on her game and not at the point where she had to step down. She retired September 1, 1997, which was nine months after we did the interview. Governor Engler filled the vacancy.

While the Riley ouster was the most notorious chapter in court lore, there were other instances where politics damaged the court's image.

Justice Mary Coleman, mentioned earlier, was ready to retire. Her term was almost over and it seemed logical to leave at the end of the year. Her party however, had a different take. Since most incumbents always win reelections , the party prevailed on her to run one more time. She did. She won. And one month later she retires giving Gov. Milliken a chance to fill the slot.

He does, with his buddy Jim Brickley. Remember, Brickley did not win the GOP nomination for governor, but Milliken made sure his long time friend landed on his feet before Milliken left office. The practice was not uncommon. In fact, John Engler did the same thing in 1997.

When Riley revealed she would leave early due to her illness, speculation quickly centered on Clifford Taylor as a replacement. Engler went through the motions of allowing other names to be part of the speculation game. But Appellate Court Judges Rick Bandstra and Rick Griffin were never in the hunt.

Taylor was a shoe-in. He and the governor were very close, not to mention the fact that Taylor's wife, Lucille, had been with Engler for years and served as his legal advisor to boot. Taylor had been loyal not only to Engler, but to the party. When they needed some unknown nobody to battle Frank Kelley for attorney general, Taylor said yes. When they needed somebody to run for Congress from the East Lansing area, Taylor said yes.

But loyalty is not the word I associated with the affable jurist. That word would be condoms.

To put that in context, you must know that Taylor has an infectious sense of humor and can laugh with the best of them. Judging him in the personal arena, you would never guess he was a judge.

In 1974, Taylor was embroiled in a three person GOP primary for the right to face incumbent Democratic congressman Bob Carr. Taylor was decidedly more conservative than one of his GOP opponents, Bill Ballenger, now the noted editor of the popular *Inside Michigan Politics*.

Taylor authorized an ad castigating Ballenger for supporting the sale of condoms on open drug store shelves. A common practice today, but in the world of right wing GOP politics thirty years ago, that was tantamount to having sexual relations on the capitol steps. The spot was a cheap shot, albeit accurate. Taylor won the primary but lost to Carr. No shocker there.

But the condom stuff was not over.

As fate would have it one night, I was attending a gala put on by a colleague from WKAR-TV. Jim Cash had been a gifted writer on our documentary unit and had parlayed his talents into a Hollywood script writing gig. On the night in question, Cash was hosting the premier of the movie *Top Gun* that he wrote with co-writer Jack Epps. The showing was set for the old Campus Theater near the Michigan State University campus. Cash, before his untimely death, also co-wrote *Turner and Hooch* starring Tom Hanks; *The Secret to My Success* with Michael J. Fox; *Dick Tracy* with Warren Beatty and they were called in to do an emergency rewrite on *Sister Act* with Whoppie Goldberg.

Cash had been gracious enough to invite me and several close friends. We rented a limo for the evening. I drove, complete with chauffeur's hat. But before the movie, Cash-eroo was feted at the home of Bill Madigan, head of the Michigan State Medical Society.

The place was packed on a breathtaking Michigan summer's eve.

I found myself in a conversation with Madigan's and Taylor's mothers. They were delightful, and asked about the new baby in the Skubick household. As I reached for my wallet to show Carly's picture, something dropped out onto the floor. It didn't bounce back up, but you can imagine what it was . . . .yep, a condom.

So here I am embarrassed, yet trying to be cool in front of these two stately matriarchs. I'm praying and hoping they both suffer from severe farsightedness as I quickly and non-chalantly reached for the rubber staring me in the face. I thought I had pulled it off as neither of them said a word.

Whew. I dodged the bullet.

As I finished the conversation and moved to another part of the room, within five minutes, here's Taylor on my trail. He's laughing hysterically and it didn't take me long to figure out why. "Way to go Skubick! Right in front of my mother. Have you no class?" And on and on he goes. I figured I had no choice but to take what he was dishing out and it wasn't long before the whole joint had heard the "rubber" story.

Thankfully it was time to head for the limo, and who should jump in, uninvited? John Engler, who picked up where Taylor left off. Well suffice it to say, it was a long night. The flick by the way was a monster hit, and Cash went on to write countless other screen gems.

But you won't believe this, the Taylor-condom connection was still not over.

Taylor, again answering the call of his party, was nominated to run for the U of M Board of Regents. That meant he would appear on our public TV debate for that contest. As it turned out, one of the hot issues on campus that fall was the insertion of . . . what else? Condom machines in U of M dorms.

With all my fingers and toes crossed, I asked Taylor during the program for his stance on the question. I wondered if he had the guts to bring up the Skubick-condom story? He did not and I think he opposed the selling of maize and blue prophylactics at his alma mater. He did remind me of the story afterward.

As a reward for helping the party, Engler eventually helped Taylor by plucking him from the Appeals Court and giving him the Supreme Court spot.

Another appointment that stirred the waters was that of Conrad

Mallett, Jr. Jim Blanchard was headed out the door after losing to Engler in 1990 and just like Milliken before him, Blanchard appointed one of his closest friends to a seat on the court as he was turning out the lights.

Mallett had served as a savvy confidant to Detroit Mayor Coleman Young before joining Blanchard as his legislative lobbyist and then as his legal advisor.

"Connie," as he was known, was a total hoot to cover. Sharp wit, sharper mouth and even sharper mind, Mallett was good for a story or two. You could yank him aside and get the low-down on what was going on and he never pointed me in the wrong direction. He was a load of laughs and just fun to be around.

The timing of his appointment to the bench drew some media criticism on several fronts. Blanchard was tagged with failing to "rise above petty partisan politics" by the *Detroit News*, when Mallett was picked. And wasn't it ironic that Blanchard was being tagged for making an eleventh hour appointment, just as he had done to Milliken eight years earlier. Blanchard dismissed that and other remarks as "partisan drivel." He noted that even though Mallett had never been a judge, the same could be said for Jim Brickley, Soapy Williams, former U.S. Senator Bob Griffin and Dennis Archer, whom Mallett was replacing. Blanchard, always the student of government, suggested "anytime you encourage new faces to assume some power, you get criticized . . . . The media seems to suggest there's only room for one black leader in the state . . . Coleman Young, and anytime anybody else crops up, it's very interesting. Because they are new they get beat around."

He brushed aside the flap, suggesting the Mallett would serve with distinction. In fact, Mallet eventually became the 60th Chief Justice and the first African American to hold that post. He also set into motion a court reorganization plan that had languished in the legislature for eons.

But while Democrats applauded Mallet's judicial expertise, the jurist opened a real political can of worms when he decided to take a lucrative position in the private sector. The firestorm blew up because the vacancy allowed GOP governor John Engler to name a replacement and take firmer control of the high court.

Even before Mallet's December 11 decision in 1998, the GOP

won enough seats in the previous month's election to take a 4–3 edge. Mallet's departure and Engler's appointment of another African American, Jurist Robert R. Young, Jr, gave the Republicans a hefty 5–2 edge. It's that advantage that had some Democrats stewing.

Mallet addressed the issue saying had the Democrats stayed in control, "I don't think I could have left then."

As for the criticism in 1990 that he did not have bench experience, which Blanchard defended, Mallet confessed in his swan song news conference that "I wish I'd had more trial experience . . . but I was fortunate that other justices had experienced that, and could convey that experience to me."

Keeping that 5–2 edge was a top priority for the GOP in 2000, and Democrats were just as committed to wrestling it away. The stakes were high as both parties proceeded to make the court race even more political than before.

Three GOP bench sitters were up for reelection. Taylor, Steve Markman, and Young, Jr. The Democrats put up an impressive field with Marietta Robinson, a savvy and successful trial lawyer from Detroit, E. Thomas Fitzgerald who sat on the state appeals court and flirted for years about running for the high court, and a Detroit attorney Edward Thomas.

The major players on the sidelines ready to bankroll the candidates were the Michigan Chamber of Commerce and allies fighting for the GOP, and the Michigan Trial Lawyers and associates helping to finance the Democrats.

The Democrats, in what one of the candidates called a major blunder, began an ad campaign lumping all of the Republicans into one bunch. The infamous "Markman, Taylor, and Young. Oh My" commercial was a take off on the "Lions, Tigers, and Bears, Oh My" line from the *Wizard of Oz.*

The ad got plenty of media attention because it was unique as Democrats tried to paint the three GOP'ers as extreme conservatives, chipping away at the rights of the little guy. But candidate Tommy Fitzgerald contends the spot, conjured up by the same folks that did Bill Clinton's advertisements, only served to make the trio a household name in an electorate that knows squat about judicial candidates. In other words the ad was ill-conceived.

Republicans had some ads of their own. One spot targeted the likable Judge Fitzgerald. It would cause a stir because it left the impression he was a pedophile which, of course, he was not.

The TV spot suggested Fitzgerald had given a "slap on the wrist" to a man who sexually molested a seven year old girl and had seven earlier convictions." As the script is read, there is a picture of an older man and the word "pedophile" is under the picture. The word gets bigger as the spot goes on.

If you did not know what Judge Fitzgerald looked like, and who the heck did, the viewer might assume that he was the pedophile in the ad.

The announcer concluded that "Fitzgerald has voted to reverse criminal convictions more than fifty times and now he wants us to put his team on the court. That's scary. Fitzgerald, Robinson, and Thomas: weak on crime . . . wrong for the court . . . wrong for our kids."

The GOP also sent out a mass mailing with the same tone and misrepresentation. One such piece arrived in the home mail-box of Fitzgerald. His pre-teenage daughter got the mail that day and came into the house in tears. She wanted to know about this pedophile stuff. Fitz was livid. His wife was even more angry. She had urged her husband not to run because she knew it would get nasty, and this was proof she was right.

"My wife was absolutely furious," he remembers. His daughter got an unsolicited lesson in hardball politics.

GOP Chair Rusty Hills took credit for the spot, saying he was going after Fitzgerald because he was considered to be the strongest of the three Democrats due to his popular judicial last name.

Fitz's media guy Mike Shore called the spots "clearly over the edge . . . gross charges, and beyond the pale." Shore also called it a smearing.

It was against that backdrop that public TV prepared to produce the only televised debate of the campaign. The six contenders posed for pictures before the program. It was the only time they were together all fall.

The pedophile ad would dominate the Fitzgerald/Young segment, but before we got to that, it was Justice Taylor and challenger Robinson in the barrel first.

The two were meeting each other for the first time in our studio.

There were no rules for the exchange, which left the door open to a free exchange. Robinson was clearly the aggressor as she clobbered the court. At one point Taylor suggested, "The damage that this woman is doing to the judicial institution of this state is breathtaking. These claims are simply not true."

One of Robinson's claims was that the three Republicans on the court are "embarked on a political agenda the likes of which we've never seen on our highest court." She went on to accuse Taylor of being biased.

I turned to Taylor, "Guilty?"

"Gosh, ah, no [with his voice raising on the "o"]. He blamed the Democratic Party Chair Mark Brewer with distorting the courts record. "They claim we're corrupt. This is really unprecedented since this state came into being," he said with a frustrated tone.

She won't say the trio of jurists is corrupt but she asserts that their decisions are made with one eye on the law and the other on the special interest groups the judges support, namely "big business, insurance companies and not the little guy."

Taylor will have nothing to do with that. "It's a lie," he protested. He on the other hand declined to charge her with being a pawn for trial lawyers and big labor but he does add, "I think she gets an inappropriate amount of money from one law firm and from one narrow segment of the bar, meaning the trial lawyers.

It is a lively exchange. Her attacks clearly keep him on the defensive and several times he asserts his desire to get a word in edgewise. "Are we going to have time here for me to make a presentation?" he pleads his case with me.

On one hand, Taylor tries to stay on the high road not wanting to appear too aggressive. He says, "I don't want to impugn her integrity at all. I don't know her well enough to do that. And then add a little zinger coda: She's never been on the court."

She can find nothing nice to say about him or his partners. "I've been ashamed and disgusted at what this group has done to the judiciary in Michigan," she continued.

Taylor accuses her of being the Paladin of the rich personal injury lawyers who "are willing to do anything, say anything. No charge is too outrageous and in Ms. Robinson they have found a vehicle for this."

"This is an absolute outrageous lie," she fires back.

As I am sitting there, I'm thinking I've done a lot of judicial debates, but this one has the most slings and arrows of all them. Robinson figured this was her only shot, so she bores in. But Taylor comes up with the line of the night, or at least the sound bite that got into my story.

"She has said repeatedly this court has been bought and paid for. These things are just plain amazing." That's the set up and here's the kicker, "If she thinks this court is corrupt, she shouldn't be talking to Tim Skubick, and she should be talking to the sheriff."

After their closing remarks, I can't remember if they shook hands. I know they didn't hug.

Next up was incumbent Justice Robert Young, Jr., the only African American on the high court and veteran Court of Appeals judge Tom Fitzgerald. I took a different tack with them and asked the challenger what question he wanted to ask his opponent.

"Bob, what's the number on your parking pass at the court? You won't be needing it after November 7."

Young quietly says, "That's kind of you to say that." Then Fitz says he was just joking. There were no more laughs as the debate quickly shifted to the TV ad—the one Fitzgerald's daughter brought in from the mail box.

Fitzgerald asks, if his party had run the pedophile ad against Young, "would you like to have your sons see it?"

Young ignores the thrust of that and answers, "About as much as I like being called a racist by Mark Brewer and the Democratic Party."

Young reveals that he has talked to the state GOP chair to complain about the pedophile spot. Then he asks Fitzgerald if has logged a similar gripe with Brewer. Fitzgerald has not, but says he will if that is legal.

Young is not satisfied and wants Fitzgerald to denounce it. "You can say it right now. I hate the kind of sleazy campaign your party is running. I hate the fact that you're using race to influence the campaign."

Fitzgerald remains mute. It's interesting that so many of these debates eventually get around to debating the commercials. In one sense, it's understandable, because so much is riding on the impression those ads leave with the voters. I strongly believe we have a lazy electorate that too often makes a decision based on those spots, so the candidates have to battle each other over the content, hoping to persuade the voters the ads are lies.

But Michigan law is strange. The candidates themselves have no control over the commercials run by their supporters or independent committees, as they are called. Attempting to influence those groups is considered by some to be illegal.

After millions of dollars were spent, the three incumbents scored impressive victories. Markman, Taylor and Young got eight more years on the bench and the GOP securely held control of all three branches of government. Democrats were in a deep funk, but could do nothing but wait for the next election cycle for revenge

Former State Appellate Court Judge S. Jerome Bronson was talking with an old friend in 1987. What the judge didn't know was that the friend was bugged. In a scout car, state troopers and the attorney general's crime unit were listening in on a court-authorized bug, waiting for the judge to incriminate himself. Bronson emerged from the meeting and into the handcuffs of the cops. He was arrested on the spot for soliciting a bribe.

All of the other stories in this chapter have been political messes. The Bronson saga was a full-fledged scandal that began with a phone call just after the 1986 election.

The Chief Judge of the State Court of Appeals, Robert Danhof, was in his office when a call came in at 9 A.M. . . . a call that would eventually tarnish the state court system as it had never been blemished before.

Judge Joe B. Sullivan, who once worked for Detroit Mayor Jerome Cavanagh, had some information to share. It was about a case that was pending in the appeals court. The phone conversation centered on the allegation that Bronson was trying to squeeze a bribe out an attorney who had a case pending before Bronson and two other judges.

Danhof and Sullivan decided to continue their secretive talk over lunch in Lansing. Sullivan says attorney James Canham had a prehearing report he should not have had. Sullivan hints Bronson may be seeking a $20,000 bribe.

Chief Judge Danhof is getting all this second, third, and fourth hand. "I'm not sure whether I've got bar talk," Danhof recalls but he knows he can not assume that it is. He calls the Michigan State Police and sets up a meeting at headquarters in East Lansing for the next morning. Before he leaves his office for the day, he calls in the court clerk and shares the information with him, "Just in case I got hit by a car going home," the judge says.

At the huddle at the cop shop, the attorney general's office is brought in and the probe commences of Judge Bronson. Danhof hears nothing about it for months, as he resumes his normal duties.

Hunting season is just around the corner and Danhof heads to West Branch where he is the first guy to arrive at the lodge. The cook is there and says there's a call for a Judge Danhof. Danhof takes the message from Stanley Steinborn, the second in command in Attorney General Frank Kelley's office.

Steinborn reports the thing is "coming down."

Local Judge Tom Brown approves the use of a bug to nab the suspected judge. There are several recorded phone conversations. The money drop is finally set. Bronson meets Canham at his office. Canham has a suitcase with $25,000 inside. Bronson takes the suitcase and walks out of the office. Two state police officers arrest him on the spot.

They shuttle him before Judge Brown. Because events are moving so quickly, Bronson does not have legal counsel. Brown steps outside his court room and sees Lansing trial attorney Hugh Clarke, Jr.

"What are you doing?" the judge inquires. Clarke says nothing. He is immediately ushered into the court to appear with Bronson, who is charged, but released on bond. The attorney general's guys ask if the judge is OK and if he needs a ride to Farmington Hills. Bronson says he's all right and gets in his state car and heads to his office, where the state believes he removes some files, and then he heads home on that fateful Friday afternoon.

After the update, Danhof remains at the hunting camp where he takes another phone call from son Bill.

"Dad, Bronson just committed suicide. I just heard it on the radio."

The senior Danhof calls the local state police post for verification and gets it. Bronson used a revolver to shoot himself in the back of the head. Danhof forgets the hunting trip and goes home to huddle with two court employees. A major scandal is bursting and he drafts a statement.

Since the Jewish religion does not allow burials on Saturday, the funeral was set for that Sunday.

Danhof takes another phone call on Saturday. This one is from the Chief Justice of the State Supreme Court. "Soapy" Williams is at the U of M football game in Ann Arbor and wants to know how long Danhof has been on this case. Williams knew nothing about it.

The two chat and the "Chiefy," as they call the Chief Justice, tells Danhoff that he has handled the matter correctly.

At the funeral, Bronson's mother berates Danhof for what he has done. But Bronson's brother Ken, who is also a local judge, tells Danhof "you did the right thing."

Leon Cohen, a former Frank Kelley aide, sees Danhof after the funeral. "Bronson's problems are over, but he left a big pile of shit for everyone else," Cohen correctly concludes. The media is all over this story that not only rocks the public, but the tightly knit legal community as well. Shortly thereafter, the lawyer who was being hit up for the alleged bribe came home, jumped in the pool and never came up. He died from a heart attack. An internal court investigation is launched parallel with a federal and state grand jury. The state and feds want to know if Bronson was involved in any other illegal activities. They paw over his bank accounts and learn that he is 'living the high life' as one investigator puts it. The judge had a house in Colorado and Florida and a life style to match.

The state judicial system has not suffered any other scandals as dramatic as this and while many of the principles are dead, the memory of this dark chapter lives on especially in Danhof's mind as the above account was based on his recollections.

The next to last court story in this chapter centers around one of the court's most hallowed principles: No opinion should be made public before the court makes it public. Getting a court verdict out of the court before it's officially released, is like trying to steal gold bars out of Fort Knox.

I got one 'bar' out that left the chief justice angry.

The state legislature, local prosecutors, the state attorney general and the pro- and anti-gun lobbies, had been tangled in a controversial struggle to rewrite the state's concealed weapon's law. The pro-gun folks wanted to liberalize the law. They complained that there was not equal justice when it came to securing the coveted Carry Concealed Weapons (CCW) permit. It depended on where you lived and who was on the local gun board, some argued.

The anti-gun lobby argued that lives would be lost if this proposed new law took effect. The rhetoric was getting hot.

"We'll return to the days of the Old West," was a favorite line. Each anti-gunner predicted a body count that got higher with each passing day.

The other side chimed in that lives would actually be saved as criminals would think twice about attacking anyone who might be hiding some heat. And so it went, until the legislature finally adopted the measure.

As predicted, the matter went into the courts before it went into effect. Eventually it got to the Supremes, where that body would rule on whether the law would go on the books on July 1.

This was one of those stories that impacted everyone, so the pending court ruling had everyone's attention, including mine.

Bit by bit, the decision story started to fall into place for me. Remember, there are plenty of folks working at the court and while the security was tight, there were ways to get the information, if you made the right calls.

It was the day of the expected court decision and I was pretty sure I had this one nailed. I was pretty sure five justices would vote for the new law with two against.

At noon time I phoned the radio desk in Detroit. "I've got the court decision on the CCW law," I told the WWJ editor and within minutes I was on the air announcing the 5–2 ruling. The report was also aired on the Michigan Radio Network, which feeds the state capital news to sixty-plus stations.

En route to Harbor Springs, Appeals Court Judge E. Tom Fitzgerald was listening to the radio and heard my report. He rang his secretary asking her to call me with a "way to go" and to find out "How the hell I got that story." It was the same question the supreme court jurists were asking as they were still hours away from releasing the formal opinion.

I repeated the story about three more times, milking it for all it was worth. You know the drill, "WWJ News radio 950 with this exclusive report out of Lansing" the anchor would say. But all the while I'm reporting, I'm hoping I'm correct. By this time the court was aware of my reports. Other reporters were calling the court media office for confirmation, which of course they didn't get. All the P.R. guy would say was that was Skubick's story, not the court's.

The three hours ticked off very slowly as every imaginable scenario rumbled around in my head. Maybe they would pull back the decision. Maybe somebody would change his or her vote. Maybe I'd be looking for work the next day. My little behind was sitting out there ready to be shot off by a concealed weapon or something else as 4 P.M. rolled around.

Finally the court released the decision. 5–2. The law would take effect. I was relieved.

But there was some serious fallout from the bench over breach of security. The Chief Justice said she was "angry and upset. That is the first time that had happened" and she took steps to make sure it didn't happen again. She warned if it occurred again, she would call in the state police to investigate.

Actually that was my second "leak" out of the high court. In the '70s a history-making decision on the state gasoline tax got out early and I had it on the air days before the court ruled. If you do the math, two leaks in thirty-four years means the high court is way ahead in this "who can get it first" game.

This final story gives you a peek at the impact that *Off the Record* has in one judicial household in the state. The participants will go nameless for reasons that will be obvious as you read on.

The unidentified judge tells the story of one Friday night when he knew his children would be gone. On the way home he picked up a bottle of champagne and worked on the twinkle in his eye as he looked forward to a night of romance with his wife.

"We seldom have time alone," he noted. It got to be 9 P.M. and the judge was ready, but his spouse was not. "She told me she had to watch *Off the Record*," the frustrated jurist reports as he stood there with a glass of bubbly.

He couldn't believe it and blurted out, "Either Skubick has one hell of a show or I'm one hell of a lousy lover."

He did not report how his wife responded but she watched our show . . . .not his. Upon learning of this, I scraped together enough pennies to send them a bottle of champagne with this note, "Thanks for watching *OTR*. . . . now go do something different."

I got a return thank you note with this inscription, "You are the greatest . . . we are going to enjoy."

16
Mr. Show Business

Frank J. Kelley began his law career in Alpena. But he almost didn't have one. In fact, up until age 11, he just wanted to be a cowboy, but the sisters at St. Theresa had different plans. They allowed him to skip the eighth grade and boosted him right into high school where he graduated at the tender age of sixteen. He entered the University of Detroit and proceeded to flunk out after one semester.

"I did not know how to study, and college pointed that out to me rather quickly," he recalls. So there he was at the tender age of seventeen, out on the street with no career path to follow.

Enter Divine intervention.

After a stint in the Merchant Marines, Kelley was walking down Jefferson Ave in Detroit and happened by a bulletin board on the U of D campus. A priest saw him standing outside and wondered if there was anything he could do for the young man.

Kelley said, "No Father, I don't think you can, for I have already had my chance at U of D, and I blew it.

"Young man, that's why I am here. My job is to give second chances to young people like you."

Within fifteen minutes Kelley was enrolled, on probation, for ten hours of courses in the evening school. It took him seven years but he finally got his undergraduate and law degrees. He headed off to Alpena where he was plucked out of total obscurity by then Gov. John Swainson to be attorney general and the rest, as they say, is history. And after his thirty-seven year record run, the national association of attorneys general renamed its annual award in his honor.

Truth be known, a young Mr. Kelley, besides wanting to be a cowboy, also wanted to go into show business as a talent manager. In fact he concedes show biz "ran in our blood." His mom was a model often appearing in *Ladies Home Journal* and *Women's Home Companion.* One of his uncles was a drummer with Wayne King and other big bands of that era. His aunt was the first woman to sing on radio and his daddy used to manage prize fighters, but became a "Great Public Servant." Dad was also a Democratic Party activist and wanted his son to be a lawyer, so the two compromised. Kelley would go to law school and use the degree to be a "manager of talent" as he puts it.

That's how the *Detroit News* described Frank E. Kelley who wanted his son to be a lawyer and not a "manager of talent."

A wife and three kids later, those plans fell by the wayside. "My father and I agreed being a talent manager was not a good idea for a man with three children. I gave it up."

But he really didn't. He just took his act to the legal stage where he performed with ease and style and every four years he gave the voters an encore after they reelected him. He was a political star because during his third, fourth, and fifth grades in school, a weekly visitor came to the Kelley home in Detroit.

"Dad hired an elocutionist, nobody today knows what that is anymore, to come to the house and teach us to stand up and speak on our feet." Kelley was a good student. He knew in the back of his head that his Irish ancestors valued such talent, so he practiced real hard and got real good.

"Public service was a high calling for the Irish," he reflected. One of the traits they honored was the ability to get on your feet and give a speech . . . to be a public person.

By the time Kelley got to high school he was starring in plays and reprised that in college. "I was good enough," he says, "to get the roles."

Kelley continued to dabble in the arts in college and even roomed for a time with the old *Tonight Show* host, Steve Allen. The two even dated the same girl . . . but not at the same time. They later had a philosophical falling out and never spoke to one another after that. Allen went to the right and Kelley stayed on the left.

Once he arrived on the Lansing scene it was obvious the A.G. loved being in the news. One of his former assistants instituted a policy whereby every news release began with the words, "Michigan Attorney General Frank Kelley today announced . . . ." They call that top billing.

Kelley says he never ordered that format but confesses that Leon Cohen did it to "impress me and he certainly did," he says with laughter.

Even though he was often center stage, Kelley lived by the advice he got one day on the campaign trail from John F. Kennedy.

"It was his last visit to Michigan before he died," Kelley recalls. The scene is the old Sheraton Cadillac Hotel in Detroit. Because the attorney general was doing so well in the polls, Gov. Swainson hooked JFK to Kelley's wagon for the day. When the trio stopped for sandwiches the conversation turned to egos and who had the most and least.

The president looked Kelley in the eye and said, "Frank, we are all egoists. The winner is the one who hides it the best."

"It was a pretty good line and it's true," Kelley figures. He says the Kennedys were masters at it. "It always appeared that they had to be forced to run," when in reality they lusted for the power.

Kelley adds the president was also suggesting that humility in politics was important and it was best "not to let your ego get the best of you."

Throughout his tenure Kelley developed a knack for selecting issues that got him plenty of attention and ink. He made a career out of fighting the nasty utilities in this state. Everyone pays a monthly bill and anything Kelley did to keep those bills down made him a champ with the little guy and the enemy of the corporate profit mongers.

When electronic scanners at the grocery store became all the rage, there was Kelley raging about their inaccuracies. He invited every TV camera in the Western Hemisphere to record his denouncement of the rip-off. Sometimes it was only pennies, but who was counting. It was good TV.

He contends over a five year period, millions of dollars were lost and he did such a good job of exploiting the story that NBC's *Dateline* did a national report on it and won an Emmy for its coverage of Kelley's crusade.

He pleads guilty to attaching his wagon to issues that gained him public notoriety. He says that's because the average person has a better chance of being cheated in consumer fraud than being criminally assaulted.

He ran every four years for reelection and defeated ten opponents, most of whom nobody can remember. That's because all of the big names never had the nerve to take him on. Asked to reveal which challenger he enjoyed beating the most, he dead panned, "I don't want to get sued for libel."

His 1994 opponent, John Smietanka, "lacked a sense of humor. I never knew why John was always so dead serious. I liked John but the day after he lost, he started campaigning for the office again and lost the second time to Jennifer Granholm."

Smietanka was getting under Granholm's skin when she ran for A.G. after Kelley retired. He aired an ad linking her to Geoffrey Fieger. Rather than answer the ad herself, the neophyte Granholm asked Kelley to do the dirty work. He readily agreed.

He flew to Buffalo, New York to tape the thirty second spot. The commercial opens with Kelley sitting on a stool watching a TV screen. On the screen is the tail end of the Smietanka ad.

Kelley turns to the camera, "That ad is garbage. I've spent thirty-seven years protecting the people of Michigan from cons. I know one when I see one. John Smietanka is running a dishonest campaign." He utters the line with all the indignation he can muster.

It's always tough to determine what contributes to a victory, but there are a host of Granholm loyalists who point to that Kelley performance as a key factor. He also recorded the spot in five minutes, which in and of itself reveals how much talent he has. Most politicians are less polished and take hours.

Kelley had a slight flirtation with national office, but never the governor's chair. "It never appealed to me." Some heavy weight labor types in 1964 wanted Kelley to derail George Romney, the popular GOP governor.

"I was summoned to a meeting with Walter Reuther [UAW president] and others and they asked me to run."

"Gentlemen," he began, "I'm sorry. I'm just not interested and I never will be." Kelley preferred lawyering to being the "political spokesman for the state."

He did run for the U.S. Senate, however. "That was more my father's sort of thing. He bragged that was the most exclusive club in America." But with liberal Democrat George McGovern on the top of the ticket in 1972 and with Kelley on the "wrong" side of the cross district busing [he was for it] he never had a chance. It was his one and only attempt to move up the political food chain and GOP Senator Robert Griffin devoured Kelley.

"I remember talking with Ohio Senator Bill Saxby after the election and I thought he was trying to comfort me. He said he was going to quit. That it wasn't the way it used to be. Another senator said the same thing." Then and there Kelley buried the senate bug.

I always wanted to do the following story on Kelley. Whenever he called, the capital press corps for one of his announcements, he would begin by reading a carefully prepared statement. [That elocutionist stuff paying dividends.] He was in total control. His Irish relatives would have loved him up there on his feet. However, often times once the reading was over and the heavy questioning began, Kelley could be seen leaning to this side or that. He was searching for the answer from his assistants, who had more knowledge than him. Those folks always stood off to the side so as not to be in the picture with the boss, but they were still close enough so if he needed a life line, it was within reach.

In his defense, it was impossible to know every detail about every item, but for a guy so concerned with his image, it always struck me that he was vulnerable, and if a good opponent could have gotten some footage of his performance, he or she could make a point with the voters. To underscore this image thing, I had a run in with the Kelley gang over an elevator story. Kelley's office was on the top floor of the Law Building in the capitol complex. There were four elevators that serviced the seventh floor and there was usually a wait before you got on.

One day I noticed a little button in a spot where no little button had existed. It was right next to the elevator on the far right. My reporter's natural curiosity was aroused and since I had nothing else going that day, I asked some questions.

Turns out Kelley had ordered the installation of a bypass device that speeded the elevator directly to his floor leaving all the other peasants on the other floors cooling their heels. It was a clear violation of JFK's rule about hiding your ego and arrogance. It was my opinion that the device was proof he had both and I said so in the column.

We got the figures on how much the taxpayers paid for this little perk and ran the story in the weekly newspaper column. Well, you would have thought we had accused him of robbing a bank.

A few days later a letter to the editor appeared in the paper from one of his henchmen, Assistant Deputy Attorney General Haywood W. Julian. Woody, a former cop out at MSU, was the designated hitter. Kelley would never respond himself. That would add too much credibility to the story. So the letter did not begin with "Frank Kelley announced today." Instead it politely started with, "Please allow me the opportunity to respond to a grossly [oh oh] inaccurate [double oh oh] and misleading article by Tim Skubick giving the false impression that Attorney General Frank Kelley has a private elevator on demand."

Whoever wrote this thing was obviously not a writer. The letter explains the elevator in question is for one department and another is for the law library and, "thus, one elevator, while serving six of the nine levels within the building, does bypass the third, fourth and fifth floors."

What???

Julian tries to divert blame away from his boss by suggesting the decision was made by the Supreme Court and a group representing the lawyer's in Kelley's office. How lame.

The defense was a joke. Kelley wanted the express elevator because he didn't want to stand around, and taxpayers picked up the tab. He should have ignored the story but when his office responded, I knew I hit a nerve. To this day Kelley defends the installation of the device and strongly argues he was not seeking special treatment. "It was not my personal elevator," he protests.

Mr. Kelley also had an organized crime division headed up by Vincent Persanti. The mob was always a good story, but frankly, over the years Kelley's gum-shoes had not produced many headlines or, more importantly, any major convictions.

The unit was costing taxpayers about $300,000 a year for a bunch of attorneys sitting around, "clipping newspaper articles and attending funerals [ala that scene in the *Godfather*]" one inside source recounts while adding, "They were doing useless shit."

Then one day, Mr. Persanti ends up on the unemployment line. He proceeds to berate the attorney general for losing interest in organized crime. It was a rare frontal attack from a credible witness and it caused some nervous moments in the inner sanctum. But the story went away. The unit was dismembered and shifted to the state police, which also had paper clippers and funeral attenders of their own. Years later Kelley and Persanti patched up their differences, says Kelley.

The one race for attorney general that everyone in town wanted to see was Kelley against Brooks Patterson. It was 1982. The advance billing conjured up visions of fist fights, verbal brick bats, and a good ole fashion tough guys contest. Patterson was Mr. Law and Order and had a mouth to match. He often laid into Kelley, but nothing stuck. And then there was the debate before the Oakland County Bar Association.

The place was packed with about two hundred lawyers, media, and others hoping to see some fireworks. As the debate nears the end, Patterson delivers his closing statement. He brings to the podium a suitcase filled with $14,000, but the audience doesn't know that and neither does Kelley.

Patterson accuses Kelley of taking a recently awarded $14,000 pay increase and with that he opens the suitcase and tosses all the money into the audience, which the TV cameras dutifully recorded. Talk about your good visuals.

Patterson closes his remarks and Kelley, who has been madly figuring on a pad of paper steps up to the microphone. He tells the audience that over the last four years Brooks Patterson has received raises as well . . . that came within fourteen dollars of what Kelley got. In other words Patterson was just as guilty as Kelley.

Kelley says that night, pictures of the flying money appeared in the TV accounts, but it was Kelley's remarks that got aired, thus turning a possible disaster into a wash.

Of all the officeholders I've covered, I watched Kelley for nineteen years. He never ducked any of our public TV debates, and he appeared on the regular *OTR* seventeen times in sixteen years. Told you he liked the cameras.

After one debate, I wrote a column in which I described Kelley's arrival at the studio. There was this aide and that staffer and the driver and then I added the phrase, "and other hangers-on."

I soon heard through the grapevine that the two accomplished secretaries who guarded the door for Kelley felt that term applied to them. Pat Anderson and Sandy Szul were no hangers-on.

When I learned they were offended, I bought two potted plants and personally delivered them with the appropriate note, which I think read in part, "Dear Hangers-on: So sorry for the mistake. Please forgive me."

They were touched. We all had a good laugh. I vowed to strike 'hangers on' from my lexicon. Pat, by the way, still has her plant in Kelley's private sector office. Unfortunately for Sandy, there was a fire on the seventh floor of her office building years ago, and the plant didn't make it.

As you run from one story to the next, you seldom get the opportunity to just shoot the breeze with the folks you cover. That happened one day in the penthouse office of Mr. Kelley . . . you know the office with the express elevator service?

It was a beautiful day and the news conference was over. There were just the two of us. He got up to look out into the beautiful midday sunshine. Seemingly out of nowhere he advised me, "You know sometimes you have to take the time to smell the roses." I thought at the time he might be going through a mid-life crisis or something, but afterward I concluded he was probably talking more to himself than to me. It was a reminder that no job is so important that you can't stop from time to time to breathe it all in. It seldom happens in this town.

Later on, as he prepared to leave office, he demonstrated that he had acted on his own "smell the roses" advice. As he tells the story he was coming out of a state Democratic Party convention in Detroit's giant Cobo Hall. To get out he has to walk through the annual boat show. A brilliant red cigarette speedboat catches his eye. He buys it on the spot. Twenty years ago, he explained, he would have taken more time to weigh the pros and cons, but he figured, why wait? There might not be another chance tomorrow. The 'rose' cost a pretty penny but he didn't care.

Kelley possessed a fiery temper. While he never lost it during a news conference, you could always tell when he was getting defensive. His rate of speech would go up along with his voice. A highly competitive sort, he was quick to shoot back if some reporter shot at him, so you could always tell when you "got him."

In private, his staff knew when he was angry. During a controversial investigation into the private life of a state senator, Kelley lost it when he learned his office was involved, even though he had told everyone to stay out of it.

His assistants got a tip that Highland Park Democrat Basil Brown was allegedly buying and peddling cocaine in Detroit. The local prosecutor's office joined the probe, which was taken to a higher level when a bug was placed on a prostitute who was friendly with Brown. Enough evidence was recorded to make a case. But when Kelley found out, he refused to prosecute.

"It was a tainted investigation. I was very much upset because of the ethics of the investigation," he says. He ordered his people off the case and let the Ingham County prosecutor's office proceed without state aid.

Kelley did not want any publicity from that but as noted before, he was more than happy to appear on *OTR*. Most guests prep the night before, hoping to anticipate every possible inquiry. The trick for reporters is to find that one question they had not anticipated.

I had such a question.

Kelley liked the image of crime fighter and public defender, so it seem logical to ask him, "In your many years in office, what's the single most important thing you've done to fight crime?"

Do you recall the Roger Mudd interview with Teddy Kennedy when he was running for president? Mudd asked, "Why do you want the job?" Kennedy is still searching for the right answer.

That's how Kelley looked as he frantically searched his mind to answer my question. Instead of saying he had convicted thousands of crooks, hecame up with this: "I helped to create the Law Enforcement Training Council."

The viewers at home are going, "Law Enforcement what?"

It was not the best answer, and Kelley and company knew it. It just sort of laid there.

Word got back to me afterward that, as he left the studio and was out of earshot, he unloaded on everyone in sight for not anticipating that question. The wrath of Mr. Kelley was not a pleasant thing to feel . . . so they say.

Even though he was formally out of elective office in 2002, he still couldn't stay away from the lights . . . that family blood thing again. During the Granholm for governor campaign, he watched our show as she fumbled around on the role of the attorney general in launching investigations.

The next Monday, on his own, he calls in the press corps in an attempt to defend her. But he only muddied the waters and makes a bad situation for her even worse. That kind of shaky performance was rare for him as he came out of retirement to do commercials for a host of candidates and issues.

When a local Democrat, Gretchen Whitmer, made her first bid for a house seat from East Lansing, Kelley did an ad for her, too.

When the state's health care community got greedy and tried to earmark money in the constitution for their services, there was Kelley again.

David Waymire, the fine former capital reporter for the Booth Newspaper chain, was doing the P.R. for the anti-Proposition Four campaign. He was assigned to birddog Kelley in the recording of some hard hitting commercials.

"It was unbelievable," Waymire recalls. "I didn't have to do anything. Frank did it all including a hard nosed read on the tag line for the campaign, "Stop the robbers at the door. Vote No on Proposal Four." The commercial and Kelley's performance helped turn the race around. At one point the yes side had 68 percent. When it was over 68 percent said no. A historic flip-flop and Kelley shared much of the credit.

Since he was the A.G. for George Romney, Bill Milliken, Jim Blanchard, and John Engler, Kelley always got this question: Who did you like the most? And he always deferred for obvious reasons. He didn't want to offend anyone. But he did have a take on each.

Romney "was dogmatic but when he gave you his word, he stuck by it"; he was a man of convictions. Kelley tells of the time the two were in Flint to support a new Open Housing law. It was one of the toughest civil rights issues these two had worked on, illustrated by the fact that, "we were both stoned by the crowd at the rally." It was then that I knew he truly fought for what he believed in.

Kelley found Milliken to be a "gentleman and a natural politician." The two got along very well.

Poor Jim Blanchard has lived his entire political career under the notion that he was Kelley's driver. Granholm made the charge during a primary debate, but Kelley says that's a "bad rap" on his former assistant.

"I never let him drive much because he talked all the time. I was afraid he'd go through a red light." Kelley says he was proud of Blanchard's eight year record in Congress and eight years in the governor's chair.

Regarding the last governor he served, Kelley notes "Engler was the most conservative, but a pragmatic one." In other words he knew when to bend a little, unlike dyed-in-the-wool conservatives who would rather lose than compromise. "We agreed that all our work would be done in private with no leaks."

Even though Kelley won't confirm it, my guess is he liked Milliken the best. You can put money it.

There was only one time when Kelley couldn't get his story straight. That related to the emotional issue of assisted suicide. Here was a guy who took controversial stands on issues as easily as you drink a glass of water, but in May of 1996, he took a hike.

It was only a three minute interview that began with, "What's your stance on assisted suicide?" "I don't have a personal opinion on it one way or the other," he surprised me.

Why not?

"I can't give opinions on law . . . on prosecution of criminal cases," he stammers. Now he's sounding like a judge hiding behind the Canons of Ethics, which does prevent them from taking a public stance.

"So you're going to punt on the issue?" I asked.

"That's correct."

He was dancing as if his first name was Gene not Frank.

I tried to get him on the record on how he would vote on the issue when it was on the statewide ballot. Foolish me.

"Oh, I don't know. I would have to study it . . . I wouldn't comment on that. I have to live with all these things."

When I left him, I went to Senator Bill Schuette who was considering running for attorney general in two years and he promptly chided Kelley. "I'm not going to punt on you. You know the people across the state want clarity on this," and he says he'll oppose it.

With that in hand I go back to Kelley for a reaction to Schuette's take. Suddenly Kelley gets off the fence. So I ask why he didn't do that in the first interview.

He explains he had just come out of a news conference on a "major bribery case and I was preoccupied at the time." In other words, he's saying I caught him off guard.

After first saying he needed to study it, now he confesses he did a term paper on euthanasia and had confronted that issue in his own family. Bottom line, he now says, "I am against assisted suicide—but not totally." He would favor it in the case of a life threatening illness or when someone is in great pain.

It was a rare flip-flop, but a flip-flop nonetheless. In our exit interview done in 1998, I asked the question again and he remained opposed to the concept.

We did that exit interview because months earlier, he had decided enough was enough. Again, his father played a role in the decision, even though dad died before Kelley became an attorney.

"He always told me to leave while they want you to stay." His family told him it was better to retire "when you are vital and in full command." Once the decision was made, he says he never looked back.

Came the day of his announcement, the G. Mennen Williams building was filled with emotions and friends. The ground floor was packed with staffers, onlookers, media, and others who wanted to see a part of history unfold.

Kelley was quoted in the media as having two scripts. That was not accurate. His decision had been firm for sometime.

"It's now incumbent upon me to make a decision," he told the hushed audience. "I've anguished greatly about all the implications of this decision. I know the people had to grant me office by actively voting for me. For now, let me just say thanks for the memories."

Calling it a "wonderful adventure" he went on to confess, "I get all the credit [while] they do all the work" referring to the circle of friends who were now standing as close as they could get.

The next paragraph he must have delivered with his daddy in mind, because it reflects his father's wisdom about leaving. "I'm blessed with good health. There's ample time for me to have another career."

He was asked to endorse a successor, but he begged off. He eventually would sign on with Granholm.

He left his office at the end of the year, only to show up on the platform as a private citizen at the Inauguration festivities on New Years day.

The impact of the day left Kelley with what he termed a "mixed feeling." On one hand it was like graduation day he said, leaving a life behind him. On the other, "I'm graduating to a new life so I'm looking forward to that as well."

Always ready with a quick one-liner, he was asked what he would miss most? Mr. Show Biz, answered, "the driver."

17

The Presidents of MSU

The first time I saw John DiBiaggio in action he was working the crowd at the Elks Club on the west side of Lansing. He was making his first appearance in town after being tapped by the Michigan State University Board of Trustees to run MSU.

I was there to pick him up for a TV interview we were going to do in about a half hour.

"Hi. I'm Tim Skubick. How would you like a ride to the station?"

He graciously revealed that he had "heard about me," but was going to take me up on the ride anyway.

We jumped in my convertible and headed to East Lansing on a wonderfully sunny afternoon.

"I used to have a convertible, too," he begins our first real conversation.

"Used to?" I inquire.

"Yeah. After I got this job, the President of the State AFL-CIO Frank Garrison told me to get rid of the MG. Guess he frowns on foreign cars," he sort of chuckled.

"Welcome to Michigan," I chuckled back.

With that I began the coverage of my eighth president of my alma mater.

Located just down the street from the State Capitol, MSU has been in a unique position compared to the other fourteen major universities in this state. Being in the backyard of lawmakers has its pluses and minuses. Having thirty-five some reporters in the capital press corps living next door, makes MSU a great source for news and an easy target. In other university towns, officials have to cope with two or three nosey local reporters at the most.

Consequently MSU has found itself in the headlines on countless occasions and most of the stories have been, shall we say . . . interesting reading.

During the turbulent 70s, when there was a war in Viet Nam and another one on the campus, MSU came under sharp fire from conservative lawmakers who detested the violence that anti-war students perpetrated on their own school.

I recall Oakland County senator Bob Huber formed a Campus Violence Committee. He made lots of noise, made lots of headlines and made lots of university leaders nervous. Since MSU depends on financial aid from lawmakers, anything that triggers unrest with the folks who dole out the dole also triggers ulcers in the ivory tower.

John Hannah was the first president I covered. Anybody who has spent more than five minutes in this state knows that the one time chicken farmer turned the sleepy cow college into a Big Ten powerhouse, both academically and on the playing field, too.

He was not flamboyant and had a fatherly image about him. In the early '60s, when I was on the campus, he was the personification of the concept of 'en loco parentis.' That was the notion that when mom and dad sent their kids to college, the university would be 'in place of parents' or surrogates. That meant women had to be back in the dorm on weeknights at 11 P.M. The theory was: if the women are safely inside, the man will go back and study.

I remember the freshman convocation my first night on campus in 1963. Hannah stood at the front of the old auditorium alongside the winding Red Cedar River, and told us we were not a number. That was hard to swallow given the 4,000 apprehensive high school seniors trying to look like college students sitting next to me.

There is one story involving Dr. Hannah and the MSU concert band that also involved me, although I never knew it at the time. For years, the revered Director of Bands, the beloved Leonard Falcone, had tried to secure money from Hannah to replace band uniforms that went back to WWII. Falcone had always struck out, until one concert that Hannah attended.

One of the highlights of the afternoon was the playing of "Perpetual Motion," which featured the first six clarinetists in the band, including me. We stood in front of the band trying to hit all the notes of this challenging piece that started allegro, and got faster as the measures moved on. Anyway, my uniform was too short. Legend has it that after Hannah saw my uniform he called Falcone the next day, and within six months the MSU band had new duds. I'm getting this story twelfth hand, but let's assume it's true.

During my undergraduate years, I never figured I'd end up in Hannah's office as a radio reporter. I was hoping to get an interview with him as he was surrounded by about one hundred other students who had dropped in to protest the war . . . and take over his digs!

He seemed unfazed but he clearly wanted those protesters out of there. After all, children don't commandeer daddy's office.

Hannah spoke in sympathetic terms about the students' demands. He later went on to head the U.S. Civil Rights Commission, so he was no dummy when it came to fielding complaints about inhumane conditions.

Somehow or other the students left. I got an interview with him and that's about the extent of my Hannah coverage because soon thereafter he left for the federal government and the Agency for International Development, which I think was sometimes a front for the CIA. That was 1969. Coming in behind Hannah was Dr. Walter Adams.

"Skubick!" he would shout out in a gruff, yet friendly voice, as he chewed on his cigar and tolerated all my obnoxious questions about his interim presidency. If Hannah was distant, Adams let you in.

He invited me into his inner sanctum on numerous occasions, as I covered labor unrest, student uprisings, and what not, during his brief one year tenure as head of the school he loved. I think he liked me. I knew I really liked him.

I was smart enough not to take any of his economic courses during my undergraduate years. I wanted to keep a 3.0 grade point average and knew he was flunking kids left and right. His classes were legendary, and he refused to stop teaching them, even though he was president.

He and I also hooked up on the marching band field. During my days as a celebrated clarinet player in the MSU marching band, you would see Walter in his little hat with the feather coming out of it tapping his feet to the fight song. He would march with us every Saturday over the bridge, past Sparty, and eventually to the tunnel entrance to the stadium. We made him an honorary band jock, complete with a band jacket that he loved.

I never suspected I'd be trading that clarinet for a microphone. One day I interviewed my second MSU president as he marched down Michigan Ave. one chilly fall day with 10,000 students behind him.

These were obviously well educated students because they could count . . . and swear. One-two-three-four, we don't want your f— war.

It was the largest anti-war march since the war began and it was headed toward the state capitol. Lawmakers who had only seen a student protest on the tube, saw one live outside their window. If higher-ups in the university were worried about the impact such a march would have, nobody told Adams.

Hannah would not have been caught dead in a protest march. But there was Adams right in the front row as he was locked arm in arm with labor leaders, at least one state senator, Jackie Vaughn III, MSU Board members, and for a time, me.

I had been covering the march from the sidewalk along the main drag leading to the capitol steps. As far as they eye could see they kept coming and coming and then, without thinking, I moved into the front row next to Adams. We chatted for a moment and then, in his own fatherly way, he said, "Skubick you're not to supposed to be here." I had momentarily forgotten my journalistic credo of not getting involved. He was concerned enough for me to yank me back to reality. A fine picture that would have made: "Journalist Chucks Objectivity to Join War Protesters."

I sheepishly retreated to the sidelines, still trying to figure out what moved me to do that. I don't think I ever thanked him for setting me straight, but he certainly deserved it. Suffice it to say, I never got personally involved again.

While Adams ran the place, the MSU Board searched for a permanent replacement, although there was strong sentiment in many corners to keep Walter right where he was.

"Let him have the interim title forever," was one battle cry. This was promptly ignored by the board, which chose Clifton Wharton, Jr. instead.

Getting your facts right is job one for any reporter, so when the campus paper boldly announced "Clifford Wharton" as the new president everyone in the press corps had a good laugh.

Clifford . . . er . . . Clifton was mild mannered, as polite and dignified as you can get, with a friendly smile. If you had to find one word to describe him it would be formal. In light of that, if you were looking for a newsmaker, Dr. Wharton was not your guy. He was low-keyed and was not fond of controversy. But he quickly found himself picking up where Dr. Hannah left off.

Anti-war protesters were one of his first challenges, and once again the legislature and governor had a ring side seat to evaluate how the president performed under fire, figuratively and literally.

May 7 1970. Governor Milliken held a news conference in the Capitol and invited two MSU students. Susan Carter was president of the Women's Residential Council and Harold Buckner was chair of the Associated Students of Michigan State University (ASMSU), the student governing body.

I knew neither of them, but would eventually get to know Ms. Carter. She became a radio reporter for WVIC-radio in town and would eventually ascend to even greater heights. She was Gov. Blanchard's first media secretary and much later became the executive assistant to MSU President Peter McPherson.

She and Buckner were with Milliken that day because protesting students down the road were "striking" at MSU. Milliken met with them and called them outstanding people who "make no bones about their position with respect to the President's decision in Cambodia." President Nixon was hoping to bring the Viet Cong to their knees by dropping bombs on their heads in that Southeast Asia country.

"Students have the right to stay out of classes if they wish to," the governor began and quickly added, "I'm very pleased that President Wharton takes a very strong position on this . . . no student should be denied the opportunity to attend a class by intimidation or otherwise."

He and the MSU president were in telephone communication and Wharton reported that about 15 percent of the 40,000 plus students were skipping class.

The latest round of protests grew out of the killing of innocent students by Ohio National Guardsmen at Kent State. Milliken was asked his stance on President Nixon's invasion of yet another country.

Milliken walked the tightrope. On one hand he said the president was making strategic judgments with more facts than the governor had, however, "I have honest and I have very deep reservations about the decision to send American troops to still another country."

There were 6,000 protesters at MSU who were even more concerned. They might be going there, too. Wharton and Milliken certainly talked about sending in the state police or the guard to end the strike, but the governor said he wanted to avoid that.

Asked if he would send them in with weapons, Milliken suggested, "The lessons of Kent State have not been lost on me."

Between May 7 and the 20, protesters took over university buildings. The Reserve Officers' Training Corps (ROTC) center was a favorite target. President Wharton had seen enough and on the night of May 19, he sent in the police. 127 arrests were made.

Wharton earned high marks from the governor for the move. "I am convinced that taking this kind of approach, this kind of a firm but fair approach will avoid, hopefully, problems there and elsewhere in the future."

It was during all these protests, that I found myself one night in the demilitarized zone (DMZ). Not the one in war torn Viet Nam, but the median on Grand River Ave. which snakes its way through East Lansing on the north border of the campus.

On the left, appropriately, were disgruntled war demonstrators armed with signs. On the right, the Michigan State police armed with weapons. In the median, were members of the press corps armed with cameras and microphones.

The tension was thick as each contingency eyed the other. While I was there, there was no violence, just an uneasy peace that could dissipate at the drop of a tear gas canister. When the students rushed the business district and started popping windows at Jacobson's department store and other locations, the canisters dropped. No shots were fired and eventually the riot ended.

When I surveyed the damage the next day, the boarded up windows and all, I was glad I had missed it. I filed a report and hoped I would never see any live action.

Wharton stayed around until 1978. He went about one year beyond the normal stay of a university president. He was well liked by most folks and when they built a new concert hall/theater, they named it after Dr. Wharton and his wife Delores.

Then came Dr. Edgar Hardin. He had been a player, as they say in this political town. The former president of Northern Michigan University was well connected in the legislature and Lansing business community, from his leadership post with the longest running Oldsmobile dealership in the area.

He was a consummate schmoozer in the best sense of the word, very approachable and always willing to fill me in on what was going on. To survive in this town, you have to have those sources for scoops.

There wasn't much to report on him since he was only around from 1978 to 1979.

The selection of a new president was always a good story and at MSU it seemed as though we were always covering that process. Between the Hannah departure and the Wharton arrival, the selection process became very controversial.

August "Gus" Scholle was head of the Michigan AFL-CIO. He was from the old school of getting things done. When he told you to do something you did it, or you suffered the consequences. That's why they call them union bosses. Well, a pal of his was out of work and the crafty union president thought he could find Soapy Williams a job . . . as president of MSU.

The MSU Board at the time was dominated by Democrats who-held a comfortable 5–3 edge over the GOP. Gus could count and he was counting on his "friends" to come across for the former governor.

The word went out through Board Member Claire White that the five Democrats were to vote for Williams. There were no meetings with Scholle. No phone calls. And he would not take no for an answer.

Democrats Claire White, Warren Huff, and Frank Hartman fell in line. East Lansing dentist and former MSU football star Blanche Martin and fellow Democrat Don Stevens did not. They had earlier agreed with the rest of the board, that only candidates who had gone through the screening process would be considered. Williams had not, but that didn't bother Gus.

White told Martin and Stevens, "We're going to be in trouble if we don't vote for Soapy," recounts Martin who tells his story here for the first time.

"But I told him I was elected to do what was best for the university and not the Democrats," Martin says. He and Stevens held tough.

Of the two, Stevens was in a tighter spot. He worked for Gus. One of his fellow workers, Tom Downs says his friend was under "tremendous pressure." But the quiet Stevens, who used to live in the same apartment as me, remained strong. Ironically, I saw him every day when all this was coming down, but had no inkling that he had a gun aimed at his noggin.'

With the search process coming to a head, the two Democrats sent word that they wanted to meet with the three Republicans, Ken Thompson, Steven Nisbet, and Frank Merriman. In those days there was no Open Meetings Act, so there was no concern about meeting in secret. Martin and Stevens were worried stiff, however, that they might be discovered huddling with the enemy.

The five met at Thompson's office building near Butterfield Hall on the west side of campus. Martin says he and Stevens were so nervous that when the elevator door opened to take them to the office, they were afraid of who might jump out. If Gus had walked out it would have been curtains for the turncoats, but he did not. The five members discussed the situation and a week or so later when the vote on Wharton was taken, it was 5–3.

It was a rare loss for Gus.

After Wharton, Dr. Cecil Mackey moved from the faculty side of things into the president's chair in 1979. He lasted until 1985. With all due respect, he was not the most accessible or popular president. You sort of left him alone and frankly I can't recall any major stories other than some labor unrest and budget stories that were common back then.

That brings us to Dr. Gordon Guyer. He was what they call a permanent fixture around these parts. He worked for governors, for the university, and awmakers loved him. When an interim guy was needed between Mackey and DiBiaggio, Guyer was the perfect choice. He was well respected and nobody seemed to have any unkind words to say about him. From a reporter's vantage point that made him boring. That was just the way he liked it.

He was a good source however. He had some inside knowledge on the Blanchard administration and gave me guidance when I needed it on university issues, but much like Mackey, he didn't make much news. He did give me his number at the cottage up north, and was always gracious, but cautious.

That can't be said about the dentist from Anchor Bay. Dr. John DiBiaggio came to campus with one stated goal: to retire here. Silly man.

After our convertible ride, I got my first peek at how he performed under fire. He was a natural.

We arrived at the WKAR-TV studio for his first TV appearance. It was a one hour program and I tossed everything but the kitchen sink at him to test his mettle and his savvy.

The one question he hated the most was the one on abortion.

"Man, that was awful," he confided to me afterward.

At first blush you might wonder what did that have to do with running a university. In the politically charged era around 1985 when he was hired, Right to Life was honing in on medical practices everywhere, including university health clinics.

It was an "awful" question for him because whatever he said, he'd offend someone. If he said he was pro-life, the choicer's would go nuts and vice versa. If he turned on the fog machine in front of me, I would have bored in.

So what did he do? With only a catch pause after hearing the question, he answered it straight up. He was pro-choice. That said a lot about the guy I was going to cover for the next seven years.

Since it was obvious to me that this guy had a ton of charisma, it seemed only natural to ask about his political ambitions. He ruled out running for office, but former board member Larry Owen contends, "He told me he would run for the U.S. Senate. He absolutely did."

When Dr. B. left his job at the University of Connecticut, he brought with him his close professional and personal advisor David Kimball. Kimball became DiBiaggio's first crisis.

Kimball was on university business in San Diego when he got a phone call. The cops back home had a warrant out for his arrest. Kimball's image had been recorded on some hidden video cameras at a rest stop near the MSU campus. He was not the only one on candid camera. Forty-one other males were photographed performing various alleged sex acts.

I remember the story because I was working for WJBK-TV at the time and since the rest stop was in my backyard, I was assigned to cover the round-up. I recall being awakened at a ridiculous hour and told that the police were busy hauling in suspects and our crew was to tag along.

The first stop was in Williamston. The police knocked on the door with our cameras rolling, but the man they wanted was not there. I could see the wife and kids were in shock. Eventually at the Army National Guard Armory, the police brought in all their captives. Kimball was not among them.

When his name showed up on the arrest blotter, the president of MSU discreetly farmed him out to the College of Agriculture, which was a lower profile spot than Kimball's old job as Secretary to the MSU Board. After a year, DiBiaggio said good bye, as Kimball left the school.

Kimball, quoted in the *City Pulse* newspaper in Lansing said, "I have nothing to say against John DiBiaggio. He's a wonderful person. He was in a very difficult position politically."

As personal as that decision was for the new president, the battle he got into over university athletics was more trying and provided the first hint of friction between the board and its hire.

The new president was smart enough to understand the interrelationship between college sports and the rest of the university, and especially the alumni. He joined the Knight Commission, which quickly went on a mission to reduce the impact of sports on the college campus. That did not endear him to the jocks and other athletic supporters on or off the campus.

Ironically, his most visible confrontation with the board turned into a power struggle over the appointment of football coach George Perles to the Athletic Director's (A.D.'s) post. Some on the Board wanted to phase the coach off the sidelines and into the A.D.'s office over two years. The president would have no part of that.

"I had him over to my home for lunch," Owen recalls. "I told him the board wanted to work this out. He told me there was no room to negotiate." The two sides went at it and the whole thing spilled into the public. I recall thinking nobody was looking good in this. It was just one more example of MSU making news . . . the kind it did not want to make.

Many observers feel that flap over Perles sealed DiBiaggio's fate. "That's not true at all," he clarifies the popular wisdom. But there was something else going on at the same time that played a more significant role. In 1998, some members of the board suggested it was time to write a contract. The president had been working without one and without tenure. The intent was to supply both sides with some security and a draft was composed keeping him at MSU for four more years. He says the deal was offered "because of the history here, of conflicts between the board and the administration." He noted that since the board is elected there could be changes that "would place anyone in jeopardy."

But negotiations never got off the ground "because the events that occurred immediately thereafter" shifted the focus. That was the Perles matter which dragged into 1999.

As a result of that protracted debate it was clear DiBiaggio's relationship with those who hired him was shaky. He was going around the state telling editorial writers that the board was trying to usurp his authority. Owen says he learned that after the fact, when former *Free Press* Editor Joe Stroud told him that's what the president said.

When the two sides finally got back to the contract issue, the dynamics changed. This time the president was offered a one year extension . . . not four.

DiBiaggio, in our exit interview, said he was offended by the offer. I said, "This is, you know, in a way, an insult to even suggest this." The board asked him to consider it nonetheless and he did, but even his attorney concluded it was not "rational." Without knowing it just then, the dye was cast for his departure, but it would not come overnight.

Instead of signing a contract, the president asked the board for something simple. He wanted a public statement of support—a verbal pat on the head. The university was involved in three delegate issues including a budgetary crisis, and DiBiaggio felt there needed to be "a signal that I was going to be supported in whatever steps I took . . . "

He made the request. The board turned it down. At that point he reveals "the message was very clear to my wife and me, that perhaps we should at least explore other possibilities."

His account of how this relationship unraveled gives you a rare if not unprecedented peek at how tough it is for presidents to get along with governing boards. He had heard about MSU's reputation. Now he was an eyewitness.

During his seven years at MSU, he says he rejected twenty-five different overtures and offers from other schools. He wanted to retire at MSU, but he puts his resume in play by hiring a head hunter.

One of resumes landed at Tufts University. Leaders there were instantly interested, but DiBiaggio was in a delicate situation. He could not be an official candidate, because that could damage his already rocky marriage with the MSU Board. So he visits the school as an unpaid consultant. Leaders got to interview him, but he had the cover he needed, if anybody asked about him being a candidate. The whole thing was a ruse.

As soon as he got back to East Lansing, the chair of the Tufts board calls requesting another meeting with trustees in New York. Dr. DiBiaggio is uncomfortable about the proposal and tells the chair that a private firm is also interested in him. The chair and another trustee fly to Detroit and the MSU president meets with them to discuss a "formulated offer," which was "extraordinarily attractive."

He and his wife Nancy agree to consider it but they make no commitments. He says, "Remember Tim, I have a lot of reasons for staying here. I have an elderly mother in Detroit. I have a home in northern Michigan that we love. I have dear, dear and close friends in this place."

The DiBiaggios ask for two weeks to mull it over. The Tufts chair wants an answer in four days. DiBiaggio asks if this can't wait for the next board meeting. He is told the board meets only three times a year. "That's a telling point" Dr. B. concluded, since he was dealing with the MSU Board almost on a daily basis in one form or another. Three sessions a year sounded pretty good.

But the situation became more complex. Businessman Eli Broad, who has made a substantial contribution to MSU, discovers that the president may leave. Broad calls the governor, state senators and some MSU trustees.

DiBiaggio is "very angry." He's lost all of his cover and now a quicker decision must be made. MSU officials worry he might leave, so hints are made about a long term contract, but he says, "quite frankly, Tim, that's not my style. I don't negotiate one offer against another."

The impending decision to stay or go is so grueling that he and his wife are not sleeping. "We are walking the campus, you know, feeling the internal conflict." They did that between eleven at night and one o'clock in the morning.

All of the turmoil he had confronted while at MSU was a factor in the final decision. "The only conclusion that we could come to that a . . . that they really wanted us badly at Tufts and ah . . . and it was an opportunity that we just had to accept."

Owen is quite harsh in his own analysis of the former president. "He was one of the better gladhanders I've seen. He was a charmer . . . but he was a megalomaniac and wasn't substantive on the academic side." Owen concludes the president had a problem with the board and "skated before he got pushed out."

In the exit interview I asked about the knock that "You were too P.R. oriented."

"I felt that was one of the critical needs of the university," he responded. He wanted to improve on the cow-college image and the lack of appreciation for the quality of education at MSU . . . I was external and I delegated freely."

He ended the broadcast expressing his hope that maybe he had "improved MSU's quality a little bit . . . I just am, will be always thankful throughout my entire life that I had this opportunity to serve in my native state where my father would have been so proud to see me at one of the great land grant universities of the world."

I wished him luck on the new assignment and he replied with a tear in his eye, "Thank you, Tim. Thank you very much for being such a good friend." My eyes were red, too.

On May 9 2003, I was scrounging around for a TV story to do when I got a call from the news director at TV-10. "Peter McPherson is leaving to go to Iraq. Check it out." He, of course was the guy who replaced DiBiaggio.

My usual chatterbox sources at MSU suddenly put a lid on it. Nobody would say anything on the record, and certainly not on camera. Only one long-time insider took me aside and confirmed it. MSU's nineteenth president would be given four months to help rebuild Iraq's war-torn economy. The White House had not formally made the announcement, which is why everyone clammed up. "Nobody wants to upstage the White House" was the party line.

With a fat "no comment" on my note pad, I needed more than that to flesh out the huge story. I got on campus and went to Cowles House where the president resides. I knew he was in Washington putting the finishing touches on his new assignment as "financial coordinator for the Office of Reconstruction and Humanitarian Assistance in Iraq." I hoped that his desk was long enough to handle that name plate.

Desperate for anything to put into the story I thought maybe his wife would talk. So with cameraman Bassar in back of me, I walked up to the side door of the McPherson residence.

Knock. Knock. Knock.

A maid and a man I did not recognize opened the door. I explained who I was and asked to talk with Joanne McPherson. I was told she was not available at the moment. I said I would be back in an hour.

I returned and the same guy answers the door. This time he has a more definitive answer. "She doesn't know who you are." Door closes.

O.K. a good ego bruising is required from time to time to keep one humble and that did the trick.

I eventually slapped something together and confirmed the story during a noon live shot on the tube and radio. I never did get a chance to talk to the president, because on May 9 he arrived in Iraq where he said the assignment was "fun."

I knew he wasn't kidding. This was right down his alley. During our first interview after he was hired he talked about the MSU job being fun because, "you try to figure out what we should be and how best to work to get there." That was precisely what he was doing in the middle east. He loves working on complex situations and loves it even more when they are solved.

McPherson was an unlikely candidate for the MSU post after DiBiaggio's departure. He did not possess a Ph.D., but he had something more important—he had green and white blood. His grandfather, Melville, was on the MSU board when it picked John Hannah to run things. Peter McPherson was two months old at the time.

His family sent a steady stream of offspring to Moo-U, and McPherson graduated in 1963 and joined the Peace Corps, where he helped bail out another floundering country, Peru. After a master's degree at Western University and a law degree from American University, McPherson eventually convinced the Reagan administration to let him run the Agency for International Development, John Hannah's old job.

McPherson's Washington experience brought him into contact with Cliff Wharton who suggested he might want to think about a university presidency.

The MSU Board had its sights on a man from Florida but it didn't work out. So board member Joel Ferguson calls McPherson at his Bank of America office and asks if he is interested.

"I was very careful not to absolutely commit myself until the very end, because I saw what a public process could do," he says. What it can do is ruin your career where you're at, if the new post doesn't pan out.

Anyway, he gets the job and brings his special brand of dealing with issues to his alma mater. His mantra is "stay away from controversy." He'd make one heck of a CIA agent because you can't get anything out of him, and believe me I tried in that first TV interview.

I hit issue after issue and drilled successive dry holes.

Should the selection process for a university president be closed or opened?

"I have been staying out of that debate."

I pressed for more and got nothing.

"I'm going to stay out of this. You won't get anywhere," he firmly explains the obvious to me.

Compare MSU to the U of M.

"It is a mistake, in my judgment, for us at MSU to see ourselves in comparison with others," he suggests.

Was the Knight Commission correct when it argued there was too much emphasis on college sports?

"It's hard for me to say. On any given day you might conclude it is, but I don't know about being out of balance."

Should the board be appointed or elected?

"I've worked with what I have . . . I'm not going to take a position on this now . . . .I think a president should be careful about what he says about his own bosses," he continues to dodge a direct answer.

Good thing I'm not paid by the answers or I'd be on the unemployment line. Unwilling to take no for an answer I try a different tack.

"You're a very cautious politician aren't you?" as I state the obvious.

Even on that one, he's uncomfortable. "Oh, I don't know. Being drawn into a debate can distract you from what you need to do. If you're not careful, you get distracted in ways that hurt your institution and hurt your ability to perform your mission."

He was well aware of the difficulties MSU suffered in the past and he did not want to create problems. There would be enough that just popped up on their own.

Even though he can give a frustrating interview, he still felt his media treatment had been "good" but he suggested: I don't think it will last. Mistakes will be made."

And news would be made.

He took a hit for not joining the U of M and hundreds of other universities when they filed briefs in the Affirmative Action suit that was decided by the U.S. Supreme Court in 2003.

MSU got a national black eye when students rioted in the streets after MSU basketball teams played for the national title. Binge drinking among students made headlines, as one student celebrated his twenty-first birthday by drinking himself to death.

While he may not be the best self-discloser in the world, he is still good company, and since he loves the political game, we sometimes had lunch during the summer where I picked his brain and vice versa.

His political acumen started early. He was a page in the Michigan House and later worked as a janitor in the capitol building and even though he has told the story a thousand times, it still bears repeating. It reveals how he parlayed that background into an entree with the chair of the senate budget committee.

McPherson instinctively knew that when he landed his job, much of his time would be spent lobbying. Even though MSU's location near the capitol has its drawbacks, it also makes it easier to pop in on a moment's notice.

Over the years I could count on one hand the number of times I saw a president of U of M, Wayne State, or the other thirteen schools. I got the impression that some of the omniscient presidents felt it was beneath them to grovel for money at the knees of lawmakers. I am convinced the arrogance cost them millions of dollars in the long haul .

McPherson wasn't bashful about getting his hands dirty. If anything he was more than eager to visit the capitol which he did soon after he arrived on campus. One of his first port of calls was to see Sen. Harry Gast, a crusty but likable cuss from west Michigan. The former farmer was tilling the legislative fields as head of the senate appropriations committee, which controlled the purse strings for higher education.

The two had never met before. As they stroll into the stately appropriations room with its 100 foot high ceilings and decorative chandeliers befitting the royalty that works there, McPherson breaks the ice by saying, "I've been in here before."

Gast takes the bait and asks why.

"I used to empty the wastebaskets in here when I was a janitor years ago." In an instant the two have a rapport based on this little story that says a lot about McPherson as a person. Gast can relate to hard work because he is sitting in his cushy chair for the very same reason. You don't get to run the budget panel unless you have paid your dues.

Several years into the job, McPherson revealed his political savvy by holding a very unusual meeting. He invited twenty MSU grads to a "Prominent Spartans" breakfast. Nothing unusual about that, you might say, but what made the guest list so interesting is that each of them was a registered lobbyist for a host of companies, associations, and other special interests.

The president asked them to come over so he could extol the wonders of MSU and solicit their free advice, which they gave.

"Really good move." "Good idea." "Brilliant move." Those were some of the observations from some of those in attendance. During the hour long sit-down he also asked for any critical comments from the experts eating MSU eggs and drinking MSU milk. There were none. One of those in attendance noted that McPherson was quite facile as he talked about all the players in the house and senate as if they were old chums.

Before it was over, a hidden agenda surfaced. At the time MSU was embroiled in a battle for an extra ten million dollars that Gov. Engler wanted to direct to his alma mater. Other schools, including the one down the road, as the U of M is often referred to, were trying to block it.

McPherson mildly suggested to the lobbyists that if in their daily rounds they bumped into any lawmakers who were not on MSU's side, well, you know . . . give them a little push. And he conveniently supplied the names of twenty lawmakers who were on the fence.

He was asking for a little free lobbying which led one participant to complain, "That's what we get paid for doing." Nonetheless it was still a good move and if he turned around only one or two votes as a result of the breakfast it was worth it. Do the math: a couple of hundred bucks for breakfast vs. ten million dollars for MSU coffers. That must have appealed to McPherson's banking instincts.

While the first TV interview was long on evasive answers, there were two times when he was direct. He was not interested in running for office, and on the matter of race relations in our country, he opined, "It is maybe getting worse. Our country hasn't escaped the problem."

There was one other issue that was pressing. Earlier in the week McPherson had announced that Marilee Dean Baker, the school's first female athletic director, had decided to leave. Her departure was yet another example of a P.R. nightmare for MSU.

DiBiaggio brought her in and left for Tufts shortly after she unlocked her office door at Jenison Field House. The welcome mat was not out, and her tenure was on thin ice from the opening gong. McPherson had engineered a deal so she could move on to some other school. They held a news conference, for which he gets points. But there were a ton of questions left unanswered, and I wanted to change that.

Even though I was zero for life in the interview I charged in.

"Did she get a bum wrap?"

Warm up the fog machine. "Well, I was very pleased that we've been able to work through this set of issues. I haven't commented about [her] for a long time. I think she's a very nice woman . . . a very nice person.

"So nice that you nudged her out?" I inquired.

"Well, you know the public story on this . . . "

"I'm not sure that I know the full story on this, which is why I'm asking."

"I'm not going to comment about this."

I am a glutton for punishment. "Wait a second," I continued. That's a public policy issue. You serve at the taxpayer's pleasure, and that's a legitimate question, isn't it."

"I think that we publicly have dealt with that many times . . . ."

. . . etc., etc., etc.

One of the viewers who saw the exchange was long time friend and veteran political columnist George Weeks, who noted that I tried an additional ten times to get more out of McPherson, before tossing in the towel.

He wrote that his initial skepticism about McPherson had been replaced by his "impressive moves" including his "working the Capitol budget-writers as Hannah used to do."

Although he has never said it publicly, I'm darn sure McPherson went to school on the trials and tribulations of DiBiaggio and vowed not to make the same mistakes. DiBiaggio did not shy away from questions. McPherson does. DiBiaggio got into a power struggle with the board. McPherson has found away to avoid it. DiBiaggio fell into disfavor with the jock crowd. McPherson has had his problems, but never let it get out of hand. DiBiaggio was seen as arrogant. The farm boy from Lowell has not been tagged with that. The worst you hear is that he is a workaholic and what board member would complain about somebody burning the midnight oil.

His tenure has been a textbook example on how to navigate the choppy waters of running a university within the shadow of the capitol dome.

18

Class Clowns, Characters, and Class Acts

A nytime you have 148 individuals in a legislative body and toss in a whole raft of folks in the governor's office, you're going to get a good cross section of society in general. Frankly, that makes a better legislature, because it more accurately reflects the make up of the general population.

Some of the names in this chapter, you probably won't recognize. But you don't need to know them to capture the diversity of talent and non-talent, and how it impacts the legislative process.

Edgar Geerlings

Rep. Edgar Geerlings . . . a character from the Muskegon area and a Republican. Geerlings had a propensity to take a walk. That's legislative parlance for running and hiding whenever a controversial vote was taken. In fact it got so bad that on one occasion, former Gov. Milliken personally went after Geerlings to get his vote.

The issue was a temporary income tax increase back in the '70s and Milliken needed one more GOP vote. It was 7 A.M. and the house was still in session but Geerlings was nowhere in sight. Picture this: Milliken comes out of his second floor office in the capitol where he pulled the all-nighter along with the rest of us. With camera crews and reporters tagging along, he walks into the morning sunlight to the old Jack Tar Hotel, which sits across the street from the Capitol.

Milliken goes up the elevator to the seventh floor where Mr. Geerlings is sleeping. The Governor of the State of Michigan, without fanfare, knocks on the door. A crack in the door appears . . . some inaudible words are exchanged. Milliken leaves and moments later who shows up on the floor to vote? Eddy baby.

Geerlings contends he had told his leaders that he would be a yes vote, he just didn't want to sit through all the debate. And it turns out that he played a pivotal role in lining up other GOP votes for the tax hike.

During a closed door caucus meeting before the final vote, Geerlings came up with a different title for the increase. He wanted to call it a "temporary emergency surcharge." It was a concept he swiped—he says he borrowed it—from former President Johnson who once used the term to mask a tax hike at the federal level.

The theory was if you didn't call it a tax increase, the public could be misled into thinking it wasn't, and by attaching the words "temporary" and "emergency" it gave the tax hike a different and illusionary feel. The caucus loved it, because this vote was coming on the eve of their reelection bids, and who wanted to run with a tax hike vote hanging over their heads? Nobody.

And to make it even more attractive, the GOP decided to kill the tax in October . . . one month before the election. So even if some stupid voter figured that it was a tax hike, it would be gone by the time they got to the polls. Talk about spinning an issue to make it as painless as possible.

By the way, the final vote came on Good Friday. You can make of that as you wish. It passed.

George Montgomery

Rep. George Montgomery. You want crusty and old school? George is your guy. Montgomery was an institution in the legislative institution. He chaired the taxation committee and ruled it with an iron fist, which he often jammed in the face of uncooperative committee members to get his way.

I didn't know the Detroit Democrat from Adam when I arrived on the scene, but we had a quick introduction. I had done a program with Milliken in which I innocently asked if some lawmakers had been around too long? Milliken took the bait but took me only halfway there. He answered yes, but refused to answer the follow up.

Who are they?

No dummy he. Milliken had to work with all those old you know whats, and to name names was a no-no. I thought his comments had the ingredients for a good little story, but it needed a little more pop . . . some names.

I proceeded to get the names of all the lawmakers who were well up in years. I can't remember the cut-offage, but I think seventy and above was the floor.

I composed the story using Milliken's quotes to set it up and sent it out to the Associated Press which promptly ran it statewide.

Montgomery's name made the list, and come to find out the old guy could still read. So when he read the story, I got a phone call. He wanted to see me in his office the next night. This was a first for me. I had not been on the capitol beat long enough to be called on the carpet, but that was about to change. Was I nervous? Heck yeah. So I asked my executive producer from the public TV station, Dave Rice, to be my second. We showed up, ahead of schedule, at Montgomery's stately office on the first floor of the Capitol. Without a smile, he let us in. I sensed this was not going to be fun.

There on his desk was a copy of the AP story and next to Montgomery was another guy I didn't know, Senator Billy Huffman. Billy Sunday, as he was called, was there for one reason . . . intimidation . . . of me. Huffman chaired the Senate budget subcommittee on higher education. WKAR-TV was a part of Michigan State University. Huffman was there in a thinly disguised attempt to make it clear that my little story might cost MSU some money.

Of course, Huffman had no intentions of doing that. He was good friends with MSU's lobbyist Jack Breslin. But they didn't share that little bit of information with me and proceeded to scare the heck out of me. Montgomery was not happy about having his name in print and being lumped in with "lawmakers who had been in office too long." Hey if you were a thousand years old, you wouldn't like it either.

They had their fun and I acknowledged that the story could have been misinterpreted, and it was certainly not my intention to embarrass the old coot . . . although I probably used a different word.

Everyone shook hands. I left. Billy and Georgie must have laughed themselves sick all the way to the local watering hole, where I am certain they had a wonderful laugh at my expense. I went on to have a fruitful working relationship with them both but the subject of age never came up again.

Maynard and Fitzpatrick

Rep. John Maynard and Rep. Richard Fitzpatrick. You honest to goodness won't believe the tale surrounding these two house Democrats. The Speaker of the House was about to be elected. He was Alabama transplant and good ole boy Gary Owen of Yspilanti. But Maynard and Fitz didn't think Owen was the best guy for the job. They figured that one of them was. So they proceeded to plot an overthrow. They did so by going to the Republicans.

They went into the meeting with House GOP Leader Mike Busch at about midnight, the day before the vote for Speaker. Rep. Gary Randall was also in the room along with Representatives Ernie Nash and Bill Bryant. Sometime during the meeting, Maynard and his sidekick retired to the hallway to make a critical decision: Which one would be Speaker. They flipped a coin. Fitzpatrick would become Speaker and Maynard would get to chair the house budget committee. They returned to the room to announce the outcome of the coin flip. The discussion on how to engineer the ousting of Owen is moving along, when the phone rings.

Randall picks up the phone and asks who it is. Randall blurts out, "Oh shit, it's Owen!"

Owen wants to talk with Busch and promptly tells him that he knows what's going on. Owen advises against the coup . . . no surprise there. . . . and orders Busch to end the discussion. Busch refuses.

Nobody is sure who clued Owen in, but it was somebody who had left the room momentarily. For years there's been speculation it was Nash or Bryant. They both deny it.

Owen won't reveal the name because he made a promise to the snitch. "The only thing he asked for was a promise to never reveal his name until he died," Owen recounts while sticking to his word.

But the story doesn't end there. Owen is slightly rattled and does not want to risk losing his powerful post. At 3 A.M. he awakens his floor leader Lew Dodak and orders him to round up any and all Democrats for the critical vote later that day. One of those votes was in a Brighton hospital drying out from a bout with alcoholism. The lawmaker's name was Dennis Dutko.

Owen made a personal call to the center and requested the temporary release of the legislator. The clinic director refused, citing a long-standing policy against it. Owen then demanded it. He said he would "close the site" . . . in other words put it out of business, if the director did not cough up Dutko.

The director thought about it for a minute and recanted, but under one condition: Dutko would need an escort to and from the facility. Owen sent his buddy Rep. Mike Griffin to play nursemaid.

Safely re-elected, Owen went on with his next assignment . . . to get even with everyone involved.

His first target was the GOP leader Mr. Busch. Owen informed Busch that the Democrats were going to elect a new GOP leader, Ed Geerlings. Busch's extra leadership pay would go to Geerlings, along with the title. Owen really liked Busch and let him swing in the wind for awhile before he reversed his threat.

Next Owen called in the two turncoats. Owen had helped both of them get re-elected, had funneled campaign checks into their hands, and had done nothing, he thought, to offend the two. So when Maynard came in, Owen wanted to know, "Why did you vote against me, John?"

Owen quotes Maynard as saying, "I guess I'm just a prick!"

Owen told the St. Clair Shores Democrat that he would let him back in the caucus but he had to promise to always vote with the Speaker on so called procedural issues. If he didn't, Owen warned, Maynard would lose all his committee assignments. Maynard agreed.

Fitzpatrick was next. Owen was really angry with him and laid out a different deal. There was a vacant field near the Capital City Airport and Owen said, "Let's you and me meet in that field and if you whip my ass, I'll forget everything. Or I'll give you the same deal I gave Maynard on voting with me."

Smart man that he was, Fitzpatrick opted out on the ass whoopin'.

The story underscores to what lengths political leaders will go to cement their power. Owen had to send a strong message to make sure this never happened again. And it never did. To this day Owen laughs about it, but it was not funny at the time. By the same token the Republicans had to take a chance because they wanted to control the House if they could.

By the way, Owen reports the snitch has not died . . . I did find out who it was—Rep. Ernie Nash.

Brown and DiNello

Senators Basil Brown and Gil DiNello. Collectively and individually there are enough stories about these two guys to fill another book. Brown was an African American from Highland Park. There were actually two Basils . . . the good one and the bad one. Before you approached him you always tried to determine which one had shown up that day.

There was only one DiNello, but that was enough. A staunch conservative from Macomb County, DiNello made a career out of bashing Detroit, the most popular indoor sport in his home county.

The pair was involved in one of the most contentious floor fights ever when the senate had to vote on funding a Detroit subway study. Public TV was doing a documentary titled "Day at the Capitol" and we had three cameras on the senate floor. That was in the days before live gavel-to-gavel coverage. It just so happened that the subway vote was on the agenda.

Detroit Mayor Coleman Young had been trying for years to get a subway and with his new found friend, GOP Governor Milliken, there was now a real chance. The debate quickly narrowed down to acrimonious exchanges between the man from Highland Park and the one from east Detroit.

DiNello fired the first shot. "The people of this state are having something shoved down their throats they don't want." He labeled the project a "grave mistake" noting that it would be "hardly used by anyone." The implication was not missed . . . who in the suburbs would ride a subway into Detroit? DiNello advised that the money could be better used for "troopers on the freeways" where his constituents did drive.

Brown had heard enough. "I'd like to say this to the previous speaker," at which point he delivered a verbal raspberry by making a blowing noise with his tongue.

Not one to shy away from any confrontation, DiNello rose. "The senator made a noise with his mouth and I don't appreciate it. He's not fit to be called a senator if he can get up and make those kinds of sounds."

Now the Senate is in a total hush awaiting the next volley. Bad Basil is on the floor.

Brown glared at DiNello with our cameras rolling and referred to what he termed, "your racist nit-picking. If you don't like it, you do something about it. Get your best hold" and he repeated the raspberry.

"I stand ready anytime you do," DiNello shot back.

Having seen more than enough, Lt. Governor James Brickley intervened, gaveling both combatants into their seats. The vote was eventually taken, but was deadlocked 19–19. Brickley stood tall and cast the deciding vote. The subway study was funded, but a shovel for the project never got into the ground.

As a sidebar to that confrontation, DiNello was involved in one more argument that went beyond the verbal phase to actual fisticuffs, giving new meaning to the term floor flight. DiNello and Detroit senator John Kelly actually duked it out right in front of the senate podium.

The fracas, like those in many families, did not happen spontaneously. It simmered to a boil, over a four hour stretch. DiNello wanted to cut property taxes by 33 percent and Kelly pulled his pal aside and advised that the financial loss to cities and schools would be tremendous. Kelly says DiNello responded, "They are going to have to make do with less."

Gil could never be accused of letting the facts get in the way of his conservative efforts to reduce government to the tiniest level possible. Unable to nudge DiNello to back off, Kelly says he devised an amendment to cut the taxes by 50 percent! "That was designed to make the whole concept untenable and make it so onerous that nobody would vote for it," Kelly recalls.

His self-described "provocative" amendment was adopted and DiNello commenced his slow burn. When DiNello complained, Kelly warned him "I'm going to do this to you every step of the way." DiNello's fuse got shorter. Now he is scurrying around the floor trying to line up votes to rescind the Kelly amendment. Finally GOP leader John Engler agrees to help DiNello and the 50 percent is killed.

The 250 pound DiNello sashays over to the 150 pound lightweight Kelly. "See, I told you, I'd get it off. You can't beat me," he boasts as he lifts Kelly off the floor with both hands placed convincingly around Kelly's neck. In the commotion DiNello knocks over Senator John Pridnia, who has a ringside seat. Then DiNello proceeds to slam Kelly's head onto a Senate desk. This pre-dates the World Wrestling Federation. Kelly sustains a couple of hits, then out of nowhere, he unloads an uppercut to DiNello's nose, which responds by bleeding all over DiNello's shirt.

Watching all this, Senator George Hart bellows out to Kelly, "That was lucky!"

By this point, the Sergeant at Arms has yanked the two apart and peace is restored. It all happened in a twinkle of an eye, and when it was over, I thought, did that really happen? Oh yes, it did! DiNello is no longer with us, but Uppercut Kelly is alive and well and recalls the whole ordeal that took over four hours to explode and twenty minutes to retell!

Bullard and Ferguson

Rep. Perry Bullard and Rep. Rosetta Ferguson. The lesson we learn from these two is that just because you are both Democrats it doesn't mean you see eye-to-eye on everything. Bullard was the prototypical liberal Democrat from Ann Arbor where there is no such thing as a conservative. Ferguson was from Detroit and was a Bible thumper before the term was invented. One night her thumping bumped into his liberalism.

In the early '70s, the marijuana issue was a political hot potato in the legislature. There was some talk of doing away with all the anti-grass laws and every time it came up, the issue stirred deep emotions on both sides.

Bullard was at the microphone doing his bleeding heart liberal routine about relaxing the laws, which got Ms. Ferguson to her feet. She had heard enough and proceeded to take an ash tray . . . .smoking cigarettes was still allowed on the floor then, and whacked Bullard on the head.

He was probably more stunned by it than injured, but the two struggled for a moment before the Sergeant at Arms pulled them apart. The next day all the Republicans wore yellow hard hats to session.

Hillegonds and Hertel

Paul Hillegonds and Curtis Hertel. Here was a class act. The Holland Republican was out of the Milliken mold. He tried to bring warring factions to the table to iron out their differences in a civil manner. For years, Rep. Hillegonds labored as the minority leader for the House GOP until lightening struck. The stars aligned just right and Republicans took control of the House for the first time in twenty some years. Hillegonds was the odds on favorite to assume the speakership, and he did.

He held the post for a measly two years, because during the next election cycle, Michigan voters produced a bit of history. They delivered a deadlocked house. Each party having 55 votes each, with 56 votes required to select new leaders.

The tie touched off a furious effort to find a defector to provide that 56th vote. Republicans, led by their Governor John Engler, went after a downriver Democrat who had a conservative bend. Rep. Joe Porreca was wined and dined by the GOP and was probably offered everything, including a bedroom at the governor's residence on Mackinac Island. Engler even spent time in Porreca's living room just before a crucial vote on organizing the House.

Democrats somehow kept Joe in the fold, which forced Hillegonds and his Democratic counterpart, Curtis Hertel, to explore an unbelievable alternative . . . shared power. Unheard of. Heretofore one party called all the shots and shared nothing with the minority party. Now these two guys were seriously considering forging a new deal to allow both sides to run the show.

Rep. Hertel was a Detroit Democrat and was from a long line of Hertel politicians. Brother Dennis had served in the U.S. Congress and brother John had been in the state senate. Curtis had been speaker before the GOP got lucky. Hertel and Hillegonds did not share the same party label, but they shared something much more important . . . they loved the House and were prepared to go where no leader had gone before to preserve the integrity of the body.

The lesson in this story underscores the importance of trust, which is needed to make the legislative process work. Hillegonds and Hertel had worked with each other before, but never under these circumstances with so much at stake. There were lingering doubts as the 'shared power' negotiations began. There were fears the other guy might pull a fast one when the other wasn't looking. The temptation to do that was huge. Democrats wanted to get back control and Republicans, having tasted it for only two years, were still thirsting for more.

The bond of trust was finally cemented one night at an unannounced meeting at the Paddock bar in Holt, which is about ten miles south of the Capitol. Nobody in the press corps knew anything about it.

The end result was an agreement that one party would run the house one month, then turn over the gavel to the other party for the next month. Hillegonds and Hertel sealed the deal in public by staging a joint news conference in which they both held the gavel and told the entire state they would make sure this history making deal would work.

And they did.

The 1994–96 session was a textbook example of how cooperation and compromise can really work in the legislative process. Sure there were plenty of bumps along the way, but the two stepped in and kept their troops in line for the most part. The session was productive; lots of good legislation was adopted, but during the next election cycle, shared power became a thing of the past. The GOP regained power and Hillegonds re-ascended to the Speaker's chair and Hertel became minority leader again with shared power only a faint memory.

Hillegonds was an interesting guy to cover. Mild mannered, very slow to anger and easy to work with were just some of personal traits. That set him apart from other Republicans, who in those days were more conservative. Hillegonds was the son of a preacher man and was quickly dubbed St. Paul by those in the media and his colleagues on both sides of the aisle.

As his term dragged on, speculation turned to whether he would run again for his house seat. Everyone in the press corps believed Hillegonds was governor material. But the state had one, and John Engler wasn't leaving. Hillegonds at one point was considered for lt. governor but he never took the bait Engler offered. He had a new wife, children, and was committed to making his second marriage work. He chose them over higher office.

With nowhere to go but out, or stay for another two years, rumors circulated on what he would do. I was hot on the story along with thirty-four other news hounds. Hillegonds had been elusive during the whole cat and mouse game until one day.

After listening to him say, "The decision has not been made" for the umpteenth time, it dawned on me what was going on. Here's where years in the trenches counted big time.

I recalled talking to Milliken, after he left office, about telling the truth. Did you ever lie to us? I asked. He smiled and said he could honestly say no but . . . and then there was a big but. He explained that even though he may have made a decision, he decided that the decision wasn't really "made" or "official" until he got before the microphones and actually revealed it. It was a wonderful dodge that allowed him to make a decision whenever he wanted to, but he could "honestly" tell the media the decision had not been made.

Remembering that, I confronted Hillegonds one afternoon in the cloak room in the back of the House chambers.

"You're pulling a Milliken on me, aren't you?" I began the cross-examination.

"A what?" he glibly responded.

"You know. You really have made your decision on whether to run again, but you don't consider it official until you announce it, right?"

There was this pause. I could see St. Paul searching for divine guidance. He knew I had nailed it, but like any politician he did not want me to know it. I don't know if he thought about lying, but in the end, he didn't. He told me I was right, which allowed me to ask, so you are not going to run?

He confirmed that, too. "No."

Great. I had an exclusive story, but so far only two people knew it . . . him and me. My job was to spread the news, but I did not rush off. I felt compelled to let him in on what I was about to do. I wanted to run the story on the radio and get it in the local newspaper. We agreed that before I did that, I would get back in touch with him. I was more than willing to do it. I promised I would not use his name in the story.

I called the *Lansing State Journal* and spoke with editor Steve Crosby. He obviously loved the story since nobody else had it and running it would end the three months of speculation that had engulfed this town. There was only one problem. The paper had an ironclad rule: No stories without attribution. In my column they gave me broader latitude to run stuff without a name. But this one was different. It would appear on the front page and needed some named source.

I told Crosby I had only one source and I had promised to conceal his identity. Crobsy did the smart thing. He found a way around the rule. "Tell me who it is and if it's a good source," we'll run with it without the name.

Now it was my turn to seek help from heaven. I had never revealed a secret source to anyone, but I trusted Crosby so with a slight grin on my face I said, "It's Hillegonds." Crobsy agreed that was a good source.

Feeling pretty confident, my next call was back to Hillegonds, per our agreement. I read him the story over the phone and then out of nowhere he says, "Who is your source on this?"

Say what, as I brought my heart back up from the floor?

He jerked me around pretty good. I said you are my source don't you remember? He played with me a little more and then basically let me know, I could run the story. I never anticipated the firestorm of criticism I was about to get.

The story ran the next day and all hell broke loose in town. First there were my colleagues who demanded to know how I knew it was right. I remember one in particular, Steve Harmon, who not only worked at the *Lansing State Journal*, but had been bird-dogging the Hillegonds story for weeks.

"Come on Skubick. I've been talking to the same sources you've been talking to. Where did you get the story?" he demanded.

I remembered the 11th commandment of political reporting, "Thou shall not gloat." I remained tight lipped.

The next wave came from lawmakers who were also upset. Rep. Shirley Johnson was especially livid, and gave me the what for.

"How could you do that to Paul? We don't even know what he's going to do, so how can you be so reckless to speculate on his future when he has not made his decision. [Oh yes, he has Shirley baby, I thought, but of course never put it into words.] I just stood there and let her have at me, and then others got in line too.

The reaction was completely unexpected, but it reflected the depth of affection in the legislative ranks for this man. When all is said and done, the legislature is still a human institution and there is a sense of family. When one of the members is violated, his brothers and sisters come to his aid. Instead of getting a 'way to go Skubick,' I was shown which way to go.

Sure it felt uncomfortable, but so be it. I knew the story was right and also knew there was only one guy left in town who could bail me out . . . and Hillegonds wasn't talking. Why should he, his decision was not final.

Finally, after about a month, Hillegonds summoned the press corps to his office. He sat at the head of the long table as the reporters took their seats along the parameter. I sat down in the back. He and I exchanged smiles and then his press guy handed me the release. It read, "House Speaker Paul Hillegonds Announces Today That He Will Seek Re-election This Year."

There went the ticker again.

Hillegonds had his eyes on me as I read. What he didn't tell me is that all the other reporters got a different release: "House Speaker Hillegonds Announces He Will Not Be a Candidate for Office This Year." He got me! We had a huge laugh between us, but we couldn't explain to anyone the origins of the laughs.

I waited until everyone had pretty much left the room and went over to him. "You got me big guy," we laughed some more. It was a special moment. Hillegonds had been a very special lawmaker to cover. We had a lot of years together and it would soon move to a different phase. I thanked him for helping me on the big story and assured him I would always protect him as my source. There was no goodbye because he had months to go before he left, but we shared a brief hug and moved back to our respective corners . . . his to run the house and mine to cover it.

Years later, I sought and got, his permission to share this with you. He's one class act.

Joyce Braithwaite

Saying good bye has never been easy. As a journalist you are supposed to remain emotionally detached from the folks you cover. I've always considered Bill Milliken to be more than a class act and when it came time for him to leave, it was impossible to obey the rule.

I've never seen the capital press corps more circumspect than on that day in 1981. Everyone knew he would not run again. But his decision wasn't final until he stood up there and told us. I stood in the back of the room . . . on purpose. I didn't want anyone to see the redness in my eyes and the tears that quickly formed.

He read the statement. Everyone listened as if we were in some kind of church. I flashed back to that day he was sworn in. I didn't know a Bill Milliken from a George Romney and felt no emotions whatsoever. It was just another story. What a difference fourteen years can make.

Milliken finished reading. There must have been some questions, but I don't even recall if I had one. Everyone left and I retired to my office to file the story.

The phone rang. It was the Dragon Lady on the other end. That, among other things, is what we called Joyce Braithwaite. She was the hatchet person in the Milliken front office, even though she was truly a lady.

"Tim. Come down to my office, would you?" she asked.

God. Now what had I done? I wondered. I said I would be right down.

I had no idea what she wanted. As a reporter you quickly try to rifle through all the possibilities so that you don't get caught flat footed—especially in front of her.

Braithwaite's tiny office, really a cubbyhole, was a couple of doors down from the governor's. She could be one tough hombre when she wanted to, so the words she shared with me were out of character.

She began quietly.

"I wanted to see you to thank you for caring. You really care about him don't you?" she slowly began.

Chucking the rule about unemotional detachment to the wind, I nodded yes.

"I saw your tears," she went on. "Thank you," she looked me in the eyes.

We said something about all the memories, fun, and all the other stuff your mind dredges up as you reflect on all of it coming to an end. She said thank you for coming down and I said thank you for inviting me. There was nothing left of my public, hard-hitting, take-no-hostages political reporter persona as I left her office. Fact is, I was going to miss the Milliken gang and to this very day, I still miss the climate of civility he brought to this town but more importantly the good persons who brought it to life.

Bill Marshall

When they invented the word "character" they must have had the former state AFL-CIO president in mind. Marshall rose from being a bus driver in the south and experiencing the smarmy side of segregation from the front of the bus, he became a champion of the little person, black or white, in the back.

If you called central casting to send over a typical labor union leader, you'd get Billy Boy, as I sometimes called him . . . and then ducked when I did. He returned the favor by often calling me a "beady-eyed little bastard." You won't believe this, but for him . . . and me . . . that was a term of endearment.

Marshall was built like a house, and it was not beneath him to use it to get his way. He could be gruff, profane, bullheaded, and ornery and that was just before lunch.

He once got in a verbal shoving match with a man who was his equal, Detroit Mayor Coleman Young. When Marshall felt he was right, and that was most of the time, he took nothing from anybody, not even the powerful mayor of Motown.

Marshall forged a real good working relationship with Bill Milliken. The two had nothing in common except the desire to have government work for the betterment of man and woman kind. I'm positive that Marshall voted for Milliken and maybe even helped raise some cash quietly behind the scenes.

After he left his labor post, he put his bus driver's expertise to work on the state transportation commission. When he passed on, the AFL-CIO President Mark Gaffney called.

Skubick do you have any tapes from when Marshall was on your show, and if you do, would you put together a piece that we could show at his memorial service?

I told him I would look and sure enough found the program. I proceeded to lift out the best clips that captured the crusty laborer's flair. At one point in the program we were talking about some bill he wanted that was headed for the legislative graveyard. Marshall advised us that before long, "the corpse would wink."

The panel erupted in laughter and I put it in the highlights tape for the memorial program. Then it dawned on me. It would be bad form to have a dead man saying anything about a corpse at a wake. Billy Boy probably scolded me for not having the nerve to leave it in, but I just couldn't.

The 800 or so Marshall loyalists in the room loved the tape. He was a reporter's joy. He spoke his mind, but did it from his heart and whatever came out, you just knew would make news. Even a beady-eyed little bastard can't complain about that.

Bob Bobier

Rep. Bob Bobier. A character. What are the chances that a marijuana grower from Hesperia, Michigan can win a seat in the Michigan House? Apparently pretty good cause he did it. "Billy Bob" as the press corps often labeled him was a piece of work. A liberal Republican, with commune experience. But he was not a pot head. At a time when the House GOP caucus was moving even more to the right, Bobier moved in and captured the affection of his less liberal colleagues.

In fact they liked him so much that when it came time for his reelection bid, the caucus actually rented some cattle and placed the animals on his farm, to give more of an appearance that he was actually a farmer. Can you believe it? Bobier says don't, cause it is not true, however, the story has become part of the folk lore of Lansing.

Bobier does share something that is true. During his race the Democrats sent out a mailing that attempted to trash the 'ex-hippie.' There was some dandy stuff in this pamphlet. It underscores the lengths to which the opposition will go to unseat an incumbent.

Here's what it said. Bill Bobier describes himself as "One of those people who lives on the edge. In France, they might call it avant-garde. In other areas they might call it the lunatic fringe" the document begins.

Turn the page and you discover that Bobier, "has fond memories of his hippie commune days—and lived in his farmhouse about eight years without adding indoor plumbing." Good stuff hey?

But the Democrats are only warming up. Then voters are told, "The Bobiers are part of a twenty family cooperative called Happy Farmers, which collectively buys farm tools and supplies and makes toy trucks, play equipment and school furniture. "He seems to believe in the kind of collective economy that is finally being thrown out in eastern Europe and even in Russia."

As if that character assassination is not enough, the copy says he was "born in blue jeans and the necktie he was forced to wear on occasion, because of the primary campaign, now hangs with disrespect on the top corner of a door in the kitchen."

Imagine, this is a Democratic publication lamenting the fact that he "won't even put on a tie in order to influence government for your benefit."

Despite the verbal onslaught, he won, which gave him a chance to appear on a special edition of *OTR*. Periodically when we had to put an undated program into the can to allow me a week off, we'd call in some lawmakers and allow them to grill me.

There wasn't a politician in town who did not want a chance to take a couple of shots at me . . . like the clown in the dunk tank.

Frankly, in all the years of doing it, I prepared very little because no one had really laid a glove on me . . . .that is until Billy Bob showed up.

The show was rolling along in it's usual vein as the others on the panel tried to pin me down for being too liberal, or not letting the facts get in the way of a good story when Rep. Bobier jumps in by pulling a sheet of paper from his pocket.

Like a wily prosecutor closing in for the kill, Bobier started off innocently enough.

"You believe in voting, don't you?" he asked.

[What a lame brain question I thought and proceeded into the trap.]

"Well, of course," I confessed.

"Well, if that's the case, how come you have missed five of the past eleven elections in your hometown?"

Pow. Bang. Zoom.

He had me dead to rights. This guy actually did some research, unheard of by most, and he nailed me between the eyes.

"Duh? Say What? Missed five what? I stumbled looking for shelter and demanded to see the evidence that he promptly put in my hands. He didn't say "Gotcha," but the rest of the panel and the entire audience of politicians in TV land did.

There it was in black and white. I had missed 46 percent of the last eleven elections. But it wasn't until after the show, when I had a chance to review the document more closely,that I discovered that he had deceived me. Just like a reporter might do to a mark.

Bobier had used selective information from my voting record to make me look bad. What he conveniently left out was the rest of my attendance at the polls dating back to 1982. When you factored in those votes, my absenteeism rate dropped from an embarrassing 46 percent to a more respectable 12 percent, but of course he never reported that. Hey why ruin a good story with the facts!

It was a brilliant piece of reporting proving the old adage that figures don't lie, but liars sure as heck can figure. I figured turnabout was fair play.

I fired up the phone and got the local clerk on the horn from Ferry Township where one Robert Bobier resides. I asked her to recount the elections from November 1972 to the present and his attendance at same. I knew I had him now.

Wrong.

The former pot head never missed a one . . . a perfect 31 for 31.

David Jaye

Macomb County has fed a steady stream of clowns and characters into the legislative pipeline. You had Senator Kirby Holmes who championed the death penalty to no avail. There were Senators John "The Fox" Bowman who refurbished his office complete with mirrors, sofas, and credenzas; Gil DiNello whom you've read about earlier, and Senator Doug Carl, who got the speed limit changed from 55 to 70, before his untimely death.

But by far it was David Jaye who attracted the most media attention and also found his niche in the state history books by being the first modern day senator to be voted out of office. The Jaye saga is filled with laughs, pathos, and a host of other human emotions.

In a town where the moto was, "Go along, to get along" Mr. Jaye steadfastly marched to his own drummer . . . being out of step for him was a badge of courage that he used to get reelected time after time. All he had to do was say nobody liked him in Lansing and the anti-government crowd loved it.

During budget debates in the House, it was not uncommon for Jaye to single handily add hours to the debate by offering hundreds of amendments. He would go after the limos used by members of the Detroit Board of Education and when Mayor Coleman Young was in office, Jaye had his honor in his sights all the time.

Jaye was a pain in the butt not only to Democrats, but to members of his own party. None of the Republicans would go on the record, but you didn't have to dig very deep to unearth anti-Jaye sentiment all over the place. One of his most famous moments, was when a gun supposedly fell from his pocket, while in a closed door GOP caucus. Fortunately it didn't go off.

Jaye's life took a distinct turn for the worse when he left the house and won a seat in the senate where tradition, collegiality, and conformity abound. They don't call it the House of Lords for nothing.

Jaye was more of a misfit in that body. Underscored by the fact that two of the senior senators, John Schwarz and Harry Gast, tried to get him to fall in line. It was wasted breath. Jaye continued with his amendments, headline grabbing sound bites and an attitude that seemed to say, I don't need any of you guys. I can do this on my own. You could count on two fingers the number of 'friends' he had in that body, and that was on a good day.

Like any human institution the legislative process works on trust developed between folks willing to cooperate from time to time. Jaye didn't get much done because he refused to play the game, but that didn't do him in. Falling in love did.

Jaye met a fiery woman named Sonia Kloss. You could tell he was madly in love, but the chemistry between the two was over the edge. They had alleged fights and one of the encounters caught the attention of the Senate Majority leader Dan DeGrow. He concluded that what Jaye did amounted to physical abuse and the leader put into motion one of the most emotional battles in senate history. DeGrow would lead the charge to expel Mr. Jaye, and DeGrow had plenty of supporters. Jaye did not.

It is an unwritten rule: Legislative bodies don't like airing any dirty linen in public and that includes having to kick someone out. It not only damages the person involved but everyone else in the process. The drill is to quietly go to the person and ask them to resign. Sometimes they dangle incentives such as continuing health care and retirement benefits. Jaye would not deal. He felt he had done nothing wrong. If they wanted him to leave, they would have to do it, not him.

That led to a series of public hearings that commenced on May 8 2001. Jaye's legal counsel called it a "public lynching." The testimony went on for what seemed like forever. The hearings were staged in full view of the media and the entire state. Jaye looked haggard, as his personal life with Ms. Kloss was dragged through the media gutter.

The last thing a reporter wants during such an ordeal is to be drawn into the story. Despite my best intentions, it happened to me. It was a very uncomfortable place to be . . . very uncomfortable.

While covering the hearings, I often retired to the back of the giant hearing room to chat with folks who might be there. In one such conversation, I was told that a videotape existed. It supposedly showed Jaye and his finance in a scuffle outside a bathroom inside a gas station along I-75.

The tape was potentially the smoking gun in the DeGrow case against Jaye. It's one thing to accuse a man of physical abuse where it can turn into a 'He said, she said' battle of words. It was quite another to show it on tape.

I reported the existence of the tape and Jaye's lawyers went bonkers. They accused the Republicans of sitting on the evidence. They almost called me to the stand to reveal my source. GOP leader Dan DeGrow said he didn't know the tape existed until one of his aides told him. He insisted he was not covering up anything. For a time however, I became a sideshow in the main event. I can recall coming home and expressing my concerns to Gayle about being drawn into this nasty melodrama.

The tape eventually surfaced, but no one could agree on whether it was a smoking gun. That didn't stop the committee from its appointed duty. Eventually there was a vote and to no one's surprise, there were enough votes, 5–1, to recommend Jaye's removal. The list of particulars against the maverick senator was as long as your arm and leg.

He was tagged with abusive and violent behavior; intimidating employees; multiple criminal convictions including time in jail; a recurring pattern of personal misconduct; misusing his Senate position and being "unfit to continue as a member of this esteemed body." About the only thing left off the list was stealing paper clips from the Senate supply room. A Senate source also reveals that they "had other stuff from his ex-wife that they did not use." Leader Dan DeGrow said, "We will rise above that and get him on the information we have," although he was pressured to use that ex-spouse stuff. It was at that point that the behind the scene negotiations for a deal apparently went into high gear. At one point a deal was offered, and I happened to be in Jaye's office as he ran it by some friends back home.

It is also being revealed here for the first time that Jaye's supporters allegedly investigated members of the committee and DeGrow. DeGrow claims he was shocked to get a phone call one day from his Port Huron police chief reporting that DeGrow was being linked to a murder that he never committed. At least three other members of the GOP Senate were also "threatened," according to DeGrow including Senators Hoffman, Schwarz and McCotter, who chaired the expulsion panel. None of the intimidation worked and nobody at the time went public about that aspect of this unseemly story.

DeGrow says Jaye was given the chance to "resign with honor" but no deals were consummated. Jaye's attorney said at the time his client, "Would not take the thirty pieces of silver." On May 24, the final senate vote was taken after Jaye made an 11th hour plea for his political life, taking a full hour to do it. In vintage Jaye style he did it his way by attacking senators and claiming he was the victim of a "political payback" for all his anti-establishment behavior. He conceded he had made some mistakes, but none justified what was about to be done.

As the long awaited vote came, Jaye got up out of his seat and moved to the back of the chambers before the final vote was announced. He turned and looked at the voting board and walked out the door for the last time as the Secretary of the Senate announced the expulsion vote . . . Jaye got a whopping two votes out of thirty-eight . . . his own and that of Upper Peninsula Democrat Donny Kovisto. Jaye was toast. The senate was rid of a him. In reality Jaye had a great mind and lots of potential, but it could not save him. He became a part of history as the first state senator to be expelled in 164 years.

Everyone outside the media kept saying, wow this must have been a great story to cover with allegations of sex, lies and videotapes. Frankly, it was not. I think it had an emotional impact on many of us and most were happy to see it end. Given a chance to do it over again, I would not.

Chuck Yob

Chuck Yob. You can't do a chapter on characters and not discuss the National GOP committeeman named Yob. The Chuckster is one of a kind. He doesn't have the edge that David Jaye had, but he made just as many headlines and caused just as many headaches for his fellow Republicans.

Yob's fault was he spoke his mind and removed the B.S. filter before he did. That's why capitol reporters loved to have him around. You knew when his mouth opened, eventually something controversial would come out.

Ask Ronna Romney. Back in May of 1994, she was eager to nail down the GOP U.S. Senate nomination. Yob went on *OTR* and gave this analysis: "She's riding on George Romney's name. She's going nowhere. She's running to be vindictive" because the state GOP ousted her as National committeewoman. And to top it off Yob suggested, "Ronna will be brown-nosing around Washington" and won't do her job if elected.

Yob, who was backing Spencer Abraham who got the nomination, later called Ms. Romney and sort of apologized and offered a truce after he had trashed her. He did it in order to discredit her candidacy and give Spence a boost.

The delightful Mr. Yob broke all records during another appearance when he managed to offend eight, count'em eight other politicians. During 1998 it was not clear that John Engler would run again so Yob was asked to assess other possible contenders if Engler retired.

"I haven't heard a name yet that I'm really sold on," he warmed up his quote machine.

What about Oakland County Executive L. Brooks Patterson, the clown prince of the state GOP?

"He can't win it," Yob lobbed back. He complained that L. Brooks didn't stand for much as he stopped just short of labeling him "wishy-washy."

Regarding his fellow west Michigan colleague Dick Posthumus, Yob complained, "He doesn't attend any events. He is not in touch with his constituents."

At the time of his remarks, Posthumus was deeply involved in a senate battle over state aid to Detroit and Grand Rapids. Posthumus was the GOP leader in the fight. Yob accused his pal of "sitting on the fence" and being perceived as a "Detroit guy." Dickie must have loved that.

Then he turned his sights on the chances of Lt. Governor Connie

Binsfeld running for governor. "Connie can't do it," he suggested as
he stopped just short of calling her too old for the job. He did note
she could not keep the hectic schedule a governor had to keep.

He proceeded to upset Engler next, by suggesting he didn't care
who got the nomination for president. "He (Engler) doesn't care if
he is vice president under Dole or Gramm" referring to former U.S.
Senators Bob Dole and Phil Gramm.

On his buddy Spencer Abraham, Yob said he is "on an ego trip"
and Congressman Nick Smith, who was flirting with running for
the U.S. Senate, was a loser. He rounded out his record shattering
appearance by calling the Mayor of Detroit Dennis Archer "arrogant" and state senator Matt Dunaskis was accused of running for
anything that was out there.

He left reporters breathless from hurriedly jotting down all those
quotes. That was in 1995. Three years later he got in plenty of hot
water with Engler as the two locked horns over who would run for
attorney general. Yob opposed Engler's choice. Yob's guy won.

Ironically on the eve of that 2002 election, Yob again appeared on
the show as reporters were in the midst of the bi-annual guessing
game, who is running for what? Yob was more than eager to play.

Secretary of State Candice Miller was running for Congress, so
there was an open seat for that post. Yob supported a woman named
Terri Lynn Land. Yob told the startled panel that he felt Land was
right for the post "because women like that kind of work" in the
Secretary of State's office.

Female panelist Amy Bailey went through the ceiling as she pur-
sued Yob for his apparent sexist remarks. I, on the other hand, was
in the midst of committing one of the most grievous sins of interviewing. I wasn't listening. I missed the "like that kind of work" line.
Amy didn't and after the program blasted the story all over the
Associated Press wires and before too long, Mr. Yob was up to his
you know what in alligators.

Remember, the women's vote was critical that election year and
his off handed remarks produced a firestorm of male bashing from
female columnists who had a field day at Chuck's expense. The
Democrats weren't far behind in blasting this gray-haired man for
being out of touch with modern day politics, and the Engler gang

just stewed for a few days, before calling for Yob's resignation as national committeeman.

Posthumus, who would run against Jennifer Granholm, was super sensitive to the female factor in the race. So sensitive that he took over a week to join in the criticism of his pal Yob. It made Posthumus look bad. When he finally got on the resignation bandwagon, he suggested that Yob's remarks were offensive. That lead the critics to wonder, if Posthumus really felt that way, why did it take him so long to speak out?

During the whole flap, I talked with Yob who truly felt he had gotten a bum wrap. "Skubick, my track record on bringing women into the party is solid." He was correct. There had never been even a hint of sexism in any of his other flamboyant remarks over the years. He conceded it was a poor choice of words but he refused to resign. I also asked him to come back on the show to tell his side of the story. He declined. See he wasn't totally insane.

Peter Secchia

Peter Secchia. Yob's political soul mate from west Michigan was Peter "Call Me Millionaire" Secchia. I had the chance to cover two Secchias: The one before he became Ambassador to Italy during the senior George Bush administration and the guy who returned to the states after that.

Secchia was a true insider. He was close to former President Ford and dropped Ford's name at the drop of a hat. If you needed the inside skinny on state GOP politics and could only make one or two calls, one of them was always to Secchia.

In his pre-ambassador days he appeared on the show years ago and was as tart-tongued as always. We were running out of time and I jumped in with this zinger, "What do you think of the governor's suggestion [Jim Blanchard] that your party is run by right wing extremists?"

"That's absolutely ridiculous . . . They're not going to take over the party." At this point he reaches into his coat pocket and brings out a gun . . . a squirt gun as he continues his answer. "They're going to be part of our party. We welcome them." Now he takes aim at me and as I kiss off the show, he dusts me off with some water from the gun right on my glasses!

That was a first and last.

Secchia became a different man during his overseas assignment. The old Secchia was still kicking when he took the job. He told the folks in Italy that if they wanted to see the Italian Navy they would need a glass bottom boat in the Mediterranean Sea. What a way to launch an ambassadorship.

By the time he returned home, this lovable old politician had turned into a diplomat. Ugh. He refused to be drawn into any flagrant verbal assaults and probably tossed his trusty squirt gun down there with the Italian Navy.

Coleman Young

Coleman Young. If you took the curse words out of the former Detroit mayor's lexicon, you would have had one dull politician. Coleman A. Young was anything but. I got to know him when he was still in the state senate. After the courts cleared the way for him to run for mayor, because there was confusion over whether a sitting lawmaker could run for that office, our contact dropped off. But we would bump into one another when he made lobbying trips a.k.a. hand-out-for-money sojourns to the capitol.

Young was once in Hawaii where he delivered a speech to the folks back in Detroit. He opened the address with the provocative, "Aloha M—— F——ers!" He also called President Ronald Reagan, "prune face" and once, accused former Governor Blanchard of not having any testicles although he used a more common term that rhymes with halls.

Sometime after that he appeared on the big screen again, only this time, he was in Detroit and I was with three other politicians on Mackinac Island. It was the annual soiree sponsored by the Detroit Regional Chamber of Commerce and I was interviewing the mayor, Wayne County Executive Ed McNamara, Oakland County Executive Dan Murphy, and Macomb County Commission Chair Mark Steenberg, who were on the stage with me.

This was in June 1989 and a fierce battle was unfolding about the

Detroit Tigers leaving downtown Detroit. It was a story ripe for plucking, and since all the parties involved in the flap were there, I proceed to pluck away.

I grilled McNamara on wanting to move the team to his turf and asked Murphy the same thing. Then the mayor, bigger than life on the screen, boomed into the conversation.

"I wouldn't take that crap from you, Tim" he burst in.

I shot back, "I'm glad you're back in Detroit, Mr. Mayor."

The 200 or so business types loved it.

Then the questioning turned to whether politicians can stay in office too long and I went to Young for the first response.

"Funny, you should ask me that," the seventy-one year old mayor snapped back. "I suppose so," he went on. "Do you have anyone in mind?"

I refused to take the bait. I didn't want him to retire. He was great copy and fun to be around. And so it went. The hour flew by and the exchange went down as one of the more controversial, entertaining, and informative Big Four sessions in chamber history.

Detroit Free Press writer Teresa Blossom covered the event and wrote some critical comments about my role in questioning the mayor and others. Hey, you live by the sword, you die by the sword.

Two weeks later Mayor Young announced a new addition to his media staff . . . .Teresa Blossom.

Bill McMaster

Bill McMaster is not a household word, but he's certainly well known around the capitol as the proverbial gad-fly and sometime newsmaker. Like the time he and a fellow Republican found themselves in an altercation in the middle of Woodward Ave. near Berkley, Michigan.

McMaster was running for the state senate and was embroiled in a campaign with three other Republicans including Doug Cruce. For several weeks the frontrunner Cruce had noticed that many of his campaign signs had been destroyed. He was content to let it ride, but after his wife complained, he decided to do something about it.

He and a campaign staffer got in the car and took up watch along a stretch of Woodward Ave. the main drag in his district. They took along some "imbibements" as Cruce retells the story and within ten minutes they spotted somebody in the median going to work on one of his signs.

That somebody was Bill McMaster. He contends he was not destroying any of the signs but was looking to see if the sign had the legal disclaimer disclosing who had paid for the advertisement. McMaster was prepared to file a complaint against Cruce if the sign was improper. Then out of nowhere, he recalls, came two men who proceeded to jump him. "They were over six feet and I was 150 pounds and a little over five feet," the scrappy McMaster described the mismatch.

Cruce says he didn't know who it was until McMaster turned around. The trio proceeded to scuffle with no hits exchanged, but Cruce ended up sitting on top of McMaster "like you used to do to your little brother," Cruce goes on. McMaster started banging his feet against Cruce's back, so the other guy sat on McMaster's feet.

Remember these are grown men not some hooligans out of some reform school.

Some motorists slowed down and Cruce told someone to call the cops. Within minutes three scout cars show up . . . one from the sheriff's department, one from Berkley, and one from Royal Oak. Now, in what is slowly turning into a Keystone Cops remake, the three officers debate who has jurisdiction. They decide it's the Berkley's cop gig, so the other two head for the hills.

The officers ask for identification and an explanation. Cruce alleges that McMaster was destroying his signs and McMaster contends he was only looking at them. The officer asks if the two are opponents in the race. They answer in the affirmative.

At which point the cop informs the two that they need to work this out. That's his parting wisdom as he jumps in the patrol car to fight crime in some other part of the county.

McMaster says several days later somebody offered him a $1000 not to proceed with charges against Cruce.

For his part Cruce calls his P.R. guy and reports, "We may have a problem." For the next two days Cruce goes into hiding to avoid any fall out from the incident, which eventually appears in print and makes the rounds of the radio talk shows. Now Cruce is really worried, but in the end he finishes first and McMaster comes in fourth, but their tussle along Woodward Ave. is firmly embedded in state capitol lore.

Stallworth and Vaughn

Rep. Keith Stallworth and his pal Rep. Ed Vaughn of Detroit, were involved in one of those events much like the Kelly-DiNello fight. You couldn't believe it was happening.

The senate education committee, chaired by the mild-mannered Loren Bennett, was conducting, or at least, trying to conduct a hearing on legislation to abolish the Detroit School Board. Gov. Engler was behind the effort to install an appointed board, but to do that, he had to get rid of the one the voters in Detroit elected. Many of the Detroiters didn't like the idea any more than they adored the author.

It was a classic civil rights issue and protesters from Detroit were in the committee room where things quickly got out of hand. Demonstrators chanted and halted the proceedings before Bennett could take any testimony. Then out of nowhere, Rep. Vaughn swipes the gavel from Bennett and marches around the room holding the gavel high in the air with Rep. Stallworth at his side. The victory laps with the "trophy" waving in the air brought cheers from the demonstrators. Bennett was not amused but was not about to intervene either. Senators get no combat pay.

No one had ever seen that before. As the two marched back and forth dressed in traditional African garb, Bennett and other committee members looked on in amazement. Finally a female Sergeant at Arms grabbed the gavel from Vaughn's fist and returned it to Bennett. It was great TV and we captured all of it on tape. But the confrontation was not over.

The two legislators and protesters held the joint captive for nearly two hours. At the end of which the committee voted the bill to the floor where it was eventually adopted.

The story got the attention of the entire state and the entire legislature, which tends to frown on activities that make the institution look vulnerable or stupid. Vaughn and Stallworth had done both. The Speaker of the House, Rep. Chuck Perricone, was especially upset and summoned both of his charges into the woodshed.

Perricone issued this statement and leveled these penalties.

"The kind of behavior demonstrated by Reps. Vaughn and Stall-worth at the committee hearing has no place within the state Capitol and greatly hinders the Democratic process . . . we must ensure that members feel comfortable expressing their opinions on highly emotional issues without the risk of others reacting as Vaughn and Stallworth had."

The two had their travel privileges removed and they could not have any visitors on the floor during session. It was a slap on the wrist, which the Speaker said he would review at the end of the session. But if the two apologized he would rescind everything.

Stallworth appeared on *OTR* and said he was sorry and Vaughn did, too, and the story was over.

Jim Dunn

Jim Dunn was not a household name, but he actually ran for the U.S. Senate once. And when he did, he made news by suing his own party.

With all due respect, Dunn's political career was a fluke. He had won an East Lansing congressional seat from incumbent Democrat Bob Carr in 1980. He was pulled into office due to the strong showing of Ronald Reagan and the lackluster showing of Democratic presidential loser Jimmy Carter. After a two-year stint in D.C. Dunn ran for reelection but found himself all done. He lost.

In the 1998 U.S. Senate contest, no Republican with an ounce of brains wanted to tackle twenty-two year incumbent Don Riegle who by this time had a lock on the seat.

Dunn resurfaced, as did Bob Huber who almost beat Lenore Romney in 1970. We did a debate in Traverse City with the two in June and when the August vote came, Dunn secured the nomination.

There was no way he even had a chance against money bags Riegle without a sizable kitty of his own. Dunn says he was promised a boatload of money from the national party but when his ship never came in, Dunn called a news conference. His press secretary Gary Mitchell thought the gathering was to show some new campaign commercials, which the candidate had no money to air.

Prior to the news conference, however, Dunn tells Mitchell he's going to announce his intent to sue the national GOP for non-support. Mitchell can't believe it. He strongly urges him not to do it. Dunn had a strong will and when he was committed to do something, he did it. All Mitchell could do was shake his head.

Mitchell had other woes with his difficult client. A good example was when during the campaign, one of the capitol reporters wanted to spend the day with the candidate. Dunn said no. Mitchell asked why. Dunn said because he'd have to go a whole day without passing gas and telling off-color jokes, according to Mitch.

Meanwhile the lawsuit against his own party was treated as a joke, but it was still a good story, especially when he entered the room with a rubber chicken that he swung in front the cameras. He said his party was too chicken to help him out. Great visual. Great story. Bad news for Dunn.

"I thought it was a disaster," recalls Mitchell. GOP pollster Tom Shields was also there. His and Mitchell's mouths dropped when the chicken appeared.

Dunn also took a potshot at the GOP chair, at the time Spencer Abraham. Abraham claimed the race was a top priority and he promised a quarter of a million bucks, too. Dunn was down in the polls 66 percent-16 percent. There was no way the chairman was going to pour that much into the losing effort, but when asked about Dunn's criticism, Abraham was the master of the understatement, "Maybe he just had a bad day."

Riegle had more than four million dollars. Dunn ran an entire general election campaign without one TV spot and of course, he lost. He returned to his home building business and hasn't been heard from since.

One of the true joys of doing public TV is the receptiveness to producing something out of the ordinary.

On paper, my idea for a program near the end of the rough and tumble 1990 race for governor looked like a potential bomb because it involved eight different guests.

But I sensed tossing all these folks into one studio might produce some chemistry that could produce an interesting program. I was right. Check out this cast of characters.

The four GOP folks were Dick Headlee, former candidate for

governor; David Doyle, state GOP chair; Brooks Patterson, Oakland County executive; and Dan Pero, who was managing John Engler's uphill climb against Jim Blanchard.

In the other corner four Democrats included Blanchard's campaign manager Gary Bachula; Conrad Mallett Jr., one of the governor's confidants; Barbara Roberts Mason from the party leadership; and State Treasurer Bob Bowman.

I was the moderator, and the broadcast needed a lot of moderating.

We recorded the show on October 1 about one month before the vote for governor. Hugh McDiarmid from the *Free Press* described it as it offering up more melee than substance, heavy with squabbling, boasting, occasional wisecracking, and serious [though mostly genteel] eye-gouging, and only incidentally seriously addressing fairness or truth." In other words the broadcast was a metaphor for how the campaign had been going.

Headlee suggested the campaign was "incredible" in that it hardly had any facts. Just a lot of fluff and a lot of misconceptions and misinformation and he called both sides guilty.

Mallett and Patterson exchanged niceties during the one hour show. Mallett complained, "There's no real information [here]. What's going on is that Brooks is testing to see whether or not he can scream louder than me."

Patterson glibly responded, "You win, Conrad."

The GOP chair, Mr. Doyle, wondered what a lot of reporters were wondering. "Why is it that a man who says he is "tough, tested, and trusted" is too timid to show up in his own ads?" The T, T, and T line was Blanchard's slogan.

Rather than wait for a Democrat to answer Headlee suggested, "If they talk about his record, they're dead meat."

Mason looked at the GOP gang and charged Engler with starting all the negative stuff by calling Blanchard "Dr. Frankenstein and a few other names."

Igor . . . er..er Blanchard's campaign manager Bachula, blamed the media for not paying enough attention to the issues and if it "had a more responsible attitude towards the issues, that would help," he lectured the media watching in the other studio. Pero didn't like the Frankenstein reference and said so. "That's not the case." He contends what Engler really said was electing Blanchard was "like putting Dr. Frankenstein in charge of the laboratory." A distinction without a difference, don't ya think?

Doyle reminded everyone that Blanchard had once called Headlee and Patterson "jackasses." I don't recall anybody on the panel refuting the point, including the Dickster and Brookster.

And so it went back and forth. I was having a ball. These guys were engaged, there was plenty of heat, and despite what Mac says, there was also some content.

About forty minutes into the thing, I caught Bowman with his head in his hands.

"What's that for?" I inquired.

"What's what for?" he fired right back . . .

"The non-verbal thing. You bored by this?"

"You're proving why this should be only a thirty minute show."

"Now you tell me," I lamented.

Greene and Schuster

You've heard of Simon and Schuster the giant publishing house, and you may recall the Canadian comedy team of Wayne and Schuster. Well the state capital press corps had a couple of characters . . . Greene and Schuster.

Tom Greene was the guy with the walrus size mustache who worked for TV 2 in Detroit. Gary Schuster wrote for the *Detroit News* and between the two of them, they made more enemies in the legislative ranks than you could count and for good reason. Their mission was to look under every rock they could find to embarrass everyone they could find. Their critics contend they gave "muck-raking" a bad name. They could have cared less. In fact, the more lawmakers loathed their reporting, the more determined they were to unearth more rocks.

One of the stories they rode hard came around every four years. When Michigan senators were elected they had a time honored tradition of redoing their offices. Some of the senators had an attitude and that matched their office decor: expensive sofas, credenzas, side chairs and desks were the order of the day and taxpayers picked up the tab every four years. That's where Greene and Schuster came in.

One of their favorite targets was conservative Democrat John Bowman, affectionately known as John "The Fox." He refurbished his digs complete with mirrors on the wall. It looked like a French you know what.

By the time the comedy team of Greene and Schuster got done adding up the cost, Bowman was livid. The folks back in his Roseville district watched TV and some even read the paper. It was tough for him to defend the "misuse of tax dollars." What was he to say, "I deserve it because I'm a hot shot senator? Or, everyone else is doing it? Or, I want to have a nice office for my constituents when they visit?"

The dynamic duo often appeared on *OTR* and frankly, they helped to develop an audience. They did not pull their punches. They were funny and they were good. Management at WKAR got a little queasy whenever Greene called lawmakers "turkeys" and Schuster trumped him by calling them "Bozos." But they were good TV and you almost had to watch to see what they would do next. I tried to keep them in line, but to no avail.

They were really a challenge to have on the panel and on those mornings they showed up with blood shot eyes, I knew I was in for it. They were not averse to "doing the town." They bought drinks during the night for the same Bozos they were beating up during the day. It's truly amazing they were not involved in more bar fights. Schuster once got into a shoving match with an Irish appellate court judge who ruled Schuster out of order— as legend has it, they fought to a draw.

It should come as no surprise to you that reporters tend to be anti-authoritarian and anybody who is in charge doesn't get respect just because he or she is in charge. Senator Robert Vanderlaan ran the senate back in those days and he had a huge run in with Greene and Schuster, and the rest of the capital gang, over a seemingly straight forward proposal.

In the good ole days, reporters with notepads in hand, had free reign on the senate floor. They could stroll up to a senator and discuss an issue during the session and nobody complained. But with the advent of TV and radio coverage, suddenly there were more than note pads floating around. Now there were "big cameras" as Vanderlaan describes them and microphones all over. It didn't take long before the hallowed decorum of the senate went to hell.

Republican Vanderlaan hatched the idea of confining the reporters to press boxes complete with plate glass, speakers and chairs. From the outcry in the press corps, you would have thought he was sending correspondents to Siberia. It didn't take very long before the "infringement on our first amendment rights" argument was trotted out producing a wholesale civil war. The bad guys on one side and the media on the other. In the public opinion arena it was not a fair fight. It was the guys with mirrors on the walls vs. those defending the public's right to know.

Vanderlaan, being from west Michigan where they get some of their guidance directly from Heaven, was not about to cave. He dug in. Greene and Schuster dug in deeper and finally the lt. governor got into the act.

Behind closed doors Jim Brickley agreed with Vanderlaan that the senate was out of control. It was Brickley's job to preside every-day and keep order, so, by rights, he should have backed the leader. He did not.

Vanderlaan says Brickley came in and said, "We're not going to do this. Taking on the press will hurt us." Since Brickley was fixing to run for governor, he surely did not want to get wounded in the cross fire. Vanderlaan relented and the press boxes were never built. Greene and Schuster declared victory.

Long after the fact Vanderlaan now laughs about it noting that "The idea was never meant to be punitive." But as so often happens in Lansing, good ideas are not always good politics. Greene eventu-ally got out of the business and ran for the Michigan house thinking his huge name would assure him a win. It didn't. Schuster traded his poison pen for a TV microphone in the nation's capital where he covered the White House on weekends for that little network called CBS. Schuster got so good at it that he was invited to watch movies at 1600 Pennsylvania Ave. with a guy name Reagan . . . as in Ronald.

Wonder if there were any mirrors in there?

Joe Mack

If you've been a fan of state government over the years you are probably wondering, where's the stuff about Joe Mack? For those of you not familiar with the Upper Peninsula icon, read on.

Mack was one of a kind. He was forced out of office as part of a deal he struck with then Attorney General Frank Kelley.

Prior to that, Mack was a power to contend with. He had an enemies list that included lots of reporters and the entire Department of Natural Resources. Put it this way, Joe was not a tree hugger. In fact his favorite line was about hippies who came to the U.P. to camp.

"They come up here with five dollars and a pair of underwear and they don't change either," he would repeat over and over.

Joe personified the image that was common to some, but not all senators. He was arrogant, abused his power, thought the world revolved around him and if you got in his way, he would get you out of his way one way or the other. In a weird sort of way, however, he was also sort of lovable . . . well that might be too strong.

Of course the political landscape in Lansing and Washington is strewn with guys who played the game that way and got into a heap of trouble doing it. One of Joe's least favorite moments was when his name got mixed-up in the so called tug barge issue in the U.P.

It was a convoluted story that boiled down to the charge that Mack and other U.P. lawmakers got something for helping to build a tug barge up there. Mack claimed he was innocent and came on our show to prove it.

His aide, Andy Such who was a former TV reporter turned political consultant, had come up with a proposal to make sure the viewers got the message.

When the question came up, Mack reached into the pocket of his plaid coat . . . by the way all of his coats came with a volume control because they were so loud . . . and pulls out a penny and he proceeds to drop the penny on the table as he testifies, "Joe Mack [he always referred to himself in the third person ala Bob Dole] never made one red cent on that deal."

Frankly it was a good visual. Only problem was, he dropped the penny four more times during the interview! The performance was vintage Mack. Regardless of what we asked him, he dropped the penny.

Reporters gravitated to Joe not so much because they agreed with him, but because he was great copy, gave great quotes, and did outrageous things. When *Free Press* columnist McDiarmid was not locking horns with east Detroit senator Gil DiNello you could find him working over Joe. It was Mac vs. Mack and it always made for good reading.

McDiarmid had approached Such about doing an extended Sunday story on the U.P. senator. It took a while, but Such finally convinced his boss to take the plunge, but he advised his charge to take a tape recorder to the interview, which Mack did.

One portion of the piece dealt with Mack's fierce and uncompromising defense of the logging industry in his neck of the woods. Mack advised that if the industry succumbed to all the proposed state regulations that tree huggers wanted, the price of toilet paper would skyrocket to five bucks a roll. It was a good quote and Mac put it in the piece.

The Sunday morning the story ran, Such got an angry call from Mack. "Get me McDiarmid," he bellowed. Mack told Such to read the article and buried in one of the graphs was this quote, "and the price of ass wipe would go up five bucks a roll."

Ass wipe? McDiarmid told the senator when they connected, that he had written "toilet paper" and was not sure how the substitute and more colorful description found its way into print. The paper launched an investigation while Mack got an attorney and sued. The upshot of the probe revealed that some union employee had secretly made the change, which nobody caught. It cost the paper an out of court settlement and Mack got his revenge.

About six months ago, the senator called.

"Skubick!" he bellowed from Florida. "My grand kids were playing with the VCR the other day and erased the tape of my appearance on your show. Can you get me a copy?"

I knew we didn't have it, but believe me I wish we did because it was a classic moment. Suffice it to say there are no more characters anywhere in the legislature that even come close to the likes of Joe Mack. If any of you have a VHS copy of that show, please send it along.

Bill Ryan

You didn't have to cover the Michigan House very long before you bumped into Bill Ryan. He was first elected in 1958 after serving in the Marine Corps, writing for a social action newspaper, the Wage

Earner, and being financial secretary for UAW Local 104 in
Detroit.

By the time I started on the beat in 1969, Ryan had ascended to
the top job as Speaker of the House. The line on Bill Ryan was, if
you ask him what time it is, he'll tell you how to build a watch.

That was an affectionate way of explaining that he was a detail
guy. Ryan is widely credited with almost single handily turning a
backwater legislature, with an antiquated secretarial pool and no
other staff, into a modern day entity that we know today i.e., every
legislator has a secretary and several aides.

Ryan was involved in every major issue there was. His news conferences were notorious because they took forever, but if you
wanted to know what was going on, you had to be there.

But a local TV owner did not agree. Hal Gross who operated
WJIM-TV got sick and tired of seeing Ryan on the evening news so
he ordered his news department to ban Ryan from the air. Not
exactly what you would call a reasoned journalistic decision, but it
was his station.

That decision was quickly spread to the press corps by the TV-6
reporters. Everyone was appalled and somebody eventually filed a
complaint with the Federal Communications Commission, which
was the federal watch dog agency for the broadcast industry. A host
of other Gross violations were also cataloged and for a time his
license was in jeopardy, but never yanked.

Meanwhile Ryan continued to run the house while grooming his
successor Bobby Crim. Ryan eventually retired and virtually disappeared from the political landscape.

Before he passed on, he was placed in a nearby nursing home. I
visited him on several occasions and found it to be a heart wrench-
ing experience. Here was a man who was at the center of every
major piece of legislation that cleared the House; a man who had
worked closely with GOP Governor Milliken, and a man who stood
up for his pro-life and "help the little guy" philosophy for decades.

His influence in the legislative process was so pervasive that a
state senator joked about a bill that was about to clear that body and
rushed over to the House Speaker. Sen. Billy Huffman warned the
membership, "Whatever is in the bill now, won't be in it when
you're done with Father Ryan."

But now this man of immense power was reduced to a tiny 8 x 10 room with a TV, a window, a closet and his bed. He also had his faith and his only daily visitor, his wife. In the end that surpassed all the trappings of power that never much mattered to him anyway.

We talked about old times and all the characters he dealt with, many of whom you have just read about, and I thanked him for his years of service and all the help he had given me over the years.

One of the most touching moments was when he gave me a copy of a doctoral thesis that had been written about him. I asked him to sign it and even though it took some effort, he was able to scratch out these words, "To Tim, my friend. Bill Ryan."

Jim Brickley

The news conference with the Chief Justice of the Michigan Supreme Court was over but instead of heading back to his office, Jim Brickley walked over to a corner of the room where a little five year old girl was quietly reading her book. Brickley had noticed she was there during the entire conference and he knew the little girl belong to me.

"Carly, what are you reading?" he knelt down to inquire.

I can't remember what the book was . . . probably some Disney tale as those were always her favorites. But Brickley spent about five minutes with her and shook her hand and went back to work. That was Jim Brickley . . . the kind, gentle, fatherly guy who came down from his lofty position as head of the entire state court system to give a few precious moments to a little girl too young to vote. Carly remembers it and so do I.

Brickley was one of the true class acts in this town. He had done everything from running Eastern Michigan University to hunting crooks with his FBI badge and then tossing them into the slammer as U.S. attorney for southeast Michigan. And that just touched the surface of his impressive resume which of course included being second in command on two occasions as lt. governor to Bill Milliken.

There are other Brickley stories in this book which outline his tremendous contribution to state government, but I want to end this chapter on two personal notes: One from his wife and another from me.

The date was January 14, 2003. Everyone who was anyone was

gathered in the Michigan Supreme Court chambers for the unveiling of the portrait of James H. Brickley. He had died the year before and his wife Joyce Braithwaite Brickley took the opportunity to speak in her own way about the man she loved and the man who had served his Michigan so well.

By the time she was done there was not a dry eye in the house including those of the Chief Justice and Governor Engler.

Noting that during her twenty years in Lansing, she had seen other portraits and wondered, "Who is the real person behind the portrait?"

She told the assembled dignitaries, "I want to be certain that personal facts will be available to anyone in the future drawn to the striking man in this portrait," as she looks up at him.

"With Jim," she quietly began, "what you saw publicly was what you got privately . . . there was never a dark side to Jim Brickley . . . . I considered him a master in the art of living."

She related that when he joined the court he was taken back by the "camaraderie, despite often intensely different points of view . . . He took his work seriously but never himself."

"My morning paper, I'd discover, often had holes in it so I knew there must have been a picture of a snake there, of which I have an unreasonable fear. He censored the paper to spare my fearful shaking at the sight of the slippery thing."

She talked about how they exchanged envelopes on Oscar night as they sipped champagne and danced around, he in his tux and she in her "feather boas and sequins and a time or two with my granddaughter Kaitlin's rhinestone tiara."

Their favorite song contained the lyric, "The more I read the papers, the less I comprehend the world and all its capers and how it all will end."

She then summed up her "soul mate's" life in two warm paragraphs she had read somewhere.

"The master in the art of living makes little distinction between his work and his play, his labor and his leisure, his mind and his body, his education and his recreation, his love and his religions. He hardly knows which is which.

He simply pursues his vision of excellence in whatever he does, leaving others to decide whether he is working or playing. To him, he is always doing both." And with that she said thank you and sat down. So many times in this hurried world of politics, the persons get lost in the press releases, the sound bites, the endless give and take, in pursuit of that oft illusive compromise. We forget that the persons who make the laws, enforce them and interpret them are real just like us. They cry the same tears, hope the same hopes, and live the same lives as we all do, but in politics that is often forgotten, if it's known at all.

Ms. Braithwaite's loving words about her husband have special meaning as they touched another two lives. A couple of years before he died, he sent me a personal letter. He explained that Joyce was starring in a two person play with local attorney Dean Robb in Traverse City and "Joyce would be delighted and surprised if you came up."

I wrote back that I would be there for the performance of "Love Letters." I was not familiar with the play but would soon realize the prophetic nature of the dialogue between two persons in love. To make a long story short, on the way to T.C. that sunny October Friday afternoon, I realized I would get into town hours before the show, so I called a very casual acquaintance.

"Jill. This is Tim Skubick," I spoke into her answering machine in my best radio voice. "I'm in town for a play and was wondering if we could have a drink before hand. Give me a buzz at such and such."

Within the hour, Jill called back. "Tim," she began, "My name is not Jill. It's Gayle. I have a dinner date tonight, but could meet you after the play." She came with me to the post play reception and met Jim and Joyce for the first time, but not the last.

Ten months later Gayle and I were married. Without Brickley's letter to me, it would have never happened. His love for Joyce, which motivated him to write me, resulted in me finding my soul mate, too. And we talked about that at our wedding as we shared the romantic tale with Jim and Joyce.

Love begets love, which is the way it's supposed to be.

19

Good Ole Girls

If I was writing this thirty-four years ago, it would be a very short chapter. You could count on one hand and one finger the total number of women in the house. There were none in the senate.

The roster included Reps. Daisy Elliott, Rosetta Ferguson, Josephine Hunsinger, Lucille McCollough, Nelis Saunders and Joyce Symons. Not a Republican in the bunch and you've never heard much about them. Exactly, and that was the fate of the lonely six women in a household of 104 men. They made up 5 percent of the House population which was hardly commensurate with the ratio of men to women in the real world. It was difficult, if not impossible for them to make a name for themselves since men ran the joint and shared very little of the power.

Oh sure, five of the women were given committee chairmanships by the leaders, but the panels they ran were second tier at best and forgettable at worst.

Hunsinger ran State Affairs. Elliott had Constitutional Revision. Symons got Mental Health. Education was run by McCollough and Civil Rights was the domain of Mrs. Ferguson.

There were no females on the powerhouse committees that spent the money and decided the important legislation.

All of the women were from Southeast Michigan. Four were from Detroit, others from Dearborn and Allen Park.

None of them had a college degree. Four attended a university. One had an associate's degree. One had a high school degree. All of them were community activists and had paid their dues at the lower rung of the state Democratic party, although Ferguson and Symons did serve on the Democratic State Central Committee which was a leadership body.

Hunsinger and McCollough had the most seniority, having served since 1954. The others were elected in the mid '60s.

With only six females, there was nowhere for the number to go, but up, but it was not meteoric. By 1975, there were nine women in the house. From 1983–86, there were fourteen and four years later the total went to twenty. In 1993 there were twenty-seven women and the high-water mark was reached in 1997 with thirty-one females or 28 percent of the total membership.

In the senate, Lorraine Beebee was the third woman to be elected to that body in 1966. She was the first woman elected to a leadership post, assistant majority leader. But the senate was a male dominated bastion. There was no female bathroom. When nature called, they cleared out the one men's facility so the lone woman could use it.

Beebee remembers attending her first closed door GOP caucuses As soon as she sat down, they handed her a pen and a notepad and asked her to take notes. She did. By the third meeting, she came in and put the notepad on the table, making it clear she was through being the secretary. After that, the senators hired another secretary . . . a woman of course.

"The men sort of put up with me. They assumed that all I would do was vote and not be a very active player," Beebee reflects. She soon showed them, as she jumped into her committee work on labor, health, and prisons. When she didn't know something, she asked. When she believed something, she spoke.

She did champion women's issues as they related to midwives, sex education and abortion. She made worldwide headlines in June 1969 when she rose to the senate microphone. The body was debating an abortion reform bill and for the first time in state history, a woman told the senate about her therapeutic abortion in 1948. The story was transmitted to Paris, Stockholm, and other parts of the world.

But it was a speech that almost wasn't. At the outset of the debate months earlier, she decided to be quiet. " I knew if I gave the measure early support, I would turn people off."

However her attitude changed when she endured senate debate the night before the showdown vote. As she sat quietly in her seat, many of the men around her put these quotes into the record, "Women are not as responsible as men. Women are not as intelligent. Women aren't stable. They aren't capable of making major decisions."

Recall this is 1969 not 1949. She respected the men but "The tone was that we were more animal than human," she felt.

That night she went home and decided to speak out the next day.

When it came time for her comments, she noticed some men were sleeping, some were wandering around, and others reading the newspaper.

She tells writer Lynne Crandall, "I thought to myself, "Damn it, no one is paying any attention to me," so I put my notes down and said, "and I have had a therapeutic abortion." That got their attention."

The speech however, also got the attention and ire of the Catholic Church. The Council of the Episcopal Diocese of Michigan however, reaffirmed that "each woman should be given control of her own body." But in the battle of the churches, the Catholics won. Beebee was out.

"I didn't lose that election to a man, I lost it to the Catholic Church," she told Crandall. Beebee suffered tremendous harassment as a result of her speech. Her daughter Anne could not leave school unescorted. The family home was egged. At a hearing the senator was physically attacked by a group of women calling her, "that woman for abortion."

Her loss that election year made then senate GOP leader Robert Vanderlaan more than upset, he was angry. He felt had she never given that speech, she would have held onto the seat. When she lost, that threw the senate into a 19–19 deadlock. They had to roll GOP senator Charlie Zollar in on a stretcher to insure GOP control.

Through it all Beebee was one tough character and she credits her upbringing for providing the where-with-all to survive.

"I grew up with three boy cousins and it took all of three of them to lick me," she retells. I was enough of a tomboy that my grandfather let me tag along with him. He was an old time politician in Kalamazoo . . . I think I've been a feminist since I could walk."

Four years later, urged by women's groups around the state, Beebee tossed her hat into the ring for Secretary of State. The Democratic incumbent Richard Austin had refused to allow women to use their maiden names on driver's licenses. Beebee used the issue against him but it wasn't enough. She lost that, too.

Prior to that she was the executive director of the Michigan Consumer's Council but when the *Free Press* questioned her "ineffective leadership," Governor Milliken asked for her resignation on the eve of his own reelection bid.

She eventually was elected to the Women's Hall of Fame.

Between 1993 and 2002, the number of women in the senate fluctuated between three and six. Finally, thanks in part to term limits, by the year 2002 a record eleven women served in the upper chamber, or about 28 percent of that body.

In 1983, one of the most liberal and outspoken females to serve there was elected from the Ann Arbor area, Lana Pollock. There was one other woman elected that year, Connie Binsfeld. She joined the GOP ranks.

Pollack came from a local school board and recalls the senate was a "sexist institution" but not all the men in it were. She faced early challenges, but she effectively used them to stake out her credibility.

Pollack was chosen assistant caucus leader. Sounds important but in the scheme of things, she was just one step away from caucus janitor. But one day she found herself running the meeting and deciding who could talk. The acerbic Senator Basil Brown cut off another senator.

She was not about to be out "acerbic-ed" by the feisty Mr. Brown. She told him, "I'm sorry, you're next on the list. I won't recognize you."

Brown ignored her and continued to talk. Two other senators jumped in to help Pollack, but she didn't need the assistance in this battle of the sexes.

As she is retelling this story, she now raises her right hand well above her head and says, "So I took the huge gavel and slammed it down." She lowers her arm to show me. And then I said, "You'll be recognized when the chair recognizes you!" Brown backed down.

She dismisses some of the adjustments she faced because the men "didn't know how to treat me." Prime example was when she and three other male senators were standing outside the senate. A senate staffer was introducing the quartet to a visitor.

"This is Senator DeMaso, Senator Faxon, Senator Gast, and Lana," he completed the introduction.

Pollack didn't miss a beat as she protested the omission of her title as senator. Then she sternly advised the staffer, "You better practice calling me senator."

She also endured encounters with other lawmakers. Senator Joe Mack from the U.P. was one of the worst she recalls. One day he came up to her and put his hand on her upper arm and held it.

"Joe liked to get into people's personal space as a form of intimidation. So I told him to take his hands off me," she says.

"What?" the senator said.

"You heard me and don't you ever touch me again," she ended the conversation.

Not all the males in the senate were like the guy from the U.P. Pollack recalls that Senator Mitch Irwin always made her laugh and Senators Bill Faust and Art Miller were Democrats who treated her as an equal. Surprisingly, so did a conservative GOP senator. Jack Welborn was the complete opposite of Pollack on the political spectrum, but the two became the senate's "Odd Couple." They found common ground to work on teenage pregnancy problems and prison issues. They staged joint news conferences and the press corps was always interested in what they did.

Pollack found over time that the fact that she had the title 'Senator' did mean something in that body. She says most respected the fact that she had worked hard to get it and therefore deserved equal footing with everyone else.

Even so when she first arrived she found the place to have a sexist attitude and insensitivity to the impact that laws have on women. "They lacked the life perspective that women brought to that chamber," she says. One of the things you learn about legislating is that most of the deals, the compromises and accommodations are not done during floor debate. They develop behind the scenes. And in the senate that often meant the poker game.

The game room was a senator's private office, and on occasion Pollack was invited to sit in. She declined the offer. "I knew they didn't mean it when they asked me to play."

So why didn't she call their bluff by showing up?

Good reason. "I'm not a good poker player." Had she been, you could bet she would have gone.

That brings up the issue of women having to become one of the Good Ole Boys to survive. Pollack says she did not go that far but she confesses, "I became a better reader of the sports pages so that on Monday I would know something about what happened over the weekend."

A fellow female lawmaker from Pollack's neck of the woods talked with the senator one day about having dinner with male lobbyists or lawmakers. Representative Margaret O'Connor, who was just as assertive as Pollack but more conservative, said she felt that would not "be well received by her husband or her constituents."

Pollack warned O'Connor she "would be missing something big" if she chose not to use that venue to advance her agenda.

One of the hallmarks of Pollack's tenure in the senate, and one of the reasons why she was always a good interview, was that she did not censor her thoughts. What you saw and heard was what you got.

Much like Beebee before her, Pollack got the attention of her male counterparts during another abortion debate. She told them, "I'm not going to ask you to raise your hand to reveal how many of you have paid for an abortion for your wife, your daughter, or your mistress." Woo. Heavy duty stuff, but it was vintage Pollack.

She was equally tough on her assessment of former Governor Blanchard. "He got arrogant" in the 1990 race against Engler she believes. "He didn't need Coleman Young. I tried to call his campaign manager and never got a return call."

In fact Pollack was so depressed when John Engler won, that instead of attending the swearing in ceremony, Pollack got on a plane and headed to Texas.

"I wanted to do something fun, so I went to the inauguration of Ann Richards, the new governor of Texas. On the same trip, Pollack discovered another state senator Debbie Stabenow was doing the same thing.

We roomed together and made a deal. She wanted to run for governor and I wanted to run for the U.S. Senate. We agreed not to interfere with each other's ambitions," Pollack recounts.

A woman helping another woman, that's the way the men had been doing it for years.

One final story to underscore the unique nature of this female senator; when the Democrats fell into minority status after the recall of two Democratic senators, Democrats lost heart and attendance at caucus meetings dropped off.

In an attempt to hike that attendance back up it was decided to hold a caucus at the old Playboy Club on Lansing's west side. The guys went and so did Pollack.

"Everyone thought I wouldn't go. I did. It was a good excuse to go there."

One of the reasons women found it difficult to get into the state legislature is there was no farm system. Many did serve on local school boards like Pollack but in the early '60s there was one forum that could have spawned more female lawmakers, but it didn't.

The 1961–62 Constitutional Convention was called to rewrite state laws. One hundred forty-seven delegates were chosen. Only ten were woman or about 7 percent. Countless men parlayed their election to Con-Con into higher office. George Romney became governor. Richard Austin became Secretary of State. Twelve became state legislators: Farnsworth, Faxon, Kelsey, Kuhn, McCauley, Powell, Sharpe, Snyder, Stamm, Stopczynski, Young, and Youngblood.

Three ended up in the U.S. Congress: Brown, Ford and Hutchinson. One woman advanced to the Michigan House. Representative Daisey Elliot of Detroit was the only one. Over time, as more women got elected to the House, they were given the power to run committees, which expanded their influence in the legislative process.

Representative Susan Grimes Munsell was elected in 1989 when a woman in the House was no longer a novelty.

"I didn't think it was tough," she reflects. For her coming into that body was a vast improvement over where she had been. At the Arthur Anderson company there were about 800 employees. When Munsell left, she left behind one other woman. So when Munsell arrived in the house she discovers her vote is equal to all the men. That was an improvement she says.

It was common practice for men to get together after session, but it took some time before women decided they needed time together too. One year as the men headed to the woods for hunting season, a group of women, including Munsell headed to Chicago.

They scheduled a train trip where the female lobbyists who were invited picked up the hotel tab, but each lawmaker covered the food tab. Munsell believes it "improved the communications between female legislators" and also gave them a chance to shop, visit museums, while the guys were out in the cold killing deer. She figured the women got the better part of the deal.

However, back in the political world, Munsell got a raw deal from her own Republican Party. She wanted out of the Michigan House after a ten year run, and was thinking about running for the U.S. Congress. She knew she would have to defeat Democrat Debbie Stabenow who had money, organization, and plenty of party support.

Munsell wanted the same commitment from party chair Betsy DeVos. The two met and Munsell cam away with assurances she'd have the financial support to tackle the Stabenow machine.

Munsell ran unopposed in the primary and when she revved up her fall campaign, she waited for the party check. It never came. Munsell thinks she knows why. She was a pro-choice candidate. DeVos was a staunch Right-to-Life supporter.

"She couldn't bring herself to support a pro-choice Republican," Munsell figures. Consequently the paltry $300,000 she raised looked like peanuts to Stabenow's war chest. Munsell, of course, lost.

But she got a modicum of revenge. During the writing of this book, Munsell reports she got a phone call from the state GOP asking her to renew her dues.

"Is Betsy DeVos still chair?" she asked knowing the answer.

The caller said yes.

So her answer on the dues question was clear and joyful, "No!"

The Michigan Right to Life has dominated state GOP politics ever since Roe vs. Wade and a west Michigan pro-choice woman found out how powerful when she ran for a seat on the University of Michigan Board of Regents.

Judy Frey was no stranger to the political process. She served from 1975 to 1983 on her local school board. When Right-to-Life launched an effort to shut off state abortion payments to the poor,

Frey found herself the spokesperson for a huge coalition trying to preserve Medicaid funded abortions.

There were eighteen different organizations in the coalition, and Frey says she was scared at her first Lansing news conference and during her first appearance on *Off the Record*.

"Yes I was nervous. I knew you asked a lot of pointed questions," she now laughs.

During this same time she began to attend the Kent County GOP executive committee meetings where she was sometimes verbally abused by the Right-to-Lifers in the group. She refused to give in and eventually became the group's secretary.

Frey's side lost the Medicaid battle and it wasn't until 1996 that her political ambitions were rekindled. GOP leader Chuck Yob, who was also from west Michigan, recruited her to run for the U of M Board. She was a graduate and was eager to win the nomination at the party convention where the candidates are selected.

She and Yob worked hard and arrived at the convention with no opposition. All that changed however as the anti-abortion wing of the party found an eleventh hour challenger.

It was widely reported, as it turns out incorrectly, that John Engler was in there fighting for Frey. "He never approached me," she recalls. "We never got his endorsement in writing. But he did give a speech on my behalf fifteen minutes before the convention vote on Saturday."

Frey was prepared to give her own speech but was never given a chance. The party chair Mrs. DeVos called for the vote and that was that. Frey was out on her nose. She was upset by the hardball tactics, but there was no way she could have won even with a brilliant speech. Right-to-Life had the GOP under it's finger and it would not lift it for a pro-choice women even for an obscure board seat that nobody else really wanted.

Frey eventually won an election as mayor of East Grand Rapids.

Just as there are incompetent men in the political game, that malady is not limited to them alone. Rep. Ethel Terrell (D-Highland Park) provided lots of comedy and headaches for the Democratic leadership when she served from 1989 to 1990 in the Michigan house.

Soon after she was elected, she entered the office of then House

Speaker Bobby Crim. She told him that she liked his office and wanted one just like it. The surprised Crim, who had worked years to win his leadership post and the office perks that went with that, forcefully advised her that her office would be determined by a lottery.

Next she requests three or four staffers to handle her heavy workload. Crim tells her she gets one secretary.

During one house session, Terrell is trying to pass one of her bills and not having much luck. She turns to her seatmate Representative Rick Sitz and asks him what to do. He says she should ask the chair to invoke Rule 426.

"What's that?" she asks.

Sitz, with a straight face, explains that once the rule is invoked, her bill would automatically become law without a vote of the legislature and moreover, the governor could not veto it, either.

Elated by this good news, Terrell takes to the microphone.

"Mr. Speaker," she boldly begins, "I want to invoke Rule 426."

Of course the person in the chair doesn't know what that is since there is no such rule.

The Democratic floor leader Joe Forbes, whose job it is to run the floor debate, comes over and asks her what's going on. She refers Forbes to Sitz, who by this time can't contain his laughter. Forbes gets the joke. Terrell does not.

This next story is not funny. It turned out to be a huge embarrassment to house Democrats. From time to time lawmakers are absent and they are given an automatic excuse even though nobody asks where they are or why they are missing. Call it professional courtesy. The so-called excused absence is also a total and unadulterated farce. It misleads the citizens who assume an absence is justified. It is not.

Anyway, the excused absence is extended to Terrell, but after a few days, the leaders want to know where she is. By the time her string of missed sessions hits 100 days in a row, the leaders are not only embarrassed, they are angry, too. The media is banging the story pretty hard.

Floor leader Forbes, who is now in his sixties and has one heart surgery under his belt, was told, "Joey, I'm writing about Ethel Terrell." He says, "Oh shit." Thinking back he recalls that for a time he couldn't find her but eventually discovered she was in the hospital where he visited her.

"The doctors told me there was nothing wrong with her. She didn't agree. When I saw her I said, "Ethel, you look so sexy, can I jump in bed with you?" She said are you crazy? There were some who said the same thing about her.

Uncle Joey, as he was affectionately known, was sorry he couldn't be more helpful on this section of the book, but he did give me one of his famous jokes.

Speaking of beds, "A man is on his death bed and calls his wife to his side. Honey, when I die I want you to marry Harry."

"But you hate Harry," the wife proclaims.

"I know," the husband smiles.

Thank you Uncle Joey. There's never been another floor leader like you.

Even though their numbers were small, female lawmakers tried to compensate for that. Lt. Gov. Connie Binsfeld who was like a mother to many new lawmakers when she first served in the house, made some history in 1991 when she convened the first all female legislative banquet. It was not publicized. She organized it to "give us an opportunity to know each other better as human beings." It was vintage Binsfeld and a theme and variation on the train trip that women in the house staged.

She outlawed any speeches at the event but took the opportunity to ask one question, "How much power does the lt. governor have?"

Then she answered her own question, "John [the governor] had to ask me when he could take his honeymoon just to make sure I would be around to run the state." The group loved it and in the best tradition of Lansing gatherings, the female lobbyists on the guest list paid for it. That's one thing male and female lawmakers share in common.

If a woman got into the legislature, she had to figure out how to get things done. At a recent seminar on Women in Power, U.S. Senator Debbie Stabenow and former state representative Maxine Berman were asked about how they played the game when they were house members at the same time.

Did you go out drinking with the guys after session? I asked Stabenow.

She preferred to spend time with her family. She did her legislative homework away from the downtown pubs which were really mini and informal legislatures after hours.

Berman on the other hand confessed, "Sure I went drinkin' with the men. Jake [former Rep. Dominic Jacobetti who chaired the house budget panel on which Berman had a seat] and I cut a lot of deals over a beer or two. I let him pick up the tab."

Berman by the way is the one who coined the term, "The Only Boobs in the House Are Men."

It is not uncommon for Republicans to battle a Democratic governor, but you would never expect the chair of the state GOP to lock horns with Republican governor John Engler. It happened.

Betsy DeVos had a huge falling out with Engler which marked the first time a woman took on the powerful Engler in a very public fight that captivated the media.

DeVos grew up in west Michigan where she played snare drum in her high school band. That right there told you she was independent and different. She was surrounded by wealth, which gave her the freedom to dabble in partisan politics while still riding herd on her four children.

She was elected state GOP chair in part because she had plenty of money connections and the party badly needed that. She was also a staunch backer of school vouchers and sending state tax dollars to private/religious schools.

Even though Michigan voters had over the years soundly rejected the notion, DeVos was behind a third attempt to install the new school funding concept, but her boss John Engler thought the cause was a political loser, even though he supported the concept. As a statewide petition drive was unfolding and with DeVos listening in, Engler went to Mackinac Island for a conference and proceeded to declare the voucher proposal dead. Period.

DeVos was not happy. The seeds for even more friction between the two were planted when she showed up for a news conference at the Capitol one cold day in February 2000. She announced that she was through with Engler. She was resigning her chairman's post. [She never referred to it as a chairperson or chairwoman.]

In blunt terms she in effect accused him of having no principles or convictions on the voucher issue. She suggested he was only interested in winning elections. To be sure Engler was afraid that the voucher issue on the ballot might cost his pal George W. Bush the presidency. Furthermore, Engler anticipated that the Michigan Education Association would motivate every teacher in Michigan to vote against the proposal and also oust Republicans from the legislature while they were at.

DeVos understood the political ramifications but she didn't care. She was a believer and was acting on her beliefs. In contrast she was blasting Engler for not acting on his.

It was great theater and was a one of its kind political story. DeVos argued that the party could not be a rubber stamp for the governor. She said the chair should have autonomy from the governor. Engler, who lived by the motto, "If it moves, I want to control it," must have chuckled.

DeVos left town. Engler's prediction about vouchers going down was accurate, but the GOP did not lose much ground in the legislature and the gentleman named Bush won a squeaker in the race for the White House.

After Engler split, she returned from exile. I tried to get Chairman DeVos to give me the inside story of this falling out two years after the fact, but she would not go there.

Out of the school of "If you can't beat em', join 'em" was another Oakland County woman. She rose to the highest level of power in the legislative ranks that no other female has achieved. Shirley Johnson is a self-described, "tough ol' broad." She grew up on the south side of Chicago where at the age of eleven she was assaulted in a back alley. The physical scars healed but the emotional ones still haunt her from time to time.

Her family was constantly on the move shifting her around from school to school at least five times before she graduated. She was not good at making friends so she became a loner. Her one refuge was her singing. She even appeared on *the Ted Mack Original Amateur Hour* and got gonged for her not so wonderful rendition of "I'm Lookin' Over a Four Leaf Clover."

But luck turned out to be on her side when she entered the Michigan political arena. After she married husband and attorney Cliff Johnson he advised her, "Don't back down. Don't let them intimidate you."

She was not intimidated and won a seat in the Michigan House.

It was her first foray into elective politics after paying her dues in the local GOP vineyards.

Johnson was coming in the house door as Governor Milliken was leaving and it didn't take long for the new Blanchard crowd to target Johnson for an early out. Democrats wanted her seat. She took steps to keep it.

As a freshman, Johnson was told one way to cement your reelection is to bring home the bacon to your district, the best way to do that was to win a seat on the house appropriations committee.

Johnson approached the GOP house leaders requesting a seat. She was not alone. Another house member was working to secure the same seat for someone he knew and loved. Rep. John Engler wanted Colleen Engler to sit there, too.

With the advice of her hubby Cliff echoing in her ears, Johnson did not back down from her formidable opponents. She beat them. She joined veterans on the committee including Democrats "Mo" Hood, Jr., Dick Young, Gary Owen, Jimmy O'Neill, and Republicans Don Gilmer, Ralph Ostling, and Bill Jowett.

There is a bipartisan sense of family on the budget panel. Those seats are the most coveted ones in the house and to land there says something about you. Johnson learned by listening and not moving too quickly. The men took her under their wing from time to time. She could cuss with the best of them and learned to wheel and deal, too. In her eighteen years in the House she became one of the most powerful women in that body.

But with the advent of term limits, her career would take a historic turn. In 2002, 26 members of the state senate were told to get out of town. Term limits produced the largest senate turnover in state history. Out the door was the longtime chair of the Senate Appropriations panel Harry Gast. By this time Johnson had won a senate seat and had served with Gast on that committee.

She was in line to replace Gast and become the first woman in state history to chair either the house or senate committee. She got the job.

She came into power the same year another woman made history. Johnson and Governor Jennifer Granholm, however didn't know each other from Eve.

I sensed a great story here and went to work on it.

The newly elected GOP senators were staging a closed door and unannounced retreat at the Michigan Manufacturers Association conference room about four blocks from the Capitol. I showed up with the camera.

"What do you think about the new governor?" I asked Johnson during a caucus break.

Not much. Johnson said she didn't have a relationship with Granholm because she had only met her once or twice. But based on her observations of the woman during the recent campaign, Johnson concluded that the new governor was a little heavy on the image and a little light on the substance. She stopped short of calling her a dumb blond.

Johnson revealed that Granholm had talked to her about getting together for lunch to begin work on their relationship, which Granholm agreed did not exist.

I ran a column on Johnson's biting remarks and was pretty sure the governor would respond with a call to Johnson to set up that meeting. Johnson told me the call never came and with it, Johnson's attitude toward the Democratic governor hardened.

Eventually they broke bread, but by this time others in the GOP caucus were echoing what Johnson started. They whispered in closed door caucuses, the contents of which were revealed to me by a mole therein, that Granholm appeared to be a lightweight and that her fledgling administration was in "disarray." But begrudgingly they also admitted that she was a master at P.R. and could not be beaten at her own game. They were right.

This GOP criticism of the new governor went on for months when finally the lt. governor John Cherry decided to take matters into his own hands. He summoned the governor's communication director Jeanna Gent to secure a guest spot on *Off the Record* that week. She called, asked, and I said yes.

Cherry gave a masterful performance suggesting that it was the GOP that was suffering culture shock from not having John Engler around anymore. "We are not in disarray," he argued.

Around this time Johnson was forced to deal with the governor on the budget which had to be written against the backdrop of a projected $1.7 billion barrel of red ink. Granholm had said all along she wanted to cooperate with the GOP and now it was the Republicans' turn to return the favor.

A number of shouting matches, and lost tempers later, the two sides hammered out budget targets. During the talks Johnson and Granholm got closer.

When the dust settled, I reprised my interview with the appropriations chair. Johnson revealed that she found Granholm "easy to work with . . . .comfortable . . . and not a lot of stuffiness." What about those remarks from last January hinting at Granholm's inexperience and alleged incompetence? "Did I say that?" Johnson bursts into laugher as I remind her that I did have the tape.

Johnson confesses that Granholm "still has a lot to learn" but compared to former Gov. Jim Blanchard, "she has not stumbled as much as he did. Let's leave it at that," she smiles.

So do the two of you have a relationship?

Not wanting to sound like a total Granholm convert, she ducks just a little, "It depends on how you define relationship."

Off camera Johnson has another observation. She complains about the media. "You guys just love her," she asserts implying that the new governor gets special treatment from the capital press corps. I advise her to ask Granholm about that because she would deny the supposition of special treatment.

Regardless of what disagreements they might have, one historic fact remains: All those other women that labored in obscurity for so many years laid the foundation for these two to emerge as the most powerful females in state history.

20
Leave 'Em Laughing

One of the unintended by-products of putting thirty-five or so journalists in one place is that a real sense of family evolves. The capital press corps at one time had a room where guys played cards, where everyone hung out to swap stories, rumors, and argue over the latest hot political story dominating the news.

Humor was a key ingredient and each reporter in his or her own way added to the laughs. Some were frustrated stand up comics while others were a little more shy but had a mean wit about them nonetheless.

One aspect of the humor revealed itself in what became affectionately known as the "Quote Board." It was an unflattering compilation of humorous, idiotic, and otherwise stupid remarks made by state officials and reporters on almost a daily basis. To get on the board, two persons had to hear the quote in public.

The board got so popular that numerous national publications did stories on the goofy remarks. Included on that list were *Reader's Digest, The Wall Street Journal, Time* magazine, and former late night jokester Johnny Carson gave it nationwide notoriety.

Bob Berg was the guy who started the thing when he worked for the Panax newspapers. When he went to the other side as press secretary to Bill Milliken, long time capital correspondent Larry Lee from the Gongwer News Service took over the archives. This tradition went on for seventeen years and what follows are some of the zanier quotes designed to end this book on an upbeat note.

Here goes: Rather than keep you in suspense, let's start with my favorite from over 500 quotes. The honor..small "H"..goes to the Godfather. Representative Dominic Jacobetti, during an intense debate over funneling precious state tax dollars into the Detroit Symphony, he came up with this, "The only symphony we have in the U.P. is a jukebox in a tavern."

While each quote has its own distinct twist, one theme emerges from the giant list . . . lots of politicians don't know s– about famous sayings.

"I'm worth my salt in gold." Senator David Holmes.

"We'll have the tail wagging the dog rather than the dog wagging its head." Senator Joe Snyder.

"Let's not rush into the china shop with a bull horn." Representative Mel DeStigter.

"If the proof of the pudding is in the tasting, this bill stinks." Senator Pat McCollough.

"I don't want to throw water on this train." Senator Virgil Smith.

"You are being hypothetically wise, but pound foolish." Senator Fred Dillingham.

"A lot of history has passed over the dam." Senator Steve Monsma

"Now you've hit the point on the nail." Representative Claude Trim.

"There's honor among thieves, but no honor among senators." Senator David Holmes.

"Correct me if I'm correct." Speaker Gary Owen.

"It's the only guts in this thing we can hang our hats on." Representative Tom Scott

"For most of us this is a new area. We're skating on new ground." Senator Carl Levin.

"Humane societies don't create animals, people do." Senator Al DeGrow

"It's unfortunate we're trying to pin the scapegoat on him." Senator Art Miller.

"His integrity is above reproach. Sometimes there are things better left said undone." Senator David Holmes.

Another category is a complete misunderstanding of the legislative process which every semi intelligent lawmaker should have a handle on. Not these guys.

"Our school prayer bill passed the house unanimously when first introduced . . . by a 61–28 margin." Representative Ethel Terrell. If you don't get it, dig out your government book.

Along the same lines this representative observed, "This bill was put out of committee unanimously and there were three votes against it." Representative Bela Kennedy.

Even though the state has a hard and fast open meetings law, it was ignored by this lawmaker who said, "This meeting was not closed. We just didn't want you in there." Representative Jelt Siestma.

"Our democracy is a three way street." And that was from the Chief Justice of the State Supreme Court Mary Coleman.

Redistricting was always an issue near and dear to the heart of every lawmaker because it determined where you ran for reelection. The process was sometimes used to punish those who did not cooperate with their respective parties, by creating a new district without any of their old supporters. Senator John Kelly, who was a maverick at heart, lamented one day, "I've been told if I survive the reapportionment process, moon colonies will be in my next district."

And Representative George Montgomery made this pitch for a different type of justice. "If this was a true democracy, they would have taken him out to the wood shed and shot him."

There apparently was not an abundance of math majors in the capitol as these folks could not do the math:

"If I get five votes, I'll do better than I did last time when I had eight." Senator Harry DeMaso.

"New York is losing one million dollars a day on cigarette bootlegging, which is $93 million a year." Same guy.

"We know that 90 percent of the felons in our prisons are former children." Senator Debbie Stabenow.

"Ten and ten makes seven." Senator David Holmes.

A committee chairman trying to determine the outcome of a committee vote: "I only saw three hands and two of them were yours." Senator Jerry Hart.

This next category is "I wish I had said that." Some real gems.

"This is like the kid who shoots his mother and father and then tells the judge, "Have mercy on me. I'm an orphan." Senator Joe Snyder.

"It reminds me of the fellow who was in a barrel full of horse manure up to his neck. He had another guy ready to hit him on the head with a baseball bat. He didn't know whether to duck or get hit on the head." Representative Dominic "Jake" Jacobetti.

"I feel like the man who saw his mother-in-law drive over a cliff in his brand new Cadillac. I have mixed emotions on this." Public Service Commission Chair Edwyna Anderson.

"Let's do something even if it's wrong." Senator Jack McCauley.

"There are no powerful lobbyists around here, only weak legislators." Senator Danny Cooper. How true.

"We have proposed that a monument be built for Senator Joe Mack with one condition . . . that he be under it." Representative Joe Forbes.

The State Police Director Col. George Halverson was often the target of legislative barbs. When he had enough one day he lectured a legislative committee, "We're not country cops. We don't wear white sox and move our lips when we read." Then he asked each member for their driver's license, proof of insurance, and title. Not really.

Here's my runner-up favorite from the bunch. "Everyone wants to go to heaven. No one wants to die." Senator Tommy Guastello.

"There's no PBB in turkeys, but there's plenty of turkeys affecting PBB." Senator John Hertel.

"There comes a time to put principle aside and do what's right." Senator Harry Gast.

"In the senate everyone likes to shoot the three point shot, but nobody likes to rebound." Senator Joe Conroy.

"Pork is when you don't get it." Senator Dan DeGrow.

And this one from a Monday night when the House was in session prior to a football game. "I want to remind the members, we have a schedule. We don't want to miss the first quarter." Representative Joe Forbes.

One of the ultimate powers a governor has is the power of the pen to veto one-sentence projects in any budget, which gave rise to this one, "I'm a line item. I need to be careful." I not only wish I had said that, I did.

Bodily functions and body parts generated a few good quotes starting with the former Attorney General Frank Kelley.

"I have muscles in my sh—."

"The legislature ought to show some balls, some gall, some courage." Senator Arthur Cartwright.

"I don't mind if a guy pisses on my shoes. I just don't want him to tell me it's raining outside." ALF-CIO lobbyist Si Chappell.

Former candidate for governor, Senator Ed Pierce demonstrates why he may have lost. "I have made a commitment which I can always change."

"What we do or say here is not going to have much effect on what two teenagers do in the back seat of a car." Senator Dick Allen.

"I'm winning. I'm good looking. I'm smart. I'm a perfect victim for some woman to haul into court on a paternity case." Ditto.

"Trying to take a caucus position is like shoveling solid waste into the wind." House Speaker Bobby Crim.

When former Detroit Mayor Coleman Young accused Gov. Jim Blanchard with not having a certain part of his anatomy, the Speaker of the Michigan House, Representative Gary Owen defended the governor with, "Contrary to the Mayor of Detroit, I think the governor will demonstrate that his testicles were there in this instance."

One senator had this take on the intellectual level of a fellow senator. "You don't know shit, Jack Faxon." Senator Basil Brown.

And this one from the President Pro Tem of the Senate at the beginning of the session just before the opening prayer. "Will the guests and their members please rise." Senator Jackie Vaughn III.

Senator Billy Huffman debating the dwindling support of state services suggested, "The privates are feeling the financial squeeze as much as the publics.

You could not have a list of funny quotes without some media bashing and lawmakers and reporters themselves made sure of that.

"What the hell is newsworthy about it. You're a bunch of snooping bastards. Freedom of the press ought to be abolished." Senator Basil Brown.

"The press over there [pointing to the media in front of the senate chambers] uses the iron ore to make presses out of them and then they use the wood pulp to print lies about us." Senator Joe Mack.

"I don't want to disbelieve the *Free Press* even though they are lying sons of bitches most of the time." Senator John Kelly.

"You're not a seasoned journalist until you've wrecked a few lives." AP reporter, Nancy Benac.

There is no other way to lump these next sayings other than to say they are down right stupid.

"Dick Austin's been maybe as good a Secretary of State as we've had since James Hare." Robert Tisch ant-tax zealot. At that time Austin was the only one since James Hare.

"I don't think you should take anything I say serious." Tisch again.

"I praised an animal once and then I married her." Representative Rusty Hellman.

"I may not be the most intelligent person, but I'm certainly not stupid. If I was stupid, I wouldn't have this job." Senator Gil DiNello.

"I've got some concerns on this bill. I don't know what they are specifically." DiNello, disproving his previous statement.

"I don't understand a lot of things. I think somebody should point that out." DiNello, doing it again.

"I may be gorgeous, but I'm not stupid.' Representative Margaret O'Connor.

"I've been given a summary both verbally and orally." Former Governor with the last initial B.

"I'm on both sides of the law enforcement issue." Senator Jack Toepp.

One of the effects of marijuana is on your circular system." Representative Claude Trim.

Former Governor Milliken racked up a few good ones.

"Jim Brickley's future lies ahead of him." Where else could it lie?

"They'll probably ride me out of town on their tulip." That on the eve of his appearance in the Holland Tulip Festival.

"I'm not as nice as people think I am. I can be very mean."

Former President Ronald Reagan got into the act with: "Bill Milliken is a very nice man who's got a lot to learn."

"I've said all I am going to say. Now I'm turning on the fog machine."

Senator Arthur Cartwright gets the honor . . . or dishonor of providing some of the most incongruous quotes ever. See if you agree.

"How do you know this deodorant spray is affecting the Ozark area?" Try Ozone, senator.

"The facts is beginning to submerge."

"The senate don't have to explain nothin'."

"It's already done been did."

"I'd like to be recognized as soon as you [the chair] can see me."

"Now we've got them right where they want us."

"I'm not stupid."

Unfortunately Senator Cartwright stopped giving great quotes as he was forced to resign for padding his expense account, which brings into question his last quote.